Alternate Assessments Based on Alternate Achievement Standards

Alternate Assessments Based on Alternate Achievement Standards

Policy, Practice, and Potential

edited by

William D. Schafer, Ed.D.
University of Maryland–College Park

and

Robert W. Lissitz, Ph.D.
University of Maryland–College Park

·P·A·U·L·H·
BROOKES
PUBLISHING Co®

Baltimore • London • Sydney

Paul H. Brookes Publishing Co.
Post Office Box 10624
Baltimore, Maryland 21285-0624
USA

www.brookespublishing.com

Typeset by Integrated Publishing Solutions, Grand Rapids, Michigan.
Manufactured in the United States of America by
Versa Press, Inc., East Peoria, Illinois.

The case examples in this book are composites. Any similarity to actual
individuals or circumstances is coincidental, and no implications
should be inferred.

Library of Congress Cataloging-in-Publication Data
Alternate assessments based on alternate achievement standards :
policy, practice, and potential / edited by William D. Schafer and
Robert W. Lissitz.
   p.   cm.
   Includes bibliographical references and index.
   ISBN-13: 978-1-59857-037-3 (pbk.)
   ISBN-10: 1-59857-037-4 (pbk.)
   1. Educational tests and measurements—United States—States.
2. Students with disabilities—Education—United States—States.
3. Special education—United States—States—Evaluation.
I. Schafer, William D.   II. Lissitz, Robert W.   III. Title.
LB3051.A566 2009
371.26′2—dc22   2009017290

British Library Cataloguing in Publication data are available from
the British Library.

2012   2011   2010   2009
10   9   8   7   6   5   4   3   2   1

Contents

About the Editors

William D. Schafer, Ed.D., *Affiliated Professor (Emeritus), Department of Measurement, Statistics, and Evaluation, University of Maryland–College Park,* received his doctoral degree from the University of Rochester) in 1969. He is Affiliated Professor (Emeritus), Department of Measurement, Statistics, and Evaluation, University of Maryland–College Park, specializing in measurement and applied research methods. He has also been Director of Student Assessment, Maryland State Department of Education. His professional offices include Chair of the American Educational Research Association (AERA) Special Interest Group (SIG): Educational Statisticians, Chair of AERA SIG: Professors of Educational Research, founding Chair of AERA SIG: Classroom Assessment, President of the American Counseling Association's (ACA) Association for Assessment in Counseling and Education (AACE), and editor of *Measurement and Evaluation in Counseling and Development* (a journal of the AACE). He serves on the editorial boards of *Applied Measurement in Education* and *Educational and Psychological Measurement* and coedits *Practical Assessment, Research, & Evaluation*, a free, refereed e-journal at http://PAREonline.net. He is also on staff at the Maryland Assessment Research Center for Education Success (MARCES). A professional biography, including recent publications and presentations, may be found at his home page, which can be linked from the MARCES web site (http://www.marces.org).

Robert W. Lissitz, Ph.D., *Director, Maryland Assessment Research Center for Education Success, Professor, Department of Measurement, Statistics, and Evaluation, University of Maryland–College Park,* was formerly department chairperson of the Department of Measurement, Statistics, and Evaluation at the University of Maryland–College Park. The Maryland Assessment Research Center for Education Success (MARCES) supports the Maryland state assessment program through a research effort that includes annual conferences such as the one that resulted in this book. His edited books from this series of conferences include two on value-added modeling and growth modeling and one on cognitive modeling, and he is currently working on a book on validity. Since receiving his doctoral degree from Syracuse University in 1969, he took a postdoctoral position with the psychometric laboratory at The University of North Carolina, followed by a faculty position in psychology with the University of Georgia prior to taking his current position at the University of Maryland–College Park. His research has primarily focused on standard setting and test equating in recent years. His complete vita may be found at the MARCES web site (http://www.marces.org).

About the Contributors

Douglas G. Alexander, Ph.D., *Education Associate, Office of Assessment, South Carolina Department of Education*, received his doctoral degree from the University of South Carolina in 1982. Dr. Alexander was previously the Director of Research and Evaluation, and a school psychologist, for Richland County School District One, Columbia, South Carolina. He may be contacted through the Office of Assessment portion of the South Carolina Department of Education web site (http://www.ed.sc.gov).

Joseph Amenta, M.A., *Education Consultant, Bureau of Student Assessment, Connecticut State Department of Education*, received his master's degree from the University of Connecticut in 1982 and has been involved in special education for more than 25 years as a teacher, administrator, and curriculum specialist. Mr. Amenta has collaborated on a variety of statewide initiatives, including the creation of a newly adapted alternative assessment for students with special needs. He has also been instrumental in the development of Rater Certification Training, a teacher training method that creates and provides video scenarios of students participating in the Connecticut alternate assessment.

Peter Behuniak, Ph.D., *Professor in Residence, Department of Educational Psychology, University of Connecticut*, is the former Director of Student Assessment and Chief of Certification and Professional Development at the Connecticut State Department of Education. Specializing in large-scale assessment, he has provided policy and technical support to 14 states' educational assessment programs. Dr. Behuniak was an advisor to President Clinton's proposed Voluntary National Test and currently serves on the National Assessment of Educational Progress Validity Studies Panel convened by the National Center for Education Statistics. He was the Chairperson of the Technical Issues in Large-Scale Assessment Consortium sponsored by the Council of Chief State School Officers and is a member of the Joint Committee on Testing Practices, sponsored by the American Educational Research Association, the American Psychological Association, and the National Council on Measurement in Education. He has written frequently on different aspects of assessment and its appropriate role in the improvement of teaching and learning, with articles appearing in many journals, including *Applied Measurement in Education, Educational Assessment: Policy and Use, Educational Leadership, Educational Measurement: Issues and Practice,* and *Phi Delta Kappan*.

Diane M. Browder, Ph.D., *Snyder Distinguished Professor of Special Education, Department of Special Education and Child Development, Col-*

xii ■ About the Contributors

lege of Education, The University of North Carolina at Charlotte, has done research and writing on assessment and instruction for students with severe disabilities for more than two decades. Recently, she has focused on alternate assessment and linking both assessment and instruction to the general curriculum. She is Principal Investigator for two Institute of Education Sciences–funded research projects—one on reading and the other on math and science for students with significant cognitive disabilities. She also is a partner in the National Center on Alternate Assessment. Dr. Browder has been a member of numerous national work groups. She currently serves on the technical work groups for the National Center on Education Outcomes and the National Study on Alternate Assessment. She is a member of the U.S. Department of Education No Child Left Behind National Technical Advisory Council. Further information about Dr. Browder is available through http://education.uncc.edu/access.

Dianna Carrizales, Ph.D., *Director—Monitoring, Systems, and Outcomes, Office of Student Learning and Partnerships, Oregon Department of Education,* received her doctoral degree from the University of Oregon in 2006. In her current role, she has been responsible for ensuring the valid and reliable statewide assessment of students with disabilities in Oregon. This work has involved leadership on state teams related to the development of alternate assessments as well as the evaluation and use of appropriate accommodations during assessment. Dr. Carrizales has worked in the field of specialized assessments and accommodations since 1998, when she began working as a research associate at Harcourt Assessment. Subsequently, she has worked with the research group Behavioral Research and Teaching out of the University of Oregon and has conducted research on standard setting for alternate assessments. Further information about the assessment of students with disabilities at the Oregon Department of Education can be found at http://www.ode.state .or.us/search/page/?=554.

Charles A. DePascale, Ph.D., *Senior Associate, National Center for the Improvement of Educational Assessment,* received his doctoral degree from the University of Minnesota in 1990. Dr. DePascale has been with the Center, which provides consulting services to help states and districts foster higher student achievement through improved practices in educational assessment and accountability, since 2002. He served previously as Principal Psychometrician for the student assessment unit of the Massachusetts Department of Education. His work in recent years has focused on the design and use of large-scale assessments. Additional information may be found on the Center's web site (http://www.nciea.org).

Stephen N. Elliott, Ph.D., *Professor of Special Education and Dunn Family Chair of Educational and Psychological Assessment, Peabody*

College of Vanderbilt University, received his doctoral degree at Arizona State University in 1980. Dr. Elliott teaches courses on measurement and assessment of academic and social behavior. He currently codirects three U.S. Department of Education research grants concerning the assessment of learning-focused school leadership and the validity of testing modifications and alternate assessments for students with disabilities. He also directs Peabody College's new Interdisciplinary Program in Educational Psychology and serves as Director of the Learning Sciences Institute, a transinstitutional center for externally funded research. Dr. Elliott has authored more than 130 journal articles, 22 books, 40 chapters, and 5 widely used behavior rating scales. His research focuses on scale development and 1) the assessment of children's social skills and academic competence and 2) the use of testing accommodations and alternate assessment methods for evaluating the academic performance of students with disabilities for purposes of educational accountability. Dr. Elliott, along with several colleagues, also recently designed and validated a new measure of learning-focused leadership that is being used to evaluate the performance of principals and school leadership teams.

Steve Ferrara, Ph.D., *Principal Research Scientist, CTB/McGraw-Hill,* received his doctoral degree from Stanford University in 1989. He designs grade-level assessments, English language assessments, and alternate assessments and conducts psychometric work on these assessments. In addition Dr. Ferrara conducts research on cognitive processing of achievement test items. He led collaborative projects to design, develop, and validate alternate assessments for students with significant cognitive disabilities for South Carolina and New Mexico and designed a multistate project to develop alternate assessments based on modified achievement standards. He has served on editorial advisory boards for measurement journals, as Editor of *Educational Measurement: Issues and Practice,* and on the Board of Directors of the National Council on Measurement in Education. Prior to joining CTB/McGraw-Hill, Dr. Ferrara conducted similar work for the American Institutes for Research and was Maryland's Director of Student Assessment. He was a high school special education teacher for students with mild and moderate learning disabilities.

Melissa Fincher, M.S., *Director of Assessment, Georgia Department of Education,* has worked in the field of assessment for more than 20 years. Her background includes experience with assessments in both university and K–12 settings. Ms. Fincher has developed and managed a number of large-scale, high-stakes assessment programs for both Tennessee and Georgia. In her present role, she oversees the development and administration of all Georgia assessments programs, ensuring they meet high standards for technical defensibility. Some of her recent accomplishments include managing the redevelopment all criterion-referenced assessments to comply with a state curriculum revision. Ms. Fincher has served as the principal investigator to several federally funded grants and research projects, has presented at numerous professional conferences, and serves as a peer reviewer for state assessments. Her primary research interests are building assessments that are accessible for all students and the effect of accommodations and modifications on test validity. She is currently working on her doctoral degree in educational psychology at Georgia State University.

Claudia Flowers, Ph.D., *Professor of Research and Evaluation, Department of Special Education and Child Development, College of Education, The University of North Carolina at Charlotte,* received her doctoral degree from Georgia State University in 1995. Her research focus is general curriculum access for students with significant cognitive disabilities, with an emphasis on assessment and measurement issues. She is a partner with the National Alternate Assessment Center and a member of the Research to Practice Panel for the National Center for Educational Outcomes. Dr. Flowers has published in the *Journal of Educational Measurement, Educational and Psychological Measurement, Applied Psychological Measurement, Educational Measurement: Issues and Practice, Research and Practice for Persons with Severe Disabilities,* and *Exceptional Children.* Further information about Dr. Flowers is available through http://education.uncc.edu/access.

Sharon E. Hall, Ed.D., *Education Program Specialist, Standards and Assessment, Office of Elementary and Secondary Education, U.S. Department of Education,* received her doctoral degree from The George Washington University in 2002. As Section Chief at the Maryland State Department of Education, she coordinated the development of Maryland's alternate assessment based on alternate academic achievement standards. In Montgomery County Public Schools, Maryland, she was Supervisor of Special Education Instruction, pre-K–12; a staff development specialist; and a classroom teacher in both general and special education and elementary and high school. For more information about the alternate assessment that Dr. Hall worked on in Maryland, please see http://maryland publicschools.org/MSDE/testing/alt_msa/ALT-MSA_Handbook.

Kristopher J. Kaase, Ph.D., *Deputy Superintendent, Office of Instructional Programs and Services, Mississippi Department of Education,* joined the Mississippi Department of Education in 2002 as Director of Student Assessment. Over the last 18 years, he has had a wide variety of experiences involving curriculum, testing, evaluation, research, and school accountability at the school district, state department, and university levels in South Carolina, North Carolina, and Mississippi. In addition to his state leadership, Dr. Kaase serves on the Assessment Task

Force for the National Center for Education Statistics and on the National Assessment Governing Board Policy Task Force.

Jacqueline F. Kearns, Ed.D., Principal Investigator, National Alternate Assessment Center, Human Development Institute, University of Kentucky, along with Dr. Harold Kleinert, designed the first alternate assessment to be used in a statewide school accountability system. In addition to her work at the NAAC, Dr. Kearns serves as Principal Investigator for a consortium of five states that are conducting validity evaluations for their alternate achievement standards assessments. Dr. Kearns has conducted four federally funded directed research projects involving alternate assessments. As Associate Director of the Inclusive Large-Scale Standards and Assessment (ILSSA) project, she has provided or supervised technical assistance in the design and administration of alternate assessments to more than 15 states and other entities. Dr. Kearns has coauthored many journal articles and other literature on alternate assessments, including the first book on alternate assessment *Alternate Assessment: Measuring Outcomes and Supports for Students with Disabilities* (Paul H. Brookes Publishing Co., 2001). Further information is available at http://www.naacpartners.org.

Martin D. Kehe, M.B.A., Director of Test Development, GED Testing Service, a Program of the American Council on Education, received his master's degree from the University of California, Los Angeles, in 1983. He is director of the program that is responsible for the design, development, and implementation of the GED (General Educational Development) Tests administered in the United States, in Canada, and internationally. He has also been Chief of Assessment, Maryland State Department of Education. During his tenure of service with the state of Maryland, he was responsible for the design and implementation of all of the state's K–12 assessments, including the High School Assessment end-of-course tests; the Maryland School Assessments in reading, mathematics, and science; the Alternate Maryland School Assessment for students with significant cognitive disabilities; and the Modified Maryland School Assessments (the "2%" tests). His professional affiliations include membership in the National Council of Measurement in Education, the GED Advisory Board, and the GED National Task Force. More information about Mr. Kehe and the GED Tests may be found at the home page of the GED Testing Service (http://www.gedtest.org).

Ryan J. Kettler, Ph.D., Research Assistant Professor in Special Education, Peabody College of Vanderbilt University, is also Coordinator of Data Services for the Learning Sciences Institute. He received a doctoral degree in educational psychology, with a specialization in school psychology, from the University of Wisconsin–Madison in 2005. Dr. Kettler's dissertation, *Identifying Students Who Need Help Early: Validation of the Brief Academic Competence Evaluation Screening System*, won the 2006 Outstanding Dissertation award from the Wisconsin School Psychologists Association. Prior to joining Vanderbilt University, Dr. Kettler was an assistant professor at California State University, Los Angeles, and completed an American Psychological Association–accredited internship at Ethan Allen School in Wales, Wisconsin. He has worked on multiple federally funded grants examining the effectiveness of alternate assessments, academic and behavioral screening systems, and testing accommodations. Dr. Kettler is the author of peer-reviewed publications and presentations within the broader area of data-driven assessment for intervention, representing specific interests in academic and behavioral screening, test development, reliability and validity issues, and intervention evaluation. He currently serves as a consultant to several states' departments of education, as well as to the College Board, providing expertise in the area of alternate assessment.

Harold L. Kleinert, Ed.D., *Executive Director, Human Development Institute, University of Kentucky*, has directed a broad range of federally funded demonstration and research projects, including the Kentucky Alternate Portfolio Study, the Paraprofessional Training Component for Kentucky's State Improvement Grant, the Kentucky Systems Change Project for Students with Severe Disabilities, the Personal Futures Planning Project for Individuals with Deaf-Blindness, and the Kentucky Peer Service Learning Project. Dr. Kleinert co-directed the development of Kentucky's alternate assessment (resulting in the first fully inclusive educational assessment system in the nation), and is nationally recognized for his research on alternate educational assessments. He has published widely in the area of alternate assessment for students with significant disabilities under the Individuals with Disabilities Education Act, including research on the impact of the inclusion of students with significant disabilities in large-scale assessment and accountability systems, and is the lead author of the book *Alternate Assessment: Measuring Outcomes and Supports for Students with Disabilities* (Paul H. Brookes Publishing Co., 2001). Further information is available at http://www.naacpartners.org.

Jane Kleinert, Ph.D., CCC-SLP, *Assistant Professor, College of Health Sciences, Division of Communication Sciences and Disorders, University of Kentucky*, has more than 30 years of clinical experience in working with children who experience significant communication challenges. In addition, she has provided extensive training and technical assistance in the areas of communication, augmentative communication, and language development. Dr. Kleinert is Principal Investigator of the Kentucky Youth Advocacy Project, designed to provide communication supports for the development of self-advocacy for school-age students with developmental disabilities. Further information is available at http://www.naacpartners.org.

Scott F. Marion, Ph.D.*, Associate Director, National Center for the Improvement of Educational Assessment,* received a doctoral degree in measurement and evaluation from the University of Colorado at Boulder, a master's degree in science education from The University of Maine, and a bachelor's degree in biology from The State University of New York. His current projects include evaluating the technical quality of state alternate assessment systems, exploring the instructional usefulness of interim assessment approaches, and helping states design valid accountability systems. Dr. Marion serves on the U.S. Department of Education's National Technical Advisory Committee and on a National Research Committee investigating the issues and challenges associated with incorporating value-added measures in educational accountability systems. Prior to joining the Center, Dr. Marion was most recently Director of Assessment and Accountability for the Wyoming Department of Education and was responsible for overseeing the Wyoming Comprehensive Assessment System and designing the technical and policy structures to implement a multiple-measures, locally created graduation assessment system. Dr. Marion regularly publishes and presents the results of his work in peer-reviewed journals and at several national conferences. For more information about the Center and Dr. Marion, please see http://www.nciea.org.

Lorin Mueller, Ph.D.*, Senior Research Scientist, American Institutes for Research,* received his doctoral degree in industrial and organizational psychology from the University of Houston in 2002, where he specialized in statistics and measurement. Since joining the American Institutes for Research in Washington, DC, in 2000, Dr. Mueller has worked in such diverse areas as employment litigation, measurement of individuals with disabilities, program evaluation, high-stakes testing, and educational measurement. He has presented and published work in the areas of the assessment of individuals with disabilities, alternative methods for setting cut scores, and statistical issues in employment discrimination analyses. He is a member of the Society for Industrial and Organizational Psychology, the American Psychological Association, and the Society for Human Resources Management, as well as an Associate Member of the American Bar Association. He serves as an adjunct faculty member at George Mason University, where he has taught graduate-level multivariate statistics.

Marianne Perie, Ph.D.*, Senior Associate, National Center for the Improvement of Educational Assessment,* received her doctoral degree in educational research, measurement, and evaluation from the University of Virginia. Prior to joining the Center, she worked on district, state, and international assessments as well as the National Assessment of Educational Progress as an employee of first the American Institutes for Research and then the Educational Testing Service. Her primary interests are standard setting, reporting, accountability, and validity studies. She has conducted standard-setting studies in more than 16 states, districts, and foreign countries. She taught a course in standard-setting as part of the federally funded Graduate Certificate Program and coauthored a revision of the 1982 publication *Passing Scores,* published in 2008 by Educational Testing Service as *Cutscores: A Manual for Setting Standards of Performance on Educational and Occupational Tests.* Dr. Perie is currently working with several states on exploring a validity argument on alternate assessments for students with significant cognitive disabilities and enhancing their technical documentation. For other publications, see http://www.nciea.org and click on "publications."

Rachel F. Quenemoen, M.S., *Senior Research Fellow, National Center on Educational Outcomes, University of Minnesota*, is the national technical assistance team leader for the National Center on Educational Outcomes and is Coprincipal Investigator of its primary technical assistance center. She has been a multidistrict cooperative administrator and a state department of education technical assistance provider across special and general education. During the past 15 years, she has worked at the state and national levels on educational change processes and reform efforts related to standards-based reform and students with disabilities, building consensus and capacity among practitioners and policy makers. Her current research and technical assistance priorities include alternate assessment and the causes of and solutions for "gap" issues. She has coauthored a book on alternate assessment; has written numerous book chapters, journal articles, and technical assistance materials on alternate assessment and related issues of inclusive assessment and accountability practices; and has presented research and practice findings to hundreds of audiences across the country.

Susan L. Rigney, Ed.D., *Education Specialist, U.S. Department of Education*, has two decades of experience in developing and implementing standards-based state assessments that were designed to guide instructional change. She has led portfolio assessment programs in both Kentucky and Vermont. Prior to that, she worked in the state assessment programs in Michigan and Illinois. Dr. Rigney's work during the past 8 years has focused primarily on the technical quality of state assessment and accountability systems. In addition to providing technical assistance to states, she has been directly involved in the federal review of state assessment systems under the No Child Left Behind Act and is also responsible for monitoring several research grants focused on the assessment of special populations.

Andrew T. Roach, Ph.D., *Assistant Professor, Department of Counseling and Psychological Services, Georgia State University,* received his doctoral degree from the University of Wisconsin–Madison. He currently serves as a coinvestigator or consultant on four federally funded grants on inclusive assessment and accountability strategies. Dr. Roach received the 2007 Early Career Publication Award from the Council for Exceptional Children's Division for Research for his research on the effects of curricular access on students' alternate assessment performance.

Suzanne Swaffield, M.Ed., *Education Associate, Office of Assessment, South Carolina Department of Education,* coordinates South Carolina's state alternate assessment on alternate achievement standards. She was previously with the Office of Exceptional Children at the Department of Education as a consultant for students who are blind and visually impaired. She may be contacted through the Office of Assessment portion of the South Carolina Department of Education web site (http://www.ed .sc.gov).

Gerald Tindal, Ph.D., *Castle-McIntosh-Knight Professor of Education, Department of Educational Leadership, College of Education, University of Oregon,* joined the University of Oregon in 1984 in Special Education. He is Department Head of Educational Leadership as well as Director of Behavioral Research and Teaching (BRT), a research center housing federal and state grants and contracts (http://www.brtprojects.org). His research focuses on the inclusion of students with disabilities in general education classrooms using curriculum-based measurement to develop optimal instructional programs. For the past decade, Dr. Tindal also has conducted research on student participation in large-scale testing and development of alternate assessments. This work includes investigations of test accommodations, teacher decision making using curriculum-based measurement, and extended assessments of basic skills. Much of this work on assessment has focused on development of measures for teachers to use in the classroom for monitoring progress and making appropriate decisions on participation of large-scale tests. He publishes and reviews articles in many special education journals and has written several book chapters and books on curriculum-based measurement and large-scale testing. His teaching includes both curriculum-based measurement of basic skills and concept-based instruction and problem solving in secondary content classrooms.

Elizabeth Towles-Reeves, Ph.D., *Director of Alternate Assessment Research, National Alternate Assessment Center, Human Development Institute, University of Kentucky,* received her bachelor's degree from Georgetown College with a double major in art and psychology and received her master's degree in education from the University of Kentucky.

In December of 2007, she completed her doctoral degree in educational psychology. Dr. Towles-Reeves spends most of her time in her current position conducting research investigating the technical adequacy, design, and administration of alternate assessments based on alternate achievement standards with the National Alternate Assessment Center, a 5-year, federally funded project through the U.S. Department of Education, Office of Special Education Programs. In addition, Dr. Towles-Reeves conducts the evaluations for two federally funded General Supervision Enhancement Grants aimed at researching alternate assessments based on modified achievement standards. Further information is available at http://www.naacpartners.org.

Shawnee Wakeman, Ph.D., *Clinical Assistant Professor, Department of Special Education and Child Development, College of Education, The University of North Carolina at Charlotte,* conducts research on the relationship of the principal to the education of students with disabilities, access to the general curriculum and how it is enacted for students with significant cognitive disabilities, alignment of the educational system and the policy implications of those alignment issues, and alternate assessment. She has served as a special education teacher, a middle school assistant principal, a research associate for the National Alternate Assessment Center, and an adjunct professor of special education and educational research courses. Dr. Wakeman is currently involved in several federally funded projects and publications related to alternate assessment and curriculum alignment. Further information about her is available through http://education.uncc.edu/access.

Daniel J. Wiener, M.A., *Administrator of Inclusive Assessment, Massachusetts Department of Elementary and Secondary Education,* has, since 1998, coordinated the development and implementation of the Massachusetts Comprehensive Assessment System Alternate Assessment (MCAS-Alt) for students with significant disabilities that provides a basis for these students to participate in the statewide assessment system. He has received two performance recognition awards from the governor for this work, and the educational approaches and curriculum access materials developed by Massachusetts have been recognized by the U.S. Department of Education as national models for instructing students with significant disabilities. He has written extensively on this topic and has presented at meetings and conferences sponsored by the U.S. Department of Education, the Council of Chief State School Officers, the American Educational Research Association and the National Council on Measurement in Education, and other research organizations. More information is available online at http://www.doe.mass.edu/mcas/alt.

Foreword

Alternate Assessments Based on Alternate Achievement Standards: Policy, Practice, and Potential is a treasure chest of information for those interested in assessment, accountability, policy, students with significant disabilities, and the process of change! William Schafer and Robert Lissitz have created a volume that really does, as they state in the Preface, "bring the best thinking of national experts and the best examples of state work together in one place."

It is an exciting time when a new edited volume can provide so much information and reflect so much change on a single topic—alternate assessment based on alternate achievement standards. Who would have known a mere decade ago that the "simple" requirement that appeared in the Individuals with Disabilities Education Act Amendments of 1997 (PL 105-17) would blossom into something that would change measurement and accountability practices? Certainly, the No Child Left Behind Act of 2001 (PL 107-110) catapulted the alternate assessment into the spotlight, with its regulations that allowed states to count for adequate yearly progress (AYP) those students who were proficient on the alternate assessment based on alternate achievement standards. There is little question that the alternate assessment has garnered attention and generated interest in not only how to assess students previously pushed aside by state assessments, but also how to ensure that these students receive the instruction they need to show what they know and are able to do.

Perhaps no assessment before (or likely after) the alternate assessment based on alternate achievement standards has pushed the envelope of assessment practice so far. And, it has produced an atmosphere where special educators, policy makers, and assessment experts have come together to communicate about how students with significant cognitive disabilities learn and show their learning, how states can create large-scale assessments that provide an accurate measure of what these students know and are able to do, and what needs to happen to ensure that these students have access to the curriculum and the highest of expectations. Alternate assessment for students with significant cognitive disabilities has shown those of us who thought we had high expectations for these students that our expectations were not nearly high enough.

Schafer and Lissitz have partnered with leaders in the field to provide the reader with avenues to understanding and examining alternate assessment based on alternate achievement standards. First, they have a set of chapters by authors who address the history, assumptions, policy, and conceptualizations of alternate assessment. Topics such as understanding who the children are who participate in alternate assessment, what we really want to assess and how to sample the targeted domains, the alignment of these assessments with state standards, setting performance standards, the nature of validity arguments for the alternate assessment, public policy related to alternate assessments, and the history of these assessments are all covered in the first part of the book.

Then, in Section II, the reader is invited to view the approaches that several states have taken to develop and implement their alternate assessments. Connecticut, Georgia, Maryland, Massachusetts, Mississippi, Oregon, and South Carolina all share information about their assessments. This part of the book is a wonderful exploration of the implementation of a public policy.

Section III is a unique view into the concluding thoughts about alternate assessments by some of the chapters' authors. Specifically, these short chapters touch on some critical ideas that developers of alternate assessments need to know, topics of importance for those individuals and organizations who are undertaking evaluations of alternate assessments, and comments about what needs to be learned in the next few years to ensure improved quality in states' alternate assessments.

All in all, this book is a valuable resource to readers. It documents not only what we now know, but also what we have learned during the past decade and where we still need to go to develop alternate assessments for students with significant cognitive disabilities that meet the highest criteria for technical adequacy and spur access to the curriculum and high expectations.

Martha L. Thurlow, Ph.D.
Director
National Center on Educational Outcomes
University of Minnesota
Minneapolis

REFERENCES

Individuals with Disabilities Education Act Amendments (IDEA) of 1997, PL 105-17, 20 U.S.C. §§ 1400 *et seq.*
No Child Left Behind Act of 2001, PL 107-110, 115 Stat. 1425, 20 U.S.C. §§ 6301 *et seq.*

Preface

In the dark ages of alternate assessment (about 10 years ago), there were only a handful of states that offered any sort of testing for their students who were the most severely cognitively challenged. Although phrases such as "all means all" were commonly heard, the great majority of states assessed only those students who might be expected to achieve the state's general content and performance standards (if they had any statewide assessment system at all). And those states with alternate assessments generally tested over so-called "life skills," with little or no emphasis on academics.

All that changed with the No Child Left Behind (NCLB) Act of 2001 (PL 107-110). All actually did mean all, because all students were to be included in the accountability system (up to 5% could be excluded, but only on nonacademic bases) and both reading and math were to be tested. The U.S. Department of Education reviewed states' accountability and assessment systems, using the so-called peer-review system, to make sure they implemented acceptable policies and procedures. No state at that time had an acceptable assessment system for students with severe cognitive disabilities and every state needed one. States and their consultants quickly scrambled to develop alternate assessments under less-than-ideal conditions. Some states have been quite successful and others at this writing have yet to develop a fully acceptable alternate assessment system.

The two of us felt that this was a good time to bring the best thinking of national experts and the best examples of state work together in one place. Our first step was to host an October 2007 conference on alternate assessments. We talked to prominent professionals in the field and asked about both people and states they felt the conference should include. Our contacts were unanimous in their support for our efforts and both free and frank with their advice. We are indebted to them and were very pleased that all of those whom we subsequently asked accepted invitations to speak at the conference. We are also indebted to the Maryland State Department of Education for its support of a conference on this topic as part of a series of annual assessment conferences hosted by the Maryland Assessment Research Center for Education Success (MARCES) at the University of Maryland–College Park.

Following the highly successful conference, we were extremely pleased when Paul H. Brookes Publishing Co. agreed to include the work that grew out of it in their list of titles. All of the conference speakers wrote manuscripts on their topics, and the result is the book you now have in your hands.

Like the conference, the book is divided into three sections. In the first section, this new area of alternate assessment is explored from several perspectives. This section describes the background out of which alternate assessments grew, the history of the effort thus far, and insights that have been drawn from the experience. Section I might be thought of as the current knowledge base for alternate assessment.

In the second section, several state systems are highlighted. These were chosen in three complementary ways. First, our contacts were very clear that certain state systems simply must be included; these were ones that had "made a splash" on the national scene. Second, state systems were chosen as exemplars of styles of alternate assessment. Although they do not cover all ways alternate assessment might be implemented, they nevertheless could be thought of as representative of approaches that are distinctly different, such as checklists versus performance tasks versus portfolios. Third, some professionals who have come to be associated with alternate assessments have developed their own "signature" styles. We asked each of those individuals to choose a state they felt best exemplified their approach. The combination of all three sources of input resulted in the states included in Section II. We expect you will be intrigued as we were by the variety of ways in which states have responded to the challenge of developing and documenting the success of assessments that provide useful results for this highly unique population.

The third section is unusual in books of this type. Prominent authors were asked to contribute those thoughts they felt were most salient for both theoreticians and practitioners to keep in mind as they moved forward in their own alternate assessment work. We, ourselves, wanted to see what was most important in the minds of our distinguished colleagues in this fluid but nevertheless rapidly developing field. Although the authors were free to say what they wanted, they were asked to think about such questions as

- What do developers of alternate assessments most need to know?

- What should evaluators of alternate assessments focus on?

- What new knowledge needs to be developed in the next few years?

We hope professionals in alternate assessment will use these thoughts as a look into the musings and recommendations of today's most prominent professionals. These discussions might help in the design of new and/or improved alternate assessments in your own context. They may also help identify people who agree (or disagree) with your point of view. We hope Section III will help guide further research and development efforts and give readers a peek into the future.

Thank you for picking up our book on alternate assessment. Whether or not you have worked in the area before, we believe you will find this field to be new and exciting, with some unique challenges for both special education and assessment professionals.

William D. Schafer
Robert W. Lissitz

REFERENCE

No Child Left Behind Act of 2001, PL 107-110, 115 Stat. 1425, 20 U.S.C. §§ 6301 *et seq.*

SECTION I

Conceptualizing
Alternate Assessment

CHAPTER 1

Who Are the Children Who Take Alternate Achievement Standards Assessments?

JACQUELINE F. KEARNS, ELIZABETH TOWLES-REEVES,
HAROLD L. KLEINERT, AND JANE KLEINERT

The title of this chapter might sound fairly simplistic, considering that the largest majority of students (98%–99%) who participate in statewide assessment systems represent typically developing children and youth who follow a fairly predictable and accepted path through the academic curriculum. However, for the students participating in alternate assessments on alternate achievement standards in 2000 (ranging from less than 1% of the total school population or 8% of the special education population to 3% of the total assessed population or 11% of the special education population; Thompson & Thurlow, 2000), the acquisition of traditional developmental milestones and accepted paths through academic curricula is highly varied. Since then, the U.S. Department of Education's nonregulatory guidance (2005) has capped the percentage of proficient scores that count toward proficiency in the annual yearly progress (AYP) calculations in school accountability at 1% and has defined other possible levels of achievement standards including alternate achievement standards and grade-level achievement standards. Indeed, research findings suggest that for states assessing 1% or less of the total student population in alternate achievement standards assessments, stu-

This chapter was supported in part by the U.S. Department of Education Office of Special Education Programs (Grant no. H3244040001). The opinions expressed do not necessarily reflect the position or policy of the U.S. Office of Special Education Programs, and no official endorsement should be inferred.

dent characteristics such as expressive and receptive language, vision, hearing, motor, engagement, and attendance are highly varied (Towles-Reeves, Kearns, Kleinert, & Kleinert, 2009). Researchers confirm that the academic curriculum for these students is limited primarily to sight word reading and calculator use for mathematics (Browder, Spooner, Ahlgrim-Delzell, Harris, & Wakeman, 2008; Browder, Wakeman, Spooner, Ahlgrim-Delzell, & Algozzine, 2006; Courtade, Spooner, & Browder, 2007). Decades of changing philosophical and curricular approaches for students participating in alternate assessments have contributed to a more restricted set of academic skill instruction.

KNOWING WHAT STUDENTS KNOW

We have framed our work in describing validity for alternate achievement standards assessments by using a theoretical model provided by the National Research Council's *Knowing What Students Know* (Pellegrino, Chudowsky, & Glaser, 2001). Pellegrino et al. posited that three areas of assessment—cognition, observation, and interpretation—form a reflexive triangle of components necessary to ensure the credibility of the resulting inferences. Although the work of Pellegrino et al. primarily addressed large-scale assessments for the general population, the direct application of this model to the development of alternate achievement standards assessments is an essential element in the documentation of validity of these assessments. Figure 1.1 explicates the interpretation of this model for alternate achievement standards assessments (Marion & Pellegrino, 2006; Marion, Quenemoen, & Kearns, 2006) in the work conducted by the National Alternate Assessment Center (NAAC).

The purpose of this chapter is to consider the importance of defining the population of students who may participate in alternate achievement standards assessments as a critical variable in evaluating the validity of these assessments. We explicate our interpretation of the assessment triangle (Pellegrino et al., 2001) cognition vertex as it applies to assessment design for alternate achievement standards assessments. The *cognition vertex* refers to student population and models of cognition/theories of learning; we are interested in this concept because of the reported variability in this population (Almond & Bechard, 2005; Towles-Reeves, et al., 2009). As such, we describe the participation rates and disaggregated disability categories for 11 states, including the 7 states participating as case examples in the Eighth Annual Maryland Alternate Assessment Research Conference, which are referenced in this book. In addition to these states, we report the results of an in-depth study of four other states, with extended demographic information on population characteristics. We provide profiles of students with similar characteristics and highlight our understanding of how they learn. Finally, we offer suggestions

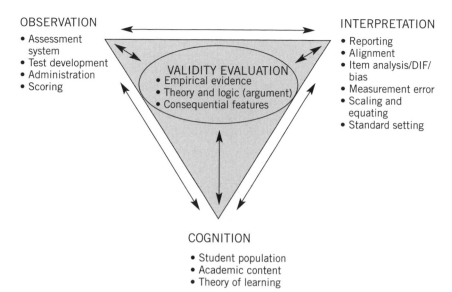

Figure 1.1.   The assessment triangle and validity evaluation. (From Marion, S.F., & Pelle-grino, J.W. [2006]. A validity framework for evaluating the technical quality of alternate as-sessments. *Educational Measurement: Issues and Practice, 25*[4], 47–57; Copyright © 2006 National Council on Measurement in Education. Reproduced with permission of Blackwell Publishing Ltd.) (*Key:* DIF, differential item functioning.)

for further research in defining the population and a theory of learning as integral to explicating validity for these assessments.

REVIEW OF THE LITERATURE

The early literature on alternate assessment suggests that alternate as-sessments implemented before 1997 were targeted primarily toward a very small percentage of the population (1% or less; Kleinert, Haigh, Kearns, & Kennedy, 2000; Kleinert & Kearns, 1999). After implementa-tion of the Individuals with Disabilities Education Act Amendments (IDEA) of 1997 (PL 105-17), the Individuals with Disabilities Education Improvement Act of 2004 (IDEA 2004; PL 108-446), and the No Child Left Behind Act of 2001 (NCLB; PL 107-110), the U.S. Department of Ed-ucation's (2005) nonregulatory guidance defined the percentage of profi-cient scores that could be counted in AYP calculations from alternate achievement standards assessments. Researchers at the NAAC conducted a comparison of participation rates, category distributions, and learner characteristics in four partner states. Learner characteristics were iden-tified by using a demographic tool designed especially for the purpose of describing this unique population (Towles-Reeves et al., 2009). In this study, the participation rates ranged from 0.55% to 1.17% of the assessed populations across the four states.

It is important to emphasize that the federal requirements in the U.S. Department of Education's nonregulatory guidance (2005) to NCLB do not limit participation in an alternate achievement standards assessment to any percentage. However, they do limit the number of proficient scores that can count toward AYP in the school accountability calculation to 1% (U.S. Department of Education, 2005). This means that in states that are assessing more than 1% of the total population, it is likely that the percentage of proficient scores in that assessment will be somewhat less than the 1% allowance.

DISABILITY CATEGORICAL REPRESENTATION

The U.S. Department of Education's annual report to Congress on IDEA in 2006 reported the percentages of students with disabilities by category for the entire population receiving special education services. These data are important because they provide a context for understanding the demographics of students participating in alternate achievement standards assessments. Specifically, the majority of the special education population comes from the specific learning disability category at 48%, followed by speech-language impairments at 19%, mental retardation at 10%, and emotional disturbance at 8% (U.S. Department of Education, 2006). However, it is important to note that describing participation in alternate assessments by disability category is problematic. The categories represent a range of functioning, but not all of the membership within a category may participate in either the alternate assessment or the general assessment. In addition, although most states use the same categories in their annual monitoring reports, some states do not use certain categories. Specifically, multiple disabilities and developmental delay are not used consistently in all states (U.S. Department of Education, 2006).

STATE EXAMPLES

For the purposes of illustration in this chapter, we have compiled the alternate assessment participation rates for the states participating in the Maryland Alternate Assessment Research Conference (MARCES) and have added an additional four states for which we collected data through the NAAC. The states participating in this conference were identified by expert recommendation as having high-quality alternate assessments. The four additional states from the NAAC volunteered to share their participation data and to consider other characteristics of their student populations at a more in-depth level. We have combined the participation rates and the disability category distributions of these states in Table 1.1. The table indicates each state, its overall state participation rate, the percentage of alternate achievement standards assessment participation based on total statewide assessment participation, and the percentage of students with disabilities who participated in the alternate achievement standards assessments. The NAAC states are indicated by the letters *A, B, C,* and *D,* and the states participating in the MARCES conference along with Wyoming, are indicated by their state postal codes.

All of the states included in Table 1.1 are assessing 95% or more of their entire populations, as required by NCLB. Most are assessing closer to 99% of their total populations. Participation rates are important because they allow the identification of missing populations. It is interesting to note that most of the states represented at the conference were assessing 1% or less of their total school populations with alternate assessments. However, two states stand out as assessing higher percentages of students with disabilities. Massachusetts and Oregon were assessing 1.5%, a higher percentage than the other states. This higher percentage, in turn, affects the percentage of participants represented in disability categories. For example, we would expect to see higher percentages of students within the higher-incidence categories (i.e., specific learning disabilities, speech-language impairments, and emotional/behavioral disorders; Towles-Reeves et al., 2009) if a state were assessing a higher percentage of students with disabilities in its alternate assessments based on alternate achievement standards (AA-AAS). Table 1.1 also illustrates the disability category distributions of the states highlighted in this volume.

As Table 1.1 illustrates, all disability categories are represented. Not surprisingly, the two states with the highest participation rates in their alternate assessments have higher percentages of students from the "high-incidence" categories. For example, Oregon and, to some extent, Massachusetts, report higher percentages of students in the specific learning disability category than the other NAAC study states and the states that participated in the conference. Although these data are helpful for understanding the population of students who participate in alternate achievement standards assessments, more information is needed to truly understand the implications of instruction and assessment for this population of students. In an effort to more clearly describe this population of students and identify assessment observation strategies that address the purported diversity of student needs within the population, we have designed a tool to provide additional demographic data about the population. These learners experience notable difficulties in expressive and receptive communication and often require augmentative and alternative communication (AAC) systems (Almond & Bechard, 2005; Towles-Reeves et al., 2009). In addition, issues with attention, engagement, and motor problems increase the challenge of item development for assessment conditions for these students. Instructionally, these students need increased time for skill acquisition, maintenance,

Table 1.1. Participation rates and IDEA categorical distribution

AA-AAS IDEA disability category distribution	A CT	B	C	D	GA	MA	MD	MS	OR	SC	WY
Mental retardation and multiple disabilities	*	72%	71%	84%	79%	50%	*	71%	27%	73%	60%
Autism	*	18%	17%	14%	13%	20%	*	12%	15%	16%	14%
Other health impairment	*	4%	5%	1%	3%	2%	*	7%	9%	3%	11%
Emotional disability	*	<1%	2%	<1%	1%	3%	*	<1%	6%	<1%	1%
Specific learning disability	*	2%	1%	<1%	<0%	8%	*	5%	23%	1%	2%
Traumatic brain injury	*	2%	<1%	<1%	<0%	4%	*	1%	<1%	<1%	3%
Speech language impairment	*	1%	0%	0%	<0%	4%	*	<1%	10%	<1%	0%
Orthopedic impairment	*	<1%	1%	<1%	<0%	<1%	*	4%	3%	3%	2%
Hearing impairment	*	<1%	<1%	<1%	<0%	1%	*	<1%	2%	1%	7%
Deafblind	*	<1%	<1%	<1%	<0%	<1%	*	<1%	<1%	<1%	<1%
Visual impairment	*	<1%	<1%	<1%	<0%	<1%	*	<1%	<1%	<1%	<1%
Other	*	X	X	X	X	5%	*	X	X	X	X
State assessment participation rate	98%	99%	99%	99%	99%	99%	100%	99%	99%	*	*
Participation rate for AA-AAS	<1%	<1%	<1%	1.2%	<1%	1.5%	1%	<1%	1.5%	<1%	<1%
Percent of students with disabilities in the state assessment	8%	8%	*	8%	14%	8%	*	7%	11%	*	7%

Source: U.S. Department of Education (2006).

Key: IDEA, Individuals with Disabilities Education Act; AA-AAS, alternate assessments based on alternate achievement standards; *A, B, C,* and *D* represent states for which data were collected through the National Alternate Assessment Center; * data not available; X, Category not used; ~ reading only (categories may not add to 100 because of rounding).

and generalization; each phase of the learning process requires specific methodology (Kleinert, Browder, & Towles-Reeves, 2009). This need for increased time, in turn, impinges on the breadth and depth of the curriculum content. In addition, students in this population experience special health care needs; these conditions present unique access challenges for instruction and assessment conditions. Finally, academic curriculum access has been significantly limited for this population (Browder et al., 2008; Browder et al., 2006; Courtade et al., 2007; Kleinert et al., 2009).

The student characteristics identified by Kearns, Kleinert, Kleinert, and Towles-Reeves (2006) include difficulties in receptive and expressive communication, presence of an AAC system, impairments in hearing, vision, motor skills, engagement, or attendance, and low estimated skills in reading and mathematics. Based on these characteristics, the following profiles represent learners who would likely participate in an alternate assessment on alternate achievement standards.

STUDENTS TAKING ALTERNATE ACHIEVEMENT STANDARDS ASSESSMENTS

This section describes students who take alternate achievement standards assessments by their communication and academic skill sets. These composite cases are intended to provide the reader real-life examples of learners with these characteristics. Megan, Jason, Skyler, and Leslie exemplify the range of students who participate in alternate achievement standards assessments.

Meet Megan

Megan has multiple disabilities that interfere with learning and assessment. She communicates using cries, facial expressions, or other body movements, but she has no clear use of symbolic forms of communication. Her cries, facial expressions, and body movements are interpreted as communication by her teachers and care providers. She does not initiate communication with an AAC system, although objects representing activities are provided to orient her to upcoming activities. Receptively, Megan alerts to sensory information (touch, visual, auditory) but requires extensive physical assistance to respond. It is not clear how much she uses her vision. However, she does respond to music by moving her head and will turn toward other auditory stimuli. She alerts to input from individuals and consistently responds to interactions with familiar people in close proximity to her. Her attendance at school is irregular because of significant health issues. She listens to stories, especially when they are read by peers, but her responses to print and her number awareness skills are inconsistent. Educational priorities for Megan include the use of AAC (e.g., objects and signs) with peers within the context of literacy and numeracy activities.

Megan represents an alternate assessment participant who fits the definition of *most significant cognitive disabilities*. Not only is she communicating at a presymbolic level, but she experiences motor, sensory, and health issues that increase the challenge of teaching and assessing her skills. It is important to note that one way to teach communication and other skills can be through reading and math activities that other students may be doing. Social engagement is a relative strength on which to build subsequent skills in communication, reading, and mathematics. Again, the general curriculum, especially as it is taught within general education settings in the presence of peers who do not have disabilities, can provide the material for engagement. The opportunity to be in "environments that promote one's communication as a full partner with other people, including peers" is emphasized in the National Joint Committee for the Communication Needs of Persons with Severe Disabilities and supports the inclusion of such students in the general classroom. Such a "collaborative consultation model," if used appropriately and in conjunction with other service delivery models, offers students with disabilities increased intensity and consistency of services (Mollica, Paul-Brown, Whitmire, White, & Kovach, 2003). Figure 1.2 illustrates the percentage of students with the most significant cognitive disabilities as characterized by levels of symbolic language use and the presence

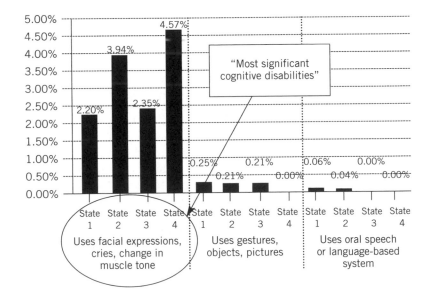

Figure 1.2.   Expressive language use and complex characteristics.

of other complex characteristics (e.g., vision, hearing, motor, engagement, health). Notably, as the level of symbolic language increases, the presence of complex characteristics decreases.

Meet Jason

Jason, another alternate achievement standards assessment participant, uses verbal and written words to respond to questions, describe objects and events, and express a variety of intentions. He has a diagnosis of an intellectual disability (IDEA category of mental retardation). He follows multistep directions independently and engages with familiar and unfamiliar people in reciprocal, sustained social interactions. His vision, hearing, and motor skills are well within typical limits, and his attendance at school is regular. Jason reads basic sight words, bulleted lists, and simple directions. He uses a calculator in math to perform addition and subtraction mathematics operations. He can write simple sentences and fill in applications with the correct personal information.

Whereas Megan represents a student with the most complex needs among the students who participate in alternate achievement standards assessments, Jason represents the more typical alternate assessment participant. Data from four states suggest that students such as Jason represent the majority of the students who participate in alternate achievement standards assessments (Towles-Reeves et al., 2009).

Meet Skyler

Skyler is a student with autism who participates in alternate achievement standards assessments. Skyler communicates using gestures and points to pictures to communicate a variety of intentions. He needs additional cues to follow multistep directions. He responds to social interactions but does not initiate or sustain social interactions. His hearing, vision, and motor skills seem to be within typical ranges. Students such as Skyler who communicate at emerging levels of symbolic language are more likely to respond receptively by following directions with prompts or cues. Skyler's attendance at school is regular; in school, a structured routine is essential for managing his complex behavior. Skyler orients to books correctly, follows print directionality, fills in words for cloze sentences, and points to pictures. He identifies some environmental print. He can repeat counting sequences and match objects in patterns.

Skyler is an emerging symbolic language user—the second-largest group of students participating in the states' sample. It is important to note that students with autism, like students with intellectual disabilities, represent a continuum of development. That is, not all students with autism have the same ability sets and skills as Skyler. Similarly, not all students with intellectual disabilities have the same skills and abilities as Jason. Indeed, several of the skills for each of these students could be interchanged with others and still be representative of the population of students who participate in alternate achievement standards assessments. It is important to note that expressive and receptive language development seems to be an essential distinguishing characteristic of students who participate in alternate achievement standards assessments.

The majority of students communicate at a symbolic level of communication (see Figure 1.3) and follow at least two-step directions independently (70%). Students communicating at presymbolic levels of language development represent the smallest group (slightly more than 10%), followed by students communicating at emerging levels of language development (fewer than 20%).

Receptively, students fall into two groups. Students who follow directions independently and those who require cues to follow directions represent the largest group, whereas those who alert to sensory input or have inconsistent responses represent the smaller of the two groups. Figure 1.4 highlights receptive communication from the NAAC study (Towles-Reeves et al., 2009).

As illustrated in the previous student profiles, Megan represents a student who communicates at a presymbolic level of language development and alerts to input from others. Jason uses symbolic communication and follows directions, whereas Skyler uses emerging symbolic language and requires cues to execute directions receptively. These levels of expressive and receptive communication skills are very descriptive of the range of student participants in alternate achievement standards assessments. With perhaps a few notable exceptions, communication development distinguishes these students from typically developing students who engage in the entire breadth of curricula and participate in general assessments.

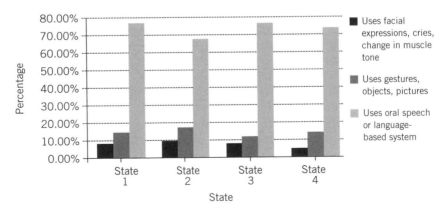

Figure 1.3.   Expressive language skills distribution for alternate assessments based on alternate achievement standards population.

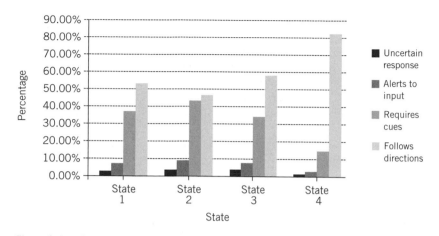

Figure 1.4. Receptive language skills distribution for alternate assessments based on alternate achievement standards participants across population.

Meet Leslie

Like Megan, Leslie has multiple disabilities and a fragile medical condition. She breathes with a ventilator, has limited motor functioning and low vision, and attends school only 3 days per week. For many years, it was believed that she, too, was limited in her communication to cries, facial expressions, and occasional eye gazes. However, with careful and extensive observation, an appropriate AAC system was developed for her and was flexible enough to include academic content from her classes. Using a head-control switch and a clocklike dial, she responds independently to questions that have multiple-choice responses. Her team was excited to learn that she could indeed choose a mathematical pattern when they gave her three examples. Members of her team do not recall teaching her about patterns or ever asking her such a question. With the communication system, Leslie communicates at a symbolic level of language development that previously went undetected. Her team had *thought* she was a presymbolic learner, but in reality she had the capacity to be a symbolic learner all along.

CHARACTERISTICS TO CONSIDER

The following sections discuss some common characteristics of students who take alternate assessments.

Augmentative and Alternative Communication Systems

Although AAC goes back decades and includes pictures and objects, since the advent of assistive technology in the early 1990s, AAC systems (high-technology, computer-based systems; low-technology pictures, object boards, and so forth) have allowed students such as Leslie to demonstrate communicative competence, knowledge, and skills at much higher levels than expected. For students such as Leslie who fall within the very small percentage of students who might be described initially as presymbolic or even emerging symbolic communicators, certainly AAC systems are key to enabling them to demonstrate what they know and can do.

Sadly, our research suggests that of the students communicating at presymbolic or emerging levels of symbolic language, only 50% or fewer have any type of AAC system (Towles-Reeves et al., 2009). In the early days of accountability, alternate achievement standards assessments required demonstration of communication. A number of validity studies touted the increase in communication systems among this population as an unintended but positive outcome of the assessment (Kleinert, Kennedy, & Kearns, 1999). When students have no way to consistently communicate their intents and purposes (including literacy), access to the general curriculum poses problems for assessment design, not to mention even more fundamental questions about the content of what they are learning!

Communication Growth and Literacy Skills

All too often, students such as Leslie are never identified as symbolic communicators, and, in cases such as Megan's, communication is viewed as a prerequisite to learning academic content instead of teaching communication through academic content activities (Browder, Wallace, Snell, & Kleinert, 2005). Erickson, Koppenhaver, and Yoder have addressed this issue in their 1997 longitudinal case study of a student with severe communication and physical disabilities who also was considered to have moderate to severe cognitive impairments. Appropriate literacy interventions, use of technology in classroom settings, adaptation of the curricula, and active interactions with same-age peers "in academic aspects of the curriculum" (p. 148) were all implemented during a 2-year period. The student showed consistent progress in a variety of literacy skills. Sturm et al. (2006) noted the importance of exposing students who use AAC devices to the "core literacy learning opportunities across grade levels that foster development of conventional literacy skills" (p. 21). These authors posit that lack of exposure to communication, reading, and writing tools is one reason that students who require AAC often do not develop literacy skills or develop such skills only to a second-grade level.

To compound the problems created by a lack of communication systems, the results of the NAAC study indicate little change in the distribution of communication levels from presymbolic to symbolic across the grade span from elementary to high school. Figure 1.5 illustrates the distribution of communication functioning from elementary school to high school.

Although these are cross-sectional and not longitudinal data, they do suggest that even after years of schooling, the percentages of students communicating at presymbolic and emerging levels of symbolic language do not seem to change. Most important, the percentage of students who communicate at a symbolic level of language increases only slightly from elementary to high school (from 67.0% to 72.6%). Couple these data with the lack of AAC systems for many of these students, and serious instructional and assessment problems emerge. Clearly, students such as Leslie are getting to high school all too often without communication skills essential for accessing the general curriculum and without having a wide range of functional intents.

This lack of communication, together with limited use of technology (though it has been available to students with severe disabilities for more than two decades), severely limits not only these students' rights to self-assertion and self-advocacy but also their basic right to academic achievement. Erickson, Koppenhaver, and Yoder stated in 1997 that, for such students, literacy has been "underemphasized" and that access to literacy, like communication, is a "birthright of human beings—not something available only to those without obvious disabilities or to those for whom we predict high degrees of competence" (p. 259). These researchers stressed the availability of technology that can overcome many of the obstacles to learning faced by students with severe disabilities. This technology must be used, however, and unfortunately data on the use of AAC in schools are not strong (Towles-Reeves et al., 2008).

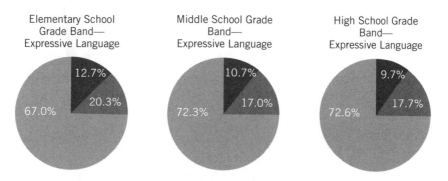

Figure 1.5. Expressive language distribution across grade bands. (*Key:* ■, student communicates primarily through cries, facial expressions, change in muscle tone; ■, student uses gestures, pictures, objects/textures, points, or similar methods to clearly express a variety of intentions; ■, student uses verbal or written words, signs, braille, or language-based augmentative and alternative communication systems.)

Reading Skills

In addition to communication, we asked teachers to select the best descriptions of their students' overall skills in reading and mathematics. Not surprisingly, students such as Leslie and Megan were most likely to be identified as having no observable skills in reading and mathematics. However, for the great majority (70%) of students who participate in alternate achievement standards assessments, including students such as Skyler and Jason, the distribution of reading and math Learner Characteristics Inventory (LCI) performance ratings also did not change across elementary, middle, and high school grades (Towles-Reeves et al., 2009). Although the LCI measures are not designed to capture precise gains in student skills, it is reasonable to assume that even global measures such as the LCI would show increasing student skill levels with age. Yet, our data suggest otherwise; students such as Jason and Skyler—whether they are in elementary, middle, or high school—still read basic sight words. A few students read with basic or literal understanding/comprehension. An extremely small percentage of students might read with critical understanding, although one state determined that students reading at this level likely would not meet the participation criteria for the state's alternate achievement standards assessment. Figure 1.6 illustrates the distributions of reading levels in the four states. With the possible exception of State 4 (in which more students are reading with basic understanding), the patterns in the data are remarkably similar.

Again, it is plausible to assume that as students spend additional years in school, the distribution of skill levels would change as the students have additional opportunities to learn. Yet, the NAAC study findings suggest that the distribution of reading skills from elementary to high school did not change. Figure 1.7 illustrates this finding.

The most likely explanation for this finding is that the newly required focus of curricula on academic content (IDEA 2004; NCLB) is very

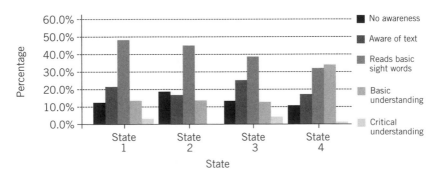

Figure 1.6. Reading skills distribution for alternate assessments based on alternate achievement standards population.

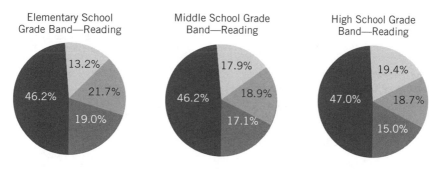

Figure 1.7. Reading skills distribution for alternate assessments based on alternate achievement standards across grade bands. (*Key:* ■, aware of print or braille; ■, reads basic sight words; ■, reads fluently with basic understanding; ▨, reads fluently with critical understanding.)

recent; schools simply have not emphasized higher-level academic skills in their curricula for these students.

Mathematics Skills

Similar to the findings in reading, students such as Jason and Skyler use calculators to perform mathematics operations, whereas students such as Megan and Leslie most likely are rated as having no awareness of numbers. Jason and Skyler make up the majority of students in the population, followed closely by students who can count with correspondence. A small number of students can apply computational procedures in a variety of real-life situations. The NAAC findings suggest that in mathematics, solving simple mathematical problems with a calculator represents the performance level of the majority of students in the alternate assessment population (Towles-Reeves et al., 2009). Figure 1.8 illustrates the distribution of skills in mathematics.

In their review, Browder, Spooner, Ahlgrim-Delzell, Harris, and Wakeman (2008) found that, according to the research literature, basic operations, calculator skills, and skills in measurement were the most predominant mathematics skills taught to students who participate in alternate assessments. A few studies referred to teaching geometry, statistics, and probability. None of the studies discussed algebra (Browder et al., 2008). As with reading, the distribution seems to mirror what is commonly understood as the "curriculum" for students with significant cognitive disabilities.

Finally, although the NAAC study found that the distribution of mathematics skills did change slightly across grade levels, the change was minimal. Figure 1.9 represents these findings.

These findings were repeated across all four states in the analysis. Although mathematical skills seem to increase slightly across grade bands,

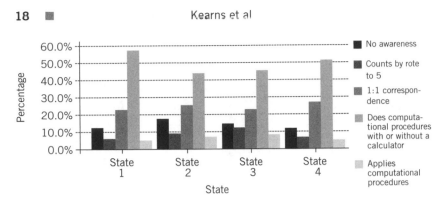

Figure 1.8. Mathematics skills distribution for alternate assessments based on alternate achievement standards population.

the distributions remain essentially unchanged from elementary school to high school. However, it is possible that even these small gains may not represent real changes in performance for students. One alternative explanation for the increase in mathematics performance at the high school level is that students with cognitive disabilities who previously were in the general assessment or a different assessment were reclassified in high school for the alternate achievement standards assessment. This could explain the increase in skills at the higher end of the age continuum and not at the other grade bands. We simply do not know enough to answer this question.

LIMITATIONS

Although these data describe the general characteristics of the population of students who take alternate achievement standards assessments, some significant limitations continue to challenge our thinking about

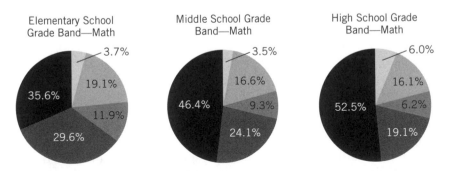

Figure 1.9. Mathematics skills distribution for alternate assessments based on alternate achievement standards across grade bands. (*Key:* ■, no observable awareness or use of numbers; ■, counts by rote to 5; ■, Counts with one-to-one correspondence; ■, does computational procedures with or without a calculator; ■, applies computational procedures.)

this student population. First, we examined a relatively small group of states and a very small population of students within those states. More statewide data are needed to solidify these findings.

Second, these states assess only slightly more than 1% of students in their alternate achievement standards assessments; states that assessed higher percentages of students in their alternate achievement standards assessments would probably show broader ranges of skills for their participating students, especially in the percentages of students at the upper skill levels of the LCI. States reporting 1% of proficient scores in their alternate assessments may well be assessing up to 3% of their populations. None of those states are represented in these data.

Third, data sources such as disability category may be interpreted differently from state to state. For example, students in the AA-AAS seem to represent a higher level of heterogeneity than the rest of the student population; in fact, they may represent at least three subgroups of children whose characteristics in receptive and expressive communication warrant considerations in assessment design. Finally, our content variables are limited, continuously resulting in data that are less precise about the depth and breadth of skills within each content domain.

More detailed information is needed to characterize the student population across a broader sample of states. In addition, an analysis of assessment results by student characteristics may reveal more about how students are learning in the academic content domain. For example, if students such as Megan who communicate at emerging symbolic levels of language development have no or low scores on certain items or continue to have low overall scores across years, technical assistance and training in instruction may be warranted. In addition, implementing a multiple achievement standards approach to highlight appropriate learning targets may lead to improved results for these students and improve their communication skills. Multiple alternate achievement standards are allowed under NCLB (U.S. Department of Education, 2005). Given that the population of students in alternate achievement standards assessments ranges from symbolic learners, who demonstrate skills in reading and math, to presymbolic learners, who display limited social engagement and no awareness of print and numbers, it would seem reasonable to consider separate alternate achievement standards for these two sets of students (Towles-Reeves et al., 2009). However, the decision to implement multiple achievement standards must consider and monitor the intended and unintended consequences of such a decision to ensure that students are assessed appropriately.

The score distributions in our reading and math items across elementary, middle, and high school suggest a lack of a cohesive and progressive academic curricula, highlighting the significant lack of research about how students who participate in alternate assessments longitudinally demonstrate academic content in meaningful and appropriate ways. For example, although using a calculator to do math represents an important life skill, Skyler and Jason still should be challenged to use increasingly complex mathematics and reading skills in authentic, real-life contexts that make the skills immediately useful for them. Both a menu of functional skills *and* a progression of academic skills are needed to keep students learning at high levels across school years.

Finally, careful attention should be paid to the determination of "proficiency" for this population. A high percentage of proficient students in an alternate achievement standards assessment may leave a false impression of achievement, and that in itself may be very dangerous. Schools might believe that all is well when, in fact, continuous progress is not occurring and high standards are minimal. This *is* the place in which children will be left behind, to do the same skills and achieve the same objectives year after year until they finally age out of school.

SUMMARY

The major challenge of evaluating students who take alternate assessments lies in the diversity of the population and the lack of a progressive academic curriculum. However, the model developed by Pellegrino et al. (2001) illustrates a compelling argument for knowing and understanding the students, and also the content, in any endeavor to build valid alternate assessments that can provide data to inform instructional decisions. In addition, continuous validity evaluation is needed to improve the instruments and to increase knowledge and outcomes for students with the most significant cognitive disabilities.

REFERENCES

Almond, P., & Bechard, S. (2005). *In-depth look at students who take alternate assessments: What do we know now?* Retrieved November 10, 2007, from http://www.cde.state.co.us/cdesped/download/pdf/FindingsDemographics_Reliability.pdf

Browder, D., Spooner, F., Ahlgrim-Delzell, L., Harris, A., & Wakeman, S. (2008). A meta-analysis on teaching mathematics to students with significant cognitive disabilities. *Exceptional Children, 74*(4), 407–432.

Browder, D., Wakeman, S., Spooner, F., Ahlgrim-Delzell, L., & Algozzine, B. (2006). Research on reading instruction for individuals with significant cognitive disabilities. *Exceptional Children, 72*(4), 392–408.

Browder, D., Wallace, T., Snell, M., & Kleinert, H. (2005). *The use of progress monitoring with students with significant cognitive disabilities.* Washington, DC: American Institutes of Research, National Center on Student Progress Monitoring.

Courtade, G., Spooner, F., & Browder, D. (2007). A review of studies with students with significant cognitive disabilities that link to science standards. *Research and Practice in Severe Disabilities, 32*(1), 43–49.

Erickson, K., Koppenhaver, D., & Yoder, D. (1997). Integrated communication and literacy instruction for a child with multiple disabilities. *Focus on Autism and Other Developmental Disabilities, 12*(3), 142–150.

Individuals with Disabilities Education Act Amendments (IDEA) of 1997, PL 105-17, 20 U.S.C. §§ 1400 *et seq.*

Individuals with Disabilities Education Improvement Act of 2004, PL 108-446, 20 U.S.C. §§ 1400 *et seq.*

Kearns, J., Kleinert, H., Kleinert, J., & Towles-Reeves, E. (2006). *Learner Characteristics Inventory (LCI).* Lexington: University of Kentucky, National Alternate Assessment Center.

Kleinert, H., Browder, D., & Towles-Reeves, E. (2009). Models of cognition for students with significant cognitive disabilities: Implications for assessment. *Review of Educational Research, 79,* 301–326.

Kleinert, H., Haigh, J., Kearns, J., Kennedy, S. (2000). Alternate assessments: Lessons learned and roads to be taken. *Exceptional Children, 67*(1), 51–66.

Kleinert, H., & Kearns, J.F. (1999). A validation study of the performance indicators and learner outcomes of Kentucky's alternate assessment for students with significant disabilities. *Journal of the Association for Persons with Severe Handicaps, 24*(2), 100–110.

Kleinert, H., Kennedy, S., & Kearns, J. (1999). The impact of alternate assessments: A statewide teacher survey. *The Journal of the Association for Persons with Severe Handicaps, 22*(2), 88–101.

Marion, S.F., & Pellegrino, J.W. (2006). A validity framework for evaluating the technical quality of alternate assessments. *Educational Measurement: Issues and Practice, 25*(4), 47–57.

Marion, S.F., Quenemoen, R.F., & Kearns, J.F. (2006, October). *Introductory presentation.* Presented at the Seminars on Inclusive Assessments, University of Minnesota, National Center on Educational Outcomes, Minneapolis.

Mollica, B.M., Paul-Brown, D., Whitmire, K., White, S., & Kovach, T. (2003, November). *Service delivery for individuals with severe disabilities.*

National Joint Committee for the Communication Needs of Persons with Severe Disabilities. (1992). *Guidelines for meeting the communication needs of persons with severe disabilities* [Guidelines]. Available from www.asha.org/policy or www.asha.org/njc

No Child Left Behind Act of 2001, PL 107-110, 115 Stat. 1425, 20 U.S.C. §§ 6301 *et seq.*

Pellegrino, J., Chudowsky, N., & Glaser, R. (Eds.). (2001). *Knowing what students know: The science and design of educational assessment.* Washington, DC: National Academies Press.

Sturm, J., Spadorcia, S., Cunningham, J., Cali, K., Staples, A., Erickson, K., et al. (2006). What happened to reading between first and third grade? Implications for students who use AAC. *Augmentative and Alternative Communication, 22*(1), 21–36.

Thompson, S., & Thurlow, M. (2000). *State alternate assessments: Status as IDEA alternate assessment requirements take effect.* Retrieved June 3, 2008, from University of Minnesota, National Center on Educational Outcomes web site: http://education.umn.edu/NCEO/OnlinePubs/Synthesis35.html

Towles-Reeves, E., Kearns, J., Kleinert, H., & Kleinert, J. (2009). An analysis of the learning characteristics of students taking alternate assessments based on alternate achievement standards. *Journal of Special Education, 42*(4), 241–254.

U.S. Department of Education. (2005). *Alternate achievement standards for students with the most significant cognitive disabilities: Non-regulatory guidance.* Washington, DC: Author.

U.S. Department of Education. (2006). *Twenty-sixth annual report to Congress on the implementation of the Individuals with Disabilities Education Act.* Retrieved February 22, 2008, from http://www.ed.gov/about/reports/annual/osep/2004/introduction.html

U.S. Department of Education. (2009). *Twenty-eighth annual report to Congress on the implementation of the Individuals with Disabilities Education Act.* Retrieved March 3, 2009, from http://www.ed.gov/about/reports/annual/osep/2006/parts-b-c/index.html

CHAPTER 2

Understanding the Construct to Be Assessed

STEPHEN N. ELLIOTT

This chapter introduces the construct—or constructs—that alternate assessments are intended to measure and the evidence needed to support construct claims. Defining the construct that a test measures is a fundamental and seminal step in test development. Often, the nature of the construct to be measured is not fully understood until a number of studies have been completed that collectively provide evidence about a test's scores and reliable inferences from those scores.

Some definitional background information can be helpful in this exploration of alternate assessments and the construct(s) they measure. First, consider the potential definitions of the key word *construct:* "1) To form by assembling parts; build; 2) To create by systematically arranging ideas or expressions; or 3) Something, especially a concept, that is synthesized or constructed from simple elements"[1] (Editors of the American Heritage Dictionaries, 2002). For the purposes of this chapter, the third definition is most relevant, given the work that has been done to develop assessments that have a number of items (i.e., "simple elements") that, when administered and synthesized, provide information about students' knowledge and skills. The first and second definitions, however, are also relevant because, once there is a vision of needs to be measured, a method is needed to carry out the assessment that will yield reliable and valid results. In other words, understanding the construct requires process and outcome knowledge!

The term *construct* has a central place in the history of testing. A few brief points from this history are relevant and provide a little more context for my subsequent comments:

- The term *construct*—logical or hypothetical—originated in Bertrand Russell's 1929 maxim that wherever possible, logical constructions are to be substituted for inferred entities (McCorquodale & Meehl, 1948).

---

[1]Copyright © 2007 by Houghton Mifflin Harcourt Publishing Company. Reproduced by permission from *The American Heritage College Dictionary, Fourth Edition.*

- McCorquodale and Meehl (1948) distinguished *hypothetical constructs* (unobservable, inferred entities) from *intervening variables* (abstractions from observations).

- In the 1954 test standards published by the American Psychological Association, construct validity was defined as "the degree to which the individual possesses some hypothetical trait or quality [construct] presumed to be reflected in the test performance" (as cited in American Educational Research Association, American Psychological Association, & National Council on Measurement in Education, 1999).

- The concept of validating a construct was more fully developed by Cronbach and Meehl (1955), who referred to a *construct* as an *attribute*. They went on to list construct-validation procedures as 1) criterion-group differences, 2) factor analysis, 3) item analysis, 4) experimental studies, and 5) studies of process.

- Messick's (1989) epic chapter united all types of validity under construct validity. As described by Messick, "construct validity is . . . the unifying concept of validity that integrates content and criterion considerations into a common framework for testing rational hypotheses about theoretically relevant hypotheses."

- Through the work of Cronbach, with contributions from Messick (1980, 1989), the common view is one conception of validity referred to as *construct validity*. Thus, the validation of a test score can be taken to include every form of evidence that the score, to some acceptable extent, measures a *specified attribute*—a quantifiable property of quality—of a respondent.

Based on this background, Figure 2.1 provides a simplified version of the logic outlined about the relations among an individual's performance, his or her test score, and an interpretation about the degree to which he or she posseses an abstracted attribution.

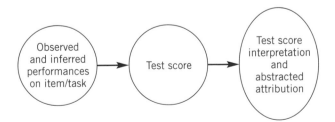

Figure 2.1.　A simplified version of the logic underlying a tested construct.

The interpretation of test scores ideally should be grounded in theory and verifiable against other measures that claim to measure the same or similar knowledge or skills. Figure 2.2 shows some possible relationships between what a test can measure and the domain space a construct can represent. This figure is from Forte Fast and Hebbler's (2004) report on accountability systems and provides a graphic illustration of three tests—A, B, and C—and each test measures Construct X. As indicated by the figure, the degree to which each test accomplishes the goal of measuring Construct X varies considerably. I suspect that, collectively, alternate assessments around the country function like these hypothetical tests. That is, some alternate assessments function like Test A in only measuring part of the intended construct, thus underrepresenting the construct. Some alternate assessments function like Test B and measure the intended construct plus additional constructs, thus reflecting construct-irrelevant variance. Finally, some of our alternate assessments probably perform like Test C, underrepresenting the intended construct and also measuring some irrelevant constructs. Gathering evidence to support a claim that an alternate assessment measures its intended construct is a challenge for all education professionals and requires better understanding of the construct(s). An improved understanding is needed to enable the improvement of these measures through revision and ongoing validation studies.

The U.S. Department of Education has provided some definitional guidance that informs one's understanding of the construct to be assessed by alternate assessments. According to the U.S. Department of Education, "An alternate assessment must be aligned with the State's content standards, must yield results separately in both reading/language

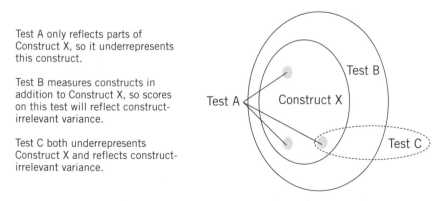

Test A only reflects parts of Construct X, so it underrepresents this construct.

Test B measures constructs in addition to Construct X, so scores on this test will reflect construct-irrelevant variance.

Test C both underrepresents Construct X and reflects construct-irrelevant variance.

Figure 2.2. An illustration of construct underrepresentation and construct-irrelevant variance. (From Council of Chief State School Officers. [2004]. *A Framework for Examining Validity in State Accountability Systems.* Washington, DC: Author. http://www.ccsso.org/Publications/Download.cfm?Filename=ValidityFrameworkFeb04.pdf; reprinted by permission.)

arts and mathematics, and must be designed and implemented in a manner that supports use of the results as an indicator of AYP (adequate yearly progress)" (U.S. Department of Education, 2005, p. 15).

I am tempted to end this chapter here with a brief statement: To understand the constructs to be measured by alternate assessments is as simple as knowing a state's content standards for reading/language arts, mathematics, and science. With a moment of reflection, however, it becomes clear that my statement does not really shed light on how people come to understand the construct being measured by an alternate assessment. Some would note that reading, mathematics, and science are complex content areas that vary throughout the course of a school's general education curriculum. Others would assert that the nature of the assessment—evidence-based rating scales, portfolios, or performance tasks—and the people involved in the assessment—one or more educators and the student—can influence what actually is being measured. Therefore, understanding the construct to be measured by an alternate assessment is more complicated than simply examining a state's content standards and knowing what the word *construct* means. Understanding the construct measured by a test or assessment actually is the central aspect of a test-validation process and the concept called *validity*.

Validity refers to the adequacy and appropriateness of the score interpretations made from assessments, with regard to a particular use. Criteria for evaluating the validity of score inferences from tests and related assessment instruments have been written about extensively, yet few studies about the validity of alternate assessment scores have been published. In 1999, a joint committee of the American Educational Research Association, the American Psychological Association, and the National Council on Measurement in Education revised their comprehensive list of standards for tests. This list stresses the importance of construct validity and describes a variety of forms of evidence indicative of a valid test. The revised *Standards for Educational and Psychological Testing* (American Educational Research Association, American Psychological Association, & National Council for Measurement in Education, 1999) includes valuable information for educators involved in testing diverse groups of students, including students with significant cognitive disabilities. In addition to the *Standards for Testing,* the U.S. Department of Education (2004) published the *Standards and Assessment Peer Review Guidance: Information and Examples for Meeting Requirements of the No Child Left Behind Act of 2001.* This latter document extends the *Testing Standards* and provides even more specific guidance concerning validity evidence for state alternate assessments. For example, the *Technical Quality* subsection (4.1) of the *Peer Review Guidance* document specifically asks,

> (b) Has the state ascertained that the assessments, including alternate assessments, are measuring the knowledge and skills described in

its academic content standards and not knowledge, skills, or other characteristics that are not specified in the academic content standards or grade-level expectations? . . .

(e) Has the state ascertained that test and item scores are related to outside variables as intended (e.g., scores are correlated strongly with relevant measures of academic achievement and are weakly correlated, if at all, with irrelevant characteristics, such as demographics)? (p. 35)

As indicated by these excerpts from guiding resources, understanding the construct being measured requires research and a development plan based on content in a state's academic content standards and intended interpretations about students' academic achievement. Here are some salient points about test-score interpretations in the world of academic achievement:

- The proposed interpretation refers to the construct or concepts the test is intended to measure. Examples of constructs are mathematics achievement, performance as a computer technician. . . . To support test development, the proposed interpretation is elaborated by describing its scope and extent and by delineating the aspects of the construct that are to be represented. The detailed description provides a conceptual framework for the test, delineating the knowledge, skills, (and) abilities . . . to be assessed. (American Educational Research Association, American Psychological Association, & National Council for Measurement in Education, 1999, p. 9)

- Education professionals should be interested in understanding student achievement—that is, the knowledge and skills students possess at a given time in the content domains of language arts, mathematics, and science.

- Education professionals gain insights into student achievement by observing the amount or quantity of knowledge and skills students possess in these defined content domains. The amount or quantity of a measured attribute takes the form of a test score.

- Education professionals attribute more knowledge or skills for samples of behavior or work in which students demonstrate correct responses to a correspondingly larger number or more complex type of items.

- Education professionals' interpretations about student attributes are situated within broad academic content domains and are framed by performance-level descriptors.

For a more complete understanding of the construct(s) measured by a state's alternate assessment, I suggest you begin by inspecting the following documents, which commonly are provided at states' department of education web sites or in technical manuals for alternate assessments:

• The state's academic content standards

• The state's academic achievement standards—in particular, the performance-level descriptors for each content area

• Validity and alignment studies as reported in alternate assessment technical manuals

• Reports to consumers of the assessment results

The state of Mississippi can serve as an example of how such information sources can contribute to an understanding of the construct being measured by an alternate assessment—in this case, the Mississippi Alternate Assessment of Extended Curriculum Frameworks (MAAECF). Examining the structure of a state's content standards (e.g., the language arts strands and competencies for the MAAECF shown in Figure 2.3) can provide a real sense of what an alternate assessment is intended to measure. As this framework shows, language arts comprises two strands: reading and writing. Moving on to the intended interpretation of scores from the assessment, Figure 2.4 provides a snapshot of the multilevel framework for interpreting the results of the MAAECF assessment. As illustrated by this performance-level descriptor, the various levels of performance are defined both by general statements of competence and by specific content skills in reading and writing. With more time and inter-

---

Language Arts Strands and Competencies

Reading Strand. Students use reading skills and strategies to decode and interpret symbols, words, and larger blocks of text. Students demonstrate the ability to use reading to acquire new information, refine perspectives, respond to the needs and demands of society and the workplace, and provide for personal fulfillment.

• Competency 1: Use word recognition skills and strategies to communicate.
• Competency 2: Apply strategies and skills to comprehend, respond to, interpret, and evaluate communication.

Writing Strand. Students develop a working knowledge of language as well as grammatical structures, diction and usage, punctuation, spelling, layout, and presentation. Students develop the ability to express personal ideas, understandings, desires, and needs in writing.

• Competency 3: Understanding and using the writing process.
• Competency 4: Mechanics of writing.

Figure 2.3. Language arts strands and competencies for the Mississippi Alternate Assessment of Extended Curriculum Frameworks (MAAECF). (From Mississippi Department of Education [2007]. *Mississippi Alternate Assessment of Extended Curriculum Frameworks [MAAECF] technical manual* [p. 14]. Jackson, MS: Author; adapted by permission.)

Language Arts Grades 3-5

Language Arts involves a number of reading and writing skills and the development of subskills in four interrelated competency areas: (1) word recognition skills, (2) skills to comprehend, respond to, and evaluate communication, (3) writing process skills, and (4) writing mechanics skills. These subskill areas vary in complexity and importance for students in these grades. In general, students in this grade cluster are expected to progress with reading instruction from awareness to recognition of symbols and begin to comprehend text read by others or themselves. In writing, these students focus on basic communication and writing skills.

To develop and demonstrate skills to read and write, students require varying levels of support especially as the complexity of tasks and materials increase. This support or accommodation is intended to facilitate students' access or responding to tasks or items so that they can demonstrate what they know and can do.

Minimal	Basic	Proficient	Advanced
Student may occasionally attend to reading by others or look at pictures, but is unable to demonstrate most discrete pre-reading or pre-writing skills. Student currently exhibits 1or 2 of the prerequisite skills and knowledge in reading at a barely existent level. For example, a student at this level typically can: • Demonstrate very limited understanding of the most basic reading and writing concepts and skills.	Student attends to reading instruction and participates in a few writing or drawing activities. Student responds or performs several skills in at least 1 language arts subskill area, typically at the emerging level in at least 1 setting. For example, a student at this level typically exhibits Level 1 subskills and can also: • Attend and respond to texts read to him or her. • Identify pictures in text.	Student demonstrates the ability to decode and comprehend some basic text and write his/her name. The student's knowledge of basic concepts and performance of many skills in 2 language arts subskill areas are typically at the progressing level across 2 or more settings. For example, a student at this level typically exhibits Level 2 subskills and can also: • Attend and demonstrate an understanding of texts read to them. • Match words to common pictures in school and community settings. • Recognize some words in his or her environment and/or texts. • Writes his/her name from memory.	Student demonstrates a consistent understanding of basic reading and writing concepts and skills. He or she performs many of the skills in 2 or more language arts subskill areas at the progressing level and some skills at the accomplished level in multiple settings. For example, a student at this level typically exhibits Level 3 subskills and can also: • Accurately spell high frequency words. • Make connections between information in a text and previously read materials or life experiences. • Read basic texts with support. • Answer appropriately to some comprehension questions. • Provides some personal information upon request.
Grade 3: 0----------------8 Grade 4: 0----------------9 Grade 5: 0-------------11	9------------------------38 10------------------------45 12------------------------53	39-----------------------119 46-----------------------122 54-----------------------124	120-------------------174 123-------------------174 125-------------------174

Figure 2.4. Example of a performance-level descriptor from the Mississippi Alternate Assessment of Extended Curriculum Frameworks (MAAECF). (From Mississippi Department of Education [2007]. *Mississippi Alternate Assessment of Extended Curriculum Frameworks [MAAECF] technical manual* [p. 20]. Jackson, MS: Author; reprinted by permission.)

est, it can be demonstrated clearly that there is a high degree of alignment among Mississippi's academic content standards, its alternate assessment, its standards for proficiency, and actual instruction in the
classrooms. Thus, theoretical and practical arguments can be made
about the constructs that the MAAECF is intended to measure.

In addition to the theoretical and practical claims about the construct
being measured by the MAAECF, there is substantial empirical evidence
to support these claims. An example from the MAAECF technical manual
is highlighted by the illustration in Figure 2.5. Figure 2.5 features the scree
plot for the factor analysis of the MAAECF Grade 3 language arts and
mathematics items combined. This scree plot (of eigenvalues and factor
numbers) indicates the hypothesized three-factor—reading, writing, and
mathematics—solution that can be supported. Similar solutions were
found at each grade level; thus, replications of this finding for multiple
grade levels create more confidence that the MAAECF does measure the
constructs it intends to measure.

More evidence about measuring the intended constructs is provided
by examining the performance of known groups of students—those who
qualify to take the MAAECF and those students with disabilities who do
not qualify to take it. Table 2.1 provides data from a larger study showing correlations regarding the performance of students with disabilities
who took Mississippi's general education test and who also took the
MAAECF. This concurrent evidence between an established measure of
language arts and mathematics achievement with a new and alternative

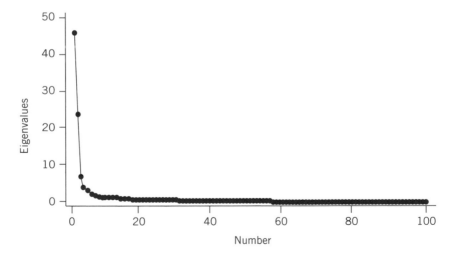

Figure 2.5.   Scree plot for the factor analysis of the Mississippi Alternate Assessment of
Extended Curriculum Frameworks (MAAECF) Grade 3 language arts and mathematics
items combined. (From Mississippi Department of Education [2007]. *Mississippi Alternate
Assessment of Extended Curriculum Frameworks [MAAECF] technical manual* [p. 37].
Jackson, MS: Author; reprinted by permission.)

Table 2.1. Results of correlational analyses of MAAECF subscale scores with Mississippi's large scale assessment (MCT) for students with disabilities who did not qualify to participate in the MAAECF.

| | MAAECF | | | |
| | Language Arts | | Mathematics | |
MCT	Grade 4 (n = 11)	Grade 8 (n = 11)	Grade 4 (n = 11)	Grade 4 (n = 9)
Reading	.20	.12	.00	−.10
Language Arts	−.05	.41	−.17	−.09
Mathematics	−.08	.19	.14	.39

From Kettler, R.J., Elliott, S.N., Beddow, P.A., Compton, E., McGrath, D., Kaase, K., et al. (2009). *What does an alternate assessment of alternate achievement standards measure? A multi-trait multimethod analysis across six states* (CAAVES Project Report). Nashville: Vanderbilt University; reprinted by permission.

Key: MAAECF, Mississippi Alternate Assessment of Extended Curriculum Frameworks; MCT, Mississippi Curriculum Test.

measure provides some promising support that, to some extent, the MAAECF measures the intended constructs. However, the magnitude of the relationship between Mississippi's general education test and the MAAECF is not large. Thus, the MAAECF might underrepresent the intended construct (like Test A in the opening example from this chapter), or it might measure some irrelevant constructs in addition to the intended construct (like Test C in the opening example). The important conclusion is that, for any assessment (including alternate achievement measures or general education achievement tests), refinements are necessary, and validation processes are ongoing.

To close, I highlight some assessment issues to keep in mind and provide a summary statement about the critical role that construct definition plays in alternate assessment research and practice. While venturing forward to understand the constructs that alternate assessments measure and to improve the reliability and validity of the inferences made about scores from alternate assessments, it is important to confront a number of issues that affect the validity of test-score interpretations. These include

• Teachers' support and prompting during the assessment

• Tests with items or tasks that are nonacademic

• Assessments that sample a limited portion of the intended domain

• Item or task rubrics that score for more than achievement

My colleagues address some, if not all, of these issues in this book. Each of these issues, if present in an alternate assessment process, can influence the construct being measured and might unknowingly alter the intended score interpretation and validity claims made about the assessment. Paraphrasing Michael Kane (2002), a validity argument provides an overall evaluation of the plausibility of the proposed interpretations and uses of test scores. To understand and evaluate a test-score interpretation, it is necessary to be clear about what the interpretation claims. And, to accomplish this clarity, it is imperative that the construct being measured is well defined.

SUMMARY

I hope that this brief chapter has helped get this book off to a good start and has created a focus on the roles that policy, theory, state documents, and data play in understanding what alternate assessments are intended to measure.

REFERENCES

American Educational Research Association, American Psychological Association, & National Council on Measurement in Education. (1999). *Standards for educational and psychological testing.* Washington, DC: Authors.

Council of Chief State School Officers. (2004). *A framework for examining validity in state accountability systems.* Washington, DC: Author. http://www.ccsso.org/Publications/Download.cfm?Filename=ValidityFrameworkFeb04.pdf

Cronbach, L.J., & Meehl, P.E. (1955). Construct validity in psychological tests. *Psychological Bulletin, 52,* 281–302.

Editors of the American Heritage Dictionaries. (2002). *The American heritage college dictionary* (4th ed.). Boston: Houghton Mifflin.

Kane, M. (2002). Validating high-stakes testing programs. *Educational Measurement: Issues and Practices, 21*(1), 31–41.

Kettler, R.J., Elliott, S.N., Beddow, P.A., Compton, E., McGrath, D., Kaase, K., et al. (2009). *What does an alternate assessment of alternate achievement standards measure? A multi-trait multi-method analysis across six states* (CAAVES Project Report). Nashville: Vanderbilt University.

McCorquodale, K., & Meehl, P.E. (1948). On a distinction between hypothetical constructs and intervening variables. *Psychological Review, 55,* 95–107.

Messick, S. (1980). Test validity and the ethics of measurement. *American Psychologist, 30,* 955–966.

Messick, S. (1989). Meaning and values in test validation: The science and ethics of assessment. *Educational Researcher, 18*(2), 5–11.

Mississippi Department of Education. (2007). *Mississippi Alternate Assessment of Extended Curriculum Frameworks (MAAECF) technical manual.* Jackson: Author.

U.S. Department of Education. (2004, April). *Standards and assessment peer review guidance: Information and examples for meeting requirements of the No Child Left Behind Act of 2001.* Washington, DC: Author.

U.S. Department of Education. (2005, August). *Alternate achievement standards for students with the most significant cognitive disabilities (non-regulatory guidance).* Washington, DC: Author.

CHAPTER 3

Sampling the Domain for Evidence of Achievement

GERALD TINDAL

Alternate assessments came into national focus when the Individuals with Disabilities Education Act Amendments of 1997 (PL 105-17) mandated that students with disabilities have access to the general education curriculum and participate in large-scale assessments with appropriate accommodations and modifications as necessary or be permitted to take alternate assessments.

BALANCING CONTENT AND METHODS OF ASSESSMENT IN SAMPLING DOMAINS

Most states had no experience in creating or administering alternate assessments; as a result, from 1997 to 2001, states diligently developed various forms of alternate assessments that reflected either of two approaches: "(a) simplify the regular standard until we can find something (anything!) that the student can do, or (b) redefine the regular curriculum standard so that it represents some type of functional skill" (Ford, Davern, & Schnorr, 2001, pp. 213–214). As a consequence, teachers have not been provided much direction regarding alternate assessments, and many have expressed confusion on the subject (Crawford, Almond, Tindal, & Hollenbeck, 2002).

Content of Assessment

Content and method needed to be balanced, if for no other reason than the reality of students' living situations (and needs as identified by individualized educational programs) and the legal mandates of the No Child Left Behind Act of 2001 (PL 107-110), which required state assessments to be aligned with grade-level standards. As a consequence, the constructs of most early assessments in this area often begged the question of what was really being measured. In striking this balance, with no history of test development similar to that available for general education tests, it is not surprising that the content domain sampled a mixture of items, tasks, or behaviors that were important for students' personal lives yet also related to academic standards. Sometimes, the content comprised prerequisite skills that, with mastery, would lead to success on the state tests and grade-level standards. For example, the early measures in Oregon sampled early skills in learning to read, write, and complete mathematical problems (Tindal et al., 2003). Many states still use this strategy after having extended the grade-level content standards. Other times, skills were embedded in functional tasks that are important in day-to-day living; for example, counting change may be a task on an alternate assessment, reflecting an appropriate grade-level standard in mathematics while representing a relevant task in the world outside of school. In fact, an entire mathematics curriculum has been developed (Everyday Mathematics; The University of Chicago Mathematics Project, 2007) to better contextualize problems that are more relevant for students and not just problems to be practiced and drilled.

Method of Assessment

Another (perhaps related) issue needed to be addressed in sampling items and tasks as part of alternate assessments: What method of administration (and scoring) should be used? Because the populations being tested in alternate assessments were so varied, and given the variety of problems these students had in accessing the tests, portfolios represented a viable strategy. With this method, administration options were left open and embedded into the classrooms, taking advantage of the routines with which the students were familiar. Furthermore, teachers were free to structure the assessment processes to maximize each student's ability to interact with the items and tasks in the assessments. Yet, such variation has been viewed as antithetical to large-scale testing because of problems in establishing reliability, a quintessential requirement for measures used in accountability systems.

In contrast, standardized performance assessments represented an option for overcoming some of the difficulties inherent with portfolios. With this assessment method, items and tasks were structured with various scaffolds made available during administration to maximize appropriate interaction with items and tasks and to provide more comparability among participating students. Given the need for some level of comparability to establish proficiency standards and still have uniform meaning, this method seemed more consistent with large-scale testing programs. Tindal, Yovanoff, and Geller (in press) described this tension between portfolios and standardized performance assessments.

The Nexus of Content and Method

These two dimensions of assessment—the content (functional living skills versus academic content) and the method (portfolio entries versus performance tasks)—reflect a larger issue in the field: The term *construct* is both a noun and a verb. As a noun, it refers to the essence of what is being measured, and as a verb it refers to the method used in the measurement. In the end, both dimensions need to be considered: A construct may be viewed as a concept within a nomological net (see Cronbach & Meehl, 1955), a set of lawful relations that help define the construct, including other measures that employ multiple methods. A fully articulated nomological net includes measures that should *and* should not be related to each other (and the target of measurement).

Perhaps the best model for understanding the evidence for sampling domains in documenting achievement came from Campbell and Fiske (1959) in their description of the multitrait, multimethod analysis (I use the term *trait* to mean *skill*). In this analysis, (several) different traits are measured using (several) different methods to provide a correlation matrix that reflects specific patterns supporting the claim being made (i.e., providing positive validation evidence that achievement is adequately documented and proficiency is appropriately established). An important perspective in this process is that

> Each test or task employed for measurement purposes is a "trait-method unit," a unit of a particular trait content with measurement procedures not specific to the content. A fully rendered analysis is needed so that disconfirmation is possible as well as the obvious confirmation. If only one method is used, it is not possible to disentangle performance as a function of the method and trait. This two-dimensional matrix provides reliability-related evidence (in each monomethod block) and validity evidence (in each heteromethod-heterotrait block). Ideally, the pattern of relations reflects a systematic ordering or relations such that the highest values are found with the same methods measuring the same traits, then different methods measuring the same trait, and finally different methods measuring different traits: "Reliability is the agreement between two efforts to measure the same trait through maximally similar methods. Validity is represented in the agreement between two attempts to measure the same trait through maximally different methods" (p. 277).

Both *content* and *method* of measurement must be considered to appropriately sample items and tasks for alternate assessments. And, in this process, two types of interpretive errors need to be considered: 1) construct-irrelevant variance and 2) construct under- or misrepresentation. In the former error, the measurement process includes components not relevant to the target skill being measured; the resultant outcome is, therefore, likely to be misinterpreted. For example, reading and mathematics performance are often highly correlated. To the extent that performance is unduly influenced by a student's ability to read, the mathematics score is misrepresented. Construct underrepresentation occurs when the sampling plan or administration and scoring of items fail to adequately reflect the full domain of items in the universe being targeted. For example, in a mathematics task on sequencing, a simple pattern used in a test may not fully reflect the domain, underrepresenting the complexity of possible items (e.g., using obvious patterns with little interpolation or comparing patterns of geometric shapes versus Fibonacci coding).

Elliott and Roach (2007) provided even more exact articulation of the process for validation of proficiency decisions from alternate assessments by considering the sampling domain. In part, their description of the process included both an analysis of the content and the methods through which assessments are operationalized. A major issue that they raised is the amount of control over the task (specifications) and the judgment of performance. They presented a very useful heuristic graph, with the Y-axis reflecting increases in task control from none (e.g., arbitrary samples entered into a portfolio) to total (e.g., externally controlled tasks as part of a performance assessment). The other dimension (X-axis reflecting judgment of performance) increases from unguided judgments to objective, machine-scored responses.

In summary, the history of alternate assessment has addressed the issues of content and method in defining sampling domains that provide evidence of achievement. Content has been balanced precariously between the full needs of students and the mandates of legislation. Methods have been bounded by the access skills of students and the grade-level standards of states. Research is only beginning to emerge on both of these dimensions. The research on content has focused on alignment, and the research on methods has focused on portfolios, rating scales, and performance tasks.

CONTENT: ALIGNMENT OF ALTERNATE ASSESSMENTS AND GRADE-LEVEL STANDARDS

As identified in the peer review guidelines (U.S. Department of Education, 2004) used to judge the adequacy of all state assessment systems, including alternate assessments,

> The current [No Child Left Behind Act] requirements include high-quality academic assessments, accountability systems, and teacher preparation and training aligned with challenging State academic standards so that students, teachers, parents, and administrators can measure progress against common expectations for students' academic achievement. (p. iii)

The key feature implicit in this language is the alignment of the assessment with the grade-level standards. Alignment is the degree of consistency between test content and subject area content reflected in state academic standards; because most states employ vast arrays of standards that cannot be completely assessed, alignment often focuses on the adequacy of sampling standards using various criteria of breadth, depth, and range (La Marca, Redfield, Winter, Bailey, & Hansche, 2000).

Probably the most ubiquitous model for alignment is that proposed by Webb (Wisconsin Center for Education Research, 1997, 1999). Webb's (2002) model combines qualitative expert judgments and quantified coding and analysis, yielding a set of statistics for each standard and grade on the degree of alignment between state content standards and state assessments. Trained reviewers individually identify the content standard objectives that match each assessment item and the depth of knowledge required by each objective/benchmark of the content standards being analyzed (using four levels: 1) recall, 2) skill/concept, 3) strategic thinking, and 4) extended thinking). Next, reviewers determine the objective/benchmark represented by each item or task on the state assessment and rate the depth of knowledge required for successful completion. Reviewers' ratings are entered into a spreadsheet and are analyzed across reviewers, producing statistics on the following four categories: 1) categorical concurrence, 2) depth-of-knowledge consistency, 3) range-of-knowledge correspondence, and 4) balance of representation.

Though developed for general education tests, this model is applicable for alternate assessments. Tindal (2006) presented a strategy for using this alignment model with three methods for operationalizing alternate assessments—portfolios, performance tasks, and rating scales. The research generally has been consistent: Alternate assessments are very capable of being aligned with grade-level standards and increasingly are reflecting appropriate levels of all dimensions (Roach, Elliott, & Webb, 2005; Flowers, Browder, & Ahlgrim-Delzell, 2006). The two major problems that seem most prominent are the need for defining *items* or *tasks* with portfolio assessments and the need for caution with interpreting the results. As Tindal (2006) noted, when the items and tasks in alternate assessments reflect complex events that take substantial time to complete, inherent problems exist in trying to reconcile an appropriate range of coverage with an adequate balance of representation.

METHOD: EARLY RESEARCH ON ALTERNATE ASSESSMENT

Much of the early literature focused on a host of administration issues, with a few studies also addressing technical characteristics of measurement (Kleinert, Green, Hurte, Clayton, & Oetinger, 2002; Kleinert, Haig, Kearns, & Kennedy, 2000). For example, researchers from the University of Kentucky were quite active in documenting perceptions of educators (Kleinert & Kearns, 1999; Kleinert, Kennedy, & Kearns, 1999). Kleinert, Kearns, and Kennedy (1997) described a number of standards for evalu-

ating alternate assessments with scoring dimensions aligned to performance, support, settings, interactions, contexts, and domains (each referenced to a professional literature base). They then reported on the reliability of their "alternate portfolio" approach across a period of 3 years,
with agreement indices of 57%, 49%, and 49% achieved on a four-point
scale. They also reported a correlation of .45 between a measure of program quality and performance on the alternate portfolio (a finding also reported by Turner, Baldwin, Kleinert, & Kearns, 2000). Kampfer, Horvath,
Kleinert, and Kearns (2001) reported on 206 teachers' perceptions of
time and effort associated with a number of variables relevant to the operation of the alternate assessment: eligibility, materials sent out, schedules, entries, progress, social relationships, access to multiple settings,
and development of natural supports. The teachers who responded reported spending 25–35 hours outside of instructional time to complete
the portfolios. Modest relationships were found among outcome performance and a number of these operational variables. In summary, this
research provides valuable information on the context of measurement
and the relations among variables, and it has potential for focusing educational programs.

In contrast to the portfolio research, the performance assessment research has focused primarily on traditional measurement issues. For example, reliability and criterion validity of alternate assessments in reading and math have been reported by Tindal, Glasgow, Gall, VanLoo, and
Chow (2002) and also by Tindal et al. (2003). Almond, Tindal, Arnold,
Stolp, and McCabe (2003) used a multitrait, multimethod matrix (Campbell & Fiske, 1959) and Yin's (2003) case study design to study assessments
across several states. Crawford, Tindal, and Carpenter (2006) studied Oregon's alternate writing assessment to determine whether the internal structure accurately reflected the six areas identified as tasks that students had
to complete in taking this assessment. Yovanoff and Tindal (2007) scaled
reading performance tasks to a 25-item statewide reading test to extend the
lower measurement range. Tindal et al. (in press) used generalizability theory (Brennan, 2001) to understand various facets of measurement (tasks
and raters) within a structured reading assessment for students with significant cognitive disabilities. All of these examples of the research from
the University of Oregon were based on the 1999 *Standards for Educational and Psychological Testing* (American Educational Research Association, American Psychological Association, & National Council on Measurement in Education, 1999) in their approaches to validation.

SUMMARY

In adjudicating the similarities and differences between the use of portfolios and performance assessments, Elliott and Roach (2007) analyzed
these approaches (including rating scales). Their analysis addressed a

number of dimensions: 1) content coverage, 2) administration and scoring, 3) results and reporting, and 4) various evidences of validity. Using the standards for testing (American Educational Research Association et al., 1999), Elliott and Roach addressed a number of technical adequacy issues that need to be addressed irrespective of assessment method. In the end, as alternate assessments gain more acceptability, as the assessments become more established with their focus on academic grade-level standards, and as the research becomes more prevalent, it is very likely that the evidence used for documenting achievement is very much the same as that used in general education.

REFERENCES

Almond, P., Tindal, J., Arnold, N., Stolp, P., & McCabe, P. (2003, June). *Alternate assessment: Research findings and implications for state practice.* Paper presented at the 2003 Large Scale Assessment Conference, San Antonio, TX.

American Educational Research Association, American Psychological Association, & National Council on Measurement in Education. (1999). *Standards for educational and psychological testing.* Washington, DC: Authors.

Brennan, R.L. (2001). *Generalizability theory.* New York: Springer.

Campbell, D.T., & Fiske, D.W. (1959). Convergent and discriminant validation by the multi-trait, multi-method matrix. In W.A. Mehrens & R.L. Ebel (Eds.), *Principles of educational and psychological measurement: A book of selected readings* (pp. 273–302). Chicago: Rand McNally & Company.

Crawford, L., Almond, P., Tindal, G., & Hollenbeck, K. (2002). Teacher perspectives on inclusion of students with disabilities in high-stakes assessments. *Special Services in the Schools, 18*(1/2), 95–118.

Crawford, L., Tindal, G., & Carpenter, D.M., II. (2006). Exploring the validity of the Oregon extended writing assessment. *The Journal of Special Education, 40*(1), 16–27.

Cronbach, L., & Meehl, P. (1955). Construct validity in psychological tests. *Psychological Bulletin, 52*(4), 281–302.

Elliott, S., & Roach, A. (2007). Alternate assessments of students with significant cognitive disabilities: Alternative approaches, common technical challenges. *Applied Measurement in Education, 20*(3), 301–333.

Flowers, C., Browder, D., & Ahlgrim-Delzell, L. (2006). An analysis of three states' alignment between language arts and mathematics standards and alternate assessments. *Exceptional Children, 71*(2), 201–215.

Ford, A., Davern, L., & Schnorr, R. (2001, July/August). Learners with significant disabilities. *Remedial and Special Education, 22*(4), 214–222.

Individuals with Disabilities Education Act Amendments of 1997, PL 105-17, 20 U.S.C. §§ 1400 *et seq.*

Kampfer, S.H., Horvath, L.S., Kleinert, H.L., & Kearns, J.F. (2001). Teachers' perceptions of one state's alternate assessment: Implications for practice and preparation. *Exceptional Children, 67*(3), 361–374.

Kettler, R.J., Elliott, S.N., Beddow, P.A., Compton, E., McGrath, D., Kaase, K., et al. (2009). *What does an alternate assessment of alternate achievement standards measure? A multi-trait multi-method analysis across six states* (CAAVES Project Report). Nashville: Vanderbilt University.

Kleinert, H., Green, P., Hurte, M., Clayton, J., & Oetinger, C. (2002). Creating and using meaningful alternate assessments. *Exceptional Children, 34*(4), 40–47.

Kleinert, H., Haig, J., Kearns, J., & Kennedy, S. (2000). Alternate assessments: Lessons learned and roads to be taken. *Exceptional Children, 67*(1), 51–66.

Kleinert, H.L., & Kearns, J.F. (1999). A validation study of the performance indicators and learner outcomes of Kentucky's alternate assessment for students with significant disabilities. *Journal of the Association for Persons with Severe Handicaps, 24*(2), 100–110.

Kleinert, H., Kearns, J., & Kennedy, S. (1997). Accountability for all students: Kentucky's alternate portfolio assessment for students with moderate and severe cognitive disabilities. *The Journal of the Association for Persons with Severe Handicaps, 24*(2), 88–101.

Kleinert, H., Kennedy, S., & Kearns, J. (1999). The impact of alternate assessments: A statewide teacher survey. *Journal of Special Education, 33*(2) 93–102.

La Marca, P.M., Redfield, D., Winter, P.C., Bailey, A., & Hansche, L. (2000). *State standards and state assessment systems: A guide to alignment.* Washington, DC: Council of Chief State School Officers.

No Child Left Behind Act of 2001, PL 107-110, 115 Stat. 1425, 20 U.S.C. §§ 6301 *et seq.*

Roach, A.T., Elliott, S., & Webb, N. (2005). Alignment of an alternate assessment with state academic standards: Evidence for the content validity of the Wisconsin alternate assessment. *Journal of Special Education, 38*(4), 218–231.

The University of Chicago Mathematics Project. (2007). *Everyday Mathematics* (3rd ed.). DeSoto, TX: Wright Group/McGraw-Hill.

Tindal, G. (2006). Alignment of alternate assessments using the Webb system. In Council of Chief State School Officers (Ed.), *Aligning assessment to guide the learning of all students: Six reports on the development, refinement, and dissemination of the web alignment tool* (pp. 35–66). Washington, DC: Council of Chief State School Officers.

Tindal, G., Glasgow, A., Gall, J., VanLoo, D., & Chow, E. (2002). *Oregon extended assessment: Technical adequacy analysis summary.* Salem, OR: Oregon Department of Education.

Tindal, G., McDonald, M., Tedesco, M., Glasgow, A., Almond, P., Crawford, L., et al. (2003). Alternate assessments in reading and math: Development and validation for students with significant disabilities. *Exceptional Children, 69* (4), 481–494.

Tindal, G., Yovanoff, P., & Geller, J. (in press). Generalizability theory applied to reading assessments for students with significant cognitive disabilities. *The Journal of Special Education.*

Turner, M., Baldwin, L., Kleinert, H., & Kearns, J. (2000). The relation of a statewide alternate assessment for students with severe disabilities to other measures of instructional effectiveness. *The Journal of Special Education, 34*(2), 69–76.

U. S. Department of Education. (2004, April 28). *Standards and assessments peer review guidance: Information and examples for meeting requirements of the No Child Left Behind Act of 2001.* Washington, DC: Author.

Webb, N.L. (2002). *Alignment study in language arts, mathematics, science, and social studies of state standards and assessments for four states.* Washington, DC: Council of Chief State School Officers (CCSSO): State Collaborative on Assessment and Student Standards (SCASS), Technical Issues in Large Scale Assessments (TILSA).

Wisconsin Center for Education Research. (1997). Alignment critical to successful reform [Electronic version]. *WCER Highlights, 9*(4), 6–7.

Wisconsin Center for Education Research. (1999). Are state-level standards and assessments aligned? [Electronic version]. *WCER Highlights, 11*(3), 1–3.

Yin, R. (2003). *Case study designs.* Thousand Oaks, CA: Sage Publications.

Yovanoff, P., & Tindal, G. (2007). Scaling early reading alternate assessments with statewide measures. *Exceptional Children, 73*(2), 184–201.

CHAPTER 4

Public Policy and the Development of Alternate Assessments for Students with Cognitive Disabilities

SUSAN L. RIGNEY

This chapter provides an overview of how federal policy has driven the design and implementation of alternate assessments based on alternate achievement standards (AA-AAS), their use as indicators of school accountability, and our understanding of the consequences to date.

HISTORICAL OVERVIEW

Throughout the 1990s, many students with disabilities were routinely excluded from state assessments. This occurred partly because of a reliance on national norm-referenced tests that did not typically include students with significant cognitive disabilities or English-language learners in the norm group. Also, many states followed the example set by the National Assessment of Educational Progress and exempted students who received less than 50% of their instruction in regular classrooms. Michigan, for instance, had a well-established assessment system based on the state's model curriculum objectives. All students were required to participate, except for some special education students and non–English-speaking students who had been enrolled in U.S. schools for less than 2 years. In 1991, the Michigan Educational Assessment Pro-

---

This chapter is intended to promote the exchange of ideas among researchers and policy makers. The views expressed in it are part of ongoing research and analysis and do not necessarily reflect the position of the U.S. Department of Education.

gram specified that the exemption of a special education student required that

> a) the student has been found eligible for special education services through an IEP [individualized education program]; and b) receives special education services prior to the first day of testing; and c) receives 49% or less of his/her reading/English instruction per week through general education instruction. (Michigan State Board of Education, 1991)

Another state with a high-stakes graduation test had statutory exemptions for students with disabilities; these exemptions were intended to protect students with disabilities from negative consequences of failing the test and, therefore, being unable to qualify for diplomas. But, because the Individuals with Disabilities Education Act Amendments (IDEA) of 1997 (PL 105-17) prohibited exclusion based on disability, students receiving special education services were permitted to take the test voluntarily. In fact, few did. Students who were excused from testing—even those who chose to take the test—were not included in school accountability calculations because, by law, their results on the general test could not be aggregated with the results from other students.

KEY FEDERAL STATUTES

In less than a decade, federal policy regarding students with disabilities has moved from an emphasis on providing instruction in the "least restrictive environment" to emphasis on inclusion in state- and district-wide assessments that emphasize students' attainment of the academic content of the general curriculum rather than functional skills (Browder, 2001). This shift in emphasis can be traced through several successive federal statutes and associated regulations.

- IDEA 1997 represented a significant advance in the education of students with disabilities by introducing the concept of access to the general curriculum—that is, the same curriculum as that provided to students without disabilities (34 C.F.R. § 300.347(a)(1)(i)). This requirement far exceeded the earlier notions of physical access to the school building and access to special education and related services intended by the original version of the statute describing educational services for students with disabilities known as the Education for All Handicapped Children Act (PL 94-142) in 1975. IDEA 1997 also required states to develop and administer alternate assessments by July 1, 2000, but the law provided no direction regarding format, alignment with content standards, scoring, standard setting, technical adequacy, or participation criteria. (Karger, 2004; Council of Chief State School Officers, 2007)

- The 1994 reauthorization of the Elementary and Secondary Education Act of 1965 (PL 89-10), known as the Improving America's Schools Act of 1994 (IASA), required development of state content standards in reading or language arts and mathematics by 1997–1998 and assessments based on those standards to be fully implemented in school year 2000–2001. In addition, IASA required the inclusion of all students in the assessments and in a state-defined accountability system that applied to Title I schools. The assessment system was to include accommodations for students with disabilities and for limited English proficient students and an alternate assessment for those students whose "IEP team determines cannot participate in all or part of the State assessments . . . even with appropriate accommodations" (34 C.F.R.§ 200.6(a)(2)). In his 2001 letter to the states summarizing the initial results of peer review under IASA, Assistant Secretary Michael Cohen emphasized that full inclusion of students with disabilities in the assessment system was important "because this is the vehicle for ensuring that schools, school districts, and States assume responsibility for educating every child to high standards."

- The 2001 reauthorization of the Elementary and Secondary Education Act, known as the No Child Left Behind Act (NCLB) of 2001 (PL 107-110), continued all assessment requirements established under IASA. In addition, NCLB defined the concept of adequate yearly progress (AYP) to include separate measurable annual objectives in reading/language arts and mathematics for the achievement of *all* students, and it required that results for all students with disabilities be used as an accountability indicator for all public schools, not just those receiving Title I funds. Alternate assessments were regarded as a way for all students with disabilities to participate in and benefit from assessment systems. However, little detail was provided in regulation or in guidance regarding the characteristics of an alternate assessment except that it

  > must be aligned to the State's content and student achievement standards, must report student achievement with the same frequency and level of detail as the State's regular assessment, and must serve the same purpose as the assessment for which it is an alternate. (U.S. Department of Education, 2003, p. 16)

- In December 2003, a new regulation provided states with the flexibility to develop alternate achievement standards for students with significant cognitive disabilities. For the first time, the regulation defined an *alternate achievement standard* as "an expectation of performance that differs in complexity from a grade-level achievement standard" (Office of Elementary and Secondary Education, U.S. Department of Education, 2003) and specified that it must be "aligned with the State's academic content standards; promote access to the general curriculum; and reflect professional judgment of the highest achievement standards possible." (34 C.F.R. § 200.1(d)(1)–(3)). The regulation limits eligibility for AA-AAS to students with the most significant cognitive disabilities. U.S. Department of Education documents describe the intended benefits for these students as follows:

> Students with disabilities, including those with the most significant cognitive disabilities, benefit instructionally from such participation. [And], to ensure that appropriate resources are dedicated to helping these students succeed, appropriate measurement of their achievement needs to be part of the accountability system. Further, when students with disabilities are part of the accountability system, educators' expectations for these students are more likely to increase. In such a system, educators realize that students with disabilities count and can learn to high levels, just like students who do not have disabilities. (U.S. Department of Education, 2005, pp. 8–9)

The regulation provides a safeguard for students by limiting the number of proficient results that can be used for AYP:

> "A limit is required to ensure a thoughtful application of alternate achievement standards and to protect IEP teams from pressure to assign low-performing students to assessments and curricula that are inappropriately restricted in scope, thus limiting educational opportunity for these students." (U.S. Department of Education, 2005, p. 28)

- The Individuals with Disabilities Education Improvement Act of 2004 (PL 108-446) confirmed NCLB's alternate achievement standards regulation by specifying that each state's alternate assessments must be aligned with the state's challenging academic content and achievement standards (Karger, n.d.; National Association of State Directors of Special Education, Inc., 2004).

- To recognize another group of students with disabilities who might be held to different expectations than the general population, *modified academic achievement standards* were approved in regulation in April 2007:

> States have the option of developing alternate assessments based on modified academic achievement standards [that] are intended to be challenging for a limited group of students whose disability has prevented them from attaining grade-level proficiency. These students must have access to a curriculum based

on grade-level content standards and, therefore, must be assessed with a measure that is also based on grade-level content standards, although the assessment may be less difficult than the general assessment. (U.S. Department of Education, 2007, p. 20)

Federal statutes and regulations have clearly established the expectation that all students with disabilities will receive instruction based on state content standards and will participate in their states' standards-based assessment systems, including alternate assessments with the possibility of less rigorous achievement standards for some students with disabilities. However, policy statements alone cannot guarantee results. To appreciate the effects of federal policy, we must consider not only the intent of the policy statement but also the implementation of policy requirements and the resulting impact on practice in the field.

IMPLEMENTATION OF FEDERAL POLICY REGARDING ALTERNATE ASSESSMENTS

Regardless of how well intentioned a policy statement may be, the policy goals can be realized only through implementation. The execution of federal education policy depends on the knowledge, skills, and good will of many diverse actors at the federal, state, and local levels. Progress is likely to be slow, particularly when substantive reform efforts are required, and effort at each level must be sustained in the face of competition for resources.

Federal policy implementation takes several forms:

- Statutes, regulations, and guidance documents are drafted and disseminated by the U.S. Department of Education.

- Compliance monitoring is carried out by multiple U.S. Department of Education offices (e.g., Office of Special Education Programs, Office of Elementary and Secondary Education, Student Achievement and School Accountability) through on-site observations and interviews. Monitoring reports are posted online, and states are required to take corrective action to address all monitoring findings such as failure to provide alternate assessments that meet all requirements in the law or failure to include all students in AYP calculations.

- A peer review of each state's Title I consolidated application is required by law. This is generally conducted as a document review. Some components of the state's plan, such as the state accountability workbook or the assessment system, are scrutinized in detail, and documentation must be kept up to date as changes are made in the state's assessment or accountability system.

- The U.S. Department of Education provides technical assistance through regional centers that work directly with state and local offices. For example, implementation of the alternate assessment policy has included the funding and evaluation of several national technical assistance centers such as the National Center on Educational Outcomes (NCEO), the Assessment and Accountability Comprehensive Center, the National Center on Accessing the General Curriculum, and the National Alternate Assessment Center (NAAC).

- The U.S. Department of Education awards funds and monitors the implementation of discretionary grant projects such as the Enhanced Assessment Grant and General Supervision Enhancement Grant. These grants have been targeted to support the development and implementation of alternate assessments.

States also play an important part in the implementation of federal policy. The state role focuses more immediately on the development, administration, and use of alternate assessments. State legislatures contribute by drafting statutes that authorize statewide assessments and by appropriating funds to operate the assessment programs. Generally, the state education agency is responsible for the day-to-day implementation of its assessment program, which usually includes activities related to curriculum and instruction. Successful implementation of an alternate assessment includes

- Assessment program inclusion policies and procedures

- Optional development and implementation of AA-AAS or alternate assessments based on modified achievement standards consistent with statute

- Support for test administration and use, including dissemination of state and federal requirements

- Infrastructure to support local implementation

  - Assessment training

  - Guidance for IEP team decisions

  - Professional development for general and special education teachers to support effective instruction

PEER REVIEW

None of the U.S. Department of Education's implementation activities have been more influential than its review and approval of state assessment systems. The U.S. Department of Education has monitored state implementation of the standards, assessment, and accountability requirements under IASA and NCLB through a peer review process. Compliance monitoring of each state's assessment system through the peer review process has focused on the participation of all students in the assessment system, the state's documentation of the tests' technical quality, and the public reporting and use of results for school accountability. As a result, substantial changes in state assessment systems, including the design and use of alternate assessments, have occurred.

Although the assessment requirements under IASA are often taken for granted, it is important to recall that, when they were developed, they represented a paradigm shift for existing state testing programs. Three fundamental changes in the characteristics of state assessments were required: a shift from norms to standards-based interpretation of results, a shift to full inclusion of all students, and the replacement of input data (such as dollars per student or number of library books per student) to the use of outcomes data (in the form of scores from standards-based achievement tests) as the basis for school quality decisions.

As the states prepared to implement alternate assessments under IASA, most planned to use a body-of-evidence approach, and most had adopted guidelines for students who should participate in alternate assessments with the expectation that the number of participants would range from less than 0.5% to no more than 2% of the total student enrollment in the grades tested. Several states had designed their alternate assessments to reflect the general academic standards, but many planned to measure basic or functional skills, and many reported that they had not yet resolved issues related to scoring procedures or to how the results would be reported (Thompson & Thurlow, 2000). At that time, most states were preparing to initiate their alternate assessments in spring 2001, and, therefore, they had little evidence confirming the content or technical quality of their alternate assessments. Each state was expected to explain how scores from alternate assessments would be integrated into the Title I accountability system, but there was variation among states regarding how the alternate assessment results were scaled, reported, and used for accountability (Quenemoen, Rigney, & Thurlow, 2002).

The U.S. Department of Education's peer review of state assessment systems under IASA focused on tests administered in 2000–2001. States had been cautioned that

> alternate assessments must be valid, reliable, and to the maximum extent appropriate, aligned to State content and performance standards. In addition, the State must monitor and collect data from school districts to ensure the proper use of alternate assessments; they must publicly report the results of alternate assessments; and they must integrate the results of alternate assessments into their accountability systems. (U.S. Department of Education, 2000)

The *Peer Reviewer Guidance for Evaluating Evidence of Final As-sessments Under Title I of the Elementary and Secondary Education Act* (U.S. Department of Education, 1999) asked only whether each state had a policy "for including students with disabilities in their assessment sys-tem" and, in particular, "What policies are provided regarding appropri-ate accommodations for students with disabilities and the use of alternate assessments?" There was no specific reference to alternate assessments in the technical quality or alignment sections of the peer review guid-ance document. By 2004, the expectations regarding alternate assess-ments were much more detailed and rigorous.

PEER REVIEW UNDER THE NO CHILD LEFT BEHIND ACT

The general assessment requirements under NCLB are virtually identical to those of IASA except for the expansion of testing to additional grades. (NCLB also requires the addition of science assessments at three grade levels by 2007–2008, but the implications for science alternate assess-ments are not discussed in this chapter.) Peer review of alternate assess-ments under NCLB has been far more detailed for two reasons. First, by 2002–2003, virtually all states had completed the development and ini-tial administration of an alternate assessment, so the emphasis could shift to the characteristics of the alternate assessments rather than simple ver-ification of their existence. Second, the December 2003 publication of the so-called 1% regulation included, for the first time, specific require-ments for an AA-AAS (U.S. Department of Education, 2005).

The NCLB peer review guidance issued by the U.S. Department of Education in 2004, along with the supplementary guidance concerning alternate achievement standards for students with significant cognitive disabilities (U.S. Department of Education, 2005), provided direction to states on the implementation of the December 2003 regulation on alter-nate achievement standards for students with the "most significant cog-nitive disabilities." Although the format of the alternate assessment was left to each state's discretion, the NCLB peer review guidance included references to the alternate assessment in the sections on achievement standards, the assessment system, technical quality, alignment, inclusion, and reports. A state could not receive approval of its assessment system unless specific requirements were met for the alternate assessment (U.S. Department of Education, 2004).

At the beginning of each review meeting, peer reviewers were in-structed to concentrate on five essential aspects of the AA-AAS:

1.   The assessment yields results separately in reading and math.

2.   Clear guidelines for student participation are provided to all local education agencies (LEAs).

3. The assessment is designed and implemented in a manner that supports the use of the results for AYP.

    • The assessment is aligned with state content standards.

    • The assessment design is appropriate for school accountability measures (e.g., the results are comparable across schools and districts; evidence includes test blueprint, test administration manual or administrator training materials, scoring rubric, and scoring procedures).

    • If local assessments are employed, requirements in 200.3(c) are met.

4. The state provides evidence of the assessment's technical quality.

    • This includes evidence of validity, reliability, accessibility, objectivity, and consistency with nationally recognized professional and technical standards.

    • This also includes a description of the standard-setting process employed, the judges who participated in standard setting and their qualifications, and the state's adoption of the resulting alternate achievement standards.

5. The assessment results are reported to teachers and parents in a manner consistent with the alternate achievement standards.

Many states were not able to satisfy these requirements, and the U.S. Department of Education extended the 2005–2006 deadline to permit states either to finish revising their AA-AAS to reflect the requirements in the regulation or to rebuild their alternate assessments completely. If a state had satisfied all other assessment requirements and had work remaining only on the alternate assessment, it was placed in "mandatory oversight" and required to provide the Department with evidence of commitment and investment of resources to resolve all outstanding issues for the 2007–2008 administration of its assessments, along with a mutually acceptable timeline for how and when the remaining work would be accomplished.

CURRENT STATUS OF ALTERNATE ASSESSMENTS BASED ON ALTERNATE ACHIEVEMENT STANDARDS

Federal policy has had a significant impact on the inclusion of students with disabilities in state assessments. Virtually all states have changed their assessment participation policies since 2001. Twenty-two of fifty states have changed their participation policies/guidelines for AA-AAS since the regulation of December 9, 2003 (Thompson, Johnstone, Thurlow, & Altman, 2005). And, the peer review of AA-AAS under NCLB has prompted linkage to academic content for all states. All states have operational AA-AAS in reading and mathematics at Grades 3–8 and in high school. The greatest challenge for completing peer review for most states has been completion of standard setting, documentation of technical quality, and demonstration of the linkage of the AA-AAS to grade-level content standards (Sheinker & Erpenbach, 2007). As of September 1, 2007, approximately a dozen states were still working toward U.S. Department of Education approval of their AA-AAS. A few of these states have new alternate assessments, introduced in spring 2007, that must be peer reviewed and approved. A few states planned to introduce new alternate assessments in 2008. The remaining states have not yet provided final documentation, primarily in the areas of alignment with grade-level content standards or technical quality. The U.S. Department of Education told these states that they must complete all statutory requirements by the end of the 2007–2008 school year.

Typically, the rigor and technical quality of AA-AAS are somewhat less robust than the levels documented for general assessments. Peer review has required documentation in the same manner as that of general assessments, but reviewers generally have not expected AA-AAS to reach the same levels of technical rigor as the general assessments, for several reasons. First, these assessments are, for most states, relatively new. Consequently, although reliability statistics are commonly submitted for peer review, important validity data have not yet been accumulated. Second, most reviewers agreed with Hill's (2001) argument that because the results from AA-AAS have limited impact on the calculation of AYP results at the school, district, and state levels, a somewhat lower standard for psychometric indicators may be tolerated. Nevertheless,

> the NCLB standards and assessment peer review process increased the requirements for documenting the technical quality of all assessments, but the biggest shift was for AA-AAS. The type of technical documentation necessary to fulfill the peer review requirements has never been expected from AA-AAS developers previously. (Marion & Pellegrino, 2006)

Federal policy also has dramatically affected the use of alternate assessment results in state Title I accountability systems. IASA did not specify the design of state accountability systems or how the results from alternate assessments should be included, and states took different approaches. Many states did not include students with disabilities in accountability calculations at all. In 2000, NCEO reported that only seven states seemed to include all students with disabilities in their accountability systems (Krentz, Thurlow, & Callender, 2000). After implementing their alternate assessments, states were not consistent in how results from the alternate assessments were incorporated into the existing state accountability systems. Kentucky, for example, applied the overall holistic score for each student's alternate assessment portfolio in each of the seven content areas included in the accountability system. In this way, every student taking an alternate assessment had the same influence on the school accountability results as the students taking seven different content tests. Another state counted results from its alternate assessment as a single composite score that combined the results from four separate domains, even though students in the general assessment contributed separate scores for each domain tested. This procedure effectively weighted scores from the alternate assessment in a way that diminished the influence of some students with disabilities in the accountability system (Quenemoen et al., 2002).

NCLB specifies the components of AYP, and although states have considerable flexibility in how the AYP calculations are carried out, all students enrolled in the grades tested are to be included in the participation rate, and all student scores are to be included when calculating the percent proficient. The U.S. Department of Education denied early requests from several states that would have effectively assigned a diminished weight to the scores from their AA-AAS and required that each student with disabilities be counted as equivalent to all other students regardless of the test taken.

Experience suggests that the 1% limit on the numbers of proficient and advanced scores from an AA-AAS that may contribute to AYP has been reasonable and consistent with state needs. For 2006–2007, only three states requested exceptions to the 1% cap on proficient or advanced scores, and one of those states based the request on its large number of very small schools.

The impact of AA-AAS on assessment practice has not been limited simply to states meeting statutory requirements. As NCLB peer review has challenged states to document the technical quality of their AA-AAS, several states have applied or adapted rigorous methods, such as Alabama's procedures for setting alternate achievement standards or the framework for documentation of technical quality developed by the New Hampshire consortium (New Hampshire Enhanced Assessment Grant, National Alternate Assessment Center, & National Center for the Improvement of Educational Assessment, 2006a, 2006b). New methodology is also emerging. Links for Academic Learning (Flowers, Wakeman, Browder, & Karvonen, 2007) was developed to evaluate the alignment of AA-AAS with state content standards. It is a set of procedures based initially on Webb's alignment model (Webb, 1997) but adapted to yield more meaningful results for AA-AAS. Another well-established tool, the Survey of Enacted Curriculum (Porter, 2002; Smithson & Porter, 1994), has been adapted to provide teacher-reported data on instruction for students who participate in AA-AAS (Karvonen, Flowers, Browder, Wakeman, & Algozzine, 2006; Karvonen, Wakeman, Flowers, & Browder, 2006). New tools, such as the Learner Characteristics Inventory created by the NAAC to gather data about the target population for AA-AAS, have generated valuable data regarding students with the most significant cognitive disabilities (Kearns, Towles-Reeves, Kleinert, & Kleinert, 2006). A growing number of articles in technical journals devoted to measurement provide evidence of increased attention among measurement professionals to assessing the academic achievement of students with significant cognitive disabilities (see Eckhout, Plake, Smith, & Larsen, 2007; Elliott, Compton, & Roach, 2007; Marion & Pellegrino, 2006; and Schafer, 2005). Technical challenges remain, but serious work based on state research and innovations in the technical quality of AA-AAS is being documented, evaluated, and incorporated in discussions of large-scale assessment as never before.

Emerging Evidence of the Impact on Instruction

As we have seen, the impact of federal policy on the format and content of state assessment systems is well documented, but the impact on teaching and learning is not yet clear. Most of the published case studies and anecdotal reports of change in instruction predate the requirements for academic content represented in NCLB. However, a few reports released early in the NCLB era suggested a positive influence on instruction. As early as fall 2003, special education teachers in a national survey reported that "the curriculum for special education is more demanding than it was three years ago" and that "students in special education are learning more content based on state academic standards for students their age" ("Quality Counts 2004," 2004, p. 21).

On the basis of teacher surveys, several studies reported teachers' perceptions of a limited but positive influence on either instruction or student IEPs (Flowers, Ahlgrim-Delzell, Browder, & Spooner, 2005; Towles-Reeves & Kearns, 2006; Towles-Reeves & Kleinert, 2006). Moore-Lamminen and Olsen (2005) reported changed teacher expectations resulting from the NCLB requirements for AA-AAS. Teachers reported feeling willing to attempt more challenging activities from the general curriculum and observing that individual students were able to meet goals that they (the teachers) previously would not have attempted. Many of these studies emphasized the need for professional development.

Some studies directly attributed benefits, such as higher teacher expectations, to NCLB's accountability focus on students with disabilities (Karvonen, Flowers, et al., 2006). Another reported benefit of accountability has been increased resources. For example, one teacher explained that

> when her students' scores began being used along with general education scores, the administrators paid closer attention to her classroom

needs in order to help students with special needs acquire the skills outlined on their alternate assessment portfolios . . . she indicated that she now has access to a greater range of materials that she can use to address specific needs. (Moore-Lamminen and Olsen, 2005)

This perspective was confirmed in a 2007 meeting of state and national experts:

Most who attended the meeting believed that NCLB has caused advances in instruction, assessment and modes of assessment for students with disabilities that would not have occurred without it. Many groups believe that accountability—as framed by NCLB—has helped to shift the pervasive cultural belief that students with disabilities cannot learn and achieve at grade level or should not be taught the general curriculum. (Center on Education Policy, 2007b)

Emerging Evidence of the Impact on Student Outcomes

Although states' AA-AAS have become more firmly linked to academic content standards, few empirical data have been accumulated to judge the impact of the alternate assessment requirements on student learning. Research is hampered because student outcomes data from AA-AAS are often limited or difficult to find. Although test results for the subgroup of students with disabilities is a required component in NCLB state and district report cards, these data usually are presented as the total percentage of students considered proficient for AYP calculations on the basis of results from all assessments combined. Few states display results from their alternate assessments alongside results from their general assessments. There are several possible explanations for this: If the AA-AAS results are prepared by a different contractor than the general assessment, the data files may not be consistent; or the AA-AAS may be "housed" in the special education office rather than the assessment office, and the report formats may be very different. Although results for individual students are sent home to parents, it is often very difficult for the public to determine state- or district-wide scoring trends for students with the most significant cognitive disabilities as a group. Maryland, on the contrary, provides an excellent data display, showing results from its alternate assessment next to results from its general assessment. Maryland's interactive Report Card web site (Maryland State Department of Education, 2008) includes a detailed presentation of alternate assessment results with a visual display of trend data, and the viewer can query any of the data elements for more information.

The lack of continuity as states negotiate the change from functional skills to academic content standards as the basis for AA-AAS has been another barrier to research. Most states' AA-AAS redesigns took effect in 2005–2006 or 2006–2007, so many states currently have only 2 years of continuous data—not enough for trends in student performance to be evident. New York, for example, historically displayed the performance of students who took the AA-AAS on school, LEA, and state reports. The New York AA-AAS results suggested stability or modest improvement during the early years of NCLB. However, after New York redesigned its AA-AAS to focus on more challenging academic content, a new trend had to be established beginning with the 2006–2007 results. Since 2005–2006, many states have implemented redesigned AA-AAS to meet the NCLB requirements that these assessments be linked to grade-level content standards. These changes are not always apparent in assessment reports, consequently; researchers and stakeholders cannot be confident that higher scores over time reflect improved learning rather than changes in the format or achievement standards of the AA-AAS (McLaughlin & Thurlow, 2007; Center on Education Policy, 2007a).

Another challenge to the interpretation of the results from AA-AAS involves the absence of data regarding students' opportunities to learn the academic content assessed. If these students previously were not exposed to academic content as part of their daily instruction, their score gains may indicate curricular changes as much as true learning gains.

Consequential validity is another aspect of AA-AAS that has not been well documented. The standards of the American Educational Research Association, American Psychological Association, and National Council on Measurement in Education (1999) state that

> it is the responsibility of those who mandate the use of tests to monitor their impact and to identify and minimize potential negative consequences. Consequences resulting from the uses of the test, both intended and unintended, should also be examined by the test user. (Standard 13.1, p. 145)

To document consequential validity for a state assessment and accountability program that is intended to improve curriculum and instruction, the investigation of several propositions may be necessary: the level of teacher and principal motivation and effort to focus instruction on standards, the quality of professional development provided, the impact on instruction and classroom assessment, student motivation, and improved test scores as a function of changes in instruction and learning (Lane & Stone, 2002). These types of data collection are difficult and time consuming. Positive and negative consequences must be considered. The consequences associated with accountability may have negative effects on teacher morale (Karger, 2004). Or, schools might inappropriately assign low-performing students who do not have significant cognitive disabilities to AA-AAS. In fact, few states have provided such detailed information regarding their general assessments, but, as a consequence of peer review, states have begun to consider what relevant data should be examined in connection with their general assessments and AA-AAS.

LESSONS LEARNED

As states have worked to design and implement AA-AAS, it has become increasingly clear that an extraordinary level of collaboration is needed to develop high-quality alternate assessments: extraordinary because the key players, including assessment, special education, and content experts, have seldom been asked to work together in this way before. They have different vocabularies and different views of skills such as reading, and each expert tends to look at standards and assessment from his or her unique perspective as a specialist. However, their combined expertise will be required to address the challenges associated with successful implementation of AA-AAS.

- Resources are needed to build local support systems. Federal and state policies provide a framework for educational reform, but the changes needed to reach those policy goals must be enacted in thousands of classrooms. Professional development, instructional materials, and informed supervision must be provided in conjunction with improved assessments. Without this type of support at the local level, assessments alone cannot improve teaching and learning for students with cognitive disabilities.

- Consequences must be documented so that education professionals can refine and, if necessary redesign, assessments intended to improve instruction. Each state needs to collect baseline data within the framework of a long-range plan to evaluate the impact of AA-AAS on students' academic opportunities and achievement.

- The interpretation of outcomes remains difficult because state systems are in flux and student results are confounded with opportunities to learn. Also, because the numbers are small for this population, some statistical analyses traditionally associated with large-scale assessment are not workable. Faced with these challenges, we need carefully designed and executed research to understand and appropriately use the results from AA-AAS.

SUMMARY

Federal statutes can provide a powerful lever for change in assessment and instruction, but even in the absence of laws and regulations, professional standards oblige states to explain individual student results to parents clearly, to document the integrity of their assessment and accountability systems to stakeholders, and to convince policy makers that students and taxpayers are benefiting from assessments. The real reason to persist in the difficult work of investigating the complex issues related to AA-AAS is the children—the very children who were "invisible" just a few years ago in our public reports of school quality. Because they keep surprising us with their accomplishments, we owe these students our high expectations, the most effective instructional practices, and the best measures of their learning achievements that we can devise.

REFERENCES

American Educational Research Association, American Psychological Association, & National Council on Measurement in Education. (1999). *Standards for educational and psychological testing.* Washington, DC: Authors.

Browder, D. (2001). *Curriculum and assessment for students with moderate and severe disabilities.* New York: Guilford Press.

Center on Education Policy. (2007a, June). *Answering the question that matters most: Has student achievement increased since No Child Left Behind?* Retrieved August 6, 2007, from http://www.cep-dc.org/index.cfm?fuseaction=document.filterDocumentList&sortby=Title&topicOnly=&topicRadio=subTopic&topic=&subTopic=28&docTitle=&docAuthor=&publishState=&docDescription=&docPublishYear=getAllYears&presentationSite=&FilterDocumentType=&FilterKeyword=&parentid=481&nodeID=1

Center on Education Policy. (2007b). *NCLB's accountability provisions for students with disabilities: Center on Education Policy roundtable discussion May 1, 2007.* Retrieved August 8, 2007, from http://www.cep-dc.org/index.cfm?fuseaction=document.filterDocumentList&sortby=PublishDate&startrow=11&topicOnly=&topicRadio=subTopic&topic=&subTopic=28&docTitle=&docAuthor=&publishState=&docDescription=&docPublishYear=getAllYears&presentationSite=&FilterDocumentType=&FilterKeyword=&parentid=481

Council of Chief State School Officers. (2007). *Handbook for developing alternate assessment technical adequacy (DAATA).* Retrieved March 4, 2007, from http://www.ccsso.org/publications/details.cfm?PublicationID=358

Eckhout, T.J., Plake, B.S., Smith, D.L., & Larsen, A. (2007). Aligning a state's alternative standards to regular core content standards in reading and mathematics: A case study. *Applied Measurement in Education, 20*(1), 79–100.

Education of All Handicapped Children Act of 1975, PL 94-142, 20 U.S.C. §§ 1400 *et seq.*

Elementary and Secondary Education Act of 1965, PL 89-10, 20 U.S.C. §§ 241 *et seq.*

Elliott, S.N., Compton, E., & Roach, A.T. (2007). Building validity evidence for scores on a state-wide alternate assessment: A contrasting groups, multimethod approach. *Educational Measurement: Issues and Practice, 26*(2), 30–43.

Flowers, C., Ahlgrim-Delzell, L., Browder, D., & Spooner, F. (2005). Teachers' perceptions of alternate assessments. *Research and Practice for Persons with Severe Disabilities, 30*(2), 81–92.

Flowers, C., Wakeman, S., Browder, D., & Karvonen, M. (2007). *Links for academic learning: An alignment protocol for alternate assessments based on alternate achievement standards.* Retrieved January 5, 2008, from http://www.naacpartners.org/LAL/documents/NAAC_AlignmentManualVer8_3.pdf

Hill, R. (2001). *The impact of including special education students in accountability systems.* Retrieved March 10, 2007, from http://www.nciea.org/publications/CCSSOSpecialEd_Hill01.pdf

Individuals with Disabilities Education Act Amendments (IDEA) of 1997, PL 105-17, 20 U.S.C. §§ 1400 *et seq.*

Individuals with Disabilities Education Improvement Act of 2004, PL 108-446, 20 U.S.C. §§ 1400 *et seq.*

Karger, J. (2004). *Access to the general curriculum for students with disabilities: A discussion of IDEA '97 and NCLB.* Retrieved October 8, 2007, from http://www.cast.org/publications/ncac/ncac_discussion.html

Karger, J. (n.d.). *Access to the general education curriculum for students with disabilities: A discussion of the interrelationship between IDEA and NCLB.* Retrieved October 8, 2007, from http://www.cast.org/system/galleries/download/ncac/NCLB_IDEA04april05.doc

Karvonen, M., Flowers, C., Browder, D.M., Wakeman, S.Y., & Algozzine, B. (2006). Case study of the influences on alternate assessment outcomes for students with disabilities. *Education and Training in Developmental Disabilities, 41*(2), 95–110.

Karvonen, M., Wakeman, S., Flowers, C., & Browder, D. (2006, April). *Measuring the enacted curriculum for students with significant cognitive disabilities.* Retrieved August 2, 2007, from http://www.naacpartners.org/products/presentations/national/NCME/7000.pdf

Karvonen, M., Wakeman, S., Flowers, C., & Browder, D. (2007, April). *Validation studies on the curriculum indicators survey (CIS): Preliminary results.* Paper presented at the annual meeting of the American Educational Research Association, Chicago.

Kearns, J., Towles-Reeves, E., Kleinert, H., & Kleinert, J. (2006). *Learning characteristics inventory report.* Lexington: University of Kentucky, National Alternate Assessment Center.

Krentz, J., Thurlow, M., & Callender, S. (2000). *Accountability systems and counting students with disabilities* (NCEO Tech. Rep. No. 29). Minneapolis: University of Minnesota, National Center on Educational Outcomes.

Lane, S., and Stone, C.A. (2002). Strategies for examining the consequences of assessment and accountability programs. *Educational Measurement: Issues and Practice, 21*(1), 23–31.

Marion, S.F., & Pellegrino, J.W. (2006). A validity framework for evaluating the technical quality of alternate assessments. *Educational Measurement: Issues and Practice, 24*(4), 47–57.

Maryland State Department of Education. (2008). *2008 Maryland report card.* Retrieved October 1, 2007, from http://www.mdreportcard.org/Assessments.aspx?WDATA=State&K=99AAAA#ALTsnapshot

McLaughlin, M.J., & Thurlow, M. (2007). *Profiles of reform: Four states' journeys to implement standards-based reform with students with disabilities.* College Park, MD: The Institute for the Study of Exceptional Children and Youth.

Michigan State Board of Education. (1991). *Michigan Educational Assessment Program administration manual.* Lansing: Author.

Moore-Lamminen, L., & Olsen, K. (2005). *Alternate assessment: Teacher and state experiences.* Retrieved September 5, 2007, from http://www.osepideasthatwork.org/toolkit/ta_teacher_state.asp

National Association of State Directors of Special Education, Inc. (2004). *The Individuals with Disabilities Education Act: A comparison of P.L. 105-17 (IDEA '97) to H.R. 1350 as passed by Congress on November 19, 2004.* Alexandria, VA: Author.

New Hampshire Enhanced Assessment Grant, National Alternate Assessment Center, & National Center for the Improvement of Educational Assessment. (2006a, October). *An annotated workbook for documenting the technical quality of your state's alternate assessment system: Volume II: The validity evaluation*. Retrieved March 3, 2008, from http://www.naacpartners.org/ products/workshops/materials/16310.pdf

New Hampshire Enhanced Assessment Grant, National Alternate Assessment Center, & National Center for the Improvement of Educational Assessment. (2006b, October). *Documenting the technical quality of your state's alternate assessment system: An annotated workbook: Volume I: "Nuts and bolts"*. Retrieved March 3, 2008, from http://www.naacpartners.org/products/workshops/ materials/16320.pdf

No Child Left Behind Act of 2001, PL 107-110, 115 Stat. 1425, 20 U.S.C. §§ 6301 *et seq.*

Office of Elementary and Secondary Education, U.S. Department of Education. (2003, December 9). *Title I—Improving the academic achievement of the disadvantaged: Background and analysis of comments and changes*. 68 F.R. 68698–68701, 68703–68708.

Porter, A.C. (2002). Measuring the content of instruction: Uses in research and practice. *Educational Researcher, 31*(7), 3–14.

Quality counts 2004: Count me in. (2004, January). *Education Week, 23*(17). Retrieved January 4, 2008, from http://www.edweek.org/media/ew/qc/archives/ QC04full.pdf

Quenemoen, R., Rigney, S., & Thurlow, M. (2002). *Use of alternate assessment results in reporting and accountability systems: Conditions for use based on research and practice* (Synthesis Rep. No. 43). Minneapolis: University of Minnesota, National Center on Educational Outcomes.

Schafer, W.D. (2005, August). Technical documentation for alternate assessments. *Practical Assessment Research & Evaluation, 10*(10). Retrieved August 8, 2007, from http://pareonline.net/getvn.asp?v=10 &n=10

Sheinker, J., & Erpenbach, W.J. (2007). *Alternate assessments for students with significant cognitive disabilities—Strategies for states preparation for and response to peer review*. Retrieved August 5, 2008, from http://www.ccsso.org/ content/PDFs/AltAssmntsCriteria%20051607.pdf

Smithson, J.L., & Porter, A.C. (1994). *Measuring classroom practice: Lessons learned from efforts to describe the enacted curriculum—The reform up close study* (CPRE Research Rep. Series No. 31). Madison: University of Wisconsin, Consortium for Policy.

Thompson, S.J., Johnstone, C.J., Thurlow, M.L., & Altman, J.R. (2005). *2005 state special education outcomes: Steps forward in a decade of change*. Minneapolis: University of Minnesota, National Center on Educational Outcomes.

Thompson, S.J., & Thurlow, M.L. (2000). *State alternate assessments: Status as IDEA alternate assessment requirements take effect* (Synthesis Rep. No. 35). Minneapolis: University of Minnesota, National Center on Educational Outcomes. Retrieved September 6, 2007, from http://cehd.umn.edu/nceo/Online Pubs/Synthesis35.html

Towles-Reeves, E., & Kearns, J.F. (2006). *Alternate assessment impact survey (AAIS) report*. Lexington, KY: National Alternate Assessment Center.

Towles-Reeves, E., and Kleinert, H. (2006, Summer). The impact of one state's alternate assessment upon instruction and IEP development. *Rural Special Education Quarterly, 25*(3), 31–39.

U.S. Department of Education. (1999). *Peer reviewer guidance for evaluating evidence of final assessments under Title I of the Elementary and Secondary Education Act*. Retrieved September 6, 2007, from http://www.ed.gov/policy/ elsec/guid/cpg.pdf

U.S. Department of Education. (2000). *Summary guidance on the inclusion requirement for Title I final assessments. April 2000*. Retrieved August 8, 2007, from http://www.ed.gov/policy/elsec/guid/inclusion.html

U.S. Department of Education. (2003). *Standards and assessments: Non-regulatory guidance, March 2003*. Washington, DC: Author.

U.S. Department of Education. (2004). *Standards and assessments peer review guidance: Information and examples for meeting requirements of the No Child Left Behind Act of 2001*. Retrieved September 6, 2007, from http://www.ed.gov/policy/elsec/guid/saaprguidance.pdf

U.S. Department of Education. (2005). *Alternate achievement standards for students with the most significant cognitive disabilities: Non-regulatory guidance*. Washington, DC: Author.

U.S. Department of Education. (2007). *Modified academic achievement standards: Non-regulatory guidance, July 2007*. Washington, DC: Author.

Webb, N. (1997). *Criteria for alignment of expectations and assessments in mathematics and science education*. Retrieved January 27, 2009, from http://www.ccsso.org/publications/details.cfm?PublicationID=65

CHAPTER 5

Alignment of Alternate Assessments with State Standards

DIANE M. BROWDER,
SHAWNEE WAKEMAN, AND CLAUDIA FLOWERS

Alternate assessments for students with significant cognitive disabilities were first mandated in the reauthorization of the Individuals with Disabilities Education Act Amendments (IDEA) of 1997 (PL 105-17) and scheduled to begin in July 2000. Although IDEA 1997 also required all students to have access to the general curriculum, many states did not apply this requirement to the development of their alternate assessments. Instead, these states focused early development of alternate assessments on skills related to daily living (also known as functional skills; Lehr & Thurlow, 2003). With the authorization of the No Child Left Behind Act (NCLB) of 2001 (PL 107-110), states were required to include students with disabilities in their accountability systems and to report outcomes for the areas of reading, math, and, most recently, science. This chapter addresses the issues surrounding the alignment of alternate assessments with state academic content standards in reading, math, and science and provides information (e.g., alignment criteria and state outcomes) about one alignment method specifically designed for alternate assessments based on alternate achievement standards (AA-AAS).

ALIGNMENT CHALLENGES

Alignment methods are the procedures used to describe the degree of intersection, overlap, or relationship among the content embedded in state standards, assessments, and instruction (Webb, 1997). Logical and empirical evidence are important to document the extent to which alternate assessments reflect the process or skills that are specified by the domain definition (American Educational Research Association, American Psychological Association, & National Council on Measurement in Education, 1999). Most alignment methodologies were designed for general state assessments (e.g., Achieve, Inc., 2001; Porter, 2002; Webb, 1997) and examine criteria such as the focus of the content, the articulation across the grades, and pedagogical implications. Some of these general assessment alignment methods have been used to study the alignment of AA-AAS, with mixed results. In an alignment study using Webb's alignment criteria, Flowers, Browder, and Ahlgrim-Delzell (2006) reviewed three states' AA-AAS and found that none of the states met the criteria established for general education assessments, although all showed evidence of intersection with their state standards. Roach, Elliott, and Webb (2005) also applied Webb's model and evaluative criteria to Wisconsin's alternate assessment and found that "the rating scale is generally well aligned with the skills and knowledge represented by Wisconsin's Model Academic Standards" (p. 227). Whereas the general assessment alignment models primarily examine the content validity of assessments, there are other challenges or issues related to the AA-AAS system that may influence alignment outcomes. Browder et al. (2007) and Wakeman, Flowers, and Browder (2007) identified several of these challenges including the diversity of the population of students with disabilities, the curricular changes and challenges, and the format of the assessments.

Diverse Populations

The final regulations of December 9, 2003, describe alternate assessment as "an assessment designed for the small number of students with disabilities who are unable to participate in the regular State assessment, even with appropriate modifications" (U.S. Department of Education, 2003, p. 68699). Whereas AA-AAS are intended for use with small numbers of students, these students are more heterogeneous than homogeneous in their characteristics. Almond and Bechard (2005) surveyed teachers about the capabilities of students who participated in AA-AAS. They found that most students 1) were identified as having intellectual disabilities (with a third of the students having two or more disabling conditions), 2) required some form of assistive technology (e.g., picture schedules, electronic voice output devices), and 3) had a range of physical impairments. Kleinert, Browder, and Towles-Reeves (2005) described this population as having individualized capabilities and needs, with limitations in short-term memory. The authors also described this population as needing extensive explicit instruction in metacognition, practice, and feedback and requiring multiple opportunities for generalization. Because eligibility for participation in AA-AAS is not based on categories of disabilities, the students who participate in these assessments can be identified as exceptional with several different labels (e.g., other health impairments, autism, mental disabilities, multiple disabilities). The needs of the students participating in these assessments can be as varied as the services needed to support them.

Curricular Challenges

The focus of the content of alternate assessments, as described earlier, was changed from that of a functional curriculum to the academic content required for reporting adequate yearly progress. A shift in thinking about content has occurred broadly within special education. Nolet and McLaughlin (2000) explained that special education students historically have received alternate curricula but can receive access to general curricula through diversified instruction. Browder et al. (2003, 2004) described the evolution of curricular expectations for students with significant cognitive disabilities that led to the expectation for general curriculum access. As shown in Table 5.1, the first curricular approach in the 1970s adapted early childhood or infant curricula. This developmental model was rejected in the 1980s with the emergence of a functional, life skills approach. Social inclusion and self-determination were integrated with the functional curriculum in the 1990s. Although this focus is still valued today, the 2000s brought an additive focus on academic content, as reflected in state standards.

Although the last three curricular phases were additive, with functional skills, inclusion, and academic learning all having ongoing importance, the reality is that most states have changed the focus of their alternate assessments to what must count in school accountability—reading, math, and science. In 2005, Thompson, Johnstone, Thurlow, and Altman found that more than 60% of states were focusing their alternate assessments on grade-level content standards or expanded/extended content standards; this rate represented a dramatic increase from 38% in 2001 (Thompson & Thurlow, 2001). With U.S. Department of Education peer review of state assessments systems' adherence to NCLB requirements, nearly all states have initiated or completed this shift in focus.

The inclusion (and potential prioritization) of academic content has not gone without controversy. The Center for Policy Research on the Impact of General and Special Education Reform (1996) found that states were "wrestling with how to be inclusive (of students with disabilities) while acknowledging that for a small percentage of students, high academic standards are not relevant to their lifelong goals" (p. 10). Agran, Alper, and Wehmeyer (2002) found that teachers did not consider access to the general curriculum important for students with severe disabilities; instead, teachers ranked functional and social skills as most important for these students. Browder et al. (2007), however, outlined four reasons for promoting access to the general curriculum: 1) the promotion of adult

Table 5.1. A summary of changing curricular expectations for students with significant cognitive disabilities

Time frame	Curricular focus	Conceptual foundation	Examples of what assessed	How related to prior era
1970s	Developmental curriculum	Mental age can be used to plan interventions	Checklist of infant and early child development	First public education services for the population
1980s	Functional curriculum	Use students' chronological age; teach for community living	Ecological inventory of skills needed in job site; checklist of functional skills	Replaced the focus on mental age; new thinking—"age appropriate"
1990s	Social inclusion and self-determination	Students should be full members of schools and have choices	Person-centered plans with goals; preference assessments	Complemented functional curriculum but more in inclusive settings
2000 to present	Learning in the general curriculum	All students should have instruction in state academic content standards	Alternate assessments with alternate achievement, but also ongoing individualized educational program	Person-centered planning and functional skills continue to be important, but with an increased focus on academic learning

competence, 2) an increase in achievement expectations for this population of students, 3) the creation of equal educational opportunity, and 4) an increase in opportunities for self-determination.

In addition to this rationale for promoting learning in the general curriculum, there also is research suggesting that students with significant cognitive disabilities can learn academic content, although outcomes are limited to the functional academic focus of the last two decades. Comprehensive reviews of the literature in reading (Browder, Wakeman, Spooner, Ahlgrim-Delzell, & Algozzine, 2006), mathematics (Browder, Spooner, Ahlgrim-Delzell, Harris, & Wakeman, 2008), and science (Courtade, Spooner, & Browder, 2007) demonstrated that this population can learn academic skills through repeated opportunities for practice with systematic prompting that is faded across time. In contrast, Browder, Wakeman, et al. (2006) found that the majority of the reading research conducted with this population focused on vocabulary, including sight words. Browder et al. (2008) found that most of the research in mathematics was identified in the strands of numbers and operations (e.g., number identification) and measurement (e.g., money), with very little research in geometry, algebra, and data analysis and probability. Finally, Courtade et al. (2007) found only 11 studies related to instruction in science for this population, and most were focused on personal and social perspectives.

Format Challenges

AA-AAS have a wide range of approaches across states, which include portfolio, body of evidence, performance assessment, checklist, traditional, or a combination of several approaches. AA-AAS provide flexibility to help accommodate individual needs, and teachers, who have the greatest knowledge of their students' educational needs, often determine the content and level of complexity of the items. This lack of standardization across students adds complexity in the alignment process. When teachers vary the content and complexity of assessments, adjustments to the alignment procedure (e.g., a strategy for sampling portfolio entries) must be made.

RESPONDING TO THE CHALLENGES

For educators to be able to plan instruction and assessments that target state standards, resources are needed that offer examples and conceptual guidance. Some of the first resources by Kleinert and Kearns (2001) and Thompson, Quenemoen, Thurlow, and Ysseldyke (2001) illustrated how to make state academic content standards accessible to students with disabilities—for example, by using critical skills, adapting content, and providing alternative modes for responding (e.g., assistive technology). Browder, Ahlgrim-Delzell, Courtade-Little, and Snell (2006) recommended several ways to access general curriculum content: 1) using universal design of curriculum for all students, 2) promoting self-directed learning, 3) applying direct, systematic instruction, 4) developing standards-based individualized educational programs (IEPs), 5) becoming familiar with grade-level curriculum, 6) promoting active participation, and 7) using functional activities to address academic skills. Browder, Ahlgrim-Delzell, et al. (2006) also introduced the concept of applying students' symbol use to plan instructional targets. They described and illustrated how instruction can be differentiated for students at a presymbolic, early (concrete) symbolic, and expanded (abstract) symbolic level. Whereas students at an abstract symbolic level have mastered some sight words, numbers, and other symbols that can be used to demonstrate knowledge of academic concepts, students at a concrete symbolic level will probably need symbols that have immediate applicability to the context. Students at a presymbolic level will be learning symbol use (e.g., meaning of pictures) concurrently with academic content and may need alternative ways to show what they know.

Browder, Wakeman, et al. (2007) provided conceptual thinking about how access to grade-level content with alternate achievement can be defined. Although it can be difficult to grasp, the distinction between grade-level achievement of grade-level content and alternate achievement of grade-level content is the essence of AA-AAS. Browder et al. used federal policy on AA-AAS and the needs of students with disabilities to propose that alternate achievement is academic in content and that some fidelity with this original content can be ascertained. Alternate achievement is also defined and differentiated by grade level or grade band. In contrast, the expectations for achievement differ in depth of knowledge (DOK) and breadth of content, and there are multiple levels or ways for students to access this content.

Besides these early illustrations and conceptualizations, some research demonstrated methods for students to learn general curriculum content. Several researchers demonstrated how peer supports might promote learning in the general curriculum (Carter, Cushing, Clark, & Kennedy, 2005; McDonnell, Mathot-Buckner, Thorson, & Fister, 2001; McDonnell, Thorson, Allen, & Mathot-Buckner, 2000). Dymond et al. (2006) described how principles of universal design could be used to include students in a high school science class. Some researchers also showed how systematic instruction strategies could be applied to grade-level content (e.g., Browder, Trela, & Jimenez, 2007; Jimenez, Browder, & Courtade, 2008; McDonnell et al., 2006).

LINKS FOR ACADEMIC LEARNING: A METHOD TO EVALUATE ALIGNMENT OF ALTERNATE ASSESSMENTS BASED ON ALTERNATE ACHIEVEMENT STANDARDS

Although the requirement of linking to grade-level content standards gives states flexibility to determine the content of alternate assessments, it does not exempt states from designing assessments that measure academic domains with interpretable results and accurately reflecting what students know and can do (e.g., appropriate inferences being made from the assessment outcomes). For this reason, criteria for judging alignment among expectations, alternate assessments, and instructional practices and resources should be as strenuous as those used for assessing students in the general population. Because of the unique characteristics of the population of students with disabilities, testing approaches, instructional practices, and opportunities for alternate achievement standards, additional alignment criteria need to be considered for alternate assessments. For example, peer review notes from the U. S. Department of Education (2004) clearly indicate that each state must provide documentation of the alignment of all assessments (including alternate assessments) with its academic content and achievement standards (p. 18). Because these assessments vary across states on multiple issues (e.g., format, level of standardization, participation requirements, included content standards, etc.), alignment methodologies must be sensitive to the flexibility states have for capturing the understanding of students with significant disabilities and to the technical requirements of the assessments.

Using the conceptual model of Browder, Wakeman, et al. (2007), Flowers, Wakeman, Browder, and Karvonen (2007) developed the Links for Academic Learning (LAL), an alignment methodology for AA-AAS. Their model is based on the following definition:

> To be linked to grade level standards, the target for achievement must be academic content (e.g., reading, math, science) that is referenced to the student's assigned grade based on chronological age. Functional activities and materials may be used to promote understanding, but the target skills for student achievement are academically focused. Some prioritization of the content will occur in setting this expectation, but it should reflect the major domains of the curricular area (e.g., strands of math) and have fidelity with this content and how it is typically taught in general education. The content will differ from grade level in range, balance, and depth of knowledge, but the expected achievement is for students to demonstrate learning of grade referenced academic content. Some differentiation in content across grade levels or bands should be evident in the standards and assessment. Issues of sources of challenge present in the assessment should be minimized or resolved prior to implementation. Finally, the alignment between the instructional program including professional development and the academic content standards should be evident (p. 10).

Table 5.2 outlines the eight alignment criteria that are used to guide the LAL alignment process. These criteria are described briefly in this chapter. A full delineation of each criterion can be found in Flowers et al. (2007), which is available online (http://cehd.umn.edu/nceo/OnlinePubs/AlignmentManual.pdf).

Criterion 1: The Content Is Academic

The core domain of an AA-AAS's academic content is not assumed; instead, it is evaluated as a first step in the process. As described earlier, academic content has been underrepresented in past instruction and research among students with significant cognitive disabilities. Sometimes, the translation of content standards produces targets that are not "really" language arts, mathematics, or science. The LAL uses guidance from the national curricular professional societies—the National Council of Teachers of English (n.d.), the National Council of Teachers of Math-

Table 5.2. Criteria for instruction and assessment that link to grade-level content

Criteria	Evaluation
1. The content is academic and includes the major domains/strands of the content area as reflected in state and national standards (e.g., reading, math, science).	1. Nearly all of the extended or alternate standards should be considered academic. The remaining nonacademic items should be rated as foundational.
2. The content is referenced to each student's assigned grade level (based on chronological age).	2. There is no evaluation, but there is descriptive reporting of what is occurring.
3. The focus of achievement maintains fidelity with the content of the original grade-level standards (content centrality) and, when possible, the specified performance.	3. Nearly all of the extended standards and items should be rated as near or far on content centrality and performance centrality.
4. The content differs from grade level in range, balance, and DOK, but it matches high expectations set for students with significant cognitive disabilities.	4. Range, balance, and DOK will not meet the same acceptable levels established for general education assessments, but the results should match the state's intended alignment.
5. There is some differentiation in content across grade levels or grade bands.	5. Most of the materials used should be rated as age appropriate. Each strand should show primarily differentiated content with minimal redundancy across grade bands.
6. The expected achievement for students is for the students to show learning of grade-referenced academic content.	6. Scoring rubrics should focus on student performance alone, and standard setting should also support accurate performance with minimal assistance.
7. The potential barriers to demonstrating what students know and can do are minimized in the assessment.	7. Alternate assessment items or guidance for their modification are inclusive of students with sensory and physical impairments and differing symbolic levels.
8. The instructional program promotes learning in the general curriculum.	8. Professional development emphasizes how to teach to grade-level standards and promotes overall program quality.

Key: DOK, depth of knowledge.

ematics (n.d.), and the National Research Council (1996)—to define what is *academic.* It is recommended that nearly all alternate assessment items and extended standards be academic.

Although it is recommended that nearly all items be academic, 100% is not expected. As assessments should be inclusive of all students, it is important to have a few items that capture the performance of students who do not yet have symbolic communication. This may require using items that target the beginning points for academic learning. Nonacademic items are reviewed to see whether they are *foundational skills.* Foundational skills are those skills that are the assumed competence at all grade levels specific to an academic context (e.g., not simply sitting in a chair). They are commonly embedded in academic instruction (e.g., orienting a book, turning a page, reacting to chemical changes in a science experiment, placing items on a jig to be used for mathematical computation). Foundational skills are not what have been called *access skills*—motor responses such as grasp and release or passive responses such as being exposed to content. Although foundational skills are considered important to capture progress toward a standard, these alone should not count as proficiency. In the LAL, foundational skills were omitted from the rest of the alignment study because they were not considered academic in a review by content experts.

Criterion 2: Content Is Referenced to the Student's Grade Level

Because students with significant cognitive disabilities often have been served in ungraded classes, thinking about content by grade level can be new for some educators. The LAL provides feedback on the extent to which states intend for any extended standards and alternate assessment tasks/items to be referenced to specific grade levels or grade bands. No judgment is made about whether the components actually do align at this second step.

Criterion 3: Fidelity with Grade-Level Content and Performance

Extending content and defining performance for the heterogeneous population of students who participate in AA-AAS is challenging and can produce learning targets that miss the mark. In the LAL, when a state uses extended standards, these are compared with the state standard for content and performance centrality. If the extended standards are aligned with the grade-level standards, the alternate assessment items are then aligned with these extended standards. If they do not align, or if the state does not use the extended standards, the alternate assessment items/tasks are aligned with the grade-level standards. Content centrality (Achieve, Inc., 2002) is rated using a three-point scale (i.e., near, far, none) in which experts rate the quality of content links. Content reviewers examine each extended standard (if applicable) and each alternate assessment item/task and evaluate whether the subject area content is a near, far, or no link as described in the corresponding grade-level standards. See Table 5.3 for examples of content centrality across the strands of math. Performance centrality (Achieve, Inc.) also is reviewed by content experts to judge the degree of equivalent performance (i.e., all, some, none) between the extended standards and state standards and between the alternate assessment items/tasks and the extended standards. Because the expectation is alternate achievement, some of the performance from the standards should translate to the linked items. See Table 5.4 for examples of performance centrality across strands of English/language arts.

The National Alternate Assessment Center (2005) introduced "Is it plumb? Is it square?" to consider whether instructional targets link to state standards. Within the LAL model, it is recommended that close to 100% of the extended standards and alternate assessment items match (near or far) on content centrality. In contrast, the performance central-ity match may be lower because of the difficulty of creating ways for students who do not yet have fluent use of printed symbols (e.g., words, pictures) to show achievement. For example, if the content standard is *Compare and contrast genres of literature,* for content centrality, the al-ternate assessment item should incorporate an activity with different types of literature rather than survival sight words. Many students can also be taught to compare and contrast poems, stories, and so forth. For example, a student with extensive communication challenges may be able to identify types of genres but not be able to compare and contrast. Whenever possible, a performance match is the goal. Determining how far below 100% performance centrality is acceptable requires some pro-fessional judgment about whether enough attention has been given to the use of assistive technology and symbol options so that more students can show what they know.

It is important to note that, within the LAL, only items that are iden-tified as academic are considered for content and performance central-ity. An item can be academic but not have content centrality for several reasons. It may be *mismatched* to the wrong grade-level standard (e.g., clerical error or misidentification). Sometimes, the target item has been *overextended* or watered down so that the link is lost. Sometimes, be-cause of *backmapping* or *retrofitting,* the content is the functional activ-ity. The use of functional contexts for the academic items within AA-AAS should be encouraged, but the focus should be on whether students are learning to respond in ways that show academic learning (Tables 5.3 and 5.4).

Criterion 4: The Content Differs in
Range, Balance, and Depth of Knowledge

This criterion most closely resembles the work of Webb (1997). Measures of categorical concurrence, range of knowledge, balance of representa-tion, and DOK are included in Criterion 4. The range and balance should match each state's priorities, with consideration given to some coverage in all major strands of academic content. The LAL is based on the as-sumption that the DOK levels between the alternate assessment items and any extended standards should match, but the DOK levels of the al-ternate assessment items and extended standards should be skewed to lower levels than the state standards. This is a key difference between grade-level achievement and alternate achievement.

Table 5.3. Examples of content centrality across strands of math

National strand	General education standard	Near content centrality	Far content centrality	No content centrality
Number sense	Develop understanding of fractions as parts of unit wholes, as parts of collections, as locations on number lines, and as divisions of whole numbers	Explain the meaning of the fractions one half and one fourth using various visual representations (e.g., number line, sets, diagrams)	Locate and label fractions on a number line	Locate points on a number line
Statistics	Gather, graph, and interpret data	Collect, graph, and answer questions about data	Collect data	Sort according to characteristics
Algebra	Write and evaluate algebraic equations	Given word problems, write and solve simple algebraic equations	Solve simple algebraic expressions (e.g., $n + 3 = 10$)	Solve simple addition problems
Geometry	Identify, describe, and/or accurately represent a variety of polygons	Describe and accurately represent polygons up to 10 sides	Identify and accurately describe quadrilaterals in the environment	Draw a line
Measurement	Recognize and use customary units of measurement	Use the appropriate units to measure length, weight, capacity, and temperature	Associate ounces and pounds to weight	Hold two objects and identify which is heavier

Table 5.4. Examples of performance centrality across strands of English/language arts

National strand	General education standard	Near performance centrality	Far performance centrality	No performance centrality
Reading	*Decode* words	*Match* letter and sound	*Repeat* sound stated by teacher	*Attend* to sounds stated by teacher
Writing	*Compose* text through the writing process	Use picture cards to *compose* text	Use picture cards to *restate* what has been said	*Color* a picture
Speaking	*Communicate* ideas required to complete a task	*Compose* directions to complete a task	*Restate* procedure followed	*Follow* directions
Listening	*Comprehend* story read aloud	*Answer* questions about story read aloud	*Restate* events from a story read aloud	*Read* story aloud
Viewing	*Use* picture journal or graphic organizers to *make* comparisons	Given two pictures, *compare* cultural differences	Use graphic organizer to *record* examples of culture	*Respond* to pictures representing a variety of cultures
Research	*Retrieve* and *analyze* multiple types of resources	*Identify* and *use* one of a variety of resources to find specific information	*Explain* what a resource could be used for	*Color* a map

Criterion 5: Differentiation Across Grade Levels or Grade Bands

The nonregulatory guidance for alternate achievement standards (U.S. Department of Education, 2005) sets the expectation that any student with significant cognitive disabilities should be assessed on content that is linked to the student's chronological grade level. Whereas Criterion 2 captures the AA-AAS's reference to the grade-level standard, it also is important to consider whether the actual alternate assessment tasks show changing expectations over time and are age appropriate. For example, students may learn to recognize and use coins in elementary school, but there should be some change in expectation by the middle and secondary levels (e.g., using dollars, recognizing prices). Extending standards for access among students with significant cognitive disabilities should not lead to achievement of the same academic skills year after year.

The LAL examines the expectation for age appropriateness and differentiation in two ways. First, special education experts examine the materials used within each task or as evidence for each task for the level of age appropriateness. Items are classified into one of three categories: 1) appropriate for all students, 2) appropriate for the grade band, or 3) not appropriate for the grade band. Second, Webb (2005) described five types of vertical relationships: 1) *broader*—higher-grade standards reflect broader application of target skills or knowledge; 2) *deeper*—higher-grade standards reflect deeper mastery of target skills or knowledge; 3) *prerequisite*—lower-grade standards reflect different prerequisite skills for mastery of higher-grade standards; 4) *new*—the higher grade is a new skill or knowledge unrelated to skills or knowledge covered at prior grades; and 5) *identical*—higher-grade standards seem identical to lower-grade standards. The LAL provides a description of the type of relationship within the extended standards and alternate assessment items. Differentiation is expected to be shown with all but the last category—identical items. A four-point rating scale is used to summarize the strands within the extended standards and alternate assessment items (very strong, strong, adequate, and needs improvement).

Criterion 6: Expected Achievement of Students Is Grade-Referenced Academic Content

States' alternate achievement standards must link to grade-level content. The LAL assumes that what is actually counted toward a score classified as "proficient" should be clearly linked to academic content. Inferences about student learning are more difficult to make when these scores incorporate aspects of teachers or program performance. The strongest inference that a student learned the necessary content can be made if 1) there is evidence that the student did not already have the skill (e.g., through use of pretest, baseline, or previous year's learning), 2) the skill is performed without teacher prompting, and 3) the skill is performed across materials and lessons to show mastery of the concept versus rote memory of one specific response. Typically, the criteria or rubric used to score each student response and the overall assessment provide information on what "counts" for proficiency.

The purpose of this criterion is to measure whether the expected achievement aligns with grade-level standards and not something less. For example, if a child selects a picture for the main idea by pointing or eye gazing, this can be considered the child's performance. However, if a student selects a picture after his or her teacher already has pointed to the correct answer or with the help of a peer, then something other than the student's performance is being measured. Some consideration of these other variables is given in Criterion 8 as part of instructional alignment because it is desirable to provide students with prompts to learn tasks, with inclusive opportunities, and with a means to self-evaluate.

Criterion 7: Barriers to Performance

Because of complex disabilities that students with significant cognitive disabilities sometimes have, it can be difficult to demonstrate achievement. This especially may be true if the only means to show learning is through symbolic representation such as words and pictures. Some students may need to show learning in a meaningful context using everyday objects. Consideration also needs to be given to how students with sensory and physical challenges can access the assessment materials and show learning. The LAL examines whether the alternate assessment items/tasks are difficult because of the knowledge and skills they target or because of other factors not related to the item/task content, such as sensory and physical challenges. This criterion considers whether a student's performance accurately reflects the intended content standard rather than his or her disability.

Criterion 8: The Instructional Program
Promotes Learning in the General Curriculum

The LAL gives consideration to the alignment of instruction to content standards. This is especially important because of the conceptual shift many educators must make to teach students with disabilities content that links to state standards. In the LAL, consideration is given to the content teachers are addressing through the use of the Curriculum Indicators Survey (CIS; Karvonen, Wakeman, Flowers, & Browder, 2007), quality indicators reflected in professional development, and whether teachers are trained to align instruction with grade-level standards. Some of the best practice indicators considered are promotion of inclusive opportunities, self-determination, and collaboration with general educators. The CIS is based on the Surveys of Enacted Curriculum (Porter & Smithson, 2002) and collects information about academic content taught, intensity of instruction by content area, and other instructional practices. The survey has two distinct parts: Part 1 contains demographic information regarding the teacher and the classroom, and Part 2 addresses the enacted curriculum for a specifically selected student who participates in the alternate assessment. Part 2 of the CIS contains three different surveys (one each for English/language arts, math, and science). Teachers are trained (either in person or online) in how to complete each part of the survey. States can select the form of the survey (long, with fine-grain descriptors under each topic strand; or short, with descriptions of each topic strand), the method to use to collect the data (e.g., electronic versus paper), and the number of teachers who will participate. In addition to surveying teachers about their instruction on state content standards, the LAL includes a review of professional development materials to determine whether teachers have received instruction on teaching to the standards. Best practice considerations for the overall quality of the educational program are also considered such as promotion of self-determination, use of assistive technology, inclusion in general education contexts, and applications in functional activities. Sometimes, these quality indicators have been used instead of, or combined with, student performance in rubrics used to score alternate assessments. The LAL promotes retaining these quality indicators through professional development or, when scored, with a separate score from student achievement.

STATE ALIGNMENT OUTCOMES

In our partnership with the National Alternate Assessment Center, we have completed six state alignment studies using the LAL methodology in collaboration with Meagan Karvonen at Western Carolina University. An example of a state report can be found on our web site (http://education.uncc.edu/access). Through these applications, the LAL was refined for use by vendors and states. These applications also provide an interesting snapshot of how states align alternate assessments and ways this alignment sometimes misses the mark.

How States Align

During the state alignment studies, a panel of content and special education experts applied each of the criteria of the LAL. One of the findings from the alignment studies was the extent to which states could meet the expectation for having grade-linked academic content in their alternate assessments. As mentioned, the target is for 90% of the items to be academic and for the 10% not rated as academic by content experts to be foundational. All academic items should have content centrality with the original standard, although not all may have performance centrality because they might be inclusive of students with more complex disabilities. Figure 5.1 provides an example of a state's English/language arts alternate assessment items. As shown, the state did not quite meet these criteria, and it needs to review the items that are neither academic nor foundational and those that were rated academic but lacking content centrality with the designated, linked standard. With some fine tuning of these items, the state could have a well-aligned alternate assessment in this content area. The state received additional information on how the DOK compared with alternate achievement expectations (a comparison with extended standards) versus grade-level achievement (how extended standards compared with grade level) and on how well the content was differentiated across grade levels or grade bands.

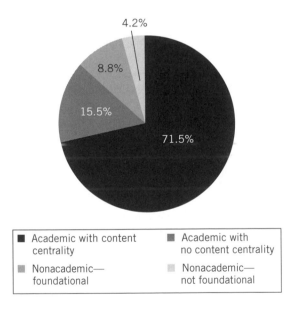

Figure 5.1. An example of one state's link to academic content. This state has 87% alternate assessment items rated as *academic;* this percentage suggests a need for item review. Items that are neither academic nor foundational should be changed or eliminated. Within the academic items, those that lack content centrality also need further review. These items might be matched to the wrong standard or be overstretched.

Why States Miss the Mark

Whether the items are standardized or whether they are written by testing vendors, states, or teachers, the issue of content centrality is a primary concern for any AA-AAS. As described previously in this chapter, there may be several reasons why some states do not adequately create sound links to the standards. The first is backmapping or retrofitting. This process may become less common as states realize that starting with a functional task and forcing it into a standard can misrepresent the content standards. For example, if an item writer begins with the task *Follow steps of washing hands* and tries to retrofit it to the standard *Demonstrate knowledge of microorganisms in human disease,* the primary content—knowledge of microorganisms—is lost. Although washing hands is a necessary skill for all individuals to learn, it has little to do with microbiology unless these concepts are explicitly taught and tested. To avoid this problem, states should encourage item writers first to extend the standards and then to identify tasks that are important for students with disabilities and that clearly link to the standards.

A second reason that states may need to readdress some items involves overstretching of the standards. If, for example, a grade-level content standard is *Apply strategies to comprehend text* and the extended standard is *Choose text for exploration,* the content of comprehension is lost. The extended standard, although possibly an academic skill, is written in a manner that no longer resembles the content of the grade-level standard. It has been extended too far from the original standard. Collaborating with general educators who know the content will help eliminate the risk of losing or misrepresenting the content.

A final, common reason involves mismatches between identified standards and extended standards or items. For example, the extended standard *Explore, observe, and investigate how living things are connected* is linked to an alternate assessment item *Indicate correct weather symbol.* This type of mistake is easily corrected and may simply require professional development or a consensus model of judging the item links.

ALIGNMENT CONSIDERATIONS DURING TEST DEVELOPMENT

Although alignment studies are important in building validity arguments for existing alternate assessments, it is equally important to give additional consideration to alignment in the development or refinement of these assessments. Several points should be considered in this initial development. First, it is important to give attention to the components of Universal Design for Learning (UDL) and to be inclusive of all students in test development. When thought is not given to the various subgroups of students who may participate in an assessment, inferences about student learning and performance cannot be made. The issue then becomes the inaccessibility of the assessment itself and its inability to glean information about students. The Center for Applied Special Technology (1998) described three components for UDL: representation, expression, and engagement. If consideration is given to how students interact with the assessments (e.g., how questions are presented to students and how answers are given by students—such as braille or the use of sign language), what the acceptable response accommodations are (e.g., Will eye gaze or pointing to pictures be accepted?), and how students engage with assessment materials (e.g., objects or other familiar representations), states can plan more inclusive AA-AAS for the varied population of students with disabilities.

A related issue involves considering symbolic communication for participation in AA-AAS. Table 5.5 illustrates how students at the presymbolic, concrete, and abstract levels may demonstrate learning. As the table illustrates, it is not correct to assume that simply providing objects will meet the needs of students at a presymbolic level. Objects can vary in complexity from concrete (a cup for *drink*) to highly abstract (e.g., representational models of science concepts). Students at the presymbolic level also should be allowed to use symbols to ensure that competence in this area is not overlooked during assessment and taught during instruction. Alternative representations such as symbolic objects also may enable students with visual impairments to understand questions or demonstrate understanding. As the table indicates, some differentiation may be needed for students who do not understand abstract concepts to show some learning of the grade-level content.

One resource that can be developed in conjunction with an assessment is a process for how to work standards into meaningful activities that retain links to the original content standards. Browder, Wakeman, et al. (2007) introduced the concept of creating options by symbolic communication levels for accessing grade-level content for students with disabilities. This "Work It Across" method (see Table 5.6) requires collaboration among general education content educators and special educators so that the critical content is retained while consideration is given to students' symbolic levels. The process uses a general education standard and teaching activity and literally works it across the page to plan activities for students with significant cognitive disabilities using the students' own levels of symbolic communication.

A clear benefit of this process is that it allows teachers to mold general education standards and activities into instructional activities for students with disabilities while maintaining alignment with the original standards and activities. The example in Table 5.6 shows the anchor or general education standard in data analysis and probability and follows with the essence of that standard (collecting information and summariz-

Table 5.5. Understanding symbolic levels of communication

Stimulus materials	Response mode options	Presymbolic or first symbols example	Concrete symbolic example	Abstract symbolic example
An array of written words; may be in braille	Point to the word. Say the word as someone else points for you. Eye gaze to indicate the correct word (words on clear frame). Sign the correct answer. Find the word on a voice output device (or spell it).	None (if a student can read words; not at the presymbolic level)	"What comes next? Yes, lunch." (familiar schedule words; student can point to next item in sequence) "Find the folder with your name—*Dan*." (student does this every day)	"What did the boy do after he found the dog?" Answers by selecting the words *walked home* (comprehension) "Which is a type of precipitation?" Answers by selecting the word *rain* (science)
An array of pictures; may be raised pictures (adaptation for visual impairment)	Point to the picture. Say the name of the picture as someone else points to it. Eye gaze to the correct picture (pictures on clear frame). Sign the name of the picture. Find the same picture on the AAC device.	"Which do we eat?" (Student points to the picture that looks exactly like a familiar food; it may be paired with real food items; distractors may be highly discrepant items such as socks.)	"Who found the dog?" (points to picture of boy on the page of the story just read) "Who is your friend?" (finds photograph of friend) "Which of these do we eat for lunch?" (selects food from nonfood)	"Which picture shows the layers of the earth?" "How did Joan feel after she lost her coat?" (Feeling pictures) "What do you think will happen next?"
An array of objects	Point to the object. Say the name of the object as someone points. Eye gaze to the object. Sign the name of the object. Find the picture for the name of the object on an AAC device.	"What do we need for lunch?" (selects a napkin) "The cat ran up the tree. Find the cat." (realistic stuffed cat is paired with objects that are not animals)	"What was this story about?" (selects the hat for a story about hats) "Today, we learned about rain. Which do we need for the rain?" (selects umbrella)	"Which of these can be used as a lever?" "Which of these has more?" "Which of these items might have been found in our story?" (antique items versus modern ones for a historical story)

Key: AAC, augmentative and alternative communication.

Table 5.6. Example of Work It Across for a math standard

Standard: *Mathematics Standard 6. The student will demonstrate through the mathematical processes an understanding of the relationships between two variables within one population or sample.*

Essence of the standard (expanded standard): *Collect information and summarize in chart/graph.*

		On grade level expectation (not adapted)	Abstract symbolic	Concrete symbolic	Beginning symbol use
Grade level: Fifth grade	Teaching activity	Students have projects to design investigation and summarize outcome (simple survey research).	Create and implement a survey; summarize outcome using choice of plot or bar graph.	Make choices to help in creating and implementing survey (e.g., who to survey, what to ask); administer (may use AT); choose between picture or symbol graph.	Make choices to help create survey; use AT to help administer questions; summarize each response as received using choice of picture or symbol.
	How student shows mastery	Design a mathematical investigation and analyze data using mathematical computations.	Compose overall survey question. Uses words and/or picture symbols to create survey questions (e.g., who, what, when); use graph of choice to answer prediction and comparative questions.	Uses selection response to identify 3 or more key survey questions; administer with AT; tally responses onto bar graph (or other format); use graph to indicate which is more/less.	Use selection to make at least one choice about survey (e.g., who—boys or girls); administer by independently activating AT or passing out paper; summarize response as received using concrete manipulatives (e.g., object graph); place "more" symbol on appropriate column of graph.

Bree A. Jimenez contributed to the design of this table.

Key: AT, assistive technology.

ing it in a chart/graph). Because one of the challenges in the alignment of AA-AAS involves special educators' lack of familiarity with academic content standards, the essence of the standard serves as a translation for practitioners of the critical component(s) of the grade-level standard. The on-grade-level expectation, whether it is a state standard or a teaching activity, should be generated from general education resources (e.g., general education teacher, curriculum framework, state standards). Practitioners should then consider how students working within the abstract symbolic, concrete symbolic, and beginning-symbol-use levels of communication could engage in the content.

As the "Work It Across" method addresses accessibility at set grade levels or bands, differentiation of content across the grade levels or bands also must be occurring. Although the vertical progression of strands and standards across grades is common in general education instruction and assessment, it traditionally has been uncommon in the education of students with significant cognitive disabilities. Instead, these students tend either to experience repeated instruction of the same skills across grade bands if mastery does not occur (e.g., instruction in shape identification through the high school years) or to encounter catalog approaches to instruction in which teachers pick and choose isolated skills (which can be on or below grade level) to teach. Therefore, a resource is needed to help inform teachers how academic content progresses across the grades. Table 5.7 includes an example of this "Work It Up" process. Grades K, 2, 5, 8, and high school are represented in the table. The process again begins with the grade-level expectations and then follows the progress of the standard through either the grades or the grade bands. Once the grade-level progression is established, the process of working it across at each grade or grade band begins.

One important aspect of this process that needs restating is the need for collaboration among general educators and special educators throughout these activities. Reviewing the links from the translated activities to the grade-level standards or activities is critical. As special educators work a standard or activity across, it is important that fidelity checks are conducted by individuals knowledgeable in the content area to prevent overstretching of the standard or instruction. For example, in a review of the content within Table 5.7, general educators who reviewed this "Work It Up" method noted that the vertical progression was clear and that the differentiation was evident and logical. Table 5.8 contains the content experts' ratings for academic, content, and performance centrality for the standard and activities presented in Table 5.7. In Table 5.7, all items were academic (i.e., they were coded as academic with links to the national standard of Earth and Space), most had near links for content between the activities and the original grade-level expectations (i.e., only the concrete symbolic for high school and all of Grade 5 had far links), and all activities had at least some performance of the original grade-level expectations.

Table 5.7. Work It Up for science

Standard: *Identify the structure of the earth system*
Essence of the standard: *Recognize the materials that compose the earth's surface.*

		On grade level expectation (not adapted)	Abstract symbolic	Concrete symbolic	Beginning symbol use
Grade level: Kindergarten	Teaching activity	Sort water, rocks, and soil.	Sort water, rocks, or soil using two categories (e.g., water and rocks or rocks and soil) using at least three different types or sizes of rocks and types of soil.	Sort water, rocks, or soil using two categories with models (picture or object).	Match water, rocks, or soil to same.
	How student shows mastery	Independent grouping of materials.	Able to sort a variety of materials.	Able to match a variety of materials to model.	Match materials to same.
Second grade	Teaching activity	Describe characteristics of water, rocks, and soil[a] (compare and contrast using Venn diagram).	Describe different characteristics of each material (one at a time) using a bubble map and picture cues or objects for abstract representations (i.e., hard). Verbal prompts and kinesthetic opportunities should be provided when needed.	Given a bubble map with no more than three bubbles and two picture cues or object representations (e.g., crumbs for soil) at a time, identify the correct characteristic of the material (e.g., for soil, the choices could be crumbs or a paperclip) using a model on the map if needed.	Given a bubble map with no more than three bubbles, and two object representations (e.g., crumbs for soil) at a time, match the correct characteristic of the material (e.g., for soil, the choices could be crumbs or a paperclip) to the material in the bubble map.

Fifth grade				
How student shows mastery	Complete Venn diagram.	Complete bubble map for each type.	Identify the characteristics for each material.	Match the characteristics.
Teaching activity	Observe topsoil with a hand lens. Look for fragments of organisms. Note the odor and clumping attributable to organic components. Compare components. Compare components that support plant growth across soil types (topsoil versus sand).	Plant seeds or young plant in topsoil and sand. Observe and note changes/difference.	Plant seeds or young plants in topsoil and sand. Answer weekly *yes/no* questions posed by teacher about changes (e.g., is the plant in the soil growing?) to create class chart.	Participate in planting seeds or young plants in topsoil (e.g., *Which is soil?* with soil and pencil presented to student. Once identified, student will help put soil in pot).
How student shows mastery	Describe plant supporting components by soil type.	Identify at least two changes/differences from a list for soils.	Correctly answer a *yes/no* question: *Is the plant growing in this soil?*	Active participation in steps to plant seeds/plants in topsoil. Communicates *growing* as appropriate using AT.

(continued)

Table 5.7. *(continued)*

Standard: *Identify the structure of the earth system*

Essence of the standard: *Recognize the materials that compose the earth's surface.*

		On grade level expectation (not adapted)	Abstract symbolic	Concrete symbolic	Beginning symbol use
Grade level: Eighth grade	Teaching activity	Explain how weather is the most significant source of erosion and can affect the shape of rocks and create landscapes depending on the weathering process and climate.	Identify changes in a variety of landscapes from weathering elements and natural events (e.g., Grand Canyon, shorelines, volcanoes, waterfalls, landslides).	Match landscapes shaped by weathering elements and natural events (e.g., shorelines, Grand Canyon, volcanoes, waterfalls, landslides) when presented to photographs or representations.	Use a computer to find pictures/photographs/videos of landscapes shaped by weathering elements and natural events (e.g., shorelines, Grand Canyon, volcanoes, waterfalls, landslides).
	How student shows mastery	Create visual presentation of the impact of specific weathering events on soil and rocks.	Sequence three photographs of the effect of wind/waves on a landscape.	Match three types of landscapes.	Participate in the selection of media (e.g., click the mouse, answer *yes/no* to select information).

Grade level: High school				
Teaching activity	Discuss how earth changes can be short term (during a human's lifetime), such as earthquakes and volcanic eruptions, or long term (over a geological time scale), such as mountain building and plate movements.	Categorize natural events and processes according to how they change the surface of the earth, using picture symbols or written words.	Identify a natural event (*Which one is a volcano erupting?*) when presented with two photographs or representations.	When presented with visual models or representations (e.g., teacher simulating the moving of plates) or computer simulations or videos of natural events (e.g., a flood), student will identify which events are fast by answering *yes/no* (with use of AT if necessary).
How student shows mastery	Create poster of impact of one identified change to earth's surface and surrounding communities.	Complete fast/short time and slow/long time chart.	Identify two events.	Answer questions correctly.

[a]All students can be given opportunities to explore soil's property through touch, smell, observe through lens, and so forth.
Key: AT, assistive technology.

Table 5.8. Expert content and performance centrality ratings for Earth and Space standards

Grade	Academic			Content centrality			Performance centrality		
	Abstract symbolic	Concrete symbolic	Beginning symbol use	Abstract symbolic	Concrete symbolic	Beginning symbol use	Abstract symbolic	Concrete symbolic	Beginning symbol use
Kindergarten	1-ES	1-ES	1-ES	2	2	2	2	2	2
2	1-ES	1-ES	1-ES	2	2	2	1	1	1
5	1-ES	1-ES	1-ES	1	1	1	1	1	1
8	1-ES	1-ES	1-ES	2	2	2	2	1	1
High school	1-ES	1-ES	1-ES	2	1	2	2	1	1

Key: Academic column: 1 = academic, 0 = nonacademic, ES = Earth/Space Standard; Content centrality column: 2 = near, 1 = far, 0 = none; Performance centrality column: 2 = all, 1 = some, 0 = none.

SUMMARY

Federal policy requires that AA-AAS be clearly related to grade-level content, although the content may be restricted in scope or complexity or take the form of introductory or prerequisite skills (U.S. Department of Education, 2005). That is, alternate assessment items must link to grade-level content standards. The criteria for this linkage probably will be different from those for general assessments. In some of our early work, we discovered that the expectations for alignment proposed for general assessments, such as range and balance, were nearly impossible to achieve when the content was prioritized for alternate achievement (Flowers et al., 2006). We also concluded that the DOK should not match the grade-level performance indicators for the content standards because this would be grade-level achievement. Gong and Marion (2006) advocated for increased flexibility in the technical considerations of AA-AAS. We concur that such flexibility is needed, but we advocate for boundaries as well. The LAL is the method we developed and field tested with six states to define the criteria for alignment of AA-AAS. In all six states, some areas of their alternate assessments met our criteria more closely than others, and specific feedback could be provided from content experts' reviewing of items that needed further development to reflect the original content standard. These criteria can be used at the outset in developing a new alternate assessment to focus on alignment with content standards.

From our work with state alternate assessment systems and professional development, it is clear that teachers need much more help in understanding general curriculum content and how to diversify instruction for the students they serve. Even if they are "highly qualified" per NCLB requirements, special education teachers still often lack the deep content knowledge needed to teach to the standards. An important way to compensate for this gap is for general and special education teachers to collaborate in planning how to include students with significant cognitive disabilities in general curriculum instruction. When planning state resources on teaching to the standards, or when developing alternate assessment items, close collaboration with content experts is essential to preserve fidelity with the original standards. We have provided two tools in this chapter, "Work It Across" and "Work It Up," which may help school or state teams plan for extensions of standards. Both require knowing the general curriculum content before creating extensions.

In our work, we also have advocated for students to be active versus passive learners. For example, in our sixth criterion of the LAL, we focus on whether inferences can be made about what a student learned versus systems that intermix teacher and program performance indicators with student achievement. In contrast, we also have advocated for systems in which students at different symbolic levels can meet achievement expectations. Federal policy permits setting multiple alternate achievement standards, but not a different one for each student (U.S. Department of Education, 2003). Creating multiple expectations during standard setting may not be feasible, given the small number of students with disabilities. In contrast, developing an AA-AAS system with multiple levels of entry (as in the Pennsylvania Alternate System of Assessment [PASA]) makes it possible for students who are just beginning symbol use to show what they know. Table 5.5 in this chapter may help educators consider what these different symbol levels mean and how the symbol levels might be used in our "Work It Across" and "Work It Up" tools.

Although we have worked diligently to show how to extend standards for students who are just learning to use symbols and who may rely primarily on nonsymbolic communication, we acknowledge that, for some students, identifying any observable, consistent response is a challenge. We sometimes have referred to this subgroup as those at an *awareness* level because the only responses that may be measurable are indications of being alert to the stimuli presented (e.g., opening eyes, changes in respiration, changes in vocalizations). This is a small subgroup within the 1% (possibly the 0.1%), but it is one that continues to challenge state developers of AA-AAS and teachers who try to address state standards. These students often are medically fragile and have complex combinations of physical and sensory disabilities (e.g., deafblindness and cerebral palsy). From our perspective, because this is the population for whom it is most difficult to ascertain what is being comprehended, it is especially important that these students receive instruction in grade-level academic content. Popular media sometimes have depicted individuals who had no way to show what they knew but who indicated full understanding once a response could be established (e.g., the movie *My Left Foot*). Although teaching state standards can be justified, there simply is no way to evaluate achievement until a reliable response mode can be established with the help of assistive technology or other means.

In summary, state alternate assessments have evolved from focusing on separate functional content to linking to grade-level content standards. Although consideration of functional and other individual needs should be an ongoing part of IEP planning for students with disabilities, evidence exists that these students can learn academic skills. More resources are needed on how to extend the academic content reflected in state standards and how to apply evidence-based practice to this learning. This chapter has summarized our approach to evaluating the alignment of AA-AAS and has offered some tools for educators to extend state standards.

REFERENCES

Achieve, Inc. (2001, April). *Measuring up: A benchmarking study of the Minnesota comprehensive assessments.* Retrieved July 13, 2005, from http://www.achieve.org/files/Minnesota-Benchmarking4-2001.pdf

Achieve, Inc. (2002). *Measuring up: A standards and assessments benchmarking report for Oklahoma.* Retrieved June 29, 2005, from http://www.achieve.org/files/OK_Benchmark.pdf

Agran, M., Alper, S., & Wehmeyer, M. (2002). Access to the general curriculum for students with significant disabilities: What it means to teachers. *Education and Training in Mental Retardation and Developmental Disabilities, 37*(2), 123–133.

Almond, P., & Bechard, S. (2005, April). *Alignment of two performance-based alternate assessments with combined content standards from eight states through expanded benchmarks.* Paper presented at the 2005 meeting of the National Council on Measurement in Education, Montreal, Canada.

American Educational Research Association, American Psychological Association, & National Council on Measurement in Education. (1999). *Standards for educational and psychological testing.* Washington, DC: Authors.

Browder, D., Ahlgrim-Delzell, L., Courtade-Little, G., & Snell, M. (2006). General curriculum access. In M. Snell & F. Brown (Eds.), *Instruction of students with severe disabilities* (6th ed., pp. 489–525). Upper Saddle River, NJ: Prentice Hall.

Browder, D.M., Flowers, C., Ahlgrim-Delzell, L., Karvonen, M., Spooner, F., & Algozzine, R. (2004). The alignment of alternate assessment content to academic and functional curricula. *Journal of Special Education, 37*(4), 211–223.

Browder, D.M., Spooner, F., Ahlgrim-Delzell, L., Flowers, C., Algozzine, R., & Karvonen, M. (2003). A content analysis of the curricular philosophies reflected in states' alternate assessments performance indicators. *Research and Practice for Persons with Severe Disabilities, 28*(4), 165–181.

Browder, D.M., Spooner, F., Ahlgrim-Delzell, L., Harris, A., & Wakeman, S.Y., (2008). A meta-analysis on teaching mathematics to students with significant cognitive disabilities. *Exceptional Children, 74*, 407–432.

Browder, D.M., Trela, K.C., & Jimenez, B.A. (2007). Training teachers to follow a task analysis to engage middle school students with moderate and severe developmental disabilities in grade-appropriate literature. *Focus on Autism and Other Developmental Disabilities, 22*(4), 206—219.

Browder, D.M., Wakeman, S.Y., Flowers, C., Rickelman, R., Pugalee, D., & Karvonen, M. (2007). Creating access to the general curriculum with links to grade level content for students with significant cognitive disabilities: An explication of the concept. *Journal of Special Education, 41*(1), 2–16.

Browder, D.M., Wakeman, S.Y., Spooner, F., Ahlgrim-Delzell, L., & Algozzine, B. (2006). Research on reading instruction for individuals with significant cognitive disabilities. *Exceptional Children, 72*(4), 392–408.

Carter, E.W., Cushing, L.S., Clark, N.M., & Kennedy, C.H. (2005). Effects of peer support interventions on students' access to the general curriculum and social interactions. *Research and Practice for Persons with Severe Disabilities, 30*(1), 15–25.

Center for Applied Special Technology. (1998). *What is universal design for learning?* Retrieved July 11, 2005, from http://www.cast.org/research/udl/index.html

Center for Policy Research on the Impact of General and Special Education Reform (1996, June). *Standards-based school reform and students with disabilities* (ERIC Document Reproduction Service No. ED398713). Alexandria, VA: Author.

Chief Council of State School Officers. (2005). *Using curricular measures for description and analysis.* Retrieved August 16, 2005, from http://www.ccsso.org/content/pdfs/JohnSmithsonsecTampa05.ppt

Courtade, G.R., Spooner, F., & Browder, D.M. (2007). Review of studies with students with significant cognitive disabilities which link to science standards. *Research and Practice for Persons with Severe Disabilities, 32*(1), 43–49.

Dymond, S.K., Renzaglia, A., Rosenstein, A., Chun, E.J., Banks, R., Niswander, V., et al. (2006). Using a participatory action research approach to create a universally designed inclusive high school science course: A case study. *Research and Practice for Persons with Severe Disabilities, 31*(4), 293–308.

Flowers, C., Browder, D.M., & Ahlgrim-Delzell, L. (2006). An analysis of three states' alignment between language arts and mathematics standards and alternate assessments. *Exceptional Children, 72*(2), 201–215.

Flowers, C., Wakeman, S.Y., Browder, D.M., & Karvonen, M. (2007). *Links for academic learning: An alignment protocol for alternate assessments based on alternate achievement standards.* Charlotte: University of North Carolina at Charlotte.

Gong, B., & Marion, S. (2006). *Dealing with flexibility in assessments for students with significant cognitive disabilities* (NECO Synthesis Rep. No. 60). Minneapolis: University of Minnesota, National Center on Educational Outcomes.

Individuals with Disabilities Education Act Amendments (IDEA) of 1997, PL 105-17, 20 U.S.C. §§ 1400 *et seq.*

Jimenez, B.A., Browder, D.M., & Courtade, G.R. (2008). Teaching an algebraic equation to high school students with moderate developmental disabilities. *Education and Training in Developmental Disabilities, 43*(2), 266–274.

Karvonen, M., Wakeman, S.Y., Flowers, C., & Browder, D. (2007). *Curriculum Indicators Survey (CIS).* Charlotte: University of North Carolina at Charlotte.

Kleinert, H., Browder, D., & Towles-Reeves, E. (2005). *The assessment triangle and students with significant cognitive disabilities: Models of student cognition.* Retrieved December 12, 2007, from http://www.naacpartners.org/products/whitePapers/18000.pdf

Kleinert, H.L., & Kearns, J.F. (Eds.). (2001). *Alternate assessment: Measuring outcomes and supports for students with disabilities.* Baltimore: Paul H. Brookes Publishing Co.

Lehr, C., & Thurlow, M. (2003). *Putting it all together: Including students with disabilities in assessment and accountability systems* (Policy Directions No. 16). Retrieved May 23, 2006, from http://education.umn.edu/NCEO/OnlinePubs/Policy16.htm

McDonnell, J., Johnson, J., Polychronis, S., Riesen, T., Jameson, M., & Kercher, K. (2006). Comparison of one-to-one embedded instruction in general education classes with small group instruction in special education classes. *Education and Training in Developmental Disabilities, 41*(2), 125–138.

McDonnell, J., Mathot-Buckner, C., Thorson, N., & Fister, S. (2001). Supporting the inclusion of students with moderate and severe disabilities in junior high school general education classes: The effects of classwide peer tutoring, multielement curriculum, and accommodations. *Education and Treatment of Children, 24*(2), 141–160.

McDonnell, J., Thorson, N., Allen, C., & Mathot-Buckner, C. (2000). The effects of partner learning during spelling for students with severe disabilities and their peers. *Journal of Behavioral Education, 10*(2–3), 107–121.

National Alternate Assessment Center. (2005, June). *Access and alignment to grade level content for students with the most significant cognitive disabilities: A training module for large-scale use.* Presentation at the annual meeting of the Council for Chief State School Officers Large-Scale Assessment Conference, San Antonio, TX.

National Council of Teachers of English. (n.d.). *Standards for the English language arts.* Retrieved May 25, 2006, from http://www.ncte.org/standards

National Council of Teachers of Mathematics. (n.d.). *Principles & standards for school mathematics.* Retrieved May 25, 2006, from http://standards.nctm.org/index.htm

National Research Council. (1996). *National science education standards.* Washington, DC: National Academies Press.

No Child Left Behind Act of 2001, PL 107-110, 115 Stat. 1425, 20 U.S.C. §§ 6301 *et seq.*

Nolet, V., & McLaughlin, M.J. (2000). *Accessing the general curriculum: Including students with disabilities in standards-based reform.* Thousand Oaks, CA: Corwin Press.

Porter, A.C. (2002). Measuring the content of instruction: Uses in research and practice. *Educational Researcher, 31*(7), 3–14.

Porter, A.C., & Smithson, J.L. (2002). *Alignment of assessments, standards, and instruction using curriculum indicator data.* Retrieved June 14, 2005, from http://cep.terc.edu/dec/research/alignPaper.pdf

Roach, A.T., Elliott, S.N., & Webb, N.L. (2005). Alignment of an alternate assessment with state academic standards: Evidence for the content validity of the Wisconsin alternate assessment. *The Journal of Special Education, 38*(4), 218–231.

Thompson, S., Johnstone, C., Thurlow, M., & Altman, J. (2005). *2005 state special education outcomes: Steps forward in a decade of change.* Retrieved December 7, 2005, from http://education.umn.edu/NCEO/OnlinePubs/2005State Report.htm

Thompson, S.J., Quenemoen, R.F., Thurlow, M.L., & Ysseldyke, J.E. (2001). *Alternate assessments for students with disabilities.* Thousand Oaks, CA: Corwin Press.

Thompson, S., & Thurlow, M. (2001). *State special education outcomes, 2001: A report on state activities at the beginning of a new decade.* Retrieved December 12, 2007, from http://cehd.umn.edu/nceo/OnlinePubs/StateSpecEduc Outcomes2001.pdf

U.S. Department of Education. (2003). *Title I—Improving the academic achievement of the disadvantaged; Final rule.* 68 Fed. Reg. 236 (December 9, 2003).

U.S. Department of Education. (2004). *Standards and assessments peer review guidance: Information and examples for meeting the requirements of the No Child Left Behind Act of 2001.* Retrieved May 2, 2005, from http://www.ed .gov/policy/elsec/guid/saaprguidance.doc

U.S. Department of Education. (2005). *Alternate achievement standards for students with the most significant cognitive disabilities.* Retrieved August 12, 2005, from http://www.ed.gov/policy/elsec/guid/altguidance.doc

Wakeman, S.Y., Flowers, C., & Browder, D.M. (2007, November). *Aligning alternate to grade level content standards: Issues and considerations for alternates based on alternate achievement standards* (Policy Directions 19). http://cehd .umn.edu/nceo/OnlinePubs/Policy19/PolicyDirections19.pdf

Webb, N.L. (1997). *Criteria for alignment of expectations and assessments in mathematics and science education.* (NISE Research Monograph No. 6). Madison: University of Wisconsin-Madison, National Institute for Science Education.

Webb, N.L. (2005, November). *Alignment, depth of knowledge, and change.* Paper presented at the annual meeting of the Florida Educational Research Association, Miami, FL.

CHAPTER 6

Conceptualizing and Setting Performance Standards for Alternate Assessments

STEVE FERRARA, SUZANNE SWAFFIELD, AND LORIN MUELLER

The No Child Left Behind Act (NCLB) of 2001 (PL 107-110) and the Individuals with Disabilities Education Act Amendments (IDEA) of 1997 (PL 105-17; updated in 2004 as PL 108-445) require that all students participate in annual, statewide assessments and that performance on those assessments be reported as part of each state's accountability system. NCLB requires assessments in reading and mathematics in Grades 3–8 and one time in high school; assessments in science are required in at least one grade each in elementary, middle, and high school. NCLB requires states 1) to develop alternate assessments based on alternate achievement standards (AA-AAS) that are 2) linked to grade-level content area standards so that 3) students with significant cognitive disabilities can be appropriately and meaningfully assessed on extended grade-level academic content and achievement standards.

Students who are appropriately eligible for AA-AAS cannot participate meaningfully in grade-level academic achievement tests because their significant cognitive disabilities do not enable them to access grade-level academic content. This does not mean that they cannot learn any academic content, however. NCLB requires that students with significant cognitive disabilities are taught academic content that is "clearly related to grade-level content, although it may be restricted in scope or complexity or take the form of introductory or prerequisite skills" (U.S. Department of Education, 2005a). Grade-level content standards that are restricted in scope or complexity to make them accessible and appropriate for these students may be referred to as extensions of grade-level academic content standards. Extended standards must retain their link to grade-level content standards. The National Alternate Assessment Center defines extended academic content standards that are linked to grade-level content standards:

> To be linked to grade level standards, the target for achievement must be academic content (e.g., reading, math, science) that is referenced to the student's assigned grade based on chronological age. Functional activities and materials may be used to promote understanding, but the target skills for student achievement are academically focused. Some prioritization of the content will occur in setting this expectation, but it should reflect the major domains of the curricular area (e.g., strands of math) and have fidelity with this content and how it is typically taught in general education. The alternate expectation for achievement may focus on prerequisite skills or some partial attainment of the grade level, but students should still have the opportunity to meet high expectations, to demonstrate a range of depth of knowledge, to achieve within their symbolic level, and to show growth across grade levels or grade bands. (Browder, Wakeman, & Jimenez, n.d.)

This focus on retaining the link between extended and grade-level content standards is intended to ensure that students with significant cognitive disabilities receive challenging academic instruction. Historically, the instructional content for these students has focused on functional or life skills (e.g., personal hygiene, food preparation, and other independent living skills).

The target examinee population for AA-AAS has become familiar to some educational measurement specialists who work on grade-level academic achievement tests, but only since 2003 or so. This target population is surprisingly diverse—some would say more diverse in terms of cognitive and social functioning than students in the general population. As examples, this chapter discusses hypothetical cases for the fictionalized students Alex, Susan, and Ginny, who are composites of real students. (The descriptions and discussion are adapted from Ferrara, Goldberg, et al., 2006.) Alex and Susan, who are assigned to a special class for students with significant cognitive disabilities, participate in state AA-AAS:

■ It is time for the morning meeting in Ms. Olson's upper primary special day class. One by one, she greets each child:

Alex, a handsome fifth grader with Down syndrome who loves baseball, greets her enthusiastically and asks how her weekend was. The morning meeting is one of Alex's favorite activities of the day because he usually gets to change the calendar date and remind the class about upcoming holidays. Alex's least favorite time used to be math, but now that he is learning to use a calculator to do double-digit addition, it is not nearly as bad.

When Ms. Olson comes to Susan, a third grader with twinkling blue eyes and a keen sense of rhythm, her assistant immediately moves behind the child. Susan, who has been diagnosed with autism, has made pretty good progress with eye contact but still must be prompted physically for other social greetings. She can use more than 80 different picture symbols to ask for food and activities that she likes, but she is much more likely to grab a person's necklace than to smile and wave *hello*. The upcoming alphabet song is Susan's favorite part of morning meetings. She cannot say the words, but she knows every letter and points along with her communication board. Ms. Olson wishes some of that enthusiasm for letters would carry over into Susan's "reading" lessons. Susan still recognizes her own name only 70% of the time.

Including students such as Alex and Susan in statewide AA-AAS is required by NCLB and IDEA, with the specific purpose of assessing their academic achievement but also to ensure that these students receive academic instruction in addition to instruction on life skills (e.g., functioning on a job, living as an adult, performing personal hygiene tasks).

The cognitive–academic functioning of a small percentage of students with significant cognitive disabilities is so limited that innovative assessment strategies are required to enable these students to participate meaningfully in AA-AAS. They are students with the most significant cognitive disabilities (see, for example, Browder & Spooner, 2006). Individually administered diagnostic assessments (e.g., the Brigance Inventory of Early Development) yield age-equivalent estimates of cognitive–academic functioning for some students in this group in the age range of 1–3 years and younger. These students are the lowest-functioning of all students with significant cognitive disabilities. NCLB requires that even students such as Ginny participate in AA-AAS:

Ms. Olson's voice softens as she bends down to greet Ginny, a 10-year-old girl with a beautiful smile and profound, multiple disabilities. Because Ginny has no functional vision, Ms. Olson gently grips and strokes the girl's fingers to say hello. Ginny, who typically stiffens and grimaces when her chair is pushed over bumpy surfaces (but otherwise displays very little awareness of her surroundings), does not react to Ms. Olson's greeting. The one-on-one nurse who accompanies Ginny to school to tend to her ventilator and other medical needs says that Ginny likes story time the best. Ms. Olson smiles in agreement. She does not divulge to the nurse that Ginny displays none of the orienting responses shown by other children in the class who have profound disabilities. Ginny has no academic goals as part of her individualized educational program. Her parents' main hope for their daughter's education is for her to be comfortable and participate as a member of the class.

NCLB and IDEA require that all students with significant cognitive disabilities—including students such as Ginny—participate meaningfully in statewide AA-AAS and be included in state accountability systems for the same reasons that students such as Alex and Susan are required to receive challenging academic instruction. (We refer to students such as Ginny as *students with the most significant cognitive disabilities* to distinguish them from students such as Alex and Susan.)

According to estimates, 1–3% of students cannot participate meaningfully in assessments at their age and grade level, even with test administration accommodations, because of significant cognitive disabilities. For example, the U.S. Department of Education cites research to support an estimate that "1.8 to 2.5% of children . . . are not able to reach grade-level standards, even with the best instruction" (U.S. Department of Education, 2005b). For many of these students, school learning is further limited by visual, hearing, physical, and communication disabilities. The first 1% of this estimate includes students with significant cognitive disabilities. The "2% rule" by the U.S. Department of Education (Olson, 2005) suggests that an additional 2% of students with disabilities may not be able to participate meaningfully. These students are eligible to participate in alternate assessments based on modified achievement standards (AA-MAS).

Designs for AA-AAS for students with significant cognitive disabilities are relatively new and evolving. One of the earliest designs was Maryland's Independence Mastery Assessment Program of the mid-1990s. In this assessment, students were scored on their performance of tasks related to personal management, community, recreation and leisure, career and vocation, communication, decision making, and interpersonal skills (Haigh, 1996). Since then, and because of the new focus on academic achievement, three basic designs have emerged:

- Assessment portfolios, which contain collections of student academic work, video and audio recordings of students performing academic tasks, and other evidence of their performance in relation to extended grade-level content standards. Some states refer to their portfolios as *datafolios,* which seems to be a reference to the scores on the contents of a portfolio. Some states require that student performance on structured performance tasks be included in the portfolio (e.g., Rhode Island). In these cases, the performance tasks are administered as part of a classroom, school, or community activity, which can vary across students instead of being standardized for all students.

- Rating scales with supporting collections of evidence. A typical rating scale AA-AAS would include considerable numbers of items linked to extended content standards. For example, items linked to a word-recognition skills standard might include matching letters to objects or pictures, selecting the letter that matches a sound, and producing the sound that corresponds to a letter. Evidence that can be rated may be based on observing students as they complete a task, recordings of students as they complete tasks, student work samples, or interviews with other teachers and adults. Rating scales typically are multilevel (e.g., nonexistent, emerging, progressing, accomplished). The types of evidence and the items for which supporting evidence must be applied typically are prescribed.

- Performance task designs. Performance task designs are quite varied. In general, each assessment task focuses on related extended academic standards (e.g., recognizing or creating patterns in mathematics using familiar objects) and may contain 3–5 or as many as 10–15 items. Administration of assessment tasks usually is supported by manipulatives such as real objects (e.g., soil or rocks for science), response cards for nonverbal students, supported communication systems, (e.g., computer eye gaze systems for physically impaired students, dark placemats to enhance visual contrast for visually impaired students), or other assistive devices used by students during classroom activities. Items often include scaffolding; for example, response choices may be reduced in number if a student responds incorrectly, and scoring of subsequent responses may be adjusted downward accordingly. In some cases, items are calibrated to an Item Response Theory (IRT) scale, and student performance is reported on that scale.

NCLB specifies that states must assess all students, including those who can participate meaningfully only on AA-AAS, and allows each state to include up to 1% of its students in the *Proficient* category or above for adequate yearly progress (AYP) reporting based on performance on AA-AAS.

In this chapter, we discuss definitions and descriptions of performance levels for AA-AAS. We summarize the designs for AA-AAS in 31 of 51 states (including the District of Columbia). Then, we define five approaches that states have taken to define and describe *Proficient* performance on their AA-AAS, and we provide examples from actual state descriptions of *Proficient* performance. And, we briefly discuss steps proposed by another author for selecting a standard-setting method that is appropriate for each AA-AAS design.

DEFINITIONS AND DESCRIPTIONS OF *PROFICIENT* ACHIEVEMENT FOR ALTERNATE ASSESSMENTS

Performance-level descriptors are widely familiar because of their use in the National Assessment of Educational Progress (NAEP; for NAEP, they are referred to as *achievement-level descriptions*) and statewide grade-level academic achievement tests. Performance-level descriptors are crucial because they represent the 1) content area knowledge and skills that students are expected to acquire as part of schooling and 2) levels of achievement expected of students in relation to a state's content standards, as indicated by ranges of scores on a state's academic achievement tests. Because they are promulgated by state departments of education, performance-level descriptors also are states' policy statements for students' academic achievement. And, descriptors are intended to communicate each state's policy to students, their teachers, and their families and to aid in interpreting performances on statewide academic achievement tests.

Definitions of *Proficient* performance are particularly important. Under NCLB, *Proficient* is the level of achievement that all students are required to achieve by 2014. More generally, descriptions of *Proficient* performance represent aspirations for the academic achievement for school-age children. Every state has its own set of descriptors and definitions for Proficient performance in each grade level and each academic area. This applies to grade-level achievement tests, AA-AAS, and the AA-MAS that began appearing in state assessment programs in 2007.

Generic Policy Definitions

NAEP's policy definition for proficient performance on all content area assessments in Grades 4, 8, and 12 has served as a model for many state content and grade-specific definitions for Proficient performance:

> This level represents solid academic performance for each grade assessed. Students reaching this level have demonstrated competency over challenging subject matter, including subject-matter knowledge, application of such knowledge to real world situations, and analytical skills appropriate to the subject matter. [See National Assessment Governing Board, n.d.]

This policy definition exhibits three key features relevant for all descriptors. It provides a clear statement of what *Proficient* means, using memorable phrases such as "solid academic performance" and "competency over challenging subject matter." In addition, it specifies the academic domain about which test performance should be generalized: "subject-matter knowledge, application of such knowledge to real world situations, and analytical skills appropriate to the subject matter." Finally, this description of Proficient performance provides the basis for defining both *Basic* and *Advanced* performance in a vertically articulated way. In contrast to *Proficient*, performance at the *Basic* level "denotes *partial mastery* of prerequisite knowledge and skills that are *fundamental for proficient* work at each grade." The *Advanced* level "signifies *superior performance*" compared with Proficient performance. (See National Assessment Governing Board, n.d.; italics added.) Because these are generic policy definitions, they do not make reference to specific content area knowledge, skills, or conceptual understanding.

Policy definitions that accompany AA-AAS must be appropriate and attainable for students with significant cognitive disabilities. Thus, they should refer to academic knowledge, skills, and applications described in extended grade-level academic content standards that define the learning goals for students with significant cognitive disabilities. And, policy definitions should be appropriate and attainable for all students who are eligible for AA-AAS, including those with the most significant cognitive disabilities.

Content Area and Grade-Level Specific Descriptors

To these three features, we add the following features for content area and grade-specific descriptors for AA-AAS. Specific descriptions of *Proficient* and other performance levels should

- Be appropriate, rigorous, and attainable for all students at all levels of cognitive and communication functioning in the targeted grade level or grade band

- Be aligned with the extended content standards that are taught and that are targeted in AA-AAS (See Critical Element 2.5 regarding alignment of achievement and content standards in U.S. Department of Education, 2007.)

- Differentiate expectations across performance levels within and across grades or grade bands, across grades or grade bands (e.g., Hambleton & Pitoniak, 2006; Perie, 2007)

- Relate sensibly to modified and grade-level achievement standards

- Reflect input from stakeholders (See Critical Element 2.6 in U.S. Department of Education, 2007.)

Exemplar Items and Student Work Samples to Enhance Understanding of Descriptors

It is fairly common practice to provide items that exemplify what students are expected to know and be able to do at each proficiency level. Exemplar items can enhance understanding and interpretation of performance-level descriptors because they are concrete and vivid. For tests with IRT reporting scales (e.g., some AA-AAS with performance task designs), items can be selected to illustrate *Proficient* and other levels of performance using the calibrated location of each item on the test score scale.

Procedures for selecting exemplar items and student work for portfolios and rating scales is somewhat less straightforward (in the psychometric sense) but feasible nonetheless. For example, evidence from portfolios with scores in each proficiency level could be selected to illustrate performance at each level. Also, supporting evidence from rating scale total scores in each level could be selected. Although we did not examine the extent of using exemplar items and student work to support performance-level descriptors for this study, we doubt that it is widely practiced for AA-AAS.

Achievement Construct Definitions Represented by Descriptors for Alternate Assessments

It is not yet common practice to define achievement constructs for educational achievement assessments (Ferrara & DeMauro, 2006), even though it is important to do so to ensure that assessment design and score interpretations are tightly aligned with one another. The *Standards for Educational and Psychological Testing* suggest that achievement constructs delineate "the knowledge, skills, abilities, processes, or characteristics to be assessed" (American Educational Research Association, American Psychological Association, & National Council on Measurement in Education, 1999, p. 9). The uniqueness and diversity of this examinee population—students with significant cognitive disabilities—escalates the importance of defining achievement constructs for AA-AAS. For example, it is common practice to define *reading* for grade-level tests simply by describing content standards and indicators for reading comprehension, decoding, vocabulary, and so forth. Most state grade-level content standards include these subdomains, and the standards and indicators overlap significantly. As a result, achievement constructs for reading are defined in similar ways in many state assessment programs.

However, defining *reading* for students with significant cognitive disabilities requires special considerations that can yield quite different definitions of reading across states. For example, should the definition of a reading construct include decoding and comprehending text only? Or, should it also include listening comprehension? For the highest-performing students who participate in AA-AAS—students such as Alex and Susan (described previously in this chapter)—listening comprehension may not need to be included in the assessment and definition of *reading.* In contrast, comprehension of text read aloud might be the only appropriate way to define reading—and quite a rigorous expectation—for Ginny.

Similar considerations are necessary for defining and assessing achievement constructs for writing, mathematics, and science. For some students who have physical limitations and communicative limitations (e.g., students with autism), for example, the definition of *writing* might include more than the physical act of writing to communicate. *Writing* might be defined broadly to include, for example, creating a permanent record by dictation or even arranging pictures and pictographs to form a permanent communication. Widely used definitions of *mathematics* for grade-level assessments include understanding of mathematical concepts (e.g., concepts about numbers) and computation (e.g., addition). For AA-AAS, rudimentary concepts are necessary to include all students with significant cognitive disabilities (e.g., two spoons are more than one spoon; one circle is bigger than another circle). Conceptions of *science* as achievement constructs for instruction and AA-AAS are only now beginning to emerge. States have experienced difficulty in extending grade-level content standards downward and retaining reasonable alignment with the grade-level content. The challenges are significant, though probably not intractable. For example, grade-level concepts like *biotic* and *abiotic*, which may appear in middle and high school biology content standards, may be represented in extended standards and achievement constructs for AA-AAS as *alive* and *dead*.

Once these issues are addressed in achievement constructs, they can be addressed in descriptors and AA-AAS.

Relationships Among Descriptors for Alternate Assessments, Modified Assessments, and Grade-Level Assessments

Perie, Hess, and Gong (2008) urged writers of performance-level descriptors to consider the interrelationships among descriptions for grade-level assessments, AA-AAS, and AA-MAS. They highlighted the special importance of articulating performance-level descriptors for AA-AAS and AA-MAS for students who move from one assessment to the other across grade levels. This is important as a practical matter. Also, it is wise as a general principle to articulate the meaning of performance standards across all three assessments simply because establishing coherent standards is desirable for its own sake. We have heard discussions about the desirability and feasibility of trying to define, for example, *Advanced* performance on an AA-AAS so that its interpretation is similar to *Below-Basic* performance on an AA-MAS. This conceptual approach seems worthy of consideration.

CONCEPTUALIZATIONS AND DESCRIPTIONS OF *PROFICIENT* ACADEMIC PERFORMANCE

In this section, we examine selected state descriptions of *Proficient* to categorize and illustrate some approaches to defining proficient performance on assessments of alternate achievement standards.

Perie (2008; see also Zieky, Perie, & Livingston, 2008, pp. 20–25) recommend three steps in defining performance levels and writing descriptors: 1) determining the number of performance levels and labels for each level, which are primarily policy decisions; 2) developing generic policy descriptions (see this chapter's previous section, Generic Policy Definitions), which also is the responsibility of policy makers; and 3) writing full descriptors, which should be written by committee. Their recommendations make plain who is responsible for determining the content and intent in each step and that the work of defining expectations for student achievement through descriptors should be completed before designing and developing an AA-AAS or, better, in conjunction with design and development. This is a declaration of best practice, though it does not yet reflect wide practice in AA-AAS or grade-level achievement testing. In this section, we discuss conceptual approaches to defining performance levels. We focus on descriptions of *Proficient* performance. Perie (2008) provides step-by-step instructions for developing descriptors and recommendations on defining, differentiating, and describing performance levels.

States have developed a wide range of performance-level labels, definitions, and descriptions for alternate and grade-level assessments (e.g., Table 3 in Perie, 2007). Descriptors for AA-AAS can be characterized in terms of how they define and distinguish academic achievement and test performance at each performance level. AA-AAS descriptors define and distinguish performance levels by referring to extended content standards in highly specific ways, to academic achievement more generally, to academic progress, and to degree of accuracy, frequency, or mastery of content. In this section, we categorize definitions of *Proficient* performance for AA-AAS according to the conceptual approach to its definition and the design of the corresponding AA-AAS. First, to facilitate discussion of the categorizations, we summarize 31 states' AA-AAS designs in Table 6.1.

Alternate Assessment Designs

We were able to locate definitions of *Proficient* performance and identify the designs of the corresponding AA-AAS on the web sites for 31 of 51 state assessment programs (including the District of Columbia). In most cases, states identified their assessment designs explicitly or we were able to identify their designs on the basis of other information on their web sites. Of the other 20 states for which we could not locate descriptors for *Proficient,* nine indicated portfolio (or datafolio) designs, six indicated performance tasks, two identified rating scales, and two indicated portfolio designs plus standardized performance tasks. We could not identify the AA-AAS design for one state.

Table 6.1.   States' alternate assessment designs, based on information from 31 of 51
state department of education web sites

Portfolio (or datafolio)	Arkansas, Georgia, Kentucky, Maine, Maryland, Massachusetts, Missouri, New Hampshire, New Jersey, Ohio, Tennessee	11
Standardized performance tasks	Alaska, Arizona, California, Colorado, Illinois, Louisiana, Michigan, Minnesota, Montana, Nebraska, North Dakota, Oregon, South Carolina, Texas, West Virginia, Wisconsin	16
Rating scale (with supporting evidence)	Connecticut, Idaho, Iowa, Mississippi	4

Note: Information is for 31 of 51 states (including the District of Columbia) for which we located performance-level descriptors for *Proficient* during September through October 2008.

As is evident in Table 6.1, portfolio and performance task designs are the most widely used designs for AA-AAS, followed by rating scales with supporting evidence. Although we do not discuss the details of these designs, we can make some general observations about each design. Alternate portfolio assessments typically include specifications on selecting the content standards for which evidence of student work must be provided. The portfolios in some states enable teachers to select standards for which to provide evidence plus standardized components (e.g., Kentucky's attainment tasks and transition attainment records). Performance task designs are considerably diverse. Most tasks comprise approximately five multiple-choice items. Typically, the design provides tailoring to the student's level of proficiency by guiding the teacher to administer a subset of tasks that are accessible to each student. For some of these assessments, tasks are calibrated to a vertical scale using an IRT model (e.g., New Mexico, South Carolina). Rating scales typically are completed by teachers while they observe students performing academic tasks or on the basis of student work samples.

Conceptions and Definitions of Proficient Performance

We examined descriptions of the *Proficient* performance level to identify categories of states' approaches to conceiving and describing proficient performance on AA-AAS. We chose to focus on descriptions for the *Proficient* level because of its obvious importance to individual students and its centrality in NCLB annual reporting requirements. We focused on reading because it is one of the earliest academic areas on which instruction has focused. We found the following conceptual categories, which we define and illustrate subsequently. For these 31 state AA-AAS, proficient performance is defined in one of five general ways:

- A list of academic skills such as those specified in the extended academic content standards

- A general description of academic proficiency with an accompanying list of specific academic skills

- A more general description of academic proficiency

- A description of academic progress

- Specification of the degree of accuracy or frequency of performance of knowledge and skills or the percentage of mastery of knowledge and skill in an academic area

As Table 6.2 indicates, 13 of the 31 states define *Proficient* using general descriptions of academic proficiency supported by lists of specific academic skills. Five states simply list specific academic skills to define proficient performance, and another six states use general descriptions of academic proficiency. Three states describe *Proficient* in terms of adequate academic progress (since the previous annual administration of the assessment), and four use percentages of accuracy or mastery or refer to frequency of performance.

There appear to be modest relationships between these states' definitions for *Proficient* and their AA-AAS designs. First, portfolio assessments tend to be accompanied by more general descriptions—either general descriptions with lists of academic skills, or general descriptions of academic progress. Second, the performance task designs tend to be associated with more specific descriptions—lists of specific academic skills or general descriptions with lists of academic skills. Three of the four rating scale designs are associated with general descriptions plus lists of academic skills. However, all five categories of definitions for *Proficient* are associated with portfolio and performance task designs. Of course, our interpretation of the associations between AA-AAS designs and approaches to defining *Proficient* could have been different if we had been able to locate definitions of proficient performance for the other 20 states. Also, nothing in the table suggests that any single type of proficiency definition is the only one that could be associated with a particular AA-AAS or design. (And, other researchers and state assessment program staff could disagree with our characterizations of these definitions and of specific states' definitions of *Proficient*.) These observations about Table 6.2 suggest that, at least for the AA-AAS discussed in this chapter, the design of an AA-AAS does not determine or limit the approach to defining and describing proficiency levels.

We describe and exemplify each approach to defining *Proficient* in the following sections.

Defining *Proficient* by Listing Specific Academic Skills

The predominant characteristic among definitions of proficient performance that list specific academic skills is the list of skills itself. The defi-

Table 6.2. Categories of definitions of *Proficient* and corresponding alternate assessment designs

Proficient defined as	Portfolio	Standardized performance tasks	Rating scale (with supporting evidence)	Number of states
A list of specific academic skills	—	Alaska, California, Colorado, Nebraska, North Dakota	—	5
A general description of academic proficiency with a list of specific academic skills	Arkansas, Kentucky, Maine, New Jersey	Michigan, Minnesota, Montana, South Carolina, Texas, West Virginia	Connecticut, Iowa, Mississippi	13
A general description of academic proficiency	Georgia, Massachusetts, Missouri, New Hampshire	Wisconsin	Idaho	6
A description of academic progress	Tennessee	Illinois, Louisiana	—	3
The degree of accuracy, frequency, or percentage of mastery	Maryland, Ohio	Arizona, Oregon	—	4

Note: Information is for 31 of 51 states (including the District of Columbia) for which we located performance-level descriptors for *Proficient* during September through October 2008.

nition may simply list the skills, or it may include an introductory statement, but the introductory statement contributes less to the definition than the list itself does. The *North Dakota Alternate Assessment 2 (NDAA 2) Achievement Descriptors 2007–08* (n.d.) define *Proficient* for Grade 3 reading as follows: "Student recognizes nonfiction text; recognizes and recalls symbols; interacts with reading; identifies main ideas. Student selects, plans, and evaluates performance in multiple settings."

Defining *Proficient* as a Description of Academic Proficiency with an Accompanying List of Specific Academic Skills

Other definitions of *Proficient* provide general descriptions that define the level of academic proficiency and also list corresponding academic skills. The general description by itself defines levels of knowledge and skills. General descriptions may refer to consistency (e.g., Mississippi), accuracy (e.g., "independent and accurate understanding," Kentucky), or level of performance or achievement (e.g., "reasonable performance," Arkansas; "some understanding," Missouri). The additional lists of skills elaborate on the general descriptions. The general performance descriptors for language arts for the Mississippi Alternate Assessment of Extended Curriculum Frameworks (MAAECF; see *Mississippi Alternate Assessment of Extended Curriculum Frameworks,* n.d.) define *Proficient* as follows:

> Student demonstrates the ability to communicate ideas when provided moderate support. The student's understanding of basic concepts and performance of many reading and writing skills are inconsistent, but typically at the Progressing level across two or more settings. For example:
>
> - Listens to others, participates in discussions, and effectively expresses his or her opinions, ideas, and feelings using words or assistive technology
>
> - Writes or types simple short responses and stories with moderate support from adults or peers

Defining *Proficient* Using a General Description of Academic Proficiency

Six states define *Proficient* using broad statements about achievement, some of which are not specific to grade level or content area. (If these four states provide more specific descriptions of *Proficient,* we could not locate the descriptions on the states' web sites.) For example, these descriptions refer to demonstrating "understanding of fundamental skills and knowledge" (Georgia), "solid understanding of challenging grade-level subject matter" (Massachusetts), and "solid academic performance" and "competency over challenging subject matter" (Montana). The Achievement Level Description for *Proficient* performance on NAEP (National

Assessment Governing Board, n.d.) clearly is a model for these descriptors (see the earlier section, Generic Policy Definitions).

Defining *Proficient* in Terms of Academic Progress

The issue of achievement growth has received intense attention because of the opportunity to use statistical and other growth models to meet NCLB reporting requirements. There is great interest in defining levels of proficiency on AA-AAS in terms of "satisfactory [academic achievement] growth" (Swaffield, Perie, & Marion, 2008; see also Ferrara, 2007), in part because status definitions of proficient achievement may not be relevant or appropriate for students with the most significant cognitive disabilities. As of 2008, three states defined *Proficient* in terms of academic progress, academic improvement, or growth in achievement. These definitions were not specific to grade level or content area. References to the progress and targeted skills of individual students are prevalent in these descriptions. The performance-level descriptor for *Moderate Growth* on the version of the Louisiana Educational Assessment Program Alternate Assessment prior to 2008, a portfolio design, illustrates these characteristics: "A student scoring at this level has demonstrated moderate improvement in performance of individually targeted skills during the school year" (Louisiana Department of Education, 2008).

Even with this interest, two of these states changed their designs from portfolios to performance-tasks designs and defined *Proficient* in terms of attainment of the level rather than growth. It seems likely that states will postpone defining *Proficient* in terms of achievement growth until progress is made in determining reasonable growth expectations and defining adequate growth for students with significant cognitive disabilities.

Defining *Proficient* in Terms of Degree of Accuracy, Frequency of Successful Use of Skills, or Percentage of Mastery

Four states define proficient performance in terms of accuracy, frequency, or degree of mastery. Maryland, for example, defines *Proficient* as "60–89% mastery" of skills assessed in a highly prescribed portfolio, and Arizona defines its *Meets the Standard* level as "reasonable performance" on specified skills assessed on performance tasks. Oregon defines *Meets* [the standard] by referring to "frequent understanding" and "relatively consistent" performance on the Oregon Extended Assessment, which is a performance task design:

> Student scores at this level indicate a frequent understanding of reduced depth, breadth, and complexity items and relatively consistent academic performance. Student scores at this level indicate an understanding of the academic concepts linked to the state's grade-level content standards for Reading. Students demonstrate a relatively consistent

comprehension of reduced complexity text, an understanding that meaning can be extracted from text, and are frequently able to extract meaning from text. Students demonstrate an understanding of the interaction between a reader and text. (Oregon Department of Education, 2008, p. 11, Table 2)

Discussion

These descriptors highlight several conceptual approaches to defining proficient performance on AA-AAS. The approaches are quite different in how they define levels of performance and in the inferences they enable about what examinees may know and be able to do beyond the test performance, in the classroom, and in other situations. In addition to determining a student's status in relation to alternate content and achievement standards, generalizing beyond test performance is, of course, a goal in assessment. In general, approaches to defining *Proficient* seem consistent with their corresponding AA-AAS designs. Some approaches capitalize on their designs (e.g., referring to accuracy, frequency, and mastery in portfolios). However, it seems from this analysis that the design of an assessment does not require a specific approach to defining *Proficient,* nor does it preclude some approaches.

This chapter is not a comprehensive collection of conceptual approaches to defining proficient performance on AA-AAS, although Perie (2008) provided a guide for developing performance-level descriptors for all assessments and summarizes naming conventions for performance levels for AA-AAS (Perie, 2007) and Crane and Winter (2006) compared and contrasted grade-level descriptors for several states (see their Tables 2–5). A comprehensive typology of conceptual approaches for defining *Proficient* and other performance levels would be helpful to designers and developers of AA-AAS, AA-MAS, and grade-level assessments.

States should examine descriptors for their grade-level assessments, AA-AAS, and AA-MAS side by side to ensure that the descriptions are articulated reasonably well. Articulating descriptions of *Proficient* might reflect a theoretical achievement hierarchy or progression from AA-AAS to AA-MAS to grade-level assessments. Or, the articulation may reflect what we learn about how student achievement develops and how students may progress from one instructional program to another and from one assessment program to the other.

ALTERNATE ASSESSMENT DESIGNS AND STANDARD-SETTING METHODS

Numerous standard-setting methods are documented in the professional literature. For example, Cizek and Bunch (2007) included nine chapters on standard-setting methods and approaches. Perie (2007) described 17 commonly used methods that seemed relevant to various designs for AA-AAS. Perie also proposed steps to select a standard-setting method for an AA-AAS, described the results of a survey on methods used to set performance standards for AA-AAS, and recommended immediate and longer-term studies and analyses to provide validation evidence for performance standards for AA-AAS. Perie observed that choosing a standard-setting method may depend on the type of assessment (e.g., Body of Work lends itself to portfolios of student work) and does depend on the values of the policy makers responsible for approving and implementing the standards (e.g., whether standards should be set at the total score level or for component scores). Perie (2007) made several recommendations about selecting standard-setting methods for AA-AAS, among them:

- First, she prefers to use student work products or recordings of students working on assessment tasks as the focus for the judgments that standard-setting panelists will make. This recommendation favors the Contrasting Groups, Body of Work, Up and Down, Rubric with Evidence, and Judgmental Policy Capturing methods.

- If this is not feasible, then she prefers focusing on scoring rubrics. The Dominant Profile and Performance Profile methods provide this focus. As in actual scoring, examples of student work for each score profile are necessary.

- If neither of these is feasible, she advises considering item-based methods, primarily variations on the Angoff method or the Yes-No method specifically for alternate assessments that are skills checklists. She prefers the Extended Angoff method because it requires standard-setting panelists to determine the score level on the rubric that is associated with an examinee just over the threshold of a performance level.

Perie (2007) provided sound guidance on selecting a standard-setting method for an AA-AAS. The crucial considerations in making a selection are ensuring that the standard-setting method is appropriate for the assessment, that the performance-level descriptors support the method, that the method is feasible and affordable for the sponsoring agency, and that the standard-setting cognitive–judgmental task is one that standard-setting panelists are qualified and well trained to undertake.

SUMMARY

In this chapter, we discussed definitions and descriptions of proficiency levels for AA-AAS, using descriptions of *Proficient* as examples. We summarized the designs for AA-AAS in 31 of 51 states. Then, we defined five approaches that states took to define and describe *Proficient* for their AA-AAS, and we provided examples from actual state descriptions of *Proficient*. The field of educational measurement has made progress in conceptualizations and procedures for defining proficiency levels, but much conceptual and practical work remains.

REFERENCES

American Educational Research Association, American Psychological Association, & National Council on Measurement in Education. (1999). *Standards for educational and psychological testing.* Washington, DC: Authors.

Browder, D.M., & Spooner, F. (Eds.). (2006). *Teaching language arts, math, & science to students with significant cognitive disabilities.* Baltimore: Paul H. Brookes Publishing Co.

Browder, D., Wakeman, S., & Jimenez, B. (n.d.). *Creating access to the general curriculum with links to grade level content for students with significant cognitive disabilities.* Retrieved October 23, 2008, from http://www.naacpartners.org/products/presentations/national/OSEPleadership/9020.pdf

Cizek, G.J., & Bunch, M.B. (2007). *Standard setting: A guide to establishing and evaluating performance standards on tests.* Thousand Oaks, CA: Sage Publications.

Crane, E.W., & Winter, P.C. (2006). *Setting coherent performance standards.* Retrieved October 20, 2008, from http://www.ccsso.org/publications/details.cfm?PublicationID=338

Ferrara, S. (2007, June). Standards for proficient achievement growth for South Carolina's alternate assessment, SC-Alt. Presented in *Vertical Integration of Benchmarks and Standards: Including Alternate Assessments in Evaluating Growth* at the National Conference on Large-Scale Assessment, Nashville, TN.

Ferrara, S., & DeMauro, G.E. (2006). Standardized assessment of individual achievement in K-12. In R.L. Brennan (Ed.), *Educational measurement* (4th ed., pp. 579–621). Westport, CT: American Council on Education/Praeger.

Ferrara, S., Goldberg, G., Thacher, S., Swaffield, S., Alexander, D., & Siskind, T. (2006). *Research and design concepts for an alternate assessment to ensure inclusion of students with the most significant cognitive disabilities.* Paper presented at Alternate and Modified Assessments for Accountability and AYP Requirements: Policy, Technology, and Implementation Considerations, an invited symposium at the annual meeting of National Council on Measurement in Education, San Francisco.

Haigh, J.A. (1996). *Maryland School Performance Program outcomes, standards, and high-stakes accountability: Perspectives from Maryland and Kentucky.* Paper presented at the annual meeting of the Council for Exceptional Children, Orlando, FL.

Hambleton, R.K., & Pitoniak, M.J. (2006). Setting performance standards. In R.L. Brennan (Ed.), *Educational measurement* (4th ed., pp. 433–470). Westport, CT: American Council on Education/Praeger.

Individuals with Disabilities Education Act Amendments (IDEA) of 1997, PL 105-17, 20 U.S.C. §§ 1400 *et seq.*

Individuals with Disabilities Education Improvement Act of 2004, PL 108-446, 20 U.S.C. §§ 1400 *et seq.*

Louisiana Department of Education. (2008). *Interpretive guide: LEAP alternate assessment.* Retrieved February 20, 2009, from http://www.doe.state.la.us/lde/uploads/7522.pdf

Mississippi Alternate Assessment of Extended Curriculum Frameworks (MAAECF). (n.d.). *General performance descriptors: Language arts.* Retrieved September 28, 2008, from http://www.mde.k12.ms.us/maaecf/MAAECF_Performance _Level_Descriptors.pdf

National Assessment Governing Board. (n.d.). *Developing student performance levels for the national assessment of educational progress.* Retrieved February 19, 2009, from http://www.nagb.org/policies/PoliciesPDFs/Technical%20 Methodology/developing-student-performance.pdf

No Child Left Behind Act of 2001, PL 107-110, 115 Stat. 1425, 20 U.S.C. §§ 6301 *et seq.*

North Dakota alternate assessment 2 (NDAA 2) achievement descriptors 2007– 08. (n.d.). Retrieved September 28, 2008, from http://www.dpi.state.nd.us/ speced/resource/alternate/descriptor/Reading%20A%20L3-11.pdf

Olson, L. (2005, September 21). New rules on special ed. scores help schools meet NCLB targets. *Education Week, 25*(4), 25.

Oregon Department of Education. (2008, June 9). *Extended assessment: Recommended cut scores, impact data, and achievement level descriptors.* Retrieved September 25, 2008, from http://www.ode.state.or.us/teachlearn/testing/oaks/ sandards_cutscores_alds_06_08.pdf

Perie, M. (2007). *Setting alternate achievement standards.* Retrieved February 20, 2009, from http://www.nciea.org/publications/CCSSO_MAP07.pdf

Perie, M. (2008). A guide to understanding and developing performance-level descriptors. *Educational Measurement: Issues and Practice, 27*(4), 15–29.

Perie, M., Hess, K., & Gong, B. (2008). *Writing performance level descriptors: Applying lessons learned from the general assessment to alternate assessments based on alternate and modified achievement standards.* Paper presented at the annual meeting of the National Council on Measurement in Education, New York.

Swaffield, S., Perie, M., & Marion, S. (2008, June). *Establishing growth expectations on alternate assessments.* Paper presented at the National Conference on Student Assessment, Orlando, FL.

U.S. Department of Education. (2005a, August). *Alternate achievement standards for students with the most significant cognitive disabilities: Nonregulatory guidance.* Retrieved February 25, 2006, from http://www.ed.gov/ policy/elsec/guid/altguidance.pdf

U.S. Department of Education. (2005b). *Raising achievement: Alternate assessments for students with disabilities.* Retrieved February 25, 2006, from http://www.ed.gov/policy/elsec/guid/raising/alt-assess-long.html

U.S. Department of Education. (2007, December 21). *Standards and assessments peer review guidance: Information and examples for meeting requirements of the No Child Left Behind Act of 2001.* Retrieved September 20, 2008, from http://www.ed.gov/policy/elsec/guid/saaprguidance.pdf

Zieky, M.J., Perie, M., & Livingston, S.A. (2008). *Cutscores: A manual for setting standards of performance on educational and occupational tests.* Princeton, NJ: Educational Testing Service.

CHAPTER 7

An Introduction to Validity Arguments for Alternate Assessments

SCOTT F. MARION AND MARIANNE PERIE

Complex issues have emerged as states have developed alternate assessments based on alternate achievement standards (AA-AAS) to ensure that all students have access to the benefits of state assessment and accountability systems. The understanding of technical quality for alternate assessments (Marion & Pellegrino, 2006) has improved with a focus on the interactions among the primary considerations in assessment design: 1) the population and their competence in academic domains, 2) the appropriateness of the observation techniques employed to assess these students, and 3) the inferences about student performance, teaching, and learning that result from the assessment scores. There is no question that technical documentation of alternate assessments has improved during the past several years, and state leaders have conducted many studies that can legitimately be called *validity studies*. However, very few (if any) states have designed their validity studies to collect data related to articulated validity arguments or have synthesized the results from their multiple studies to evaluate the veracity of the validity arguments and judge the validity of the inferences derived from assessment programs.

Many writers of technical reports for general assessments attempt to align their analyses and results with the *Standards for Educational and Psychological Testing* (American Educational Research Association [AERA], American Psychological Association, & National Council on Measurement in Education, 1999), particularly when there are student or school stakes requiring that the inferences drawn from the assessment be valid, reliable, and fair (AERA et al., 1999). This is an obvious and important first step, but it often is not fully met. AA-AAS approaches have additional technical quality challenges because many traditional mea-surement methods may require reconceptualization to "fit" the assess-ment requirements of students with significant cognitive disabilities. For example, leading measurement theorists (e.g., Cronbach, 1971; Mes-sick, 1989), including the authors of the 1985 and 1999 standards for ed-ucational measurement (AERA et al., 1985, 1999), established validity as the most important technical criterion for educational assessment. Va-lidity is defined as the "degree to which evidence and theory support the interpretations of the test scores entailed by proposed uses of the test" (AERA et al., 1999, p. 9).

Some researchers have begun defining how to document the valid-ity and reliability of AA-AAS (Garrett, Towles, Kleinert, & Kearns, 2003; Gong & Marion, 2006; Kleinert & Kearns, 1999; Marion & Pellegrino, 2006). Validity often is discussed regarding 1) the content of the assess-ment—considering the extent to which the content is representative of the established standards (content evidence), 2) the extent to which the construct indicates or captures the attribute to be measured (construct ev-idence), and 3) the extent to which the assessment correlates to or pre-dicts another desired state (criterion evidence; Mehrens, 1997). Con-sequential evidence—the degree to which an assessment produces the desired outcomes—is an area of particular interest to researchers on AA-AAS. For example, exploring how various approaches to alternate as-sessment increase access to grade-level curriculum and improve learn-ing outcomes would provide powerful validity data. Linn, Baker, and Dunbar (1991) and Shepard (1993), in their interpretations of Messick (1989), were unambiguous in the legitimacy of consequences as a criti-cal area of validity inquiry and evidence.

The challenge, however, has moved from having states and test con-tractors conduct research/evaluation studies to investigate a particular aspect of a testing program to designing a systematic validity plan for evaluating the efficacy of a comprehensive validity argument. This ap-proach requires synthesizing the various empirical results against the theory of action and validity argument (Kane, 2006). This chapter, draw-ing heavily on Kane (2006), outlines a framework for constructing and evaluating a validity argument for a state's AA-AAS.

VALIDITY SHOULD BE CENTRAL: A LITTLE BACKGROUND

The purpose of technical documentation should be to provide data to support or refute the validity of the inferences from the alternate assess-ments at both the student and program levels. Drawing on the work of Cronbach (1971), Kane (2006), Messick (1989), and Shepard (1993), our proposed evaluation of technical quality is built around a unified conception of validity centered on the inferences related to the construct and includes significant attention to the social consequences of the assessment. Before discussing how Kane's framework might be applied to validation of AA-AAS, we review the history of validity theory.

The Content Model

Kane (2006) traced the history of validity theory from the criterion through the content model to the construct model. It is worth pausing to discuss the content model because that seems to be the model that many still employ. The content model interprets a test score on a sample of performance in some area of activity as an estimate of the examinee's overall level of skill in that activity (Kane, 2006). The sample of items/tasks and observed performances must be representative of the domain, evaluated appropriately and fairly, and part of a large enough sample. This all sounds so reasonable that one wonders why theorists felt a need to move beyond this framework. However, the content model focuses only on specific performances and not on inferences from test scores (Messick, 1989). In other words, the content model seems more like a matching exercise and does not really help us get at the inferences that users draw from test scores. But does the content model have any use? Yes, but, with the intense focus on alignment these days, content evidence appears to be the main validation focus compared with trying to create arguments for the meaning of test scores.

The Construct Model

There is little question that the construct model is the leading theoretical force in validity thinking and research. This evolution can be traced from Cronbach and Meehl (1955) through Loevinger (1957) to Cronbach (1971) and culminating in Messick (1989). The construct model focused attention on the many factors associated with the interpretations and uses of test scores (and not simply with correlations). Construct theorists emphasized the important role that assumptions play in score interpretations, and they also stressed the need to check these assumptions in validation activities. Further, the construct model encouraged falsification or at least the possibility of alternative explanations for test scores.

The construct model has been criticized for several reasons; primarily because this model does not provide clear guidance for validating test score interpretations and/or use and that it does not help evaluators prioritize validity studies. Many evaluators, test developers, and test users wondered whether Cronbach was issuing a warning to validators when he wrote that "validation is a lengthy, even endless process" (1989, p. 151).

Shepard (1993), perhaps anticipating some of the criticisms of the construct model, offered a bridge between the theoretically oriented construct model and the more practical approach offered by Kane. One of the criticisms of the construct model is that it does not help evaluators prioritize validity studies. Using an evaluation framework, Shepard (1993) suggested that the following questions be used to guide the prioritization of validity studies:

- What does the testing practice claim to do?

- What are the arguments for and against the intended aims of the test?

- What does the test do in the system other than what it claims, for good or bad? (p. 429).

The call for careful examination of alternative explanations within the construct model is helpful for directing a program of validity research. Kane's (2006) argument-based framework

> assumes that the proposed interpretations and uses will be explicitly stated as an argument, or network of inferences and supporting assumptions, leading from observations to the conclusions and decisions. Validation involves an appraisal of the coherence of this argument and of the plausibility of its inferences and assumptions. (p. 17)

A validity argument serves to organize studies, provides a framework for analysis and synthesis, and forces critical evaluation of claims through the use of falsification orientation. An argument-based approach requires the user, developer, and/or evaluator to search for reasons why the intended inferences are not supported. In practice, it is not possible to search for all the reasons, so it is necessary to prioritize studies.

KANE'S ARGUMENT-BASED FRAMEWORK

Kane indicated that validation is made up of two different types of arguments: an interpretative argument and a validity argument. According to Kane (2006), "an *interpretative argument* specifies the proposed interpretations and uses of test results by laying out the network of inferences and assumptions leading to the observed performances to the conclusions and decisions based on the performances, [while] the *validity argument* provides an evaluation of the interpretative argument" (p. 17). A major advantage of Kane's perspective is that it provides a more pragmatic approach to validation than the construct model. Explicitly specifying the proposed interpretations and uses of the assessment (system), developing a measurement procedure consistent with these proposed uses, and then critically evaluating the plausibility of these inferences and assumptions can be challenging, but it is somewhat more straightforward than evaluating the validity of an assessment under a construct model.

Kane (2006) pushed for the development of the interpretative argument in the assessment design phase. The notion of specifying purposes and uses up front and then designing an assessment to fit these intentions is certainly not a new idea. However, the concept of designing a fully coherent system built on a sound theoretical model of learning and use began receiving more attention with the publication of *Knowing What Students Know* (Pellegrino, Chudowsky, & Glaser, 2001). Most assessments do not start with explicit attention to validity in the design phase (e.g., Mislevy, 1996); therefore, many evaluators working with states are put in the position of retrofitting validity arguments to existing systems.

The Interpretative Argument

The interpretative argument is essentially a mini-theory in that the interpretative argument provides a framework for interpretation and use of test scores. Like theory, the interpretative argument guides the data collection and methods for conducting the validity analyses. Theories are falsifiable, and making the connection between the interpretative argument and "mini-theory" is intended to demonstrate that validation is not a confirmationist exercise. Kane (2006) noted two stages of the interpretative argument. The *development stage* focuses on the development of measurement tools and procedures and the corresponding interpretative argument. Kane (2006) suggested that it is appropriate to have a confirmationist bias in this stage because the developers (state and contractors) are trying to make the program as good as possible. During the *appraisal stage,* the focus should be on critical evaluation of the interpretative argument. This should be a more neutral and "arms-length" standpoint to provide a more convincing evaluation of the proposed interpretations and uses. The evaluator should have moved from the confirmationist bias of the development stage to a falsification stance in the appraisal stage, because as Cronbach (1989) noted, "falsification, obviously, is something we prefer to do unto the constructions of others" (p. 153).

Kane (2006) noted the importance of being able to put forth a clear and coherent interpretative argument:

> Difficulty in specifying an interpretative argument . . . may indicate a fundamental problem. If it is not possible to come up with a test plan and plausible rationale for a proposed interpretation and use, it is not likely that this interpretation and use will be considered valid (p. 26).

It is helpful to think of the interpretative argument as a series of *if–then* statements (e.g., if the student performs the task in a certain way, then the observed score should have a certain value). Kane also offered the following criteria for evaluating interpretative arguments: clarity, coherence, and plausibility. A clear argument is one that is clearly stated as a framework for validation with the inferences and that is detailed enough to make proposed claims explicit. A coherent argument is one that logically ties together or relates the network of inferences from the assessment design, assessment scores, and inferences to the decisions. Finally, the criterion of plausibility focuses on the assumptions underlying the assessment and inferences in terms of all the evidence for and against them.

One of the most effective challenges to interpretative arguments (or scientific theories) is to propose and substantiate an alternative argument that is more plausible. With AA-AAS, it is important to seriously consider challenging ourselves with competing alternative explanations for test scores. For example, evaluators might want to propose (and confirm) that higher scores on a state's AA-AAS reflect greater learning of the content frameworks. However, the evaluators must consider plausible alternative hypotheses: higher scores on a state's AA-AAS might reflect higher levels of student functioning, or the higher scores might reflect greater understanding by teachers about how to gather evidence or administer the test.

Test validation is the process of offering assertions (propositions) about a test or a testing program and then collecting data and posing logical arguments to refute those assertions. In essence, validation requires continually challenging the supportability of the claims put forth about a testing program. If the assertions cannot be refuted, they can be considered tentatively supported, and that is the best that can be done.

Values and Consequences

Kane and others suggested that evaluators must attend to values and consequences when evaluating decision procedures (such as when a testing program is used as a policy instrument, as is the case with essentially all state tests). When conducting such a validity evaluation, the values inherent in the testing program must be made explicit, and the consequences of the decisions made in response to the test scores must be evaluated. Many have argued (e.g., Marion & Pellegrino, 2006; Shepard, 1997) that consequences must occupy a prominent role in any validity evaluation, but consequences are especially important when the validity of an AA-AAS is being evaluated.

GETTING STARTED

Katherine Ryan (2002) suggested that having state leaders (or other assessment stakeholders) lay out a more general "theory of action" is a useful starting point for developing a more complete validity argument. This theory of action, like the more complete interpretative argument, requires the explication of the intended components of an assessment and decision system and of the mechanisms by which a test user could reasonably expect to get from one step to the next. For example, one might postulate that providing AA-AAS score reports to teachers will lead to improved teaching practices. However, unless this result will happen automatically, the evaluator and/or user should specify the mechanism by which these score reports will lead to the anticipated changes in teaching practices, such as increased professional development on how to interpret the scores and take appropriate instructional steps. We (the chapter authors) created the following scenario for an alternate assessment system (Perie & Marion, 2008b).

The general theory of action for most alternate assessments for students with significant cognitive disabilities works something like this:

1. Academic content standards reflect grade-level content at levels appropriate for students with significant cognitive disabilities.

2. Teachers provide instruction that is aligned with those academic content standards.

3. The assessment is designed to reflect those content standards and student achievement.

4. The teacher administers the assessment appropriately.

5. The students respond to the tasks/prompts in a manner that truly reflects their knowledge and skills.

6. The test is scored accurately with a rubric that appropriately reflects the content and goals of the alternate assessment.

7. Those scores accurately reflect student knowledge and skills.

8. Those scores provide meaningful information to the students, parents, and teachers.

Each aspect of the theory of action leads to claims or propositions that contribute to the validity argument. The goals of the AA-AAS also should be explicated. Examples of goals for the AA-AAS include one or more of the following:

• Increase student access to academic content

• Raise expectations for students

• Increase student achievement

• Monitor student progress over time

• Provide useful information to teachers that can be used to refine instructional methods

A validity argument will start with one or more of those goals and then trace the claims of the AA-AAS that results in meeting that goal. Specifying a theory of action is a useful—and, some would argue, necessary— first step in creating a more complete validity argument. Figure 7.1 shows a sample theory of action that we developed.

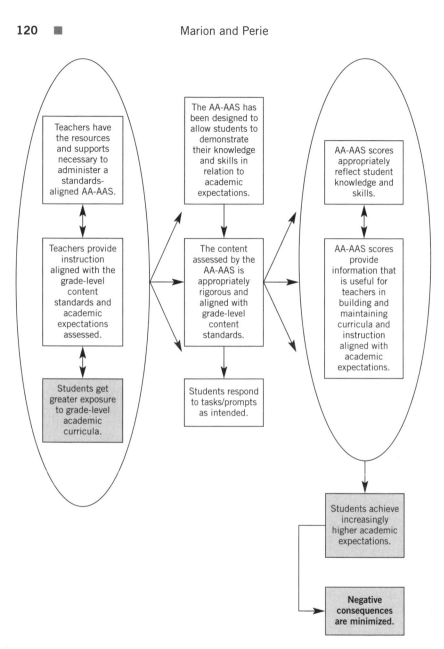

Figure 7.1. Theory of action for alternate assessments based on alternate achievement standards. (From Perie, M., & Marion, S. [2008a]. *Constructing a validity argument for an alternate assessment based on alternate achievement standards [AA-AAS].* Unpublished paper produced for an expert panel meeting of the National Alternate Assessment Center; reprinted by permission.) (*Key:* AA-AAS, alternate assessments based on alternate achievement standards.)

We separated out each claim by stage of the process, starting with classroom activities, moving to assessment development, and ending with assumptions about the scores. The end result is the goal of increasing student achievement. An interim goal is to increase student access to the content standards. Both of these goals are noted as shaded in Figure 7.1. In addition, another claim that needs to be tested is whether unanticipated negative outcomes have been minimized.

Each of the claims in Figure 7.1 will need to be incorporated into a more complete interpretative argument and then tested with appropriate studies. Some of the tests are straightforward. For example, the middle box, "The content assessed by the AA-AAS is appropriately rigorous and aligned with grade-level content standards," can be validated, in large part, through an alignment study. Others are more complex to evaluate, such as the claim, "AA-AAS scores appropriately reflect student knowledge and skills." Several propositions must be evaluated before that claim can be substantiated. Figure 7.2 spells out some of those propositions.

A complete and coherent validity argument would specify and explicate each of these claims. Studies would be designed to examine the merits of each proposition. Using the example in Figure 7.2, an alignment study that focused on the rubric could support the first proposition. Scorer reliability studies could support the second proposition. The third assumption could be supported through examining the procedural validity of the training process as well as reviewing the evaluation forms used to assess the training. A test of the scorers after training, or a

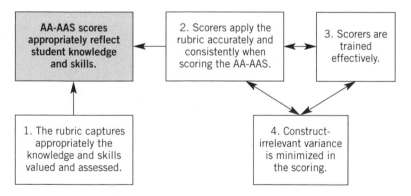

Figure 7.2. Propositions underlying a single claim. (From Perie, M., & Marion, S. [2008a]. *Constructing a validity argument for an alternate assessment based on alternate achievement standards [AA-AAS].* Unpublished paper produced for an expert panel meeting of the National Alternate Assessment Center; reprinted by permission.) (*Key:* AA-AAS, alternate assessments based on alternate achievement standards.)

pretest and posttest of the ability to apply the rubric appropriately, would also serve as validity evidence to support that proposition. Finally, a study examining how the scorers apply the rubric, such as a think-aloud study examining the thought processes of scorers, or, from a more quantitative perspective, a factor analytic study examining the structure of the score components, could address the fourth proposition.

THE VALIDITY EVALUATION PLAN

A validity evaluation cannot begin without a plan. Many states have conducted very good validity studies that yielded important and useful findings, but the usefulness of these studies could be greatly enhanced if they were conducted and considered as part of an overall validity evaluation plan to support or refute a validity argument. Creating an evaluation plan also will assist with the prioritization of the various studies when the evaluator can more easily see how each study fits into the overall plan.

Because evaluators cannot address all possible validity questions, it is crucial for each state to prioritize its evaluation questions. States and/or evaluators need to consider how to frame validity evaluations around the prioritized purposes and uses for their AA-AAS. This prioritization should extend over time so that current and future studies are discussed. The rationale for this prioritization is straightforward. The state (or other test user) cannot do everything, so it must decide what is most important to do first in terms of validating the inferences from its assessment system.

How might a state determine the priorities for its validity evaluation? Several authors (Kane, 2006; Lane & Stone, 2002; Ryan, 2002; Shepard, 1993, 1997) offered suggestions for prioritizing key validity questions. State leaders need to weigh many considerations when determining study priorities. Everyone is guided by his or her own intellectual interests, but this prioritization must go beyond the question, "What do I really want to know?" State leaders and validity evaluators must consider what the key stakeholders (including critics) want to know; there are several tools and protocols to help ascertain these priorities. However, these priorities must be considered as just one source of information and in the context of the overall validity evaluation plan. State leaders should ensure that the prioritized studies are selected to provide maximum information for the validity argument. Focusing on studies that provide only consequential evidence, for example, may shortchange the validity evaluation because of the lack of information about other important aspects of validity. Although a great deal might be revealed about the consequences of the testing program, the lack of information about other aspects of validity might not allow enough evidence to adequately evaluate the validity of the inferences from the particular assessment system. Of course, this assumes that the purposes and uses of the testing program extend beyond consequential considerations. Also, when deciding whether to invest in a study, state leaders and evaluators should conduct a thought experiment to consider how the potential study results might contribute to learning something important about the test or the program (the authors thank Rich Hill for this idea). The studies that seem likely to yield the most useful information within the particular focus categories (e.g., content evidence) should receive the highest priority. Finally, the user or evaluator must provide a rationale of how the studies cohere so that the collective results can contribute to a comprehensive evaluation of the interpretative argument.

SYNTHESIS AND EVALUATION

Haertel (1999) reinforced the notion that individual pieces of evidence (typically presented in separate chapters of technical documents) do not make an assessment system valid or not; it is only by synthesizing this evidence to evaluate the interpretative argument that the validity of the assessment program can be judged. As Kane (2006) indicated, the evaluative argument provides the structure for evaluating the merits of the interpretative argument. Various types of empirical evidence and logical argument must be integrated and synthesized into an evaluative judgment; this process can be a challenging intellectual activity. In state assessment programs, when new and varied information comes in at sometimes predictable intervals, the challenge is exacerbated. With alternate assessment programs, not only is new evidence being collected along the way, but actual understanding of alternate assessments and the students they serve evolves much more rapidly than in many other programs.

Dynamic Evaluation

In almost all studies that evaluate the validity of state assessment systems, the studies are completed across a long time span. Evaluators rarely have all the evidence in front of them to make conclusive judgments. Therefore, evaluators must engage in ongoing, dynamic evaluations as new evidence is produced. Working in this fashion requires, even more so than in more predictable evaluations, that each proposition be written to allow judgment of whether the evidence supports a particular claim. As discussed above, this always means exploring the efficacy of alternate hypotheses. However, in the context of states' large assessment systems, evaluators do not have the luxury of concluding, "The system is not working; let's start over." Rather, in such instances, when the evidence does not support the claims and intended inferences, state leaders and test developers must act as if the dynamic results were from a formative evaluation, and they must search for ways to improve the system. Of course, the evidence might be so overwhelmingly stacked against the intended claims—and this has happened in some states—that the state leaders are left only with the option of starting over.

SUMMARY

Basing validity evaluations on well-founded arguments enables dynamic evaluations to be structured in ways that allow comprehensive cases to be made for or against assessment systems. Without the structure of an argument, there is little guidance on how to weigh the different results. Through our work with our special education partners and other experts (Marion & Pellegrino, 2006; Perie & Marion, 2008b), we have offered structured guidance to help state leaders and other assessment evaluators begin the difficult but critical work of clearly articulating their assumptions, specifying their intended networks of inferences, prioritizing studies, and building comprehensive validity arguments. This systematic approach to evaluating the inferences from an alternate assessment can provide an evidence-based approach for improving assessments and, hopefully, educational opportunities for students with significant cognitive disabilities.

REFERENCES

American Educational Research Association, American Psychological Association, & National Council on Measurement in Education. (1985). *Standards for educational and psychological testing.* Washington, DC: Authors.

American Educational Research Association, American Psychological Association, & National Council on Measurement in Education. (1999). *Standards for educational and psychological testing.* Washington, DC: Authors.

Cronbach, L.J. (1971). Test validation. In R.L. Thorndike (Ed.), *Educational measurement* (2nd ed., pp. 443–507). Washington, DC: American Council on Education.

Cronbach, L.J. (1989). Construct validation after thirty years. In R.L. Linn (Ed.), *Intelligence: Measurement, theory, and public policy* (pp. 147–171). Urbana: University of Illinois Press.

Cronbach, L.J., & Meehl, P.E. (1955). Construct validity in psychological tests. *Psychological Bulletin, 52,* 281–302.

Garrett, B., Towles, E., Kleinert, H., & Kearns. J. (2003). Portfolios in large-scale alternate assessment systems: Frameworks for reliability, *Assessment for Effective Intervention, 28*(2), 17–27.

Gong, B., & Marion, S.F. (2006, June). *Dealing with flexibility in assessments for students with significant cognitive disabilities* (Synthesis Rep. No. 60). Retrieved August 1, 2006, from http://education.umn.edu/nceo/OnlinePubs/Synthesis60.html

Haertel, E.H. (1999). Validity arguments for high-stakes testing: In search of the evidence. *Educational Measurement: Issues and Practice, 18*(4), 5–9.

Kane, M.T. (2006). Validation. In R.L. Brennan (Ed.), *Educational measurement* (4th ed., pp. 17–64). New York: American Council on Education/Macmillan.

Kearns, J., Towles-Reeves, E., Kleinert, H., & Kleinert, J. (2006). *Learning characteristics inventory (LCI) report.* Lexington: National Alternate Assessment Center, Human Development Institute, University of Kentucky, Lexington.

Kleinert, H., Browder, D., & Towles-Reeves, E. (2005). *The assessment triangle and students with significant cognitive disabilities: Models of student cognition.* Lexington: National Alternate Assessment Center, Human Development Institute, University of Kentucky, Lexington.

Kleinert, H.L., & Kearns, J.F. (1999). A validation study of the performance indicators and learner outcomes of Kentucky's alternate assessment for students with significant disabilities. *The Journal of the Association for Persons with Severe Handicaps, 24*(2), 100–110.

Lane, S., & Stone, A. (2002). Strategies for examining the consequences of assessment and accountability programs. *Educational Measurement: Issues and Practice, 21*(2), 23–30.

Linn, R.L., Baker, E.L., & Dunbar, S.B. (1991). Complex performance-based assessment: Expectations and validation criteria. *Educational Researcher, 20*(8), 15–21.

Loevinger, J. (1957). Objective tests as instruments of psychological theory. *Psychological Reports, 3* (Monograph Supplement 9), 635–694.

Marion, S.F., & Pellegrino, J.W. (2006). A validity framework for evaluating the technical quality of alternate assessments. *Educational Measurement: Issues and Practice, 25*(4), 47–57.

Mehrens, W.A. (1997). The consequences of consequential validity. *Educational Measurement: Issues and Practices, 16*(2), 16–18.

Messick, S. (1989). Validity. In R.L. Linn (Ed.), *Educational measurement* (3rd ed., pp. 13–103). New York: American Council on Education, Macmillan Publishing.

Messick, S. (1995). The interplay of evidence and consequences in the validation of performance assessments. *Educational Researcher, 23*(2), 13–23.

Mislevy, R. (1996). Test theory reconceived. *Journal of Educational Measurement, 33*(4), 379–416.

No Child Left Behind Act of 2001, PL 107-110, 115 Stat. 1425, 20 U.S.C. §§ 6301 et seq.

Pellegrino, J.W., Chudowsky, N.J., & Glaser, R. (Eds.). (2001). *Knowing what students know: The science and design of educational assessment.* Washington, DC: National Academy of Sciences.

Perie, M., & Marion, S. (2008a). *Constructing a validity argument for an alternate assessment based on alternate achievement standards (AA-AAS).* Unpublished paper produced for an expert panel meeting of the National Alternate Assessment Center.

Perie, M., & Marion, S. (2008b). *Developing a validity argument for a state alternate assessment (AA-AAS) system: A guide for states.* Retrieved July, 15, 2008, from http://www.naacpartners.org/projects/validityGSEG/expertPanel.aspx

Ryan, K. (2002). Assessment validation in the context of high stakes assessments. *Educational Measurement: Issues and Practice, 21*(1), 7–15.

Shepard, L.A. (1993). Evaluating test validity. *Review of Research in Education, 19*(1), 405–450.

Shepard, L.A. (1997). The centrality of test use and consequences for test validity. *Educational Measurement: Issues and Practice, 16*(2), 5–24.

CHAPTER 8

The Long and Winding Road of Alternate Assessments

Where We Started, Where We Are Now, and the Road Ahead

RACHEL F. QUENEMOEN

Alternate assessments for students with significant cognitive disabilities were first developed in the early 1990s, were linked to standards-based reform, and had a new focus on accountability for student outcomes. This chapter is a retrospective look at how alternate assessments evolved and how they might change. Given the relatively recent development of these assessments, which were designed to measure the academic achievement of a very small group of students with highly varied learning characteristics, one could argue that a better title would be *The Short and Bumpy Road of Alternate Assessments.* Still, the road has been long for the state practitioners who have been developing and implementing these assessments to meet the policy imperative that all students count, despite a limited research base and a rapidly evolving—and startling—understanding of what these students can know and do when taught well.

The National Center on Educational Outcomes (NCEO) has documented state practices in alternate assessment through biennial surveys of state directors of special education since the early 1990s. The survey data through 2005 reflect state special education staff's understanding of state assessment systems. There was 100% participation by regular states during that time span and more varied participation by unique states (i.e., entities beyond the 50 states receiving federal special education funding). Survey responses were collected and then verified by respondents once the responses had been collated. The focus of this chapter is on the data back to 1997, when the world of special education changed (or, at least, should have changed) with the refocus of the federal special education law on the general curriculum in the reauthorization of the Individuals with Disabilities Education Act (IDEA) in 1997 (PL 105-17). There are six alternate assessment topics covered more or less throughout the span of these survey reports, including

- Stakeholder expectations and principles

- Content coverage (linkage to content standards)

- Approaches (test format)

- Scoring criteria and procedures

- Performance/achievement-level descriptors and standard setting

- Reporting and accountability

The first three topics were fully covered from the 1999 survey on; the last three became more prominent in the years after the passage of the No Child Left Behind Act (NCLB) of 2001 (PL 107-110).

NCEO synthesis reports and the NCEO survey reports are referenced in this chapter to illustrate the challenges states faced as these assessments changed to meet new professional understanding and new state and federal requirements. These challenges had their roots in the mid-1990s.

EARLY THINKING THAT SHAPED IDEA 1997 REQUIREMENTS

Maryland and Kentucky were the first two states to implement alternate assessments for students who could not participate in the general assessments, even with accommodations, adaptations, or other supports. Both states were required to develop school accountability systems based on student achievement, with the requirements initiated by the state legislature in one state (Maryland) and by legislative action following state court decisions in another (Kentucky). Both states determined that if all students were to be included in school accountability systems, then assessment systems needed to be developed that would allow all students to demonstrate achievement (Kleinert, Haigh, Kearns, & Kennedy, 2000; Ysseldyke et al., 1996).

These students were identified primarily as those considered to have the most severe and complex disabilities—students served under varying labels such as *severe-profound disabilities* and *trainable mentally handicapped.* On the basis of the research done in Kentucky and Maryland and the literature in severe disabilities, Ysseldyke and Olsen (1997) posed four assumptions that they argued should support development of alternate assessments. Excerpts from their summary rationales for each of the assumptions are included in the following citation. These assumptions and rationales affected how other states developed alternate assessments and may affect the development of similar assessments in the future.

1. Focus on authentic skills and on assessing experiences in community/real life environments. Artificial assessment tasks will not provide an indication of how well the system is preparing the students; however, "community" means different things at primary, middle and secondary levels. For a third grader, community might be the school, the playground and home, whereas community for an exiting senior would have to mean the store, bank, and workplace, for example.

2. Measure integrated skills across domains. [E]ducation, especially for students with moderate to severe cognitive disabilities, requires integration of skills. So should the assessments. For example, assessing personal and social skills separately from assessing independence and responsibility would result in redundant effort and possibly result in reinforcing a focus on isolated skills. A generic rubric that encompasses multiple skills would be more appropriate.

3. Use continuous documentation methods if at all possible. Using assessment methods that involve multiple measures over time will result in more accurate and reliable information. Students with severe challenges have greater variability in their skills from day to day than do students without disabilities or even students with milder disabilities. Therefore, a skill that cannot be observed on one day might be fully in place the next. . . . Milestones for students with severe disabilities are much farther apart than for other students, and methods that capture change rather than status will better reflect success of the educational system.

4. Include, as critical criteria, the extent to which the system provides the needed supports and adaptations and trains the student to use them. If the purpose is to hold the educational system accountable, the only way to assess the extent to which a school system is providing the needed education is to include, as one of the criteria for success, the extent to which the school system provides the needed assistive devices, people and other supports to allow the students to function as independently as possible. There is more variability in the skill levels and needs of this one percent of the students than there is in the rest of the total student population. . . . Kentucky has shown that including this criterion has the added benefit of driving effective school and classroom practice (Kleinert, Kennedy, & Kearns, in press) [in press at that time, but published in 1999]. (Ysseldyke & Olsen, 1997, pp. 16–17)

These assumptions strongly influenced states' early work on alternate assessments, and the survey data from the first years of implementation reflect them, corresponding to the early context of standards-based reform. Some of these assumptions were augmented by the requirements of the IDEA reauthorizations, by NCLB, and by changes in understanding how this small group of students learns in the academic domains. These assumptions reflect the teaching and learning literature of severe disabilities before the addition of a standards-based curriculum for these students, but they remain important in the development of alternate assessments.

IDEA 1997, building on the Improving America's Schools Act (IASA) of 1994 (PL 103-382), pushed the field into rethinking what students with disabilities should know and be able to do. IDEA 1997 also included the first federal requirement for alternate assessments. In the preamble to IDEA 1997, Congress noted that, historically,

> the implementation of this Act has been impeded by low expectations, and an insufficient focus on applying replicable research on proven methods of teaching and learning for children with disabilities. . . . Over 20 years of research and experience has demonstrated that the education of children with disabilities can be made more effective by— having high expectations for such children and ensuring their access in the general curriculum to the maximum extent possible.

Previously, federal law had required that students with disabilities have access to public school buildings, but with the passage of IDEA 1997, these students were to have access and show progress in the same challenging curriculum as their peers. Although not everyone recognized the magnitude of the shift at the time, the states that responded to the requirements with increased expectations started shedding incredible new light on what "the maximum extent possible" mentioned in the IDEA 1997 preamble really meant for students with disabilities, including those with the most severe disabilities.

POST-1997 STATE SURVEY DATA: WHERE DID WE START?

The 1997 NCEO survey of state special education directors found that although 20 states indicated they were developing alternate assessments, only two states were implementing their assessments: Kentucky and Maryland. By 1999, the survey showed that most states' alternate assessments were still in development; by 2001, nearly all states were working on development, and, by 2003, nearly all states had at least one alternate assessment in place. Eight states had two alternate assessment options, and three states had three or more options in place. During this time of rapid change, the surveys addressed early steps in development, including identification of stakeholders involved in development as well as core principles guiding development, what content the assessment covered, and the approach or format used by each state.

Stakeholders, Expectations, and Principles

In the 1999 survey, state special education directors estimated "the percent of students whose exposure to content was too limited for them to participate in regular assessment." This criterion marked a change from IDEA 1997, which defined students who required alternate assessments as those who could not take regular assessments, even with accommodations. These responses may have tapped into the status of access to the general curriculum at that time. Table 8.1 shows that only 26 state directors ventured guesses, with a wide range of estimates that went as high as 9%. The two pioneer states that already had developed alternate assessments, Kentucky and Maryland, were among the group that estimated less than 1%.

Because of the limited experience or research on large-scale assessments for these students, the starting point for building alternate assessments in many states was to identify principles to guide development, defining expectations in a general way. Most states did so, but the range of what those principles covered, as shown in an NCEO synthesis report

Table 8.1. Estimated percentages of all students whose exposure to content is too limited for them to participate in regular assessment

< 1%	> 1–2%	> 2–4	> 4%
Delaware*	California	Arkansas*	Mississippi
Kansas	Colorado	Connecticut	Ohio
Kentucky	Hawaii	Massachusetts	South Dakota
Maryland	Idaho	Missouri	Tennessee
Minnesota	Indiana	New Hampshire	Texas*
Nebraska	Florida*	New Mexico	West Virginia
Vermont	Louisiana	Utah	
	Nevada	Washington	
	Oregon	Wisconsin	
	Rhode Island		
	Virginia		

From Thompson, S., & Thurlow, M. (1999). *1999 state special education outcomes: A report on state activities at the end of the century* (p. 18). Minneapolis: University of Minnesota, National Center on Educational Outcomes; reprinted by permission.

*State-provided percentage of students with disabilities was transformed to a percentage of all students using the special education rate.

of 2000 (Thompson & Thurlow), was dramatic. Compare and contrast the principles below, taken from three states, and consider which ones are in the spirit of the IDEA 1997 shifts.

- *State #1 [#2 in original text]*
  - Expectations for all students should be high, regardless of the existence of any disability.
  - The goals for an educated student must be applicable to all students, regardless of disability.
  - Special education programs must be an extension and adaptation of general education programs rather than an alternate or separate system.

- *State #2 [#3 in original text]*
  - All children have value, can learn and are expected to be full participants in the school experience.
  - School personnel, parents, local and state policy makers, and the students themselves are responsible for ensuring this full participation.
  - The Standard Course of Study is the foundation for all students, including students with unique learning needs.

- *State #3 [#4 in original text]*
  - Meet the law.
  - Nonabusive to students, staff, parents
  - Inexpensive
  - Easy to do and takes little time (Thompson & Thurlow, 2000, pp. 2–3)

These examples illustrate that states started from vastly different belief systems as they built these assessments.

The 2000 Thompson and Thurlow synthesis report foreshadowed other challenges. In many states, stakeholders included general and special education representatives in development teams, but it was clear that in a small number of states, alternate assessment was perceived as a problem to be resolved by and for special education (see also Kohl, McLaughlin, & Nagle, 2006). Second, even at the very beginning of alternate assessment development, functional content versus academic content was emerging as a source of tension in the design of alternate assessments. Finally, the report identified the emerging challenge of understanding in state assessment offices how these "odd" large-scale tests could be scored and reported with integrity.

Content Coverage (Linkage to Content Standards)

The belief systems in some states were challenged early on by the 1997 IDEA requirement of access and progress in the general curriculum. In those states, shifts from functional content to linkage to state content standards occurred very early during the development of alternate assessments, and those shifts continued throughout the first two decades of work. Table 8.2 shows this trend across all state survey reports. Note that in 2005, some states still were revising the content covered by their alternate assessments, and in 2005 NCEO had added a response category called Grade-level Standards. The entire field of severe disabilities was shifting during this time period. States that had acted on the IDEA 1997 emphasis on access to and progress in the general curriculum by including all students with disabilities were beginning to demonstrate that these students could learn academic content in ways that surprised even long-time researchers.

Pioneers often chart new paths that others may not want to traverse. Work done by the state of Massachusetts established not only a path but a superhighway leading through the grade-level content to ensure that all students have access to the same challenging skills and knowledge (Wiener, 2005). Soon, Massachusetts and a few other early pioneering states shared student work demonstrating academic content and skills that never before had been taught to these students. That evidence increased the pressure from federal policy and from advocates for all states to move toward higher expectations for these students. Raising the bar on academic expectations for students with severe disabilities is, arguably, the most dramatic result of the alternate assessments developed in the wake of IDEA 1997. A brief summary of the changes in curricular content for students with significant cognitive disabilities is included here to provide context for the shifting content coverage of alternate assessments.

Table 8.2. Content addressed by alternate assessments: Change over time

Year	Functional skills: No link to SCS	Functional skills: Link to SCS	SCS plus functional skills	Expand/ extend SCS	Grade-level SCS	IEP team identifies content	Other	Revising
1999	16	—	1	19	—	—	24	—
2000	9	3	7	28	—	—	3	—
2001	4	15	9	19	—	—	3	—
2003	2	—	4	36	—	3	3	2
2005	—	—	1	21	10	1	7	10

Sources: Thompson, Johnstone, Thurlow, and Altman (2005) and Thompson and Thurlow (1999, 2001, 2003).

Key: SCS, state content standards; IEP, individualized education program.

Changing Curricular Content for Students with Significant Cognitive Disabilities

The field of schooling for students with severe disabilities has been in a state of constant rediscovery since school doors were forced open for these students in the early and mid-1970s through state and federal laws. Changing beliefs about the proper curricular focus have been well documented (e.g., Browder & Spooner, 2006; National Alternate Assessment Center, 2005). In the early 1970s, the field focused on adapting infant/early childhood curriculum for students of all ages with the most significant disabilities. By the 1980s, experts on severe disability began to question the validity of this approach (see Brown, Nietupski, & Hamre-Nietupski, 1976), partly because of the disconnect between the learning progressions assumed by the infant/early childhood curriculum and the actual observations of what these students could achieve despite not having developed earlier skills. The field refocused instead on age-appropriate skills and knowledge performed in authentic settings, and the functional life skills curriculum emerged. The functional, age-appropriate curricular focus was a breakthrough; as a result, these students demonstrated skills and knowledge that previously had not been thought possible (Browder & Spooner, 2006).

In the 1990s, new practices were identified as essential to further success. The practice of including students with severe disabilities with typical peers in classroom settings for purposes of social inclusion, along with a new focus on self-determination skills, reflected a new acceptance and understanding of the students. Along with the development of assistive technology, which opened the world of communication for some students and greatly enhanced the ability of teachers and students to interact, the path was prepared for the next turn: general curriculum access.

IDEA 1997 required that all children receiving special education services were to have access to and make progress in the general curriculum, but NCLB, the Individuals with Disabilities Education Improvement Act of 2004 (PL 108-446), and subsequent regulatory language for both laws clarified that the general curriculum must be based on the same standards and expectations that applied to all other students in a state. Alternate assessments were to be aligned to (or *linked to,* in later terminology) the state content standards in each grade. As the first decade of the 21st century nears an end, academics have joined earlier priorities (functional, social inclusion, self-determination) in the curriculum for students with severe disabilities across the country in principle, if not in practice, in all schools.

Although there is a strong research base to justify this blend of earlier priorities, it is startling to see remaining vestiges of the developmental infant/early childhood understanding of learning persisting despite strong evidence that this approach yields poor results. This is a distinction that people new to the issues of severe disabilities sometimes miss. References to these students in the news media or among educators sometimes include descriptions of the students in terms of "developmental age" as a rationale for low expectations. The infant/early childhood approach to teaching these students yielded very poor results, and teaching or assessment approaches based on the infant/early childhood model are not educationally defensible.

Alternate Assessment Approaches (Format)

The primary debate in the early years of alternate assessments concerned approach or format (e.g., portfolio, body of evidence, checklist, rating scale, performance assessment). Even today, active discussions of one format or the other play out as if format were an indicator of quality. It is not. There are good- and poor-quality alternate assessments of all different formats. I return to this discussion later in the chapter.

In the early development of alternate assessments, consistent with the assumptions that Ysseldyke and Olsen laid out in 1997, most states had some type of body of evidence collected over time. Table 8.3 shows alternate assessment approaches and changes from 2000 to 2005. There is some uncertainty as to how state special education directors categorized their approaches, particularly in cases of overlapping methodology across the nominal types. For example, in 1999, the category of Other specifically included performance assessments. In later years, the category choices became more descriptive (e.g., portfolio or body of evidence with or without a standardized set of performance/events/tasks/skills; checklist/rating scale with or without a required submission of student work). Some of the changes in categories across the years may reflect changes in how the directors described their assessments, as opposed to real changes in format.

A few trends are very clear. Linkages to student individualized education programs (IEPs) decreased, numbers of states with alternate assessments in revision or development fell briefly but rebounded in 2005, and there is a tendency for blurring of format boundaries as portfolios and bodies of evidence add more structure and as checklists/rating scales add more collected evidence of student achievement. The latter tendency relates to issues of scoring, reporting, and accountability, which emerged as major issues in the technical defense of alternate assessment after the NCLB-required peer review of assessment systems commenced in 2005.

Scoring Criteria and Procedures

IDEA 1997 required alternate assessments to be in place by July 2000. States had initial versions of their alternate assessments in place when NCLB was passed. NCLB increased the accountability stakes for schools,

Table 8.3. Alternate assessment approaches 2000–2005

Year	Portfolio or body of evidence	Rating scale or checklist	Individualized educational program analysis	Other	In development/ revision
Regular states					
1999	28 (56%)	4 (8%)	5 (10%)	6 (12%)	7 (14%)
2001	24 (48%)	9 (18%)	3 (6%)	12 (24%)	2 (4%)
2003	23 (46%)	15 (30%)	4 (8%)	5 (10%)	3 (6%)
2005*	25 (50%)**	7 (14%)***	2 (4%)	7 (14%)	8 (16%)
Unique states					
2003	4 (44%)	0 (0%)	1 (11%)	1 (11%)	3 (33%)
2005	1 (11%)	1 (11%)	1 (11%)	0 (0%)	1 (11%)

From Thompson, S.J., Johnstone, C.J., Thurlow, M.L., & Altman, J.R. (2005). *2005 state special education outcomes: Steps forward in a decade of change* (p. 11). Minneapolis: University of Minnesota, National Center on Educational Outcomes; reprinted by permission.

*One state has not developed any statewide alternate assessment approaches.

**Of these 25 states, 13 use standardized sets of performance/events/tasks/skills.

***Of these seven states, three require the submission of student work.

districts, and states regarding assessment results. The scoring and reporting issues in alternate assessment that states had identified earlier (e.g., Thompson & Thurlow, 2000) became critical. There also were rigorous NCLB peer review processes ahead—and most states started scrambling. Following the best practices recommended in the 1997 Ysseldyke and Olsen paper, many states had incorporated both student and system performance measures in their scoring rubrics or procedures. Figure 8.1 shows the use of these student and system measures still in place in 2005.

The first criterion listed in Figure 8.1 is the only one that has not been controversial among measurement experts, who have agreed less on the second and third criteria. These experts believe that because achievement results traditionally reflect independent student performance on content skills and knowledge, the other criteria should be seen as system measures. All of the other criteria reflect research-based understanding of effective teaching for students with severe disabilities, however, and each criterion can be defended on some level for some purpose. Whether these defenses are sustainable for purposes of system accountability is another question, which has not been fully answered.

NCEO case studies of five states with varying approaches to alternate assessment, completed in 2003, show a very complex picture of how these system versus student performance measures play out in state assessments (Quenemoen, Thompson, & Thurlow, 2003). The scoring criteria used by the states seemed very different, but when underlying assumptions and procedures for assessment instrument development (including blueprints) were examined, and when analyses of training

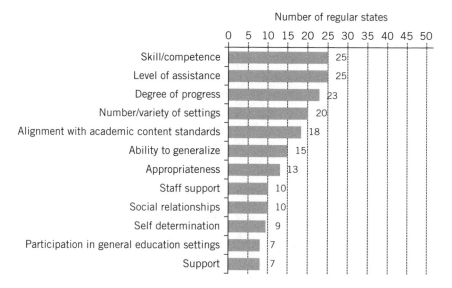

Figure 8.1. Outcomes measured by rubrics on alternate assessments—2005. (From Thompson, S.J., Johnstone, C.J., Thurlow, M.L., & Altman, J.R. [2005]. *2005 state special education outcomes: Steps forward in a decade of change* [p. 14]. Minneapolis: University of Minnesota, National Center on Educational Outcomes; reprinted by permission.)

procedures for gathering evidence or for scoring were reviewed, there were striking similarities in how the varying scoring criteria played out:

> The definitions and examples and the side by side examination of the criteria, the scoring elaborations, and the assumed criteria in the design of training materials and assessment format yield a surprising degree of commonality in the way these states define success for students with significant cognitive disabilities. Six criteria are included in all of the five states' approaches in some way, either articulated or assumed. They include "content standards linkage," "independence," "generalization," "appropriateness," "IEP linkage," and "performance." Three scoring criteria are very different across the five states' approaches. They include "system vs. student emphasis," "mastery," and "progress." (Quenemoen, Thompson, & Thurlow, 2003, p. iii)

The notion of defining success through rubric construction points to the very real challenge faced by developers of alternate assessments for students with the most significant cognitive disabilities. The scoring criteria that differed in these five states included system versus student emphasis, but the line between the two was difficult to draw. In some states, teachers would provide varying levels of prompting to ensure student responses, and the degree to which supports were provided was viewed as a system measure. In other states, the level of prompting was viewed as a student measure—the degree to which students performed independently. The distinctions between the two were not as clear as the language suggests.

Other scoring criteria that varied among the five states included mastery and progress. The term *progress* is used to define the amount of progress in learning new skills and knowledge from a student's baseline within the testing year, as opposed to the grade-to-grade or year-to-year progress assumed in growth models. Charting learning progress for students with severe disabilities has been an important long-time teaching and assessment tool. Ysseldyke and Olsen identified this as an essential challenge in their 1997 assumptions. States continue to grapple with this issue, and the definition of success continues to play out in scoring procedures and in the complexities of defining performance-level descriptors and alternate achievement standards for these assessments.

States began rethinking who should score the alternate assessments. The requirements for alternate assessments in IDEA 1997 stated that test results for students with disabilities should be publicly reported in the same frequency and format as all other student results, and IASA 1994 required public reporting of achievement results for all students. Some states built assessment scoring procedures to ensure that common scoring protocols would apply to all assessments, setting up regional or statewide scoring institutes or contracting with test publishers for scoring out of state. Other states had teachers score their own students, in some cases on checklists with no evidence required and in other cases using state-developed items or tasks that were scored according to protocols. Between the 2001 and 2003 state surveys, state special education directors reported a slight shift from teacher self-scoring of their own students to centralized scoring (Thompson & Thurlow, 2001, 2003). Other states moved toward more oversight of teacher self-scoring, including increased requirements for evidence of student work to support ratings or checklist scores, random sampling for verification of the evidence, or videotaping of assessment processes for later review by neutral, trained, second scorers. The push for these scoring enhancements was related to increased pressure from NCLB peer review processes, and it has not been determined whether these strategies increase the accuracy and reliability of scoring processes.

Performance/Achievement-Level Descriptors and Standard Setting

Beginning in 2003, the NCEO survey included questions about state plans for achievement standard setting. Regulations allowing states to set alternate achievement standards on alternate assessments designed for students "with the most significant cognitive disabilities" were released in 2003 (U.S. Department of Education, Office of Elementary and Secondary Education, 2003). Although a few pioneering states already had set achievement standards unique to these assessments, NCLB statutory requirements did not permit different content or achievement standards for any students. This new regulation added the option to develop validated and documented alternate achievement standards that reflected high expectations for this group of students. These alternate achievement standards could be used to categorize as *proficient* up to 1% of the total student population in tested grades.

The confusion in the field was rife. Special education directors generally had no experience with the concept or procedures of standard setting, and in states in which the special education section was in control of the alternate assessment, the learning curve was very steep. They had just come through a similar steep learning curve as they had grappled with the notion of curricula based on state content frameworks. In many states, special educators assumed that *alternate achievement standards* was a new name for extended content standards of some type. The confusion of content standards and achievement standards slowed progress on alternate assessments, and many states had false starts before sorting things out.

The pattern of responses in 2003 and 2005 to a question of whether states had an alternate achievement standard-setting process in place may reflect this confusion. In 2003, 52% of the regular states responded they did, and only 14% said they did not, with 10% saying they did not know, along with some reporting an informal process or other. In 2005, 55% said they did and were able to name the process. Given the intensive work being done in states in preparation for peer review at that time, it is possible that in the 2003 survey, state directors responded *yes* while thinking of their work on extending or expanding the content standards, whereas the 55% saying *yes* in 2005 actually reflected a larger increase than what the data suggest.

A few states were out in front with pioneering efforts again. Early standard-setting approaches in states reflected the necessity of adapting existing methods to these new assessments. This early work resulted in three synthesis reports documenting initial efforts (Arnold, 2003; Olson, Mead, & Payne, 2002; Wiener, 2002) and one summarizing the standard-setting approaches that could be tailored to alternate assessments (Roeber, 2002). The 2003 regulation and the release of Peer Review Guidance in 2004 (updated in 2007; U.S. Department of Education, Office of Elementary and Secondary Education, 2007) began a new phase in alternate assessment: all states began to grapple with the very real challenges of developing "real" large-scale assessments for this small group of students with varying communication requirements and varying learning characteristics. This redoubling of efforts to build technically defensible assessments was also a response to another key demand: use of the assessments in NCLB-required reporting and accountability systems.

Table 8.4 shows that, by 2005, the format of the alternate assessment had dropped from the primary focus of change, and more states were look-

Table 8.4. Alternate assessment development/revision—2005

Area	Number of regular states
Approach	8
Content	10
Standard setting	13
Scoring criteria	17

From Thompson, S.J., Johnstone, C.J., Thurlow, M.L., & Altman, J.R. (2005). *2005 state special education outcomes: Steps forward in a decade of change* (p. 16). Minneapolis: University of Minnesota, National Center on Educational Outcomes; reprinted by permission.

ing at working on refining content targets, better understanding achievement standards, and ensuring integrity in scoring. The table shows that twice as many states (17) were concerned about improving scoring criteria than were concerned about type of format as the primary issue (8).

Reporting and Accountability

Challenges in reporting alternate assessment results had been identified in the 2000 Thompson and Thurlow report, and the NCLB requirements that all student results be included in system accountability measures intensified the challenges and raised the stakes. State work on the development of alternate achievement standards was an essential step in including all scores in accountability calculations. By 2001, stakeholders across the country were seeing positive consequences for students with disabilities related to their inclusion in accountability systems, although some challenges were identified (Quenemoen, Lehr, Thurlow, & Massanari, 2001). The paper summarized the conclusions of 135 stakeholders from 39 states (plus American Samoa and the Bureau of Indian Affairs) who participated in a structured discussion of issues related to the implementation of alternate assessments. Among the findings was,

> Technical and psychometric difficulties with existing assessment systems were perceived as a major issue, but fairness of use of results is a related and complicating issue. Some of the challenges identified by participants include putting all students on the same scale versus accountability for all, a need to balance what makes sense for improvement planning with psychometric soundness, and how to compare fairly across schools, districts, and states with so many uncontrolled variables. (Quenemoen et al., 2001, pp. 5–6)

Two synthesis reports dealt with issues and methods of reporting alternate assessment scores just as NCLB was authorized (Bechard, 2001; Quenemoen, Rigney, & Thurlow, 2002), but the larger issue remained how to defend the technical adequacy of the assessment results for reporting and accountability purposes.

THE TRANSITION TO NEW THINKING

As the field continued to struggle with the issues, it became clear that retrofitting alternate assessments into existing measurement paradigms, using traditional statistical methods of documenting technical qualities, was not working well. At the 2004 American Educational Research Association meeting, a paper that described the chasm between traditional measurement tools and the challenges of alternate assessment for students with significant cognitive disabilities stimulated discussion among measurement, curriculum, and special education partners (Quenemoen, Thurlow, & Ryan, 2004). It resulted in a recognition that the challenges of alternate assessment were not going to be solved with the tools of one educational discipline alone. These challenges required collaboration that would yield educationally sound but technically defensible strategies.

In 2001, the National Research Council had sponsored a Committee on the Foundations of Assessments "to look at the advances in the cognitive and measurement sciences, as well as early work done in the intersection between the two disciplines, and to consider the implications for reshaping educational assessment" (National Research Council, 2001, p. xii). Large-scale assessment and special education colleagues around the country began investigating the application of the committee's work for application in state assessment systems. Through two federal grant opportunities, a research collaborative was formed that consisted of experts in special education (including severe disabilities), curriculum, and measurement and a dozen partner states. With funding from the New Hampshire Enhanced Assessment Initiative (NHEAI) and the National Alternate Assessment Center (NAAC), the group worked to identify key issues in developing technically defensible alternate assessments for use in NCLB-required accountability systems.

Using the assessment triangle of cognition, observation, and interpretation as the foundational conceptual framework, NHEAI and NAAC researchers, experts, and partner states developed and tested a validity framework to apply to alternate assessments. Figure 8.2 shows the assessment triangle with the key chapters of the NHEAI/NAAC-recommended technical workbook superimposed, with the validity evaluation placed in the center, drawing from and making meaning of the separate topics in the chapters. Other chapters in this book describe work that has been based on this framework (see Chapters 1, 7, 21, and 22).

WHERE ARE WE NOW?

New approaches to alternate assessments affect several key areas previously discussed under the heading "Post-1997 State Survey Data: Where Did We Start?" This section explores these topics in the context of the early 21st century.

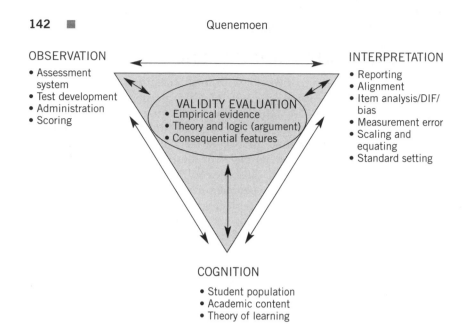

Figure 8.2. The assessment triangle and validity evaluation. (From Marion, S.F., & Pellegrino, J.W. [2006]. A validity framework for evaluating the technical quality of alternate assessments. *Educational Measurement: Issues and Practice, 25*[4], 47–57; Copyright © 2006 National Council on Measurement in Education. Reproduced with permission of Blackwell Publishing Ltd.) (*Key:* DIF, differential item functioning.)

Stakeholders, Expectations, and Principles

The NAAC at the University of Kentucky has developed the Learner Characteristics Inventory, a validated tool for capturing the learning characteristics of students who participate in alternate assessments based on alternate achievement standards (Kearns, Towles-Reeves, Kleinert, & Kleinert, 2006). The initial Learner Characteristics Inventory data from several states are presented in Chapters 1 and 21. What is alarming is that in most states for which there are data, there is no meaningful progression of skills from the elementary to high school levels. The authors of Chapters 1 and 21 attribute this lack of progression to a history of low expectations for this group of students; the historical "gold standard" held sight words and the use of calculators as the ultimate goals of academic instruction for these students.

Even more alarming are the data showing that the percentage of students who do not have meaningful communication strategies does not change from the elementary to high school levels (Towles-Reeves, Kearns, Kleinert, & Kleinert, in press). These students are not making progress in the academic content, and, apparently, they are not even able to access the content through communication tools, high tech or low. Some states have reported sharp rises in the use of assistive technology after implementation of alternate assessments. If the percentage of students who lacked communication strategies were to decrease as a result, such a change would be a powerful endorsement of the positive consequences of alternate assessments on raising expectations and outcomes.

There are other data suggesting that expectations have not yet risen universally. In 1999, stakeholders estimated that fewer than 1% to more than 9% of all students had such limited exposure to content that it would prevent them from participating in regular assessments (see Table 8.1). In 2007, with the advent of a second NCLB regulation allowing another separate achievement standard, the *2% regulation,* data from state public reports showed fewer than 1% to as many as 9% of all students in various alternate assessments. These percentages are of the total student populations, but, depending on individual state incidence figures, those populations could represent as many as 90% of all students with disabilities. Given national incidence figures showing that 85% of all students with disabilities ages 6–21 do not have cognitive disabilities (IDEA Part B Child Count, 2005), it is disheartening to see so many students being held to alternate and modified achievement standards.

Content Coverage (Linkage to Content Standards)

Since 2004, NAAC at the University of Kentucky has had content issues in alternate assessment as one of three research foci. NAAC's University of Kentucky partners continue working to define what linkage to grade-level content means in practice. They developed national training on tools that help states determine appropriate content targets, focusing on available student work as the field changed (National Alternate Assessment Center, 2005). *Is It Reading? Is It Math? Is It Science?* training materials are posted on the NAAC web site. As part of the NHEAI joint work with NAAC, Kleinert, Browder, and Towles-Reeves (in press) developed a white paper summarizing the extant literature on a theory of learning for students with disabilities as compared and contrasted with the literature base on learning theory in the National Research Council's *Knowing What Students Know.* NAAC partners at the University of North Carolina Charlotte, meanwhile, developed and validated a procedure for alignment studies on alternate assessments for students with significant cognitive disabilities (Flowers, Browder, Wakeman, & Karvonen, 2006). Links for Academic Learning is described in Chapter 5.

Although these tools have been developed during the early 21st century, states were required to have their state systems ready for peer review under NCLB requirements before tool validation. Results from peer review suggest great variability of content coverage—what the University of North Carolina Charlotte researchers called *near and far linkages,* including several states that still included broken links. These often still reflect a one-size-fits-all functional or very-low-level academic curriculum reminiscent of the infant/early childhood curriculum of years ago. Even so, there is a clear and steady trend toward more challenging academic content as more states implement alternate assessments more strongly linked to grade-level academic content standards.

Alternate Assessment Approach (Format)

Several NCEO reports called attention to the degree to which nominal categories of alternate assessment approach (e.g., portfolio, performance assessment) are not particularly useful descriptors (Gong & Marion, 2006; Quenemoen, Thompson, & Thurlow, 2003; Thompson & Thurlow, 2000). The paper by Gong and Marion (2006) was devoted to the topic; it was written after the NHEAI and NAAC expert panel had suggested that nominal categories are not useful for characterizing the technical aspects of assessments. The expert panel's technical review of partner state alternate assessments demonstrated that the evaluation of technical adequacy interacts with the types of alternate assessments being employed, but the types were better described along a continuum of standardization and flexibility in design choices rather than nominal types. Gong and Marion cautioned that this does not mean that standardization is good and flexibility is bad. Designing assessments to coherently link the nature of cognition to observation and to intended inferences for this small group of students does not lend itself to blind standardization.

This complexity of design issues is not limited to alternate assessments. In her 2007 presidential address to the American Educational Research Association, Eva Baker suggested,

> Tests only dimly reflect in their design the results of research on learning, whether of skills, subject matter, or problem solving. These test-design properties matter to researchers but rarely are observable in the tests because the naked eye is drawn to test format, not educational soundness. (Baker, 2007, p. 310)

The work of NHEAI and NAAC was meant to focus on educational soundness, not format, and the Gong and Marion (2006) paper included concepts and tools to help states focus on this concept.

Scoring Criteria and Procedures

There are many unanswered questions about what scoring criteria are appropriate for use with alternate assessments of students with significant cognitive disabilities. Basic questions remain. How can scoring protocols be designed and carried out with fidelity when tasks need to be adapted across such a broad range of student communication methods? How can degree of independence be measured in responses from students with limited response repertoires? How does one account for traditional understanding of baseline growth in a standards-based system? Who administers items or tasks and then scores responses when many of these students respond only to familiar test administrators? Who checks, and how does one verify, that consistent administration and scoring is occurring? Design of scoring rubrics and procedures, along with design of tasks, are among the greatest challenges that states face as they balance the need for flexibility versus standardization with the unusual and varied learning characteristics of the students.

Performance/Achievement-Level Descriptors and Standard Setting

Scoring and task decisions ultimately need to be driven by how proficiency is defined for these students. Here, again, basic questions still remain. What should these students know and be able to do? How well? Is the content clearly referenced? How good is good enough?

NAAC developed a paper that summarized the issues of alternate assessment and provided a framework to help states answer the questions (Perie, 2007). The paper emphasized the importance and challenges of writing detailed performance-level descriptors that clearly link to grade-level content standards while also reflecting performance expectations and addressing the context of any system supports that students require, including levels of prompting. States have struggled to accurately represent what student performance actually means. The nature of the link to grade-level content that is appropriate for students with significant cognitive disabilities and that is also appropriately challenging and consistent with what similar-age peers are learning has been both praised and ridiculed. States need to grapple with language that describes precisely what is and is not represented by various proficiency determinations, or the credibility of alternate assessments will be suspect.

Understanding and clearly describing success in academic content for these students, and then matching those descriptions to test results, is very difficult. The actual standard-setting procedures described in the Perie (2007) paper and those used in many states are relatively straightforward by comparison. Because so little is understood about what students with significant cognitive disabilities can know and do in academic content when taught well and given the support to communicate effectively, there likely will be dramatic changes in what *proficiency* means for these students. Initial descriptions and standards will require careful monitoring and adjusting over time.

Reporting and Accountability

Public reporting requirements of participation and performance of all students are defined in both NCLB and IDEA. NCEO has been compiling

IDEA-required reporting on state annual performance reports in addition to reporting on assessment data that are publicly reported by states. It is clear from these reports that some states are struggling to provide clean and clear data on the participation and performance of students with disabilities in the assessment system in either type of report. Some of the struggle comes from limited capacity for data management or communication across divisions in some states, but there is still a lack of readily comparable data on the participation and performance of students with disabilities across all 50 states, including those students who participate in alternate assessments of all types.

WHAT IS THE ROAD AHEAD?

The lack of clarity about participation and performance in alternate assessments carries across the entire alternate assessment effort. It is far more difficult to quickly peruse a state's alternate assessment description and materials and judge quality from the outside than it is for regular assessments. In NCEO's systematic analyses of state alternate assessments since 1999, it is clear that alternate assessments sometimes are more or less than initially meets the eye. A primary reason for this lack of clarity is the number of unknowns that still remain in the field about what these students can know and do when they receive appropriate academic instruction. The technical issues of these new assessments are huge, but until there is a common understanding of these students' learning characteristics, of how they can be expected to learn in the academic domains, and of what their performance looks like when they have been taught well, the technical efforts are simply attempts to put order on rapidly shifting chaos. Because of the number of uncertainties still in play, improvement is needed in the areas discussed in the following sections.

Transparency

Education professionals have not determined what will work best in teaching and assessing students with significant cognitive disabilities in the academic content. There is evidence of remarkable achievement, but this group is quite varied in characteristics, and the field of severe disabilities is still divided on what appropriate outcomes can and should be expected. It is appropriate that states vary so much in their assessment practices at this point; it is even appropriate that the content targets of alternate assessment take so much time and struggle to refine. The key to resolving this lack of clarity is transparency of processes and outcomes. It is important to know what varying practices and targets yield for student outcomes, and the only way to build that knowledge base is to ensure that assessment development, implementation, and results are transparent and open to scrutiny. Although quantitative approaches to outcome measures are valued in general assessment, as are statistical approaches to documentation of technical quality, for the numbers to be useful it is necessary to know what the desired assessment processes and outcomes are. This is not yet known for students with significant cognitive disabilities.

Integrity

Building on the need for transparency is the need for integrity. The amount of flexibility needed to ensure that all students can demonstrate what they know and can do is higher in alternate assessments for this group of students than in more typical student populations. Flexibility can mask issues of teaching and learning unless it is carefully structured and controlled. Research on teachers' ability to assess and score their own students' work with fidelity and integrity is limited. Research from the 1980s suggests that teachers can predict which items of a norm-referenced test their typical students will get right (e.g., Coladarci, 1986; Hoge & Coladarci, 1989). In the 1986 Coladarci study, teachers were right in their item-level judgments more often than not, but accuracy was higher for some tasks than others (e.g., computation versus problem solving in mathematics; literal versus figurative meaning in reading). Teachers were more accurate with higher-ability students than with lower-ability students. According to David Niemi of the National Center for Research on Evaluation, Standards, and Student Testing, research on teacher scoring of performance assessments suggests that teachers can be trained to reliably score work other than that of their own students (e.g., writing assessments), but it is less likely that they will score their own students' work as reliably (personal communication, March 15, 2007). For students with significant cognitive disabilities, the field has not established definitions of acceptable performance in the academic domains at each level, nor is there a shared understanding of how varying prompting approaches affect the content being assessed, so teacher self-scoring remains a murky issue.

Standardization as a solution carries the risk of reducing the integrity of the assessment results; this can be a concern, for instance, if the methods do not match the population being assessed. Given the uncertainties of what can be expected for these students, and the small numbers of students with highly varying learning characteristics in most states, many traditional tools of large-scale assessment development and documentation are of limited use. It is tempting to make use of tidy, traditional solutions for technical defense, but when the underlying assumptions of testing models and tools are not met, it is inappropriate to use them. Brennan (1998), in his NCME address, commented,

> In general, strong assumptions lead to strong results. . . . However, a claim that a model solves a thorny measurement problem is credible only to the extent that the assumptions engaged in addressing the problem can be shown to withstand serious challenge. Too frequently, in my

opinion, we act as if assumptions are met without question. Such unrestrained confidence can easily lead to excessive (or at least unsubstantiated) public claims about what our models can accomplish in real life educational testing contexts (pp. 5–6).

Consequential Validity Studies

Building on the issues of transparency and integrity, education professionals have an obligation to monitor carefully the effects of alternate assessments over time. Other chapters in this book address this issue well (e.g., see Chapters 7 and 22), but these chapters also reflect the considerable commitment this kind of study can be. They also document how seldom studies of this type occur in state large-scale assessment systems. It is not enough to hope that initial guesses of what will improve outcomes for these students will play out as intended. Large-scale alternate assessments of these students have been occurring for less than two decades, and there is little understanding of how these students build competence in mathematics, reading, and science.

Planned Improvement over Time

The point of consequential validity studies is to ensure that the consequences that are hoped for, and those that are to be avoided, are in fact falling into their respective places. Although formal consequential validity studies can help identify issues, ongoing day-to-day oversight of the assessment development, implementation, and use of testing results is absolutely necessary for these assessments.

Why does it matter? This chapter cited the 1997 IDEA legislation as pivotal in changing expectations for students with disabilities. The preamble to the 1997 reauthorization was cited as stating, "Almost 20 years of research and experience has demonstrated that the education of children with disabilities can be made more effective." Unfortunately, the preamble to the 2004 reauthorization includes different words simply by the addition of another decade of neglect:

> Almost 30 years of research and experience has demonstrated that the education of children with disabilities can be made more effective by—(A) having high expectations for such children and ensuring their access to the general education curriculum in the regular classroom, to the maximum extent possible, in order to—(i) meet developmental goals and, to the maximum extent possible, the challenging expectations that have been established for all children; and (ii) be prepared to lead productive and independent adult lives, to the maximum extent possible.

What is the *maximum extent possible?* Too little was expected of students with significant cognitive disabilities in the past, but much remains to be learned about what is possible. The ongoing debate over whether functional or academic instruction is the best strategy is an oversimplification of the challenges. It clearly is not an *either–or* solution, and that debate does not serve the field well. What is functional for a third grader with significant cognitive disabilities? Ysseldyke and Olsen built on the community-based instruction literature in 1997 to say, "For a third grader, community might be the school, the playground and home, whereas community for an exiting senior would have to mean the store, bank, and workplace, for example." (p. 16). Now that these students have been shown capable of mastering—and enjoying—far more than sight words and calculator use, what is functional for any third grader? What is enjoyable? For students who have very complex and challenging disabilities, what are desired outcomes? As adults with significant cognitive disabilities begin to have more normalized opportunities for supported living and work, what kinds of skills and knowledge will yield the highest quality of life? Educators have spent years practicing shopping and cooking skills with students who will need assistance lifelong to do either. Students who rarely, if ever, will drive cars or seek out hospital care on their own are taught survival signs such as *yield* and *hospital.* Meanwhile, educators have ignored the content that motivates and engages other students—and adults—such as developing deeper appreciation for creative writing, music, and other arts, developing problem-solving skills, monitoring and understanding news and current events, and understanding science phenomena. Students with significant cognitive disabilities have not yet been given sufficient access to the "rest of the content" through communications tools and assistive devices. How do expanded content targets and the use of tools and devices fit into supported life and work settings? A vignette from the Georgia Alternate Assessment technical manual profiles the possibilities:

■ *OF MICE AND MEN*—FROM THE CLASSROOM TO THE JOB SITE

Jessie Moreau & Toni Waylor-Bowen, GDOE Teachers on Special Assignment

After attending an initial daylong training session on providing access to the general education curriculum for students with significant cognitive disabilities, provided by the Georgia Department of Education, Division for Exceptional Students (DES), a high school level special education teacher and her class worked on *Of Mice and Men*. At the end of the unit, a student with autism created a multipage picture book report on *Of Mice and Men* which the teacher then turned into a PowerPoint book report. His teacher shared the PowerPoint version with the Georgia Teachers on Special Assignment who led the initial access training.

The Teachers on Special Assignment shared the adapted version of *Of Mice and Men* with other educators during follow-up trainings with a group of teachers across Georgia called "Core Access Teachers" (CATs). Penni, a high school CAT, who teaches students with severe/profound intellectual disabilities, then told us this story of her students' use of the adapted version, *Of Mice and Men.*

> I had a wonderful experience today with xxx (a student with moderate intellectual disabilities) relating to *Of Mice and Men.* When xxx was bagging groceries today at her job at Publix, she was being too rough with a loaf of bread and it was going to end up damaged. I asked her what Lennie had to do in the story and she said that "he had to be careful with the soft things." She then realized that she had to handle the bread the way Lennie had to handle the soft things. She was so excited when she made the connection!!!! She handled the bread very carefully for the rest of her shift at Publix. I was so proud of her! How exciting that she was able to make a real life comparison!!!!

Post Script

Ruth (another teacher) and Lorri-Ann (Penni's and Ruth's paraprofessional) have created another PowerPoint version of *Of Mice and Men* that includes more of the story events and character development the original book report had overlooked. Penni has now also adapted *Julius Caesar, The Scarlet Letter,* and *Animal Farm,* all of which utilize several levels of literature for access by all students. Penni and Ruth's students continue to work together and have dramatized the three additional stories, including rap and music/video versions. The students utilize AAC [augmentative and alternative communication] devices for communication, Writing with Symbol scripts, and tactile prompts/props. These high school students are having the time of their lives, are motivated to learn, are finding connections to real life, and have developed friendships with peers across the school. Can you ask any more from education than that? (Georgia Department of Education, 2007, pp. 12–13)

SUMMARY

The long and winding road of alternate assessment allows the opportunity to rethink what is possible for students with significant cognitive disabilities. Decisions on future approaches should be driven by a vision of what these students can know and do for a high quality of life, based on the wonderful new evidence of their learning. It is not enough to settle for what has occurred in the past.

REFERENCES

Arnold, N. (2003). *Washington alternate assessment system technical report on standard setting for the 2002 portfolio* (Synthesis Rep. No. 50). Minneapolis: University of Minnesota, National Center on Educational Outcomes.

Baker, E.L. (2007). 2007 presidential address: The end(s) of testing. *Educational Researcher, 36*(6), 309–317.

Bechard, S. (2001). *Models for reporting the results of alternate assessments within state accountability systems* (Synthesis Rep. No. 39). Minneapolis: University of Minnesota, National Center on Educational Outcomes.

Brennan, R.L. (1998). Misconceptions at the intersection of measurement theory and practice. *Educational Measurement: Issues and Practice, 17*(1), 5–9, 30.

Browder, D.M., & Spooner, F. (Eds.). (2006). *Teaching language arts, math, & science to students with significant cognitive disabilities.* Baltimore: Paul H. Brookes Publishing Co.

Brown, L., Nietupski, J., & Hamre-Nietupski, S. (1976). The criterion of ultimate functioning and public school services for severely handicapped children. In M. Thomas (Ed.), *Hey, don't forget about me!* (pp. 2–15). Reston, VA: Council for Exceptional Children.

Coladarci, T. (1986). Accuracy of teacher judgments of student responses to standardized test items. *Journal of Educational Psychology, 78*(2), 141–146.

Flowers, C., Browder, D., Wakeman, S., & Karvonen, M. (2006). *Alternate assessment alignment pilot study: Report to the state department of education.* Charlotte: The University of North Carolina at Charlotte, National Alternate Assessment Center.

Georgia Department of Education. (2007). *Documenting the technical quality of the Georgia alternate assessment (GAA).* Atlanta, GA: Georgia Department of Education.

Gong, B., & Marion, S. (2006). *Dealing with flexibility in assessments for students with significant cognitive disabilities* (Synthesis Rep. No. 60). Minneapolis: University of Minnesota, National Center on Educational Outcomes.

Hoge, R.D., & Coladarci, T. (1989). Teacher-based judgments of academic achievement: A review of literature. *Review of Educational Research, 59*(3), 297–313.

IDEA Part B Child Count. (2005). *Students ages 6 through 21 served under IDEA, Part B, by disability category* (Tables 1-3). Retrieved September 2008, from http://www.IDEAdata.org

Improving America's Schools Act of 1994, PL 103-382, 20 U.S.C. §§ 630 *et seq.*

Individuals with Disabilities Education Act Amendments (IDEA) of 1997, PL 105-17, 20 U.S.C. §§ 1400 *et seq.*

Individuals with Disabilities Education Improvement Act (IDEA) of 2004, PL 108-446, 20 U.S.C. §§ 1400 *et seq.*

Kearns, J., Towles-Reeves, E., Kleinert, H., & Kleinert, J. (2006). *Learning characteristics inventory report.* Lexington: University of Kentucky, National Alternate Assessment Center.

Kleinert, H., Browder, D., & Towles-Reeves, E. (in press). Models of cognition for students with significant cognitive disabilities: Implications for assessment. *Review of Educational Research.*

Kleinert, H., Haigh, J., Kearns, J., & Kennedy, S. (2000). Alternate assessments: Lessons learned and roads to be taken. *Exceptional Children, 67*(1), 51–66.

Kleinert, H., Kearns, J.F., & Kennedy, S. (1999). Accountability for all students: Kentucky's alternate portfolio assessment for students with moderate and severe disabilities. *Journal of the Association for Severe Handicaps, 24*(2), 88–101.

Kohl, F., McLaughlin, M., & Nagle, K. (2006). Alternate achievement standards and assessments: A descriptive investigation of 16 states. *Exceptional Children, 73*(1), 107–123.

Marion, S.F., & Pellegrino, J.W. (2006). A validity framework for evaluating the technical quality of alternate assessments. *Educational Measurement: Issues and Practice, 25*(4), 47–57.

National Alternate Assessment Center. (2005). Part III: Theory of learning: What students with the most significant cognitive disabilities should know and be able to do. In *Access and alignment to grade level content for students with the most significant cognitive disabilities: A training module for large-scale use.* Retrieved October 30, 2007, from http://www.naacpartners.org/products/workshops/CCSSOseminars/16600/slide1.htm

National Research Council. (2001). *Knowing what students know: The science and design of educational assessment.* Washington, DC: National Academy of Sciences.

No Child Left Behind Act of 2001, PL 107-110, 115 Stat. 1425, 20 U.S.C. §§ 6301 *et seq.*

Olson, B., Mead, R., & Payne, D. (2002). *A report of a standard setting method for alternate assessments for students with significant disabilities* (Synthesis Rep. No. 47). Minneapolis: University of Minnesota, National Center on Educational Outcomes.

Perie, M. (2007). *Setting alternate achievement standards.* Lexington: University of Kentucky, National Alternate Assessment Center, Human Development Institute.

Quenemoen, R.F., Lehr, C.A., Thurlow, M.L., & Massanari, C.B. (2001). *Students with disabilities in standards-based assessment and accountability systems: Emerging issues, strategies, and recommendations* (Synthesis Rep. No. 37). Minneapolis: University of Minnesota, National Center on Educational Outcomes.

Quenemoen, R., Rigney, S., & Thurlow, M. (2002). *Use of alternate assessment results in reporting and accountability systems: Conditions for use based on research and practice* (Synthesis Rep. No. 43). Minneapolis: University of Minnesota, National Center on Educational Outcomes.

Quenemoen, R., Thompson, S., & Thurlow, M. (2003). *Measuring academic achievement of students with significant cognitive disabilities: Building understanding of alternate assessment scoring criteria* (Synthesis Rep. No. 50). Minneapolis: University of Minnesota, National Center on Educational Outcomes.

Quenemoen, R., Thurlow, M., & Ryan, J. (2004). *I say potato, you say potahto: An AERA conference discussion paper and side-by-side glossary.* Minneapolis: University of Minnesota, National Center on Educational Outcomes.

Roeber, E. (2002). *Setting standards on alternate assessments* (Synthesis Rep. No. 42). Minneapolis: University of Minnesota, National Center on Educational Outcomes.

Thompson, S.J., Johnstone, C.J., Thurlow, M.L., & Altman, J.R. (2005). *2005 state special education outcomes: Steps forward in a decade of change.* Minneapolis: University of Minnesota, National Center on Educational Outcomes.

Thompson, S., & Thurlow, M. (1999). *1999 state special education outcomes: A report on state activities at the end of the century.* Minneapolis: University of Minnesota, National Center on Educational Outcomes.

Thompson, S.J., & Thurlow, M.L. (2000). *State alternate assessments: Status as IDEA alternate assessment requirements take effect* (Synthesis Rep. No. 35). Minneapolis: University of Minnesota, National Center on Educational Outcomes.

Thompson, S., & Thurlow, M. (2001). *2001 state special education outcomes: A report on state activities at the beginning of a new decade.* Minneapolis: University of Minnesota, National Center on Educational Outcomes.

Thompson, S., & Thurlow, M. (2003). *2003 state special education outcomes: Marching on.* Minneapolis: University of Minnesota, National Center on Educational Outcomes.

Towles-Reeves, E., Kearns, J., Kleinert, H., & Kleinert, J. (in press). *Knowing what students know: Defining the student population taking alternate assessments based on alternate achievement standards. Journal of Special Education.*

U.S. Department of Education, Office of Elementary and Secondary Education. (2003, December). *Title I—Improving the academic achievement of the disadvantaged, final regulations.* Washington, DC: Author.

U.S. Department of Education, Office of Elementary and Secondary Education. (2007). *Standards and assessment peer review guidance: Information and examples for meeting requirements of the No Child Left Behind Act of 2001.* Retrieved February 20, 2009, http://www.ed.gov/policy/elsec/guid/saaprguidance.pdf

Wiener, D. (2002). *Massachusetts: One state's approach to setting performance levels on the alternate assessment* (Synthesis Rep. No. 48). Minneapolis: University of Minnesota, National Center on Educational Outcomes.

Wiener, D. (2005). *One state's story: Access and alignment to the grade-level content for students with significant cognitive disabilities* (Synthesis Rep. No. 57). Minneapolis: University of Minnesota, National Center on Educational Outcomes.

Ysseldyke, J.E., & Olsen, K.R. (1997). *Putting alternate assessments into practice: What to measure and possible sources of data* (Synthesis Rep. No. 28). Minneapolis: University of Minnesota, National Center on Educational Outcomes.

Ysseldyke, J., Thurlow, M., Erickson, R., Gabrys, R., Haigh, J., Trimble, S., et al. (1996). *A comparison of state assessment systems in Maryland and Kentucky with a focus on the participation of students with disabilities* (Maryland–Kentucky Rep. No. 1). Minneapolis: University of Minnesota, National Center on Educational Outcomes.

Alternate Assessment in Action

CHAPTER 9

Assessing All Students in Connecticut

PETER BEHUNIAK AND JOSEPH AMENTA

This chapter describes the instruments and procedures used to accomplish the assessment of academic proficiency of all public school students in Connecticut. The discussion begins with an overview of Connecticut's assessment history. This includes descriptions of the Connecticut Mastery Tests (CMTs) and the Connecticut Academic Performance Tests (CAPTs), which are measures designed for use with the general student population, and the CMT/CAPT Skills Checklist, which is designed for use with students with significant cognitive disabilities. The next section describes the process by which the Connecticut State Department of Education (CSDE) trains the teachers who administer the CMT/CAPT Skills Checklist. The final section discusses technical documentation and the processes employed to generate supporting psychometric evidence.

THE HISTORY OF STUDENT ASSESSMENT IN CONNECTICUT

The CMTs have formed the basis for monitoring student achievement in Connecticut since their inception in 1985. Currently in the fourth generation, the CMTs have provided a stable, standards-based measure of academic progress for more than two decades. As indicated in Table 9.1, the CMTs currently are administered in Grades 3–8 and offer criterion-referenced measurement in mathematics, reading, and writing. Science was added to Grades 5 and 8 during the 2007–2008 academic year. The assessments feature mixed-item formats, including selected response, short constructed response, extended constructed response, grid response, and performance tasks.

The views expressed in this chapter by Joseph Amenta, an employee of the Connecticut State Department of Education at the writing of this chapter, are solely his own and do not reflect any official policy or position of the Connecticut State Department of Education.

Table 9.1. Student assessment in Connecticut

Connecticut Mastery Test (CMT)
First administered in 1985
Currently fourth generation
Grades 3–8 criterion reference test
Mathematics
Reading
Writing
Science in Grades 5 and 8
Connecticut Academic Performance Test (CAPT)
First administered in 1995
Currently third generation
Grade 10
Mathematics
Science
Reading
Writing

The CAPTs were developed for use with Grade 10 students and were first administered in 1995. Currently in their third generation, these assessments use mixed-item formats and cover mathematics, reading, writing, and science. The CAPT is readministered in Grades 11 and 12 to students who failed to demonstrate proficiency during their initial attempts. Although the assessment is not formally an exit test, district personnel are required to consider students' performances on the tests when determining eligibility for graduation.

CMT/CAPT SKILLS CHECKLIST

Both the initial CMT/CAPT Skills Checklist, introduced in 2000, and the second-generation Skills Checklist, administered since 2006, were intended to guide teachers through observations of student proficiency in targeted areas of the curriculum. The checklists were developed to organize and standardize each teacher's ratings of student performance in classroom settings. This section describes the development and significant features of the checklists.

Initial Checklist

The initial Skills Checklist was developed by the CSDE in the late 1990s and was administered for the first time in 2000. It was based on the philosophy of supporting individualized instruction for students with significant cognitive disabilities within general education classrooms. The measure was intended to promote greater inclusion of students with disabilities in general education settings and to improve the quality of instruction provided to these students.

The initial Skills Checklist was a single instrument designed for use with students in Grades 4, 6, 8, and 10. (Note that the CMTs were administered only in Grades 4, 6, and 8 until 2005.) The skills assessed on the checklist included

- Receptive communication

- Expressive communication

- Social interaction communication

- Basic literacy

- Basic spatial relationship

- Basic operations

- Number sense

- Measurement

Each of the measured skills was identified on the students' checklists and presented to educators familiar with the students—usually the students' primary teachers. The teachers would then rate each student's ability in one of four categories: 1) Does Not Demonstrate, 2) Developing/Supported, 3) Mastered/Independent, or 4) Not Appropriate. An excerpt of the initial Skills Checklist is shown in Figure 9.1.

Second-Generation Checklist

The passage of the No Child Left Behind Act (NCLB) of 2001 (PL 107-110) led the CSDE to revisit its approach to designing and implementing the Skills Checklist. After extensive discussions between the CSDE and the U.S. Department of Education, it was determined that the primary change required by NCLB regulations was the development of grade-specific indicators of student performance. The CSDE continued to administer the initial checklist while a new checklist was being designed and developed.

A committee of 18 Connecticut special education teachers, curriculum specialists, school administrators, parents, and CSDE staff guided the development of the second-generation Skills Checklist. The committee was charged with keeping the content of the new checklist focused on the same curricula used to develop the CMT and CAPT. Reference documents included Connecticut's content standards and frameworks, expected performances, and performance standards (Connecticut State Department of Education, 2006b, 2006c).

Content Standard 3: Basic Operations

Students will add, subtract, multiply and divide with whole numbers and fractions and apply a variety of strategies for selecting the appropriate computational and operational methods for making decisions and solving problems in daily living.

Note: When marking an item, please use a Number 2 pencil and fill the bubble completely.

Item Functional Indicators: ***Basic*** *Operations*	① Does Not Demonstrate	② Developing/Supported	③ Mastered/Independent	NA Not Appropriate
M3.1 Identifies coins and one-dollar bill correctly (for example, penny, nickel, dime, quarter and one dollar)	○	○	○	○
M3.2 Counts pennies to 10 cents, nickels to one dollar, dimes to one dollar, and quarters to one dollar	○	○	○	○
M3.3 Makes coins to purchase an item (for example, uses cue card with visual or tactile representation of coins, when purchasing item)	○	○	○	○
M3.4 Adds two numbers using a number line	○	○	○	○
M3.5 Makes purchases in school or community stores and recognizes correct change	○	○	○	○

Figure 9.1. Sample excerpt from the initial Skills Checklist. (From Connecticut State Department of Education. [2000]. *CMT/CAPT skills checklist* [p. 16]. Hartford, CT: Author; reprinted by permission.)

The discussion among committee members was further focused by framing the dialog with the following questions:

1. What skills and knowledge endure?
2. What skills are essential for progress to the next level of instruction?
3. What contributes to a student's understanding of other standards?

Through deliberation and consideration of grade-specific content, the committee organized the content on the checklist as shown in Table 9.2. Each of the content standards incorporated in the checklist closely resembles the content on which the CMT and CAPT were based. It was decided that a separate component of the checklist should address students' access skills. These skills were considered particularly important for students who might not be able to demonstrate proficiency in the academic components of the checklist.

The structure of the second-generation Skills Checklist is revealed in an excerpt for Grade 3 mathematics as shown in Figure 9.2. The main content standard presented in Figure 9.2 is Algebraic Reasoning. Each

Table 9.2.   Content on the second-generation Skills Checklist

Language arts
- Reading and Responding
- Exploring and Responding to Literature
- Communicating with Others
- English Language Conventions

Mathematics
- Algebraic Reasoning: Patterns and Functions
- Geometry and Measurement
- Working with Data: Probability and Statistics
- Numerical and Proportional Reasoning

Science

Grade 5
- Energy Transfer and Transformations
- Structure and Function
- Earth and the Solar System
- Science and Technology in Society

Grade 8
- Forces and Motion
- Heredity and Evolution
- Earth and the Solar System
- Science and Technology in Society

Grade 10
- Cell Chemistry and Biotechnology
- Genetics, Evolution and Biodiversity, Biotechnology

Access skills
- Receptive Communication
- Expressive Communication
- Social Interactive Communication
- Basic Literacy
- Spatial Relationships

content standard is represented by several performance standards. In this example, the performance standard involves patterns made with objects or symbols and is drawn directly from the corresponding curriculum documents. Next, even more finely grained statements of expected performances are used to exemplify each performance standard. All standards to this level are directly consistent with CSDE curricula associated with each grade and subject.

The next level of specificity is labeled the *essence* of each expected performance. Each essence statement represents the developers' best effort to articulate a behavioral component that reflects the target expected performance. In the example shown, the essence statement is, *Demonstrate an understanding of patterns.* After the essence statement, a series

| **Algebraic Reasoning** |
| **Grade Three** |
| **Examples** |

A. Patterns that are made with different objects and symbols and that follow the same rule may be classified together.

   1. *Use a variety of materials to construct, reproduce, describe and extend number and spatial patterns. AR 3-1*
      Essence: Demonstrate an understanding of pattern.

| Continue a pattern with elements missing (A, B, A, B, A, ___) |
| Reproduce an AB pattern with numbers, symbols or objects |
| Identify an AB pattern with numbers, symbols or objects |

Figure 9.2. Structure of the second-generation Skills Checklist. (From Connecticut State Department of Education. [2006c, October]. *CMT/CAPT skills checklist second generation: Teacher handbook* [p. 26]. Hartford, CT: Author; reprinted by permission.)

of three downward extensions provide the basis on which each participating teacher would rate each student. The downward extensions are presented in a sequence that includes an increasing level of complexity and cognitive demand. In the example shown, the lowest level requires each student to identify an *A–B* pattern, the second level requires each student to reproduce an *A–B* pattern, and the third level requires each student to continue such a pattern.

Figure 9.3 shows the format and appearance of the final instrument for the Algebraic Reasoning component of the mathematics checklist for Grade 5. The complete instruments for mathematics in other grades and for reading, science, and the access skills in all grades can be viewed online at http://www.sde.ct.gov. The checklist was originally prepared as a scannable document, but teachers now can enter their ratings online using secure web access.

The three-point rating scale was the result of an extended development process involving the advisory committee, CSDE staff, measurement specialists, and content specialists. The developers initially wanted the rating scale to capture more than one dimension. Characteristics such as consistency, frequency, and quality were considered extensively. It was eventually determined that the scale would be based on the single characteristic of independence. The final scale was defined as follows:

0. *Does Not Demonstrate.* Use this response for skills that the student does not demonstrate in any setting.

1. *Developing/Supported.* Use this response for skills the student displays only with some level of prompt support (i.e., a verbal cue, partial physical guidance, modeling). This response also

GRADE 5 MATHEMATICS ASSESSMENT

Algebraic Reasoning	Does not demonstrate	Developing/Supported	Mastered/Independent
	ⓞ	①	②

A. *Patterns can be used to identify trends and make predictions.*

   1. *Represent and analyze a wide variety of geometric and numeric patterns using words, tables, verbal descriptions, graphs and equations. State the rule for a given pattern in oral and written form. AR 5-2*
   <u>Essence:</u> **Communicate the rule for a given pattern.**

	Does not demonstrate	Developing/Supported	Mastered/Independent
Identify the rule of a pattern	○	○	○
Demonstrate knowledge of pattern rules by creating original patterns	○	○	○
Extend a given pattern (e.g., clap, clap, clap) (i.e., either a growing or repeating pattern)	○	○	○

B. *An equation or inequality may be written to describe the general relationship between two sets of data.*

   2. *Express mathematical relationships using a variable in simple equations and inequalities. AR 5-3*
   <u>Essence:</u> **Use variables as substitutes for numbers in equations.**

	Does not demonstrate	Developing/Supported	Mastered/Independent
Solve for the unknown represented by n in the equation $1 + n = 3$	○	○	○
Solve for the unknown represented by n in the equation $1 + 2 = n$	○	○	○
Solve for the unknown represented by the box in the equation $1 + 2 = \square$	○	○	○

   3. *Write and solve simple equations and inequalities to solve problems. AR 5-4*
   <u>Essence:</u> **Use simple equations to solve problems.**

	Does not demonstrate	Developing/Supported	Mastered/Independent
Given a simple addition and a simple subtraction story problem, choose the correct pictorial representation for each from three choices and solve both problems	○	○	○
Given three choices, match the correct pictorial representation to a simple subtraction story problem and solve the problem	○	○	○
Given three choices, match the correct pictorial representation to a simple addition story problem and solve the problem	○	○	○

C. *Pairs of numbers can be represented as a location on a coordinate plane defined by horizontal and vertical number lines (axes).*

   4. *Organize data in tables, graphs and scatter plots. Identify trends and analyze how a change in one variable relates to a change in a second variable. AR 5-5*
   <u>Essence:</u> **Organize data in tables and graphs.**

	Does not demonstrate	Developing/Supported	Mastered/Independent
Indicate greatest or least in a given data set on a pictograph	○	○	○
Organize a simple data set in a pictograph	○	○	○
Organize a simple data set (single digit numbers) in ascending and descending order	○	○	○

Figure 9.3. Format of the final instrument for Algebraic Reasoning in Grade 5. (From Connecticut State Department of Education. [2006a, September]. *CMT/CAPT skills checklist: Second generation.* Hartford, CT: Author; reprinted by permission.)

should be used for skills that are displayed inconsistently. If a student can demonstrate a skill occasionally but not consistently, then the skills should be rated Developing/Supported.

2. *Mastered/Independent.* Use this response for skills that the student clearly has mastered and performs independently. To be rated as Mastered/Independent, the student must demonstrate the skill consistently over time. The student does not have to demonstrate the skill every time, but, during the course of the year, he or she has to show mastery (e.g., the student successfully performs the skill 80% or more of the time without prompts or supports such as verbal cues or partial physical guidance).

The application of checklists within classrooms has both a targeted window and an extended administration window. Teachers are expected to complete the checklists in the spring of each year during the same period used for administering the CMT to the general student population—a period of about 4 weeks set by the CSDE. However, teachers are not expected to make all observations of their students on the target skills during this period. Instead, teachers are instructed to observe students throughout the year and assemble records of each student's capacity to demonstrate the target skills. During the spring administration window, the teachers use the time to record their observations and to make additional observations of the students on skills for which the ratings may be uncertain.

Standard Setting

A formal process of setting standards was employed to establish the performance levels on each component (e.g., mathematics, reading) for the checklists at each grade. A policy decision was made by the CSDE to establish only three achievement levels on each checklist, even though the CMT and CAPT each have five performance levels. This decision was based, in part, on the expectation that the distribution of scores resulting from the administration of the checklists would not support the greater number of performance levels. The checklist performance levels were labeled *basic, proficient,* and *independent.*

The procedure used to establish the standards was a generalized holistic method (Cizek, Bunch, & Koons, 2004) that consisted of elements of the judgmental policy capture technique (Jaeger, 1995) and the dominant profile judgment method (Plake, Hambleton, & Jaeger, 1997). A committee of teachers, curriculum coordinators, school administrators, and CSDE staff convened for a three-day standard-setting session. The procedures employed during the sessions were reviewed in advance and approved by the Connecticut Technical Advisory Committee.

Score Reporting

The goal in creating the battery of score reports for students participating in the CMT/CAPT Skills Checklist was to include these students in the same procedures and reports as all other students participating in the state assessments and then to supplement as needed to accommodate the unique nature of the checklist. Each student for whom a checklist is completed is included in the general CMT and CAPT reports at the classroom, school, and district levels. Each student receives a customized individual report for review by his or her parents and for placement in the student's file. The school district also receives roster and summary reports for all participating students. All reports are online at CSDE's web site but are only accessible with appropriate security clearances.

TRAINING TO ADMINISTER THE SKILLS CHECKLIST

The CSDE provides training on how to administer the checklist to all teachers who are primarily responsible for completing and submitting this assessment. This training is given annually as either a full-day workshop for teachers who have never filled out the checklist or as a half-day workshop for teachers who need to review the checklist and receive updates.

Basic Training

Training begins with a discussion of the purpose of the checklist and the intended use of the results. Participants in the training can ask for clarification of any aspect of the instrument or the identification of the student population for which it was intended. The participants are then led through a series of exercises intended to familiarize them with appropriate observational strategies and the application of the rating scales. This process focuses on a series of nonsecure videos (i.e., videos that are available for teacher review outside of the training sessions) in which teachers are shown using the checklists with their students. The participants then discuss how they would rate the students in the video on the demonstrated skills.

Certified Training

During the 2007–2008 academic year, the CSDE began offering certified rater training to teachers working with these students. This training is intended to

- Prepare veteran special education teachers to become certified raters

- Use this cadre of highly qualified certified raters to provide ongoing training to other teachers who use the CMT/CAPT Skills Checklist to increase their skills as observers and evaluators of student behavior habits

- Ensure that the rating of student performance on the CMT/CAPT Skills Checklist becomes more consistent and accurate over time

Certified training involves a more rigorous process based on the use of secure video recordings (i.e., videos that are maintained by the CSDE exclusively for use during training sessions) of Connecticut students being evaluated on a number of downward extensions in reading, writing, or math on the CMT/CAPT Skills Checklist. The secure videos were viewed and rated by an expert panel of special education consultants on the CSDE staff and advisory committee members from various districts who participated in the development of the checklist. For a video recording to be accepted as a secure video suitable for use in training teachers, the expert panel members had to reach consensus on the score of each downward extension demonstrated.

These secure videos were divided into two groups: *training videos* and *qualifying videos.* During certified rater training, participants are guided through the process of how to accurately rate a student's performance on the checklist by viewing a series of training videos and discussing the ratings they would give the students shown in these videos. Ten training videos are used to help participants determine how to score specific items on the checklist. Once the training videos have been used for practice, the participants are given a set of 10 qualifying videos to review and rate student performance. A 90% match to the ratings determined by the expert panel on these qualifying videos is required for a candidate to be accepted as a certified rater. Certified raters are individuals whom the CSDE considers qualified to provide training to other teachers on the CMT/CAPT Skills Checklist. In the future, certified rater training will be made available as an online course to increase the number of teachers who receive this level of training.

TECHNICAL CONSIDERATIONS

The first step in supporting the technical adequacy of the checklist was to make certain the instrument was used with appropriate students. The CSDE guidance to educators includes a four-part definition of the target student population. First, the student must have a significant cognitive disability. Second, the student must require intensive individualized instruction to acquire, maintain, or generalize skills that students without disabilities typically develop outside of a school setting. Third, the student must require direct instruction in multiple settings to successfully generalize skills to natural settings, including home, school, and community. Finally, the student's instructional program must include participation in the general education curriculum to the extent appropriate. The student's program also may include a functional and life skills component.

Educators receive guidance regarding unacceptable criteria for determining the appropriateness of the checklist for each student. For example, teachers are not allowed to use a student's disability category or placement as the basis for participation. Also, considering the amount of time spent with peers who do not have disabilities is prohibited. Teachers are cautioned against using the expectation that a student will not perform well on the general assessment as a basis for using the checklist.

Using these criteria resulted in 2,480 students being assessed statewide with the checklist in 2006 (the total statewide population of students in Grades 3–8 and 10 was 301,491). There were 300–400 students participating in the checklist in each of the tested grades.

Technical Manual

The development and use of the CMT/CAPT Skills Checklist is documented in an annual technical manual (CSDE, 2006b), which is available online. The structure of the manual has evolved over time and is based, in part, on the continuing collaboration of the CSDE with the National Alternate Assessment Center at the University of Kentucky. The current version of the manual includes the following structure:

- Section I: Overview, Background, Key Components of the Validity Evaluation

- Section II: Test Development, Administration, Scoring, Reporting

- Section III: Empirical Evidence

Evidence is compiled on an annual basis by the CSDE or its testing contractors and is added to the manual as appropriate. In addition, reports of separate, related research studies are incorporated by reference.

Alignment

The CSDE commissioned an independent alignment study (Assessment and Evaluation Concepts, Inc., 2006) to examine the relationship between the content of the checklists and the curriculum standards on which they were based. The study employed the methodology developed by Webb (1997, 2005) to rate items according to the following dimensions:

- Categorical concurrence

- Depth of knowledge

- Range of knowledge

- Balance of representation

The results of the alignment study indicated strong agreement between the checklists and the related curriculum standards. Most of the categories and domains were found to be closely aligned. The study's conclusions were accepted under the peer review process for NCLB by the U.S. Department of Education. The full text of the report (Assessment and Evaluation Concepts, Inc., 2006) is available online.

Content Validity

Evidence to support the validity of the content incorporated in the checklists comes from two sources. The first source is derived from the extensive efforts made by the CSDE to base the procedures used in the development of the checklists on the state's curriculum standards. These procedures required advisory committee members, consultants, and contractors to continually monitor the relationship of checklist items to the associated content standards. Further, the resulting structure of the checklist (i.e., content standards, performance standards, expected performances) closely reflects the underlying curriculum.

The second source of validity support is the independent alignment study discussed earlier (Assessment and Evaluation Concepts, Inc., 2006). This detailed examination of each item on each checklist provided considerable evidence that the content of the checklists was appropriate for the purposes of the instruments. The study concluded, "With few exceptions, the Skills Checklist is capturing the alignment with the content standards very well" (p. 25).

Additional Validity Evidence

Plans have been established to collect other evidence to support the validity of the checklists. The CSDE collected criterion-related evidence during the 2007–2009 academic years by examining the degree to which students participating in the checklist experienced greater inclusion in general education settings. Also, the CSDE is increasingly focusing on collecting consequential evidence. A multiple-state collaborative operating under an enhanced assessment grant from the U.S. Department of Education will consider avenues to gather consequential evidence of the checklists' validity. The CSDE has initiated plans to use focus groups to examine such areas as students' academic progress, students' access to the general education curriculum, teachers' access to the general education curriculum, and students' performance in nonacademic, real-life situations.

Reliability

Indicators of reliability in the form of internal consistency (alpha) estimates for students participating in the checklist are typically high. In all applications meeting minimum student population size ($n \geq 40$), estimates were .96–.99 for each measured domain. Disaggregating by race, gender, and income still yielded estimates of .93 or higher. Estimates at the content strand level were found to be .93 or higher. It seems clear that the method by which the checklists were administered contributed to these results. Discussions are ongoing regarding the use of more interpretable techniques to examine the reliability of the scores produced by the checklists.

SUMMARY

The CMT/CAPT Skills Checklist was developed to allow greater participation in statewide assessment by those Connecticut students who are significantly cognitively impaired. This purpose has been fulfilled: More than 2,000 students who previously would have been excluded were assessed in 2006. However, the work of creating and using the Skills Checklist is still in its early stages. Although the accomplishments to date in developing a workable instrument have been considerable, the need for future research and effort to improve the Skills Checklist as an educational assessment is just as critical. The CSDE will continue its developmental efforts in areas such as teacher training, score interpretability, collection of validity evidence, and improvement of the instrument's psychometric properties. Collaboration with similar research efforts at the National Alternate Assessment Center and in other states will increase the promise of future advances. Together, these research and development activities indicate Connecticut's high level of commitment to providing a valuable assessment tool to those students most in need.

REFERENCES

Assessment and Evaluation Concepts, Inc. (2006, March). *Alignment analysis of Connecticut's language arts and mathematics standards and the alternate assessment checklists summary report.* Retrieved February 23, 2009, from http://www.csde.state.ct.us/public/cedar/assessment/checklist/index.htm

Cizek, G.J., Bunch, M.B., & Koons, H. (2004). Setting performance standards: Contemporary methods. *Educational Measurement: Issues and Practice, 23*(4), 31–50.

Connecticut State Department of Education. (2000). *CMT/CAPT skills checklist.* Hartford, CT: Author.

Connecticut State Department of Education. (2006a, September). *CMT/CAPT skills checklist: Second generation.* Hartford, CT: Author.

Connecticut State Department of Education. (2006b, September). *CMT/CAPT skills checklist: Second generation technical manual.* Hartford, CT: Author.

Connecticut State Department of Education. (2006c, October). *CMT/CAPT skills checklist second generation: Teacher handbook.* Hartford, CT: Author.

Jaeger, R.M. (1995). Setting standards for complex performances: An iterative, judgmental policy-capturing strategy. *Educational Measurement: Issues and Practice, 14*(4), 16–20.

No Child Left Behind Act of 2001, PL 107-110, 115 Stat. 1425, 20 U.S.C. §§ 6301 *et seq.*

Plake, B.S., Hambleton, R.K., & Jaeger, R.M. (1997). A new standard setting method for performance assessments: The dominant profile judgment method and some field test results. *Educational and Psychological Measurement, 57,* 400–411.

Webb, N.L. (1997). *Criteria for alignment of expectations and assessments in mathematics and science education* (Council of Chief State School Officers and National Institute for Science Education Research Monograph No. 6). Madison: University of Wisconsin, Wisconsin Center for Educational Research.

Webb, N.L. (2005). *Web alignment tool (WAT) training manual.* Washington, DC & Madison: Council of Chief State School Officers & the Wisconsin Center for Educational Research.

CHAPTER 10

Georgia Alternate Assessment

A Portfolio Assessment for Students with Significant Cognitive Disabilities

MELISSA FINCHER AND CLAUDIA FLOWERS

Georgia, like other states, must ensure that all students have access to the general curriculum that encompasses challenging academic standards. The Georgia Alternate Assessment (GAA) was designed to assess the academic performance of students who traditionally had been exempted from statewide assessment systems. Under the No Child Left Behind Act (NCLB) of 2001 (PL 107-110) and the Individuals with Disabilities Education Improvement Act (IDEA) of 2004 (PL 108-446), Georgia educators, the Georgia Department of Education (GaDOE), its contractors, and the Georgia technical advisory committee designed, developed, and implemented the GAA.

In working through the design phase, the GAA developers decided a portfolio assessment would work best. There were several rationales for the selection of the portfolio format. First, individualized educational program (IEP) teams, which include students' teachers, are in the best position to evaluate which challenging academic content each student has the greatest opportunity to learn. Teachers, furthermore, have the best knowledge about how each student can demonstrate what he or she knows or can do. Finally, student portfolios allow for ongoing documentation of each student's skills, merge instructional and assessment activities, allow each student to demonstrate strengths, knowledge, skills, and independence, and provide meaningful ways to review student progress with parents.

The purpose of this chapter is to describe the GAA and the challenges that are encountered in establishing and documenting the technical quality of such an alternate assessment based on alternate achievement standards (AA-AAS). In the description of the GAA, we provide the values and rationale for many of the decisions used to develop, implement, score, and report outcomes from the assessment.

DESCRIPTION OF THE GEORGIA ALTERNATE ASSESSMENT

Before designing the GAA, a statement of core beliefs and guiding philosophy was developed.

Core Belief and Guiding Philosophy

All students, including students with significant cognitive disabilities, can learn when given access to instruction predicated on the state curriculum. Starting with this core belief, three GaDOE agency divisions, the Exceptional Students Division, the Curriculum and Instructional Services Division, and the Testing Division, partnered to design instructional resources, professional learning and support opportunities, and assessment practices for teachers and students. The inclusion of all three agency divisions was considered critical in designing an assessment system that would best serve the needs of the students and provide assessment scores to reflect what students with significant cognitive disabilities know and can do in the general education curriculum.

To help facilitate the meetings of the three state agency divisions, alternate assessment national experts were asked to guide the GaDOE discussion in the development of the GAA. The National Center for Educational Outcomes and the Southeast Regional Resource Center provided experts to facilitate communication in meetings of the three agency divisions. The purpose of these meetings was to ensure that all three divisions had a common understanding regarding inclusion of students with significant disabilities in the curriculum, AA-AAS, and use of the same language/terminology. These meetings solidified the commitment of the three divisions to ensure that students with significant cognitive disabilities had the opportunity to learn the academic content and skills embedded in the state curriculum. The GaDOE team then worked with stakeholders to develop a curriculum access methodology and an alternate assessment designed to measure student achievement of grade-level content and skills.

Selection of Portfolio Assessment Format

The GAA is a portfolio of student work that documents, measures, and reflects student performance and progress in standards-based knowledge and skills over time. The portfolio contains data sheets of academic skills, video clips and/or captioned photos of student performance, audiotapes of student responses, examples of student performance on paper-and-pencil tasks, and additional documentation of student achievement/progress.

The student portfolio is the database for documentation of reported achievement on the Georgia curriculum standards on which the students are assessed. Just as a regular assessment is a sampling of student achievement, so is the GAA. For students without disabilities, other assessments are administered to monitor progress and learning, and teachers keep samples of their students' work for assigning grades and making reports to the parents. The student portfolio serves the same purpose for students with significant cognitive disabilities who cannot participate in the regular assessment program.

DEVELOPMENT OF THE GEORGIA ALTERNATE ASSESSMENT BLUEPRINTS

NCLB and IDEA require that students with significant cognitive disabilities be assessed in the same content areas as their peers. The GAA blueprint was developed so that students would be assessed on the same curricula used in general education classrooms, *not* on alternate curricula. However, according to federal legislation, students may be assessed on alternate achievement standards that are linked to the same curricular standards at each student's grade level. Furthermore, the depth and breadth of the grade-level content standards can be reduced for AA-AAS. It was important that the reduction of the grade-level content standards be based on sound rationale that considered the importance of the curriculum and, at the same time, considered the needs of the students. The GAA assesses the content areas of English/language arts (ELA), mathematics, science, and social studies.

Content experts and special educators worked together to determine the targeted grade-level content standards for the GAA. For ELA, the reading comprehension standard was considered a *power standard* on which every student at every grade should be assessed. The reading comprehension standard was recommended as a required standard for the first of two entries for ELA. To allow some flexibility in the selection of content, it was recommended that, for each student, educators be allowed to choose a second communication standard, which could be the writing standard or the listening/speaking/viewing standard. Choice of a communication standard should be predicated on student characteristics and needs.

For mathematics, the curriculum builds students' understanding of and facility in working with numbers, numeration, and operations across grade levels. Numbers and Operations was recommended as the required strand for the first of two mathematics entries in Grades K–8.

Algebra was recommended as the required strand for Grade 11. For the second entry in math, the committee recommended a choice from several strands, which vary by grade and reflect the curriculum. Again, the committee felt strongly that teachers, who know their students' instructional needs best, should be allowed to choose appropriate strands/standards based on each student's characteristics, to allow more focused customization of instruction and assessment.

For science, the committee recommended that the content standards be paired with the Characteristics of Science standards (which represent scientific thought processes). Given that the content standards consider the content and Characteristics of Science corequisites that should be taught in conjunction with each other, this choice mirrors general education instruction and assessments.

Portfolio Entries

ELA and mathematics each require a portfolio entry that is aligned with a required content standard (i.e., reading and numbers) and an entry that is aligned with a teacher-selected content standard. Each entry consists of both primary (i.e., produced by the student) and secondary (i.e., documenting, relating, charting, or interpreting the student's performance on similar instructional tasks) evidence at two data collection points during the academic year. The intent of the two collection periods is to demonstrate academic progress within a content area. An illustration of a portfolio entry is shown in Figure 10.1. For science and social studies, only one entry is required; each entry must have two data collection periods and be aligned with the selected content standards.

An example of a math entry for Collection Period 1 is provided in Figure 10.2. This activity is only part of the student's permanent product.

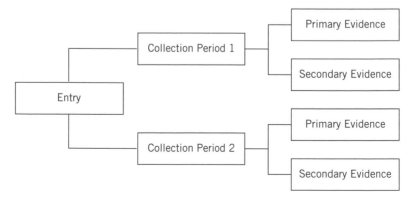

Figure 10.1. Illustration of the portfolio entry. (From Georgia Department of Education. [2006]. *School and test system coordinator's manual: Georgia Alternate Assessment* [p. 5]. Atlanta: Author; reprinted by permission.)

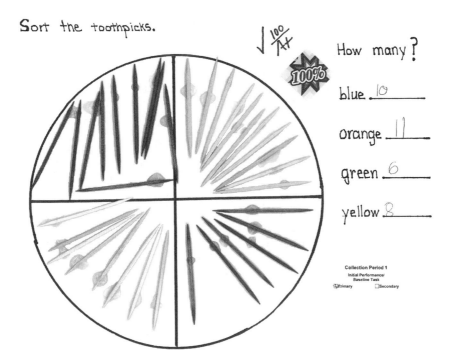

Sort the toothpicks.

√ 100/A+

100%

How many?

blue _10_

orange _11_

green _6_

yellow _8_

Collection Period 1
Initial Performance/
Baseline Task
☑Primary   ☐Secondary

Figure 10.2. Student work sample—permanent product. (From Georgia Department of Education. [2007]. *Examiner's manual: Georgia Alternate Assessment* [p. 19]. Atlanta: Author; reprinted by permission.)

Teachers and administrators are required to organize the portfolio binders using procedures described in the *Examiner's Manual.* The first divider contains student information, a validation form, and a release to use the student portfolio for training. The validation form is signed both by the person submitting the portfolio and by the building administrator, and it states that the student's work is authentic. The remaining dividers contain the academic entries by content area. An illustration of the organization for a K–2 portfolio is shown in Figure 10.3.

Participation Guidelines

IEP teams are responsible for determining the assessment program in which each student will participate. To assist IEP teams in making decisions about students' participation in the GAA, a decision tree was designed and is summarized in Figure 10.4. The criteria outlined were developed by a committee of general and special educators. Future studies are planned that will examine the accuracy of IEP teams' decisions and the characteristics of students beyond their disability categories.

Divider 1: Student information, validation form, and release to use student portfolio for training

Divider 2: English/language arts: Two standards are assessed

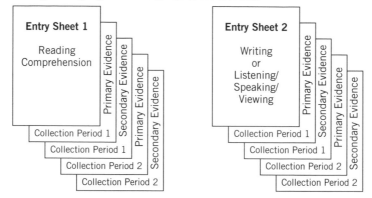

Divider 3: Mathematics: Two standards are assessed

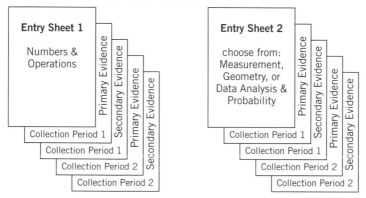

Figure 10.3.   Illustration of the organization of a K–2 portfolio. (From Georgia Department of Education. [2006]. *Examiner's manual: Georgia Alternate Assessment* [p. 21]. Atlanta: Author; reprinted by permission.)

Scoring Dimensions

All portfolios are scored on four dimensions. The Fidelity to Standard dimension, which assesses the degree to which a student's work is aligned with the student's grade-level standards, is scored on a three-point scale. This dimension ensures that all portfolios are aligned with the appropriate grade-level content standards—an essential requirement for alternate assessments. The second scoring dimension is Context. Context, which assesses the degree to which the student's work exhibits the use of grade-appropriate materials in a real-world or natural applica-

PARTICIPATION GUIDELINES FOR THE GAA

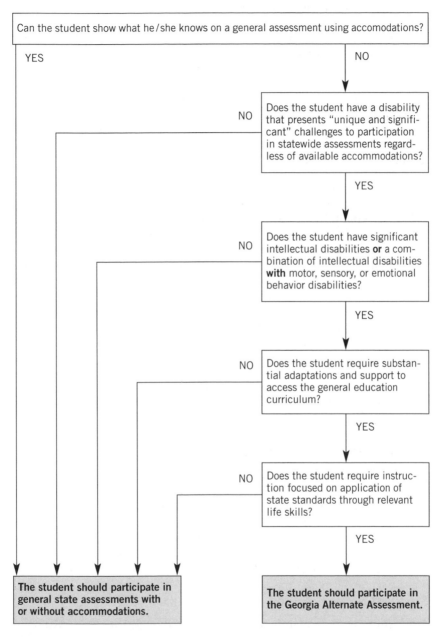

Figure 10.4. Participation guidelines for the Georgia Alternate Assessment (GAA). (From Georgia Department of Education. [2006]. *Examiner's manual: Georgia Alternate Assessment* [p. 5]. Atlanta: Author; reprinted by permission.)

tion, is scored on a four-point scale. The third dimension is Achievement/Progress, which assesses the student's increase in skill proficiency across the two collection periods and is scored on a four-point scale. The final dimension is Generalization, which assesses the student's opportunity to apply the learned skill in other settings and with various individuals other than teachers or paraprofessionals; this dimension is scored on a four-point scale. Generalization is scored only once per portfolio and considers all scorable entries in the portfolio; the other dimensions are scored for each academic content area entry (i.e., for each ELA entry, each mathematics entry, the science entry, and the social studies entry).

Rangefinding and Scoring

A Rangefinding Committee, which consisted of special and general education teachers, reviewed the scoring rubric and preliminary scoring rules. The committee reviewed, discussed, and scored several portfolios from Grades K, 1, 2, 6, and 11 to ensure consistent scoring across grade bands. The committee was then divided into two groups to score additional portfolios: Group 1 scored entries for Grades K–5, and group 2 scored entries for Grades 6–8 and 11. Representatives from the GaDOE Testing, Curriculum, and Exceptional Students Divisions served in an advisory capacity but were not voting members of the committee.

In addition to scoring entries, the Rangefinding Committee made scoring decision rules and identified illustrative examples for the scoring guide at all score points in each dimension (Fidelity to Standard, Context, Achievement/Progress, and Generalization). The Rangefinding Committee scored entries that were used to construct the scoring guides (containing annotated entries at each score point) and training and qualifying sets.

Development of Proficiency-Level Definitions

Before setting standards, the test development contractor worked with a committee of general and special educators to create preliminary definitions of proficiency levels. Three proficiency levels, Extending Progress (advanced), Established Progress (proficient), and Emerging Progress (basic), were developed and defined. The definitions, which are grounded in the rubric, describe what students at each proficiency level are expected to know or be able to do; they are displayed in Figure 10.5.

Standard-Setting Method

A portfolio-pattern standard-setting method was used to create cut scores for the three performance standards (Emerging Progress, Established Progress, and Extending Progress). This standard-setting procedure was chosen because the object evaluated for standard-setting pur-

Extending Progress (Advanced)
Based on evidence in the portfolio, the student demonstrates an increased under-standing of fundamental skills and knowledge aligned to grade-appropriate ELA, math-ematics, science, or social studies standards. He/she is working on academic content at an entry level or a level that approaches basic grade-level expectations. The stu-dent's progress extends toward the achievement of grade-level standards. The student performs meaningful tasks using grade-appropriate materials. Generalization across settings and interactions is evidenced in the portfolio.

Established Progress (Proficient)
Based on evidence in the portfolio, the student demonstrates an understanding of fundamental skills and knowledge aligned to grade-appropriate ELA, mathematics, science, or social studies standards. He/she is working on and showing progress in ac-ademic content at an access/entry level. The student performs meaningful tasks using grade-appropriate materials. Generalization across settings and/or interactions is evi-denced in the portfolio.

Emerging Progress (Basic)
Based on evidence in the portfolio, the student is beginning to demonstrate an under-standing of fundamental skills and knowledge aligned to grade-appropriate ELA, math-ematics, science, or social studies standards. The student work may not address aca-demic content or addresses it at an access level. The student performs tasks using materials that may or may not be grade appropriate. Generalization across settings and/or interactions is limited in the portfolio.

Figure 10.5. Definitions for the stages of progress. (From Georgia Department of Educa-tion. [2006]. *Score interpretation guide: Georgia Alternate Assessment* [p. 10]. Atlanta: Author; reprinted by permission.) (*Key: ELA,* English/language arts.)

poses was a complete "body of work" for an individual student, with no two content area portfolio entries being exactly alike. The entries were not alike in terms of the content standards addressed, the type of evi-dence used to demonstrate proficiency of those objectives, or the intrin-sic nature of the scoring rubric components.

The design associated with the recommended portfolio-pattern meth-odology combined critical aspects of the Body of Work (BoW; Kingston, Kahl, Sweeney, & Bay, 2001) and the Massachusetts (Wiener, 2002) mod-els. The BoW model requires participants to evaluate prescored portfo-lios of student work and assign them to performance categories while blinded to the assigned scores. The Massachusetts model uses an analyti-cal rubric transforming individual-strand raw scores into specific perform-ance levels. These strands are combinations of scores obtained using the scoring rubric for the alternate assessment. How each strand's score points are achieved directly affects the analytical rubric (i.e., performance-level designation). The GAA rubric consists of four discrete dimensions: Fi-delity to Standard, Context, Achievement/Progress, and Generalization.

To mesh the two models (BoW and Massachusetts), the test contrac-tor combined key procedural aspects of the BoW (e.g., participants re-viewing portfolios while blinded to the rubric scores, yet reporting information as performance-level designations) and the Massachusetts model (e.g., using an analytical rubric to transform individual-strand raw scores into specific performance levels). Once intense training on the scoring rubric was complete, each participant made proficiency classifications for each possible rubric score pattern, of which there were 192 possible patterns. A tabulation of each pattern matrix cell was made across participants by all content areas. Participants then were asked to assign performance levels by reviewing students' portfolios. The test contractor matched the participants' ratings with the rubric scores given by scorers. Participants then discussed their assignment of performance levels in relation to assigned rubric scores and noted the cases in which they agreed and disagreed with others.

This combined procedure (portfolio pattern) was recommended because of the nature of the GAA portfolios and the intrinsic nature of the scoring rubric dimensions. It had the added benefits of a holistic review of student work by the committee and a direct tie to the analytic rubric as applied to performance levels. This procedure, like the BoW, included advance preparation, training (practice), initial review (Vote 1), analysis, discussion, subsequent review (Vote 2), and recommendation of the final cut. Each content area committee worked by grade band (i.e., K–2, 3–5, 6–8, and 11) to recommend standards. Finally, an articulation committee met on the last day of the standard-setting event. Whereas the initial standard-setting process had involved setting standards independently within each grade band and content area, the articulation committee considered the standards collectively across all grades and content areas. In evaluating the standards, the articulation committee considered factors such as 1) consistency across grade bands and content areas, 2) expectations described in the state curriculum and alternate achievement standards, and 3) relevant policy and/or accountability implications.

Student Reporting

GaDOE reviewed several states' student reports to determine the kinds of information that would be useful to the Georgia students, parents, and administrators. The GaDOE asked participants in a development committee meeting to review the examples of student reports and answer the following questions: 1) What alternate assessment result data do you think will be most important to you? 2) Of the data in the report samples presented today, what would you like to incorporate into GAA reporting? 3) Do you have any other comments?

The participants overwhelmingly listed the following as most important: 1) scores for each dimension listing total points possible, 2) graphic representation of each student's performance, 3) simple language defining each student's performance, 4) suggestions for helping each student improve his or her performance, and 5) explanation of nonscorable entries.

EVIDENCE OF TECHNICAL QUALITY

The challenge in providing evidence of technical quality is making sense of the complex performances captured in students' portfolio entries, which include videos, student artifacts, and narratives describing each student's progress. Many (e.g., Linn, 1993, 1994; Mehrens, 1992) blamed the waning of the performance assessment movement of the 1980s and 1990s on the lack of evidence of these assessments' technical quality. Previous experiences with performance-based assessments illustrated some of the problems with providing evidence of technical quality (Linn, Baker, & Dunbar, 1991). The GAA is not a test in the traditional sense; varied tasks that target different academic content are submitted for each student. Many of the traditional sources of evidence for documenting the reliability and validity of outcomes are not appropriate for the GAA.

In the remainder of this chapter, we present preliminary descriptive statistics, evidence of reliability and validity, and future plans for documenting technical quality.

First-Year Student Results

The following results are based on the GAA's first year of administration. A total of 10,647 portfolios were submitted across all grades during the 2006–2007 academic year. Summary statistics for each of the four scoring dimensions in the four content areas are reported in Table 10.1.

The stages of progress across all grade levels are reported in Table 10.2. Between 4.8% (math) and 9.8% (social studies) of the portfolios were

Table 10.1. Scores for the dimensions of the Georgia Alternate Assessment for all grade levels

Subject	Scoring dimension	1 (%)	2 (%)	3 (%)	4 (%)	Mean	Standard deviation
English/ language arts (N = 9952)	Fidelity to Standard	7.6	66.2	26.1	N/A	2.19	.55
	Context	2.0	14.3	65.4	18.3	3.00	.64
	Achievement/Progress	12.3	39.4	45.5	2.8	2.39	.73
Math (N = 10012)	Fidelity to Standard	6.3	72.4	21.3	N/A	2.15	.50
	Context	1.6	12.1	71.1	15.2	3.00	.58
	Achievement/Progress	11.5	39.5	46.3	2.8	2.40	.73
Science (N = 7359)	Fidelity to Standard	0.1	79.3	20.6	N/A	2.20	.41
	Context	4.5	3.8	81.3	10.5	2.98	.57
	Achievement/Progress	12.4	44.9	40.7	2.0	2.32	.71
Social studies (N = 7326)	Fidelity to Standard	0.2	83.6	16.1	N/A	2.16	.37
	Context	1.5	4.9	83.4	10.2	3.02	.46
	Achievement/Progress	13.8	46.3	37.6	2.3	2.28	.72
All subjects (N = 10237)	Generalization	0.6	49.7	15.1	34.6	2.84	.92

Table 10.2. Stages of progress across all grade levels

Stage of progress	English/ language arts ($N = 10,647$)	Math ($N = 10,502$)	Science ($N = 8,126$)	Social studies ($N = 8,123$)
Not scorable	5.4	4.8	9.4	9.8
Emerging Progress	14.4	13.3	14.7	13.7
Established Progress	50.0	49.0	52.4	41.4
Extending Progress	30.2	32.8	23.5	35.1

nonscorable, suggesting that some teachers needed additional professional development. Approximately 77% (social studies) to 83% (science) of the students met proficiency levels. These percentages of proficiency were similar to those reported for the general education assessment.

Table 10.3 summarizes the correlation coefficients for the scoring dimensions and the stages of progress for each content area. The scoring dimension of progress had the largest positive correlation across all content areas, ranging from .77 to .78. The three other dimensions had small (.22) to moderate (.55) relationships to the stages of progress.

Reliability Evidence

Reliability was considered early in the development of the GAA. Consideration of replication, both structural and conceptual, was designed into the process. Two entries each are required for ELA and math, and all entries in these areas require primary and secondary evidence. Pretests and posttests of students' performance are required for each entry. Two trained readers are used to independently score at least 15% of the GAA on the four dimensions. It was anticipated that the test administrators would be the most significant source of errors. The GaDOE invested in educator training in the areas of curriculum access, design of aligned instructional tasks, and documentation of student achievement and progress. The following sections provide evidence gathered during the first year of the GAA implementation.

Rater Agreement

All GAA portfolios were scored by trained readers. A minimum of 15% of all portfolios were rated by second readers. Rater agreement and kappa values across all grade levels are reported in Table 10.3. For ELA and math, there are two entries, and agreement was calculated for each entry. Values for Fidelity to Standard and Context were high, ranging from 85% to 91% for exact agreement. Achievement/Progress tended to

Table 10.3. Correlation coefficients between the content area stages of progress scores and the four scoring dimensions

Content area	Fidelity	Progress	Context	Generalization
English/language arts	.54	.77	.55	.45
Math	.54	.78	.50	.45
Science	.25	.77	.45	.41
Social studies	.30	.78	.36	.38

Note: Sample sizes ranged between 7,326 (social studies) and 10,012 (math).

have a lower percent agreement than the other two dimensions. Generalization was calculated for the entire portfolio: the exact agreement for generalization was 85.2%, with a kappa value of .76 (see Table 10.4).

Correlation Between Entries

The correlations between the first and second entry scores for each dimension in ELA and math were calculated to examine the stability of scores. For ELA, the following correlations were calculated for the first and second entries: .46 for Fidelity to Standard, .30 for Context, and .46 for Achievement/Progress. For math, the correlation coefficients were .47 for Fidelity to Standard, .26 for Context, and .51 for Achievement/Progress. In all cases, the entries measured different strands of ELA (e.g., reading and writing), which may account for lower correlation coefficients.

Generalizability Study

The generalizability study examined two basic questions: 1) What components of the GAA are associated with score variance? and 2) What is the dependability, as defined in generalizability theory, of the GAA? Because the data for the generalizability study were from an operational assessment, a People crossed with Items nested within Raters (p × (i:r)) model was estimated. The following variance components were estimated: 1) P—person variance, 2) R—rater variance, 3) I:R—item × rater variance, 4) person × rater interaction variance, and 5) RI:R—person × item interaction nested in rater variance.

The results suggested that little variance was associated with raters or rater × person interactions. The g-coefficients ranged from .57 to .77, with a mean of .69 for a single entry scored twice across four dimensions. The signal-to-noise ratios ranged from 1.31 to 3.39, with a mean of 2.27. All the estimates suggested adequate reliability of GAA scores.

Validity Evidence

The first and most basic step for documenting technical quality is thinking clearly about the content of the assessment (Lissitz & Samuelsen,

Table 10.4.   Rater exact agreement and kappa across all grade levels

	English/ language arts Entry 1	English/ language arts Entry 2	Math Entry 1	Math Entry 2	Science	Social studies
Fidelity to Standard						
Exact	86.4	84.7	88.4	88.3	88.2	89.8
Kappa	.71	.69	.70	.73	.76	.79
Context						
Exact	88.0	86.3	88.9	89.6	90.0	91.1
Kappa	.76	.73	.75	.76	.67	.77
Achievement/ Progress						
Exact	75.1	74.4	73.3	72.7	76.8	76.0
Kappa	.64	.64	.61	.61	.66	.66

2007). Teachers are the creators of the GAA. To ensure that the GAA would comprise academic content linked to grade-level content standards, and to create a high-quality assessment of student learning, 2 years of extensive professional development were dedicated to evaluating the alignment of the GAA with grade-level content standards.

Teachers were trained on using a four-step process for designing instruction and assessment activities that were aligned with grade-level content standards. Furthermore, GAA content specifications, including which academic standards to include and procedures and requirements for including multiple pieces of student evidence aligned with the content standards, were provided. The Fidelity to Standard dimension was emphasized in all training sessions.

Results from the first year of administration suggested that the teacher training was effective. Between 92% (ELA) and 99.8% (science) of the portfolios were scored at Level 2 or 3 for Fidelity to Standard. An alignment study was conducted to determine the relationship between the GAA and grade-level content standards. Results indicated that teachers are developing academic activities that content experts rated as aligned to content standards.

Interrelationships Among the Scoring Dimensions Across Academic Areas

An exploratory factor analysis was conducted to examine the internal structure of the scoring dimensions across all content areas. Only students in Grades 3–8 and 11 ($N = 7,002$) who had participated in all four content areas were included in this analysis. Different extraction methods (e.g., principal axis factoring) and rotation methods were used, all producing similar results. The following results were based on a principal axis factoring extraction method and a varimax rotation. The decrease in eigenvalues, as evident in the scree plot, leveled off at four factors with an accumulative percentage of variance of 59.7%. Pattern coefficients greater than or equal to .42 were used to determine the relationships among the items and factors. The communalities for each of the dimensions ranged from .446 (generalization) to .725 (ELA context).

Table 10.5 shows the component matrix coefficients. For the first factor, the scoring dimension of Achievement/Progress for all four content areas had high coefficients. The second factor consisted of the scoring dimension of Fidelity to Standard across all four content areas. There was one scoring dimension, ELA Fidelity to Standard, which also had a high coefficient for factor 4. The third factor consisted of the scoring dimension of Context for three of the four content areas and the Generalization scoring dimension. The final factor had high coefficients for only 2 of the 13 different academic area scoring dimensions: ELA Context and ELA Fidelity to Standard. These results suggested that the individual scoring dimensions tended to have higher interrelationships than the different scoring dimensions within content areas.

Examining Bias

Questions about curriculum accessibility for students with the most severe/profound intellectual disabilities were constantly raised during all training sessions. In designing curriculum access protocols and procedures, the Division for Exceptional Students included adaptations for three levels of students, including adaptations for students with the most profound disabilities. Also, the teachers on special assignment

Table 10.5. Rotated component matrix coefficients

Scoring dimensions	Factor 1	Factor 2	Factor 3	Factor 4
Achievement/Progress—Science	.80			
Achievement/Progress—Social studies	.78			
Achievement/Progress—Math	.74			
Achievement/Progress—English/language arts	.65			
Fidelity to the Standard—Science		.80		
Fidelity to the Standard—Social studies		.78		
Fidelity to the Standard—Math		.71		
Fidelity to the Standard—English/language arts		.56		.63
Context—Social studies			.68	
Context—Science			.65	
Generalization			.61	
Context—Math			.54	
Context— English/language arts				.81

Note: Coefficients less that .52 were suppressed.

visited multiple Georgia classrooms and videotaped students at all levels accessing the curriculum through appropriately adapted instructional tasks aligned with the state's academic content standards. These two approaches helped teachers design and implement aligned instructional tasks for the small number of students with the most profound disabilities.

To empirically examine potential bias, data were captured that allowed rubric scores to be disaggregated by degree of intellectual disability (mild, moderate, severe, and profound), as coded by teachers on the student demographic forms. Rubric scores by dimension were disaggregated and suggested that the highest rubric scores were attainable by students identified as having profound intellectual disabilities. Although the frequency of student evidence rated at the highest rubric score point decreased as disability level increased, the rubric does not appear to preclude any student from achieving the highest score point possible. Nevertheless, this will need to be monitored over time to ensure that all students have maximum opportunity both in terms of access to the curriculum and the assessment.

Another source of potential bias was the increasing complexity of the academic content standards as grade levels increase. The middle and high school standards frequently contain complex concepts representing more abstract thinking and highly specific content. The question of whether students enrolled in the upper grade levels would be able to achieve the highest score points, particularly on the Fidelity to Standard dimension, was raised. Data were analyzed by grade level and suggested that although the highest score point is achievable at all grade levels, it seems to be more difficult to achieve in the higher grades in the Fidelity to Standard dimension. This also will need to be monitored over time, and additional professional development surrounding the design of instructional tasks aligned with upper-grade-level academic standards may be warranted.

Future Studies

Studies that have been planned for the future are discussed in the following sections.

Decision Consistency and Accuracy

A study of decision consistency and accuracy was scheduled for the second year of implementation. Teachers will be asked to classify each of their students into one of the performance categories (i.e., Emerging, Established, and Extending Progress). A discriminate analysis will be used to examine the degree to which teachers' classifications correspond to the students' actual proficiency levels based on test scores.

Impact Study

An impact evaluation was scheduled for the third year of implementation. A questionnaire will be designed that examines the intended and unintended or unwanted consequences of the implementation of the GAA. Because the unintended consequences are not known, assistance from the National Alternate Assessment Center will help determine the content of the questionnaire.

The GAA is not scaled or equated as large-scale assessments typically are. Future studies will examine the comparability of the scoring process over time. A random sample of approximately 30 portfolios will be reevaluated. Teachers who were responsible for creating the portfolios will be asked, 1) Do all the entries in the portfolio reflect the performance of the student? and 2) If you could remove or replace any entries, which ones would they be? The numbers and percentages of changes will be analyzed, and the portfolios will be divided into two groups: portfolios with changes and portfolios without changes. The portfolios will be rescored, and the new scores will be compared with the original scores.

To help ensure comparability of scoring across years, scoring decisions will be documented each year, with the previous year's decisions serving as the basis of the scoring process for each subsequent year.

Alignment Study

Alignment was a major consideration in the design of the GAA. To provide an external evaluation of the GAA's alignment with grade-level content standards, an alignment study was scheduled for the second year of implementation. Using the Links for Academic Learning, an alignment methodology specifically designed for alternate assessments, evidence will be collected regarding content centrality, performance centrality, categorical concurrence, range of knowledge, balance of representation, and other measures of alignment for the GAA.

SUMMARY

Designing and documenting evaluations of technical quality of the GAA is an ongoing, labor-intensive process. Not all the validity evidence can be gathered in 1 year, so decision makers must prioritize across multiple years. Documenting the GAA's technical quality will require innovative thinking and additional development of theory about the connections among student characteristics and how students develop domain proficiency. We hope that broader conceptual underpinnings with additional methods and methodologies will be developed. The ultimate goal is for the GAA to stand up to criticism and for the accumulated evidence to be evaluated in ways that improve the educational experiences of students with significant cognitive disabilities.

REFERENCES

Georgia Department of Education. (2006). *School and system test coordinator's manual: Georgia Alternate Assessment.* Atlanta: Author.

Georgia Department of Education. (2006). *Score interpretation guide: Georgia Alternate Assessment.* Atlanta: Author.

Georgia Department of Education. (2007). *Examiner's manual: Georgia Alternate Assessment.* Atlanta: Author.

Individuals with Disabilities Education Improvement Act (IDEA) of 2004, PL 108-446, 20 U.S.C. §§ 1400 *et seq.*

Kingston, N., Kahl, S.R., Sweeney, K., & Bay, L. (2001). Setting performance standards using the body of work method. In G.J. Cizek (Ed.), *Setting performance standards: Concepts, methods, and perspectives.* Mahwah, NJ: Lawrence Erlbaum Associates.

Linn, R.L. (1993). Educational assessment: Expanded expectations and challenges. *Educational Analysis and Policy Archives, 15*(1), 1–16.

Linn, R.L. (1994). Performance assessment: Policy promises and technical measurement standards. *Educational Researcher, 23*(9), 4–14.

Linn, R.L., Baker, E.L., & Dunbar, S.B. (1991). Complex, performance-based assessment: Expectations and validation criteria. *Educational Researcher, 20*(8), 15–21.

Lissitz, R.W., & Samuelsen, K. (2007). A suggested change in terminology and emphasis regarding validity and education. *Educational Researcher, 36*(8), 437–448.

Mehrens, W.A. (1992). Using performance assessment for accountability purposes. *Educational Measurement: Issues and Practice, 11*(1), 3–9, 20.

No Child Left Behind Act of 2001, PL 107-110, 115 Stat. 1425, 20 U.S.C. §§ 6301 *et seq.*

Wiener, D. (2002). *Massachusetts: One state's approach to setting performance levels on the alternate assessment* (Synthesis Rep. No. 48). Minneapolis: University of Minnesota, National Center on Educational Outcomes.

CHAPTER 11

The Alternate Maryland School Assessment

SHARON E. HALL, MARTIN D. KEHE, AND WILLIAM D. SCHAFER

The Alternate Maryland School Assessment (Alt-MSA) is Maryland's response to the federal No Child Left Behind Act (NCLB) of 2001 (PL 107-110), which requires an assessment of reading, mathematics, and science for students with significant cognitive disabilities. The Alt-MSA, implemented in the 2003–2004 school year, was a natural outgrowth of Maryland's previous testing program for students with significant cognitive disabilities, the Independence Mastery Assessment Program (IMAP). IMAP had been administered since the late 1990s and was a program evaluation tool intent on ensuring that schools were providing students with opportunities to learn, although academic content was not the focus. With the advent of NCLB, the Maryland State Department of Education (MSDE) staff knew that the ground originally broken by IMAP must be built upon to now create an academic assessment that would provide student-level performance results in reading, mathematics, and science.

The development of the Alternate Maryland School Assessment (Alt-MSA) described in this chapter was completed while Sharon Hall was Section Chief of Special Education and Martin Kehe was Chief of the Assessment Branch at the Maryland State Department of Education (MSDE). William D. Schafer served throughout that period as a consultant.

Portions of this project were funded by the MSDE under a contract to the Maryland Assessment Research Center for Education Success (MARCES).

The opinions expressed do not necessarily reflect those of MSDE or MARCES.

The views expressed in this chapter by Sharon E. Hall, an employee of the U.S. Department of Education at the writing of this chapter, are solely her own and do not reflect any official policy or position of the U.S. Department of Education, or the United States Government.

This chapter is divided into three parts. The first part presents a description and rationale of the test design, discusses important features of the Alt-MSA, and provides an understanding of the goals that motivated Maryland's efforts. The second part discusses some of the challenges, from both policy and operational perspectives, that the state faced when creating and implementing the Alt-MSA. Actions taken to address these challenges are presented within two major frameworks: 1) NCLB mandates, regulations, and the resulting standards and assessment peer review guidance, and 2) change and constructivist learning theories. Finally, as made clear in this chapter, there are unique aspects of the Alt-MSA, as an assessment process rather than a test, that pose some unique challenges to the technical evaluation of its adequacy. Maryland's efforts to document the success of this assessment are discussed in the third part of this chapter.

DESCRIPTION OF THE ALTERNATE MARYLAND SCHOOL ASSESSMENT

As a state, Maryland has a long tradition of assessment-driven instruction (Schafer & Moody, 2004). This approach to assessment implies that the domain of the assessment can serve as a description of what is expected of instruction for teachers, curriculum writers, and even students. The state expresses its assessment-instructional domain in its Voluntary State Curriculum (VSC), which is the framework for Maryland's grade-level academic content standards, indicators, and objectives.

The foundation of the Alt-MSA, a portfolio assessment, is the grade-level academic content standards in the VSC. Because NCLB recognizes that students with significant cognitive disabilities will be assessed on alternate assessments based on alternate academic achievement standards, the Alt-MSA assesses mastery objectives in reading, mathematics, and science that are linked with grade-level content standards. In Grades 3–8 and 10, the Alt-MSA assesses three content standards in reading and five mathematics content standards; in Grades 5 and 8 it assesses five science content standards, and in Grade 10 it assesses biology content standards. Maryland's VSC can be viewed online for pre-K through Grade 8 (http://mdk12.org/assessments/vsc/index.html) and for the high school grades (http://mdk12.org/assessments/standards/9-12.html). The philosophy of the Alt-MSA is to select, for each student, instructional and assessment objectives that are 1) representative from among the elements described by each of these strands, 2) in proportions that represent the strand structures of the content areas, 3) reasonable for the individual student to attain (i.e., appropriately realistic for that student), and 4) challenging (i.e., appropriately idealistic for that student).

The Alt-MSA cycle begins at the start of the school year before instruction in reading, mathematics, and science. The Alt-MSA requires the test examiner team (consisting of the student's special and general education teachers, related service providers, and principal or designee) to identify appropriate objectives that satisfy the four criteria listed in the previous paragraph. Ten mastery objectives (MOs) are selected for reading: at least two each for decoding or sight word recognition, vocabulary, comprehension of literary and informational text, and reading strategies. Ten MOs are selected for mathematics: two each for algebra, geometry, measurement, data analysis, and computation and number sense. For science in Grades 5 and 8, 10 MOs are written: two each from the science content standards for earth/space, life science, chemistry, physics, and environmental science. Students in Grade 10 are assessed on MOs selected from biology, which is the science subject on which all 10th-grade students are assessed. Each student's performance from the previous year is taken into account (or, for a new student, a needs assessment is performed) to make sure the MOs are indeed appropriate for the student. These MOs essentially form the basis of the student's reading and mathematics instructional program.

To ensure that students are taught and assessed on skills not yet acquired, baseline evidence for each MO must be submitted to document that achievement falls below a 50% criterion. To receive credit for the MO, student achievement must be at least 80% at the end of instruction, which is documented by a second artifact for each MO. Four types of evidence or artifacts, each of which must meet clearly defined standardized criteria, are collected in the student's Alt-MSA portfolio: 1) student work, 2) data charts, 3) videotapes, and 4) audiotapes. At least two MOs in reading and mathematics must present videotape evidence. The evidence is collected in a portfolio and sent to the assessment contractor for scoring. Each MO is scored *pass* or *fail,* with *pass* indicating that the MO was attained at 50% or less success at the beginning and at 80% or more after instruction. The achievement levels of students in each content area are judged *basic* (5 or fewer MOs passed), *proficient* (6, 7, or 8 MOs passed), or *advanced* (9 or 10 MOs passed). As with the MOs, the achievement-level descriptions (what students at each proficiency level know and can do) for each content area are individualized for students; each student's achievement-level descriptions comprise the MOs that the student achieved.

Every October, from 2003 to 2007, 20 reading and mathematics MOs for each student (approximately 5,000 students participated in the Alt-MSA each year) were sent to the Alt-MSA contractor for a contractor-conducted, no-fault technical review to determine that each MO met scoring requirements. This technical review concentrated on identifying MOs that were considered deficient, either because 1) they did not align with the content standards they were intended to assess or 2) they were not operational definitions that could be used to measure achievement. Those that did not meet these criteria were returned to the test examiner team for revision.

EFFICIENTLY DEVELOPING ACCEPTABLE MEASURABLE MASTERY OBJECTIVES: AN EVOLVING PROCESS

In the initial years of the assessment, the Alt-MSA was based on the general assumptions that teachers of students with significant cognitive disabilities 1) knew and understood the Maryland reading and mathematics content standards and 2) were able to construct measurable goals and objectives. As previously described, the design of the Alt-MSA involved teachers writing MOs for each student from scratch, tailoring the objectives to each student's particular academic needs within the overall framework of the breadth and depth of the content standards. Nevertheless, the assessment design also included a 100% independent technical review by the assessment contractor of the uniquely constructed MOs for each student (approximately 100,000 MOs in any given year). This technical review was conducted to ensure the state that the student data could support achievement-level classifications in reading and in mathematics.

The results of the technical review in each of the initial years of the assessment demonstrated that teachers of Alt-MSA students were not well versed in the VSC, nor were they familiar with writing measurable objectives. The technical review provided feedback to the teachers to enable them to diagnose and correct problems with the MOs to ensure that student performance was accurately measured on the assessment. As a result of this process, teachers gained considerable knowledge and understanding about grade-level content and skills and the scope and sequence of the content standards. However, the process was very time-consuming and labor-intensive for the MSDE, the assessment contractor, and the teachers.

One of the issues that was noted in the MO review each year is that although there were approximately 100,000 MOs, many of them were, in fact, quite similar and were almost duplicates of each other—even those MOs submitted by different teachers. In order to decrease the burden on teachers of writing unique MOs for each student and to ensure that the MOs were aligned with content and measurable, MSDE determined that the best course of action would be to take the pool of existing custom MOs, analyze it, and create a bank of MOs that would meet the needs of the vast majority of students. Teachers would be encouraged to select items from this bank that were appropriate for their students. The advantage of using a banked MO is that it was known to be aligned and measurable, and therefore it would be preapproved upon selection and would not need to undergo the assessment contractor's technical review. Teachers would always have the option of writing one or more unique MOs for a student if the situation warranted it.

MSDE assembled teams of local educators, including Alt-MSA facilitators (special educators from each local central office charged with coordinating, implementing, and providing professional development for the Alt-MSA in their school system) and teachers of Alt-MSA students, to work in consultation with MSDE assessment, special education, and content area staff. This team of individuals, facilitated by MSDE Alt-MSA staff, examined the existing pool of approximately 300,000 unique MOs and simplified it into approximately 10,000 MOs per content area, each aligned with/linked to the VSC and measurable. The assessment contractor built a web-based application, known as Alt-MSA Online, which allows teachers to select or write MOs, local administrators to review and approve MOs, contractor staff to review and provide feedback on uniquely written MOs, and teachers to revise MOs upon receiving feedback and to print final MO test documents for each content area—all within a much-reduced time frame. Reaction from the field has been overwhelmingly positive. And now, armed with the results of a recently conducted alignment study, MSDE is refining the very few areas that needed adjustment to ensure that this item bank is fully aligned with strand-based links to grade-level content standards.

Using the Alt-MSA system, Maryland has an assessment that guides each student's reading, mathematics, and science instruction and that is linked and aligned to grade-level content expectations. Each student can achieve success but is not guaranteed success before instruction. Students are presented with instructional tasks that are achievable, but no tasks are achieved before instruction takes place. Maryland did not want a system in which some students would fail no matter what they did and other students would be successful without any instruction at all; such a system would be inconsistent with the principles of assessment-driven instruction and would violate what has been called the fundamental accountability principle: assess all students on what they are supposed to be learning (Schafer, 2004). We believe that Maryland, using the Alt-MSA, has accomplished these goals.

A FRAMEWORK TO ADDRESS CHALLENGES OF DEVELOPMENT AND IMPLEMENTATION

Two conceptual frameworks guided the development and implementation of the Alt-MSA. The NCLB mandates embodied in the standards and assessment peer review guidance served as the framework for the development of this assessment. This guidance requires that all assessments, including alternate assessments based on alternate academic achievement standards (AA-AAS), meet the federal requirements for academic content standards, academic achievement standards, technical quality, alignment, inclusion, and reports. However, we also recognized that a second framework was needed to guide the effective implementation of the new Alt-MSA. To guide our implementation of the Alt-MSA, a process we recognized would take 3–5 years, we selected components from two conceptual models: 1) the Concerns-Based Adoption Model (CBAM)—specifically, the components that facilitators of change must consider—and 2) constructivist learning theory.

CBAM's foundation for school improvement encompasses six assumptions of change: 1) change is a process and not an event, 2) change is accomplished by individuals, 3) change is a highly personal experience, 4) change involves developmental growth, 5) change is best understood in operational terms, and 6) the focus of facilitation should be on individuals, innovations, and context. In CBAM, the role of a change facilitator is to "guide the change process to a point of successful implementation" (Hord et al., 1987). We intended to build the capacity of the Alt-MSA facilitators and the local accountability coordinators (LACs) so they could successfully facilitate change in their districts and schools. Hord et al. provided the Checklist of Suggested Change Facilitator Actions to Support Change. Figure 11.1 describes three of the six actions. Although we were cognizant of many of the actions that needed to be taken immediately within the framework for developing supportive organizational arrangements, training, and monitoring, we also knew that unless the concepts of constructivist learning theory were embodied in our practice, we would miss opportunities for deeper understanding and capacity building among school- and district-based staff and administrators; missing these opportunities would directly impact our intent of deep and lasting change. The strategies we enacted leveraged the federal mandates to serve as opportunities to meet our goals. Our goals were not merely to be in compliance with the mandates but actually to eliminate barriers to collaborative efforts among departments and staff in special education, general education, assessment, and curriculum and instruction so that students with significant cognitive disabilities could receive appropriate instruction and their teachers could have the necessary resources.

Processes to foster these sea changes to increase learning opportunities for students with significant cognitive disabilities reflect concepts of constructivist learning theory (Lambert et al., 1995):

- Intention is shared meaning and values among peers.

- There should be pluralistic, emerging knowledge bases informed by action research, observation of teaching and learning, and multiple disciplines.

- Problem finding is central to an inquiring stance; understanding deepens through time.

- Objectives emerge naturally as discrepancies are addressed; objectives cannot be preset because problems are not initially understood.

Concerns-Based Adoption Model (CBAM): Checklist of Suggested Change Facilitator Actions to Support Change	
Actions to Support Change	**Definitions**
Develop Supportive Organizational Arrangements	". . . providing for space, materials, personnel, equipment or furniture-all the things needed before implementation can begin . . . Developing guidelines, regulations, and policies related to the innovation, acquiring funding and other unique resources, planning for the change, and managing the processes are all essential parts of this component." (p. 75-76)
Training	". . . training should be an ongoing process to enable teachers to grow and to continue developing new skills. To be most effective, training designs must take into account teachers' individual needs and concerns. A single generalized training session prior to a new program's initial use is rarely adequate to ensure effective implementation . . ." (p. 76)
Monitoring	"Seeking objective data helps assess progress in implementing new programs. The data provide information about what assistance may be needed." (p. 77)

Figure 11.1. A checklist of suggested change facilitator actions. (*Source:* Hord, Rutherford, Huling-Austin, & Hall, 1987.)

- Changes evolve from current practice, knowledge bases, and problem finding.

- Everyone is a leader; skills in reciprocal processes are needed by all.

- There should be multiple, sustained opportunities for participation.

- Participation involves multiple professional development opportunities.

- Parameters serve emerging goals rather than being limited by them; teams challenge and redefine parameters.

- Partnerships exist among equals.

- There should be self-monitoring based on internal criteria.

These categories of action and associated concepts of constructivist learning theory cited within these categories provide the structure for the following discussion of the challenges we faced and the strategic actions we took to implement the Alt-MSA. Typically, multiple actions across these categories were implemented simultaneously.

DEVELOPING SUPPORTIVE ORGANIZATIONAL ARRANGEMENTS

Although we recognized that several immediate changes to key organizational structures would support the transition from the previous alternate assessment, IMAP, to the Alt-MSA, other organizational challenges emerged through the ongoing process of problem finding with key stakeholders. As these challenges were uncovered, strategies to address them were identified and implemented to support positive changes.

Challenge: Broad Ownership of the Alternate Assessment

This challenge resided at the state, district, and school levels. Specific actions to increase collaboration and shared ownership had to be modeled at the state level as well as captured in policy statements to influence changes in practice at both the district and school levels. We recognized that shared ownership would be critical for successful implementation of the Alt-MSA at each of these levels. Yet, how could we shift the responsibility of the development and implementation of an AA-AAS that meets the NCLB requirements, from special education to all stakeholders at the state, district, and school levels? We recognized that NCLB provided the leverage we needed to effect a system change. We also knew it would be wise to build on existing structures and to involve stakeholders during the process.

Prior to NCLB, the MSDE division of special education led all aspects of development, training, scoring, and reporting of the previous alternate assessment, IMAP. Neither the division of assessment and accountability nor the division of curriculum and instruction were involved in any aspect of the alternate assessment. Because the previous alternate assessment was not based on academic content and did not assess reading and mathematics (it assessed functional life skills such as hand washing and making snacks), there was no formal need to collaborate with staff in other divisions. However, the expectations of NCLB were clear: An AA-AAS must be aligned with grade-level reading, mathematics, and science content standards and meet technical requirements for validity and reliability. Only with the strong involvement of content and assessment staff would we be able to develop a technically adequate assessment.

Similar organizational structures existed at both the district and school levels. At the district level, IMAP coordinators, who were district-level special education administrators and teachers, were in charge of district-level implementation of this previous alternate assessment and served as district liaisons to the MSDE. There was no involvement of the LACs, although they were the liaisons to the state for all other statewide assessments. Typically, staff in departments of curriculum and instruction were not involved in curricular development for students with significant cognitive disabilities.

At the school level, the Alt-MSA requirements needed to provide structures to communicate the expectation that the education of students participating in the Alt-MSA is a shared responsibility and not just the responsibility of special education teachers. At the school level, the special education teachers who administered the alternate assessment performed all the functions typically performed by school test coordinators (STCs) for all other assessments. Like LACs, the STCs had no responsibility for the alternate assessment, but they had direct responsibility for school-based training and logistical support for all other statewide assessments. School-based principals and general education teachers were not explicitly involved in any aspects of the implementation of the alternate assessment.

Actions

State To initiate these changes, we first established collaborative organizational structures at the state education agency and then incorporated these practices into policy decisions that would provide the impetus to replicate them in local school districts. Demonstrating collaboration among the departments of special education, assessment, and curriculum and instruction at the state level and also within local school districts would provide a strong foundation for Alt-MSA implementation.

Support was gained at MSDE for key staff in the division of assessment and accountability to collaborate with the AA-AAS project manager in the division of special education. Together we created a plan to develop an AA-AAS, collaborating with external experts to guide the development process, and crafted a request for a proposal for a vendor. We identified critical times in the test development process that required the direct involvement of the coordinators of reading, mathematics, and science, and we received support to collaborate with the academic coordinators.

We changed the title from *IMAP coordinator* to *Alt-MSA facilitator* to indicate that district-level special education staff did not own the alternate assessment. We shifted the previous special education ownership to one of collaboration and shared responsibility among the Alt-MSA facilitators and the LACs. Meetings for LACs and Alt-MSA facilitators are now scheduled on the same day, and the agendas for these staff meetings include time to meet together and to meet in job-alike groups. Shared and unique and responsibilities were established.

Districts Once we had established at our MSDE LAC/Alt-MSA facilitator joint meetings that both groups had roles and responsibilities for the

Alt-MSA, they strategized how they would collaborate within their districts, recognizing that although they had a shared responsibility, each had specialized knowledge and skills that would benefit the collaborative effort. These roles and responsibilities for the implementation of the Alt-MSA were identified and documented in the Alt-MSA handbook. LACs now are responsible for the receipt, disbursement, and collection of all test materials, and they manage all the data systems and records for the test files. Alt-MSA facilitators must be knowledgeable of their districts' special education policies, procedures, and programs and of the role of individualized educational program (IEP) teams in the identification of students who would participate in the Alt-MSA, instructional and assessment practices for students participating in the Alt-MSA, and those students' learner characteristics. The LAC and the Alt-MSA facilitator in each district collaborate to provide training and technical assistance on the Alt-MSA requirements to school-based and district-level staff.

Schools Previously, in schools in which the IMAP was administered, the special education teachers of assessed students managed all components of the assessment process—from obtaining test materials and conducting the assessment to packing and delivering the assessment materials for scoring. To broaden responsibility for this state assessment, and to align with similar practices used with all other statewide assessments, specific roles and responsibilities were outlined in the Alt-MSA handbook for school-based staff. With the implementation of the Alt-MSA, the STC is now responsible for submitting the test participation files for all students in the school and not just for those taking the general assessment. On the basis of the test files, the STC orders the materials needed to develop the portfolios, disseminates the materials to the test examiner team, collects the completed portfolios at the end of the test window, and prepares the portfolios for pickup.

Test examiner teams were created. Principals are required to meet with test examiner teams to plan how all components of assessments will be implemented during test periods. The typical test examiner team comprises all members of a student's instructional team, including related service providers: occupational therapists, physical therapists, and speech pathologists; general education teachers; teachers of art, music, and physical education; special education teachers; and paraprofessionals. All test examiner team members are considered teachers of reading and mathematics because children learn more effectively when reading and mathematics skills are taught throughout the instructional day. Most students participating in the Alt-MSA had multiple service providers, so the students benefited from having the teachers and service providers share the responsibilities of teaching reading and mathematics and collecting evidence of student learning.

Challenge: Communicating that Instructional Policies Apply to All Students

Although policies related to instruction, grading and reporting, and grade-level assignment existed at the state and district levels, these policies were unevenly applied to students with significant cognitive disabilities. Identifying nonenacted policies and working to implement them would foster the implementation of the Alt-MSA.

Academic Instruction and Grading and Reporting

Based on initial reactions to the Alt-MSA from teachers and administrators, it was evident that all students were not receiving daily instruction in reading, mathematics, science, social studies, health, physical education, art, and music. This was inconsistent with the Code of Maryland Regulations.

Also, teachers typically reported that the student's IEP served as the curriculum. In 2003, only 1 of 24 districts in Maryland had an academic-based curriculum for students with significant cognitive disabilities. In addition, not all students were receiving report cards; this was inconsistent with many local board of education policies. Rather, some districts and schools relied solely on IEP quarterly reports, which may not have reflected academic goals and objectives.

Action Efforts were made to identify and explain the connections among the requirements of long-standing state education regulations and local board of education policies to the requirements of the Alt-MSA and, thus, NCLB. It was important to establish that the requirements of NCLB and the Alt-MSA were, in fact, consistent with existing state and local board of education policies. Policies requiring academic instruction and grading and reporting were cited in the Alt-MSA handbook, providing notification and leverage for district administrators to implement existing related policies and to develop a grade-aligned curriculum for students with significant cognitive disabilities. As a result, by 2007 districts reported that instructional budgets and materials have been made available to schools and that content experts are collaborating with special education administrators and specialists to write an academic curriculum.

Nongraded Classes

During initial implementation of the Alt-MSA, Alt-MSA facilitators pointed out that often students were not assigned to specific grade levels. Therefore, IEP teams could not discern whether a student was in a tested grade. Also, unless a student had a grade-level assignment, teachers and related service providers did not have an instructional frame of reference related to grade-level instruction and assessment—a requirement for the Alt-MSA.

Action A policy decision was made to assign all students to grade levels instead of assigning anyone a nongraded status. The procedures to do so would be consistent with those used for newly enrolled students. This procedure was stated in the Alt-MSA handbook. This policy also influenced the natural articulation of students from elementary to middle school and from middle school to high school with their same-age peers. Previously, these students often had remained in elementary and middle school for several additional years.

Challenge: Adding Science to the Assessment to Meet No Child Left Behind Requirements

How could we prepare districts for the science assessments to be administered in 2007–2008?

Action

In 2006–2007, we made a policy decision that, before the assessment of science in 2007–2008, we would require that specific reading (vocabulary and informational text) and mathematics (measurement and data analysis) MOs be taught and assessed within the context of science content. This expectation alerted districts and schools to provide professional development in science, fostered opportunities to coteach and plan with general education teachers, and provided teachers the necessary science instructional materials. This policy applied to every student in Grades 3–8 and 10—not just students in the grades that would be assessed in science—so that every student would have access to science instruction.

Challenge: Fairness of Resources to Districts

How could MSDE disburse funds equitably to districts to support the implementation of the Alt-MSA?

Action

Alt-MSA facilitators were invited to write grants for funding to support the implementation of the Alt-MSA. Funds would be distributed based on the number of students who participated in the Alt-MSA in each district. Initially, the grants requested support for training in how to administer the Alt-MSA. However, in recent years, grants requested support for professional development in instructional and assessment practices for reading and mathematics and in the use of assistive technologies. This shift clearly reflects the intended instructional changes.

Challenge: Communicating Policies and Procedures to Districts

How could MSDE effectively communicate the Alt-MSA administration procedures, policies, and effective instructional practices to 24 districts?

Action

The Alt-MSA handbook is rewritten every year after scoring and disseminated to Alt-MSA facilitators and LACs in June, prior to the start of the new test year. Dissemination in June allows districts to prepare for curriculum writing during the summer and staff training just prior to the beginning of the school year. In this way, all test examiner teams begin the year knowing the expectations for teaching and assessing reading, mathematics, and science. Every member of the test examiner team is required to receive a copy of the handbook.

The Alt-MSA handbook goes beyond a typical test administration manual. It provides detailed descriptions of all the tasks to be completed during the test year, procedures for developing MOs and evidence to include in the portfolios, and logistical issues. The Alt-MSA handbook also addresses effective instructional practices and the use of assistive technologies in relation to the roles of the test examiner team. Matrixes are included in the Alt-MSA handbook to convey to the test examiner team the expectation that academic content must be taught and to help them consider the logical connections to the specific reading and mathematics, and science MOs, to social studies, art, music, and physical education content. Another matrix provides a structured decision-making model for members of the test examiner team to use in teaching and assessing specific MOs in reading and mathematics.

MSDE was also committed to provide ongoing, immediate, and correct responses to questions from staff who implement the Alt-MSA in a less formal and personalized manner. To accomplish this, two points of contact at MSDE—the Alt-MSA project managers in special education and assessment—provided e-mail addresses and telephone numbers with a promise of same-day response. Questions received were reviewed and clarifications were included in the next year's Alt-MSA handbook.

Brochures that explain the Alt-MSA are sent to parents, who also are informed of their children's reading, mathematics, and science MOs each fall. A videotape that describes the rationale and procedures for developing an Alt-MSA portfolio was developed for use with staff, parents, and community members.

Challenge: Involvement of Stakeholders

How could we meaningfully involve stakeholders in the development of the Alt-MSA? Stakeholders make recommendations to the state policy makers for consideration when making Alt-MSA decisions.

Action

Stakeholders representing parents/guardians, advocacy groups, special education administrators and teachers from large and small school districts, comprehensive schools and special centers, nonpublic schools, higher education, lawyers, content experts, LACs, and Alt-MSA facilitators were invited to become members of the Alt-MSA stakeholder advisory committee. Initially, we met several times each month to begin the process of developing the Alt-MSA. Tasks to build the necessary background knowledge of the advisory committee included

- Learning the requirements of NCLB and state instruction policies

- Learning the structure and vocabulary of the reading, mathematics, and science content standards

- Understanding the learner characteristics of students with significant cognitive disabilities

- Conducting a literature review of other states' alternate assessments

- Discussing implications for teachers and their current practices

After the Alt-MSA had been established, we continued to meet several times each winter and spring. We reviewed data and discussed our observations based on experiences with professional development and direct technical assistance to administrators and teachers and recommended revisions to the test design and the Alt-MSA handbook for the next test year.

TRAINING AND PROFESSIONAL DEVELOPMENT

Professional development is an ongoing process. The content of professional development and the processes implemented to build the capacity of staff to implement the Alt-MSA varied from the initial roll out of the Alt-MSA to the fifth year of implementation. Initially, the MSDE conducted the majority of the training in the districts, which centered on the requirements of Alt-MSA. As the capacity of the district-level Alt-MSA facilitators and LACs increased as a result of the multiple professional development opportunities provided by MSDE, they assumed a more active role in providing professional development to teachers throughout the test year. Although the content always included the requirements of the Alt-MSA, as teachers became more knowledgeable of the requirements, the focus could shift to instructional practices that supported the assessment.

Challenge: Providing Professional Development

How could MSDE effectively provide training and professional development to communicate the Alt-MSA administration procedures, policies, and effective instructional practices to 24 districts?

Actions

State- and district-wide dissemination and training on the Alt-MSA administration procedures is conducted collaboratively by the MSDE and the Alt-MSA facilitators and LACs.

Our audience for ongoing training and professional development is the Alt-MSA facilitators and LACs. It was critical that they deeply understand all aspects of the Alt-MSA so that they could facilitate professional development in their districts. They needed ongoing opportunities to construct their knowledge and understanding and thereby to strengthen their abilities to convey the intent of the policies, requirements of the Alt-MSA, and practical strategies for school-based implementation.

A myriad of professional development opportunities was provided to the Alt-MSA facilitators and LACs. The training sessions varied from half-day and full-day workshops and meetings to ongoing, in-depth immersion in Alt-MSA development activities. The variety of professional development fostered a depth of understanding of the content and processes for assessment and instruction that the Alt-MSA required. Professional development included meetings and workshops pertaining to

- Understanding the content, vocabulary, and scope and sequence of reading, mathematics, and science content standards

- Writing MOs

- Collecting and using data for assessment and instructional decision making

- Using prompt hierarchies and assistive technologies

- Developing curriculum aligned with grade-level content for students with significant cognitive disabilities

Alt-MSA facilitators and LACs also participated in ongoing Alt-MSA development and assessment processes, including

- The stakeholder advisory committee

- Rangefinding

- Standards setting

- Reviewing alignment of MOs with content standards, conducted in October and November

- Developing the MO bank

- Annually reviewing the Alt-MSA handbook and recommending revisions

Together we refined professional development needs annually on the basis of observation and analysis of data from the Alt-MSA results.

Challenge: Monitoring Implementation

How could MSDE monitor the Alt-MSA portfolio development process to ensure that the procedures for the Alt-MSA were appropriately implemented and that needed adjustments to the assessment could be identified and made prior to the next test year?

Action

MSDE employed several strategies to promote continuous improvement. The Alt-MSA program manager annually monitored the on-site scoring of approximately 5,000 student portfolios which provided dynamic information about test examiners' understanding of the Alt-MSA requirements and student learning needs. Staff analysis of the portfolio evidence submitted, scores, and condition codes applied helped to identify the Alt-MSA requirements that were not understood by teachers. This analysis informed needed revisions to the assessment based on teachers' evolving understanding of instruction and assessment. As a result of these analyses, more explicit direction was provided in subsequent revisions of the Alt-MSA handbook to guide test examiners to

- Include baseline data for each MO to demonstrate that students need to learn the skills indicated in the MOs

- Write MOs to include all components and ensure alignment with content standards

- Develop artifacts of student learning that are aligned with the MOs and have the required components

- Collect and display data on data charts that meet the purposes of both instruction and assessment.

- Use assistive technologies and prompt hierarchies

Scoring rules were strengthened to reflect these revisions. In addition, MSDE and Alt-MSA facilitators collaborated to plan in-depth professional development opportunities for staff to ensure expanded knowledge and understanding each test year.

Challenge: Alignment Verification

After Alt-MSA was developed, processes such as alignment studies that were previously used in general assessment development, were adapted for use with alternate assessments based on alternate achievement standards. Although the MOs in the MO bank were selected to represent the content standards, sampled at the strand level, and reviewed by the contractor for academic content match, it was deemed necessary to have a respected independent agency check the alignment of the assessment process to ensure that it would continue to meet regulatory approval.

Action

In 2007, staff at the National Alternate Assessment Center (NAAC) performed an alignment study on the 2007 Alt-MSA assessment, the second year of the existence of the MO item bank. The study used a protocol similar to those of other alignment methods (LaMarca, 2001) but with additional criteria reflecting particular issues related to assessments of students with significant cognitive disabilities. See Flowers, Browder, Wakeman, and Kim (2007) for the criteria and the full study.

The reviewers concluded that, overall, the Alt-MSA demonstrated access for students with significant cognitive disabilities to the general curriculum. In addition, reviewers concluded that nearly all MOs in the bank were academic and were acceptably linked to the grade-level content standards. Reviewers did note that, in reading, the MOs did not cover the complete range of content found in the grade-level standards. However, this was by design: The Alt-MSA was intended to ensure that all students had access to skills that previously might not have been included in their academic programs. Despite this finding, reviewers concluded that, overall, the Alt-MSA was well developed and covered the grade-level content standards.

Maryland used the findings of this alignment study to review issues that were identified and developed a plan to enhance and strengthen the alignment of the MO bank with grade-level content standards. As a result, any MOs that were identified as nonacademic or nonfoundational were removed from the MO Bank, new MOs were written for reading and mathematics indicators that had not been previously included in the MO Bank, MOs that exceeded the grade-level expectations were deleted from the MO Bank, MOs were revised to include verbs that would promote the use of higher order skills, and decisions were made to link MOs closer to their associated grade spans. An item review for new science, reading, and mathematics items was planned in February 2009 for 2010 Alt-MSA revisions to the MO Bank and will involve 35 Maryland general and special educators. In spring of subsequent years, an item review committee will convene to review new MOs.

In July 2008, MSDE convened a group of nearly 100 special educators and content experts to review the Alt-MSA performance-level descriptors and performance standards (cut scores); this meeting occurred 5 years after the assessment had been developed and the original standards had been set. As part of their work, participants viewed a sample of approximately 500 portfolios (a 10% sample) across grades and districts. The sample was representative of Maryland in terms of race/ethnicity and reflected the full range of student performance. It is significant to note that, aside from their central task of reviewing the standards, many participants also commented on the fact that students were accessing and performing successfully on academic content that had been thought unattainable 5 years previously. One participant remarked that the Alt-MSA is an excellent example of a program in which increased access to curriculum and increased performance expectations for students led to increased performance. It is the state's expectation that as the program continues to mature, the enhancement of the MO item bank and performance-level descriptors will continue to play a key role in the academic learning progress of students with significant cognitive disabilities in Maryland public schools. The existing performance standards were reaffirmed by MSDE as a result of this meeting.

TECHNICAL DOCUMENTATION FOR THE ALTERNATE MARYLAND SCHOOL ASSESSMENT

This section describes completed and planned work that provides evidence about the reliability and validity of the Alt-MSA. Much of the evidence comes from the three technical manuals for the assessment. All Alt-MSA technical manuals as well as other information about the Alt-MSA can be viewed online (http://www.marylandpublicschools.org/MSDE/testing/alt_msa). In addition, the NAAC's report (Flowers et al., 2007) about the alignment of the Alt-MSA is available online at (http://www.naacpartners.org/products/researchReports/20140.pdf).

Guidance for technical documentation specifically targeted to alternate assessments is also available in the literature. Two sources are particularly relevant. Schafer (2005) explored implications on documentation of reliability, validity, and utility of some typical differences between alternate assessments and standard large-scale assessments. Schafer made some suggestions that are consistent with the material in this section. Marion and Pellegrino (2007) developed some recommendations for alternate assessments in the more general context of building validity arguments in technical manuals for all assessments.

Need to Document the Technical Adequacy of the Criterion

In general, in order to judge proficiency on any assessment, a student's score is compared with some criterion score. On a standard, large-scale assessment, a standard-setting study is commonly used to generate one or more criteria (e.g., cut scores) that are applied to all students in a given classification (e.g., fourth graders). An implicit assumption is that the same criteria are appropriate for everyone.

For an alternate assessment, a primary question is whether the same criteria should apply to everyone who takes the assessment. As recommended by Schafer (2005), we determined that the same criteria should not apply to all students because the Alt-MSA was intended to assess quality of schooling as opposed to student achievement against fixed standards of performance. In the face of what we felt is a broad range of entry knowledge, skills, and abilities of students taking the alternate assessment, the delivery of instruction can be successful for a student whose achievement is well below that of another student for whom far higher expectations are appropriate. This meant that we needed a system with flexible criteria and, therefore, the technical characteristics (e.g., reliability and validity) of the criteria need to be considered along with the reliability and validity of the scores resulting from the assessment.

Technical Research Agenda

We are developing research that supports the technical adequacy of the Alt-MSA in four areas. These areas represent a crossed design in which one dimension is reliability or validity and the other dimension is scores or criteria. Thus, we need to consider reliability of the criteria, reliability of the scores, validity of the criteria, and validity of the scores. We consider some aspects of each of these in the following sections. Some of the work is completed, some is in progress, and some is only in the planning stage. We include a complete description so that readers can choose the most relevant aspects (or augment the list) in their own work.

Reliability of Criteria

We are interested here in whether the criteria developed for any one student are replicable. One approach would be to compare subsets of the criteria with each other, much as a split-half reliability analysis would do for a standard assessment. Because we have 10 criteria for each student, the criteria could be divided into two sets of five by some purposive process (e.g., including at least one in each half from each curriculum strand). The difficulty and cognitive demand for each of the criteria could be rated, and consistency could be noted. Although this makes most sense for individual students, it also would be possible to group students into, for instance, three levels of challenge (e.g., severe, moderate, and mild cognitive disability—perhaps assessed by reviewing IEPs, using a proxy such as age of diagnosis, or reviewing the levels of the prior year's MOs) and to evaluate the consistency for these groups. This could be replicated for lower, middle, and higher grade (age)-equivalent students.

Reliability of Scores

As reported in the 2006 technical manual, a 5% sample ($n = 266$) of portfolios were rated for scorer agreement for reading and mathematics. The agreement rates across grades ranged from 82% to 89% for reading and from 83% to 89% for mathematics. The NAAC study also concluded that the evidence of scorer reliability was strong.

Another aspect of reliability is assessed by decision consistency or decision accuracy. These are related concepts. Decision consistency is high when the same achievement-level classifications are made on two independent applications of the assessment; decision accuracy is high when students' assessed achievement levels are consistent with their (unknown) true achievement levels. These concepts have parallels with the theoretical reliability definition (decision accuracy) and a parallel forms study as a common way to evaluate reliability (decision consistency).

Following a suggestion from Schafer (2005), we evaluated the amount of evidence generated in the Alt-MSA with standard criteria for research, using a binomial sampling model. The details of this study are in the appendix to this chapter. The study estimated that the *proficient* or *advanced* versus *basic* decision accuracy of the Alt-MSA for reading is 79.1% and that the decision accuracy of the Alt-MSA for mathematics is 79.4%. The probability of misclassifying a true proficient student as *not proficient* was 4.5% for reading and 4.0% for mathematics, and the probability of misclassifying a true nonproficient student as *proficient* was 12.8% for reading and 13.6% for mathematics. These fall within the usual research maxima for Type I errors (rejecting true null hypotheses; 5%) and Type II errors (retaining false null hypotheses; 20%); we associated Type I errors with misclassification as *nonproficient* because these errors are the ones that direct resource allocations.

Validity of Criteria

Several sorts of evidence are described for the study of validity of assessments. Among these are content evidence (e.g., comparing the activities prompted by the assessment with the nature of the construct being assessed), quantitative evidence (e.g., correlating the assessment with other assessments of the same construct or of constructs with which it should be—or, perhaps, not be—associated), and consequential evidence (e.g., whether the assessment results in positive outcomes and minimizes negative ones). It seems reasonable to apply the same types of evidence to criteria that are applied to assessments.

For the Alt-MSA, the criteria are the MOs, which are unique to each student. The MO development and review process could be studied for the nine samples of students described previously in this chapter (see Reliability of Criteria). Student progress could be mapped along content standard strands over time. The use of the MO bank could be monitored and evaluated. Parents could be surveyed about whether the MOs seem modest, too idealistic, or about right. Finally, a new cut score study has been informed by experience with the Alt-MSA; MSDE secured an outside contractor for this work. Panels of judges recommended cut scores at grade levels and these were articulated vertically (among grade levels) and horizontally (across contents, reading, mathematics, and science); in the end, the percentage cut scores that had been used were reaffirmed.

Possible alternate standard-setting approaches that could be considered in other settings include developing percentage cut scores (e.g., using modified Angoff) independently for groups with different degrees of disability; establishing criterion groups using an external criterion (e.g., teacher/parent judgment) and choosing the cut score that minimizes misclassification, as in the contrasting groups method; or setting cut scores that match the percentages of students in the achievement levels on the regular assessment (equipercentile).

Quantitative evidence about the validity of criteria was generated (see the 2006 technical manual) by evaluating same-student portfolio pairs—one from 2006 and one from 2007. Of the 267 pairs, it was found that 95% for reading and 90% for mathematics showed more demanding or completely new MOs in 2007 versus 2006.

Two expected positive consequences of Alt-MSA criteria are that the curricular goals should become more focused on academic skills and that the enacted curriculum should become consistent with the state's content standards. A study of IEP goals over time would provide evidence for the former, and a study of teacher activities over time would provide evidence for the latter.

Validity of Scores

The ability of teachers to generate artifacts that are consistent with the MOs could be studied within content strands. That would provide content evidence. Consequential evidence could be generated by surveying stakeholders to find ways in which the scores have been used and misused.

SUMMARY

Planning supportive organizational arrangements, providing ongoing professional development opportunities and focused, short-term consultation, and monitoring the implementation of the Alt-MSA resulted in intended changes in assessment and instructional practices. Observable changes in practice in districts and schools include the following:

- Teachers understand the content standards as evidenced by data indicating that students are learning reading and mathematics.

- Instructional budget allocations have increased for students with significant cognitive disabilities.

- Special education teachers and related service providers are included in and attend training in academic content in districts.

- Collaboration among general and special education teachers has increased.

- The curriculum is being developed in most districts; an IEP is no longer viewed as the curriculum.

- Teachers are examining the use of academic learning time.

- IEPs include academic goals.

- The use of assistive technologies has increased.

- Portfolios receive fewer condition codes; scores are more reflective of students' work than teachers' errors.

The technical documentation of the Alt-MSA presents several challenges related to its individualization. In this chapter, we have tried to show how we have generated (or plan to generate) evidence about reliability and validity in a careful way. But there is little literature at present on this topic. We hope that our work not only will be used to improve the Alt-MSA but also will suggest new ways to address these important issues in other programs.

REFERENCES

Cohen, J. (1988). *Statistical power analysis for the behavioral sciences.* Mahwah, NJ: Lawrence Erlbaum Associates.

Flowers, C., Browder, D., Wakeman, S., & Kim, D.-H. (2007, August). *State D alternate assessment alignment report: Links for academic learning: Report to the state department of education.* Retrieved January 27, 2009, from http://www.naacpartners.org/products/researchReports/20140.pdf

Hord, S.M., Rutherford, W.L., Huling-Austin, L., & Hall, G.E. (1987). *Taking charge of change.* Alexandria, VA: Association for Supervision and Curriculum Development.

LaMarca, P.M. (2001). Alignment of standards and assessments as an accountability criterion. *Practical Assessment, Research & Evaluation, 7*(21). Retrieved September 30, 2008, from http://PAREonline.net/getvn.asp?v=7&n=21

Lambert, L., Walker, D., Zimmerman, D.P., Cooper, J.E., Lambert, M.D., Gardner, M.E., et al. (1995). *The constructivist leader.* New York: Teachers College Press.

Marion, S.F., & Pellegrino, J.W. (2007). A validity framework for evaluating the technical adequacy of alternate assessments. *Educational Measurement: Issues and Practice, 25*(4), 47–57.

No Child Left Behind Act of 2001, PL 107-110, 115 Stat. 1425, 20 U.S.C. §§ 6301 *et seq.*

Schafer, W.D. (2004. Review of the book [*Large-scale assessment programs for all students: Validity, technical adequacy, and implementation*]. *Contemporary Psychology, 49(5),* 622–625.

Schafer, W.D. (2005). Technical documentation for alternate assessments. *Practical Assessment Research & Evaluation, 10*(10). Retrieved January 27, 2009, from http://pareonline.net/getvn.asp?v=10&n=10

Schafer, W.D., Liu, M., & Wang, H. (2007). Content and grade trends in state assessments and NAEP. *Practical Assessment Research & Evaluation, 12*(9). Retrieved from http://pareonline.net/getvn.asp?v=12&n=9

Schafer, W.D., & Moody, M. (2004). Designing accountability assessments for teaching. *Practical Assessment, Research & Evaluation, 9*(14). Retrieved January 27, 2009, from http://pareonline.net/getvn.asp?v=9&n=14

Smith, J.K. (2003). Reconsidering reliability in classroom assessment and grading. *Educational Measurement: Issues and Practice, 22*(4), 26–33.

An Analysis of Decision Accuracy and Classification Rates of the Alternate Maryland School Assessment

WILLIAM D. SCHAFER

The Alternate Maryland School Assessment (Alt-MSA) is designed to assess the academic learning of Maryland students who, because of cognitive challenges, cannot be tested accurately using the regular Maryland School Assessment. In reading and mathematics, the Alt-MSA is scored for attainment of mastery objectives (MOs) that are chosen for students individually by test examiner teams. Each student is assessed on 10 MOs in each subject in order to assign achievement levels that correspond to those used for the regular assessment. For the Alt-MSA, a score of 0–5 results in a classification of *basic,* a score of 6–8 results in a classification of *proficient,* and a score of 9 or 10 results in a classification of *advanced* in the subject being tested.

No student necessarily receives the same set of MOs as any other student, so the concept of scores that can be compared, student to student, is meaningless. I considered the implications of this feature, among others, in a previous study (Schafer, 2005). In that study, I concluded that the traditional conception of reliability (true variance divided by observed variance) is not helpful for such an assessment. Instead, I suggested that the concept of sufficiency of evidence for making an achievement-level judgment be substituted for reliability, and the same perspective has been taken for the Alt-MSA. This sort of analysis adapts a method originally suggested by Smith (2003), who applied it to formative classroom assessments.

Conditional Achievement-Level Probabilities

For each student, there are 10 binary observations in a content area (reading or mathematics). It can be assumed that these observations are sampled independently from a binomial population (at the student level) of potential observations; for this reason, the number (or proportion) of MOs mastered by a student is modeled using a binomial distribution. For either content, this yields, for any value of the binomial population parameter π (the proportion the student has mastered in a hypothetical population of MOs), the probabilities of all possible observed outcomes (all possible proportions mastered in the sample). To simplify the problem, the midpoints of 10 equally spaced intervals of π in the range of zero to one—0.05, 0.10 . . . 0.95—can be used as the values of π. Because the objective is to classify students into achievement levels that are based on proportions of MOs mastered on the Alt-MSA, the assessment's cut points can be used to group the observed sample proportions into *basic* (0–0.5), *proficient* (0.6–0.8), and *advanced* (0.9–1.0). These groupings are shown in Table 11.1.

Evenly Weighted Student Distribution

Assuming that students with $\pi = 0.95$ are true advanced students, that students with $\pi = 0.65, 0.75$, or 0.85 are true proficient students, and that students with $\pi \le 0.55$ are true basic students, the rows can be grouped into those ranges. It can be assumed that they are equally numerous in the population of students (I amend this aspect of the analysis later) and that 10% of the student population has each of the true π values shown in Table 11.1. Summing the entries in Table 11.1 in these ranges and dividing by 0.1 yields the observed achievement-level probabilities for true achievement levels shown in Table 11.2.

Table 11.1. Conditional classification probabilities for students with various values

	Classification		
	Basic	Proficient	Advanced
.95	.0001	.0861	.9138
.85	.0098	.4458	.5443
.75	.0781	.6779	.2440
.65	.2485	.6656	.0860
.55	.4956	.4812	.0232
.45	.7384	.2571	.0045
.35	.9052	.0944	.0005
.25	.9803	.0207	.0000
.15	.9986	.0013	.0000
.05	1.0000	.0000	.0000

Table 11.2. Unconditional probabilities for true and observed achievement levels

| True level | Observed achievement level | | | Total |
	Basic	Proficient	Advanced	
Advanced	.0000	.0086	.0914	.1000
Proficient	.0336	.1789	.0874	.3000
Basic	.5118	.0855	.0028	.6000

The information in Table 11.2 may be used to find the decision accuracy of the Alt-MSA by summing the correct placements on the diagonal running from the lower left to the upper right. This yields a correct placement probability of 78.21% and an incorrect placement probability of 21.79%. This is interpreted to mean that the probability of a random student being placed correctly is 78% (under the assumption of true placements according to equally prevalent π values in the range used). Under these assumptions, then, the decision accuracy of the Alt-MSA is 78%.

The conditional classification probabilities are also of interest. These may be found by dividing the entries in Table 11.2 by the row totals to yield the results shown in Table 11.3.

Because certain classification decisions about schools and districts are based on proportions of students who are classified as *proficient* or *advanced* as opposed to *basic,* the conditional classification probabilities for these outcomes are also of interest. Combining these true levels yields the fourfold table of outcomes shown in Table 11.4. Each entry is the sum of the grouped cell entries from Table 11.2 divided by the sum of their associated row totals.

According to Table 11.4, a student who deserves to be classified as *proficient* or *advanced* has a 92% chance of receiving one of those classifications, and a student who should be classified as *basic* has an 85% chance of receiving that classification. A student who is proficient or advanced has an 8% chance of being misclassified as *basic*, and a student who is at the basic level has a 15% chance of being misclassified as *proficient* or *advanced*.

Table 11.3. Conditional probabilities for true and observed achievement levels

| True level | Observed achievement level | | |
	Basic	Proficient	Advanced
Advanced	.0001	.0861	.9138
Proficient	.1121	.5964	.2914
Basic	.8530	.1424	.0047

Table 11.4. Conditional probabilities for true and observed achievement-level groups

True level group	Observed level group	
	Basic	Proficient or Advanced
Proficient or Advanced	.0841	.9159
Basic	.8530	.1471

Empirically Weighted Student Distribution

The assumption of equal weights (i.e., a rectangular distribution) of students among the values of π in the population was made for convenience. It is also possible to estimate the distribution of π using the observed proportions of students in the various score ranges on the Alt-MSA. Those results are reported in this section. There are at least two reasons why this is an interesting analysis to perform. First, Schafer, Liu, and Wang (2007) demonstrated that states differ in their relative proportions of students who are proficient in reading versus mathematics. Thus, the proportions of the various true values of π are not likely to be symmetric across the contents. Second, it is helpful to be able to compare the results of this section with the results based on the rectangular distribution of students across π values assumed in the previous section.

There were 4,851 students who provided scores on the Alt-MSA in 2006. Those students were scored on both reading and mathematics. The percentages of MOs mastered are presented in Table 11.5.

In order to parallel the previous analyses, these percentages need to be converted to proportions in the 10 intervals represented by the 10 values of $\pi = 0.05, 0.15 \ldots 0.95$. That was done by splitting evenly, if pos-

Table 11.5. Mastery objectives mastered in 2006 for reading and math ($N = 4,851$)

Percent	Reading (%)	Math (%)
100	21.8	26.4
90	16.1	16.7
80	11.6	10.3
70	8.0	7.8
60	6.7	6.1
50	5.5	5.8
40	4.9	4.6
30	5.1	4.1
20	4.7	4.1
10	6.7	6.3
0	6.9	7.7

Table 11.6. Observed population proportions assigned to the values of π

	Reading proportion	Math proportion
.95	.2985	.3475
.85	.1385	.1347
.75	.0977	.0903
.65	.0735	.0697
.55	.0611	.0598
.45	.0521	.0521
.35	.0499	.0437
.25	.0490	.0414
.15	.0570	.0522
.05	.1228	.1087

sible, the proportion in each multiple of 10% between the two adjacent values of π; for $\pi = 0$ and $\pi = 1$, the full proportion was assigned to the nearest π value. The results of that operation are shown in Table 11.6.

Reading

Allocating the reading proportions according to the proportions in Table 11.1 and grouping yields the empirically weighted observed achievement-level probabilities for true achievement levels shown in Table 11.7; the data in this table can be compared with those shown in Table 11.2.

    The information in Table 11.7 may be used to find the decision accuracy of the Alt-MSA in reading using empirical weights by summing the correct placements on the diagonal running from the lower left to the upper right. This yields a correct placement probability of 79.08% and an incorrect placement probability of 20.92%. This is interpreted to mean that the probability that a random student is correctly placed is 79% (note that this is very close to the 78% that was found using equal probabilities for the percentage ranges).

    Because the proportions of students within the ranges of π differ empirically, the conditional probabilities can differ from those in the prior section. Dividing each cell in Table 11.7 by its row total yields the conditional probabilities of outcomes shown in Table 11.8.

    Because certain classification decisions about schools and districts are based on proportions of students who are classified as *proficient* or *advanced* as opposed to *basic,* the conditional classification probabilities for these outcomes are also of interest. Summing the cell probabilities in Table 11.7 and dividing by the sum of the associated row totals yields the outcomes shown in Table 11.9.

    According to Table 11.9, a student who deserves to be classified as *proficient* or *advanced* has a 95% chance of receiving one of those classifications (compared with 92% in Table 11.4), and a student who should be classified as *basic* has an 87% chance of receiving that classification (compared with 85% in Table 11.4). A student who deserves to be classified as *proficient* or *advanced* has a 5% chance of being misclassified as *basic,* and a student who should be classified as *basic* has a 13% chance of being misclassified as *proficient* or *advanced.* The slightly

Table 11.7. Unconditional probabilities for achievement levels in reading

| True level | Observed achievement level | | | |
	Basic	Proficient	Advanced	Total
Advanced	.0000	.0258	.2726	.2984
Proficient	.0274	.1768	.1057	.3099
Basic	.3414	.0486	.0017	.3917

Table 11.8. Conditional probabilities for true and observed reading achievement levels

True level	Observed achievement level		
	Basic	*Proficient*	*Advanced*
Advanced	.0000	.0863	.9137
Proficient	.0884	.5705	.3411
Basic	.8716	.1214	.0042

more favorable classification probabilities are due to the proportionally larger numbers of students in the tails of the percentage distribution (i.e., 0% and 100%) than in their nearby percentages.

Mathematics

Allocating the mathematics proportions in Table 11.6 according to the proportions in Table 11.1 and grouping yields the empirically weighted observed achievement-level probabilities for true achievement levels shown in Table 11.10; the data in this table can be compared with those shown in Table 11.2.

The information in Table 11.10 may be used to find the decision accuracy of the Alt-MSA in mathematics using empirical weights by summing the correct placements on the diagonal running from the lower left to the upper right. This yields a correct placement probability of 79.43% and an incorrect placement probability of 20.57%. This is interpreted to mean that the probability that a random student is correctly placed is 79% (note that this is very close to the 78% found using equal probabilities for the percentage ranges, and it is the same to a percentage point as the probability found for reading).

As with reading, the conditional classification probabilities for proportions of students who are classified as *proficient* or *advanced* as opposed to *basic* are also of interest. Combining these true levels as was done for Table 11.8 yields the outcomes shown in Table 11.11.

Because certain classification decisions about schools and districts are based on proportions of students who are classified as *proficient* or *advanced* as opposed to *basic,* the conditional classification probabili-

Table 11.9. Conditional probabilities for reading achievement-level groups

True level group	Observed level group	
	Basic	*Proficient* or *Advanced*
Proficient or *Advanced*	.0451	.9549
Basic	.8716	.1284

Table 11.10. Unconditional probabilities for achievement levels in math

True level	Observed achievement level			Total
	Basic	Proficient	Advanced	
Advanced	.0000	.0299	.3174	.3474
Proficient	.0256	.1676	.1014	.2946
Basic	.3092	.0472	.0017	.3581

ties for these outcomes are also of interest. Combining these true levels as was done for Table 11.9 yields the outcomes shown in Table 11.12.

According to Table 11.12, a student who deserves to be classified as *proficient* or *advanced* has a 96% chance of receiving one of those classifications (compared with 92% in Table 11.4 and 95% for reading), and a student who should be classified as *basic* has an 86% chance of receiving that classification (compared with 85% in Table 11.4 and 87% in reading). A student who deserves to be classified as *proficient* or *advanced* has a 4% chance of being misclassified as *basic,* and a student who should be classified as *basic* has a 14% chance of being misclassified as *proficient* or *advanced.* Again, the slightly more favorable classification probabilities in comparison with the equally weighted values are attributable to the proportionally larger numbers of students in the tails of the percentage distribution (i.e., 0% and 100%) than in their nearby percentages.

Conclusions and Recommendations

The theoretical (using a rectangular student population) decision accuracy of the Alt-MSA is 78%, and using empirical weights yields 79% for both reading and mathematics. These rates do not seem different enough to justify the use of empirical weights. Further research might investigate the effects of markedly different distributions of student π values, but the trivial effect found here suggests that the theoretical result is reasonable as an overall estimate.

Table 11.11. Conditional probabilities for true and observed math achievement levels

True level	Observed achievement level		
	Basic	Proficient	Advanced
Advanced	.0000	.0858	.9139
Proficient	.0868	.5689	.3443
Basic	.8635	.1318	.0046

Table 11.12. Conditional probabilities for math achievement-level groups

	Observed level group	
True level group	Basic	Proficient or Advanced
Proficient or Advanced	.0398	.9602
Basic	.8635	.1365

A discussion of the adequacy of the obtained decision accuracy for the Alt-MSA should include an analysis of the effects of misclassification and whether those effects are symmetric. Because the implications of a classification of a student as *basic* imply a greater likelihood of redirection of educational resources, it can be argued that a misclassification as *basic* has greater negative costs than a misclassification as either *proficient* or *advanced*. Borrowing from guidelines suggested by Cohen (1988), in cases in which misclassification costs are similarly asymmetric, the misclassification probability for *basic* can be considered sufficiently small if it is less than or equal to 0.05, and the misclassification probability for *proficient* or *advanced* can be considered sufficiently small if it is less than or equal to 0.20.

In my theoretical analysis (see Table 11.4), I estimated the misclassification probability for *basic* to be 0.08, which is judged not adequate because it is greater than 0.05. On the other hand, the misclassification probability for *proficient* or *advanced* was estimated to be 0.15, which is less than 0.20 and is judged adequate.

Using empirical weights, the misclassification probability estimates for reading (see Table 11.9) were 0.05 for *basic* and 0.13 for *proficient* or *advanced*. For mathematics (see Table 11.12), the estimates were 0.04 for *basic* and 0.14 for *proficient* or *advanced*. Although the use of empirical weights did not affect the decision accuracy estimate appreciably, the effects on misclassification rates were sufficient to bring them into acceptable ranges. The empirical weights are superior to the theoretical ones because the latter are oversimplified; therefore, the misclassification rates and their associated decision adequacy are judged adequate for the Alt-MSA.

This work was highly dependent on the cut scores used in the Alt-MSA program. It should be redone if revised cut scores are implemented.

CHAPTER 12

Alternate Assessment in Massachusetts

Approaches and Validity

DANIEL J. WIENER AND CHARLES A. DePASCALE

Alternate assessment is still making news, particularly regarding the ways in which states measure, interpret, and report the performance of a very diverse and difficult-to-assess student population and the validity arguments states use to justify their approaches and the decisions they make. To fully understand a state's alternate assessment, it is necessary to revisit the internal challenges it faced and the decision-making process it used to meet the assessment's stated purposes. For example, was the intent of the alternate assessment only to measure the performance of students with significant disabilities? Was it also to substantially improve teaching and learning for those students? Should the alternate assessment measure a student's performance on a given date or within a prescribed time span, or should it determine progress during an entire academic year? Should the required assessment consist of a series of standardized tasks, or should the tasks be determined for each student by the classroom teacher? There are defensible arguments on each side of these important questions, and states continue to grapple with the options before them.

Concerns over whether states are designing adequate alternate assessments, expressed in feedback from educators, researchers, the U.S. Department of Education, and others, have resulted in changes to alternate assessments in many states since July 2000 when statewide alternate assessments were first required. States with relatively stable alternate assessments are worth studying for the decision-making processes they used, for data on student performance accumulated during several years,

---

The views expressed in this chapter by Daniel J. Wiener and Charles A. DePascale, respectively current and former employees of the Massachusetts Department of Elementary and Secondary Education at the writing of this chapter, are solely their own and do not necessarily reflect any official policy or position of the Massachusetts Department of Elementary and Secondary Education.

and for their management of continuous system improvements. Massachusetts is one state that systematically has used the feedback of its practitioners, stakeholders, and technical advisors, plus made an intensive
commitment to the professional development of its special educators, in
order to fine-tune the alternate assessment each year, without making
radical changes or lurching transformations that would have disrupted
the system in major ways. The Massachusetts alternate assessment is
linked directly and intentionally with instructional improvement. Over
time, teachers have incorporated the use of curriculum resources developed by the state and new instructional practices, such as routine data
collection on student performance, to improve teaching and learning
and produce high-quality assessment products for student alternate assessment portfolios.

In this chapter, we discuss the key elements of the statewide alternate assessment in Massachusetts (the Massachusetts Comprehensive
Assessment System Alternate Assessment, or MCAS-Alt), the challenges
faced by the state in developing its alternate assessment system, and how
the state documented the validity and reliability of this system.

BACKGROUND

The developers of the MCAS-Alt had to make a number of complex decisions while designing the assessment; one such decision was to interpret the federal Individuals with Disabilities Education Act (IDEA)
Amendments of 1997 (PL 105-17) as intended to provide alternate assessments for an expanded and diverse population of students from all
disability groups who could not take the general statewide assessment.

A stakeholders group assisted the state in developing the eligibility
and participation guidelines for students taking the MCAS-Alt. One important guiding principle that sets the MCAS-Alt apart from other alternate assessments is that it is intended not only for students with significant cognitive disabilities but also for students with other unique and
significant disabilities who, even with accommodations, cannot fully
demonstrate knowledge and skills on a standard test. Most students who
participate in the MCAS-Alt are assessed according to alternate achievement standards, which are intended for students with significant cognitive disabilities who perform well below grade-level academic expectations. A smaller group of students participating in the MCAS-Alt are
assessed according to grade-level achievement standards, which are intended for students achieving at or close to grade-level expectations and
whose disabilities are significant but primarily noncognitive.

Each year, a relatively small subset of students taking the MCAS-Alt
are assessed according to grade-level achievement standards, and some
of these (about 150 high school students between 2003 and 2008) dem-

onstrated performance levels equivalent to those of students who passed the high school graduation tests. These students used the alternate assessment portfolio rather than the general assessment to meet the state's graduation requirement on the basis of the same passing standard used for students who take the tests (Massachusetts Department of Education, 2007a). (The Massachusetts competency portfolio was discussed in Wiener, 2006.)

A CURRICULUM MODEL FOR STUDENTS WITH SIGNIFICANT COGNITIVE DISABILITIES

Although the state's Education Reform Act of 1993 intended curriculum standards for all students, it was difficult at first for educators and parents to see how the standards applied equally to students with disabilities who performed well below grade-level expectations. How would such students access the skills, concepts, and subject matter described in the grade-level standards? Without explicit direction from the state, educators would naturally feel that the academic standards did not apply to their students; consequently, they would return to less academically rigorous curricula.

By developing an explicit progression of skills, concepts, and content linked with (and ultimately leading to) each grade-level standard, Massachusetts enabled its teachers to incorporate access to the general academic curriculum in each classroom. The idea of a continuum of learning allowed educators to find points of entry to the standards for each student and to progress as far as possible along the continuum from one entry point to the next, moving toward the grade-level benchmark. In Massachusetts, the progressions themselves were outlined in a publication entitled the *Resource Guide to the Massachusetts Curriculum Frameworks for Students with Disabilities* (Massachusetts Department of Education, 2006b).

The Massachusetts *Resource Guide* (Massachusetts Department of Education, 2006b) described entry points for each content standard at varying levels of complexity and difficulty; each entry point is based on the generally acknowledged essence of its respective standard. Development of the guide involved panels of content area experts, test developers, and special educators who engaged in a dialogue for several years to determine the standards' essences and entry points, making certain that each standard's entry points were linked to its essence as they spiraled down in complexity. Virtually all students, even those with the most significant disabilities, could subsequently address the standards at an appropriate level of difficulty.

The process requires each teacher first to become familiar with grade-level standards as written for all students and then to progress down from the top, rather than up from the bottom, to identify a level of complexity appropriate for each student. As a result, special educators grew well versed in the standards and became participants to a greater extent than before in the academic lives of schools. The *Resource Guide* (Massachusetts Department of Education, 2006b) has been used by several thousand teachers who engage in discussions with their general education colleagues on standards and curriculum adaptation.

STRUCTURE OF THE MASSACHUSETTS COMPREHENSIVE ASSESSMENT SYSTEM ALTERNATE ASSESSMENT

The MCAS-Alt is an organized collection of work samples, video, photos, and data charts that indicate how much a student has learned in the required areas of the assessment. Each year since 2002, Massachusetts has trained its teachers to collect data on student performance; Figure 12.1 shows a sample data chart. Portfolio scorers evaluate whether skills aligned with the standards were taught and how accurately and independently students demonstrated their knowledge. Data charts for each student's portfolio show whether the student learned a new and challenging skill in the content area rather than a skill he or she already knew;

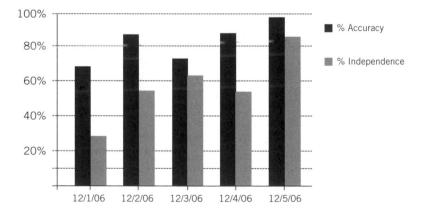

Figure 12.1. Sample instructional data chart for the Massachusetts Comprehensive Assessment System (MCAS) Alternate Assessment portfolio. (From Massachusetts Department of Elementary and Secondary Education. [2008]. *MCAS-Alt: 2008 guidelines for scoring student portfolios* [p. 16]. Malden: Author; reprinted by permission. Included by permission of the Massachusetts Department of Elementary and Secondary Education. Inclusion of this material does not constitute endorsement of this book.)

learning is indicated if there are lower values of accuracy and independence at the beginning of the data collection period than at the end.

The state's technical advisors and stakeholders believed that teachers themselves were best equipped to design the tasks required in each content area because of teachers' familiarity with state standards, the MCAS-Alt process, and their own students. Well-trained teachers also are ideally suited to conduct the necessary pretesting to determine the level of complexity appropriate for each student to address challenging and attainable academic skills.

Massachusetts has made a disproportionately large commitment to professional development and has expanded the traditional conception of alternate assessment from that of measurement tool to one that has potential for improving teaching and learning by integrating aspects of the assessment into routine classroom activities.

MEASURING STUDENTS WHERE THEY ARE

The MCAS-Alt was designed in an attempt to be true to the principles and beliefs described previously in this chapter and also to the principles of criterion-referenced or standards-based assessment. The MCAS-Alt's emphasis on improving teaching and learning through the integration of assessment and instruction had many precedents in the research on special education and assessment (Deno, 1985; Stiggins, 1997; Wiggins, 1993). Providing a clear picture of what students can and cannot do is at the heart of criterion-referenced measurement (Popham, 1978). Acknowledging the shortcomings of all performance-based, large-scale assessment systems (which are discussed later in this chapter), Massachusetts determined that a portfolio assessment system offered the best opportunity to improve teaching and learning through an alternate assessment by providing teachers with the tools to measure students in their classrooms, during instructional activities, and at times when it is possible to impact instruction.

The term *criterion-referenced measurement* commonly refers to two related but distinct purposes of measurement (Hambleton, Swaminathan, Algina, & Coulson, 1978; Nitko, 1980; Popham, 1978). One purpose, which is commonly applied to large-scale assessment for accountability purposes, is to measure student performance against a specified criterion or achievement standard. Student performance is classified as either meeting the standard or not meeting the standard. A second purpose is to describe what a student can do (and cannot do) with respect to the domain that is being measured (i.e., grade-level reading and mathematics). The first purpose provides information about whether a student has reached a certain point on a scale or continuum of skills. The second purpose provides information about where on that continuum the student's performance is located.

With general large-scale assessments designed to meet federal requirements, states commonly attempt to fulfill both purposes with a single test. Student performance is reported in terms of comparison with an established standard for proficient performance—the primary goal for most accountability systems under the No Child Left Behind Act (NCLB) of 2001 (PL 107-110). As required by NCLB, however, student performance is reported in comparison with additional established standards (e.g., basic, advanced); many states also report student performance as a scaled score indicating the location of the student's performance on a reporting scale established for the content area. Within the relatively narrow confines of grade-level content standards, it may be possible to achieve some degree of success in meeting both purposes with a single test. Much more research is needed, however, to determine just how well scores on general assessments describe student knowledge and skills in relation to specified domains.

When grade-level content standards are extended to provide access to students with significant cognitive disabilities, the range of the domain being measured is expanded significantly. Constraining the description of the domain being measured with terms such as *grade-level content standards* may give a false sense of the range of content knowledge and skills measured across the alternate assessment and general assessment at a given grade level. With a single test, it would be virtually impossible to estimate with the necessary precision an individual student's location along the continuum of knowledge and skills in the domain being measured. Interpretation problems caused by the lack of precision are exacerbated when the level of growth expected within or across years is smaller than the precision of the test.

Given the problems associated with describing an individual student's position along the continuum, many states have elected to use their alternate assessments to measure all students' performance against achievement standards established at only one to three fixed points along the continuum. The results of these assessments simply indicate whether a student's performance is above or below those fixed points. Although this approach may provide information beyond that provided by the general assessment results, the level of additional information does not seem commensurate with the costs of administering the alternate assessments in terms of time, money, and labor expended by teachers and students. There is also little evidence that such results would have the direct impact on instruction and learning valued by stakeholders in Massachusetts.

Considering the available options, Massachusetts selected an alternate assessment design focused on measuring where students are on the continuum of knowledge and skills and showing growth along the continuum within and across years.

STANDARD SETTING

After the design of the MCAS-Alt had been established, the next critical technical step was to establish achievement standards that were consistent with the design and purpose of the program. As Roeber (2002) argued,

> The nature of the alternate assessment used will help determine the type of standard-setting procedure that will be used. . . . The technique used should take into account not only technical aspects of the alternate assessment, but also the practical aspects of implementing the standard-setting technique for the alternate assessment process. (p. 9)

In Massachusetts, two key issues greatly impacted the standard-setting process for the MCAS-Alt:

1. What should the achievement levels be called?

2. How should scores on the multiple dimensions of the portfolio be combined to compute a total score for standard setting?

Naming the Achievement Levels

Although the process of implementing statewide alternate assessments was still relatively new, by the time Massachusetts was ready to set achievement standards for the MCAS-Alt a convention had emerged in the naming of achievement levels. It was commonplace for states to apply the achievement-level names used for their general assessments to their alternate assessments (e.g., proficient, advanced, novice, meeting the standard) (Roeber, 2002). This approach was consistent with the primary use of achievement-level results as indicators of success in states' accountability systems. For accountability purposes, there was no difference between classifications of *proficient* received on general or alternate assessments.

The approach of using achievement-level labels from the general assessment was not considered appropriate for Massachusetts for two reasons. As described previously, the MCAS-Alt was not designed solely for students with significant cognitive difficulties. A small percentage of students completing the MCAS-Alt would be measured against the same achievement standards as those used for students completing the general assessment. Therefore, it was important to avoid confusion caused by using the same labels. Also, Massachusetts was expending considerable resources to establish the meaning of *proficient* work in relation to the state's *Curriculum Frameworks* (i.e., content standards) with educators, students, and the general public (Massachusetts Department of Education,

2000–2005). The notion of associating the term *proficient* with a much lower level of performance was not consistent with that effort or with the goals of standards-based education reform. For those reasons, Massachusetts adopted a new set of achievement-level labels for the MCAS-Alt.

The six achievement levels used to report results for the MCAS-Alt include the three higher achievement levels from the general assessment and three additional levels that differentiate levels of performance in the lowest general achievement level. The lowest achievement level on the general MCAS tests, *warning,* was renamed and expanded to include three achievement levels labeled *awareness, emerging,* and *progressing.* These achievement levels reflected performance below the general grade-level achievement standard but increasing command of knowledge and skills linked to grade-level content standards. General achievement-level descriptors for the six achievement levels reported on the MCAS-Alt are provided in Table 12.1.

Table 12.1. Massachusetts Comprehensive Assessment System Alternate Assessment achievement levels

Level	Achievement-level descriptor
Awareness	Students at this level demonstrate very little understanding of learning standards and core knowledge topics contained in the Massachusetts Curriculum Framework for the content area. Students require extensive prompting and assistance, and their performance is basically inaccurate.
Emerging	Students at this level demonstrate a simple understanding below grade-level expectations of a limited number of learning standards and core knowledge topics contained in the Massachusetts Curriculum Framework for the content area. Students require frequent prompting and assistance, and their performance is limited and inconsistent.
Progressing	Students at this level demonstrate a partial understanding below grade-level expectations of some learning standards and core knowledge topics contained in the Massachusetts Curriculum Framework for the content area. Students seem to be receiving challenging instruction and are steadily learning new knowledge, skills, and concepts. Students require minimal prompting and assistance, and their performance is basically accurate.
Needs improvement	Students at this level demonstrate a partial understanding of subject matter in the Massachusetts Curriculum Frameworks in the content area and solve some simple problems at grade-level expectations.
Proficient	Students at this level demonstrate a solid understanding of challenging subject matter in the Massachusetts Curriculum Frameworks in this content area and solve a wide variety of problems at grade-level expectations.
Advanced	Students at this level demonstrate a comprehensive and in-depth understanding of subject matter in the Massachusetts Curriculum Framework in this content area and provide sophisticated solutions to complex problems at grade-level expectations.

From Massachusetts Department of Education. (2006b). *Resource guide to the Massachusetts curriculum frameworks for students with disabilities* (p. 56). Malden: Author; reprinted by permission. Included by permission of the Massachusetts Department of Elementary and Secondary Education. Inclusion of this material does not constitute endorsement of this book.

For school and district accountability purposes, students completing the MCAS-Alt who are assessed with alternate achievement standards are assigned points toward the state's composite performance index; student performance classified at the *progressing* level of the alternate standards receives the same points as student performance at the *proficient* level of the state's grade-level achievement standards (Massachusetts Department of Education, 2007b).

How and Whether to Compute a Total Score

A second major decision in the standard-setting process was how and whether to compute a total score. Portfolios submitted for the MCAS-Alt are scored across multiple dimensions including level of complexity, demonstration of skills (accuracy), independence, self-evaluation, and generalization of performance. Initial planning called for the computation of a total score by combining scores across the dimensions. It was assumed that this total score would form the basis for assigning achievement-level classifications to MCAS-Alt portfolios. This approach was consistent with the general assessment and with analytical scoring of portfolios used in general assessments.

After lengthy consideration of the appropriate weighting of each dimension, it was determined that a profile of scores across portfolio dimensions would provide a more accurate reflection of student performance than would a combination of scores. That is, combining scores across level of complexity, demonstration of skills, and the other dimensions would reduce the interpretability and, therefore, instructional usefulness of the portfolio scores (Wiener, 2002). The scoring dimensions on the MCAS-Alt did not represent compensatory skills that could be combined easily into a single total score to convey actionable information about student performance to teachers. Based on experience with the general assessment, there was reason to believe that a reported total score on the MCAS-Alt might become the primary focus or reporting at the expense of information provided by the dimension scores. Consequently, each student's scores on the MCAS-Alt portfolios are reported as a profile of scores across the five scoring dimensions.

Assigning Achievement Levels

After establishment of the achievement-level labels (and descriptors) and the decision not compute a total portfolio score, the task of assigning achievement-level classifications for MCAS-Alt performance remained. Given the nature of the data and the design of the assessment, a reasoned judgment approach was used to establish achievement standards. A complete description of the approach was provided in *Massachusetts: One State's Approach to Setting Performance Levels on the Al-*

ternate Assessment (Wiener, 2002), a synthesis report published by the National Center on Educational Outcomes. Another National Center on Educational Outcomes synthesis report (Wiener, 2006) described the method used to evaluate MCAS-Alt portfolios according to grade-level achievement standards. A brief overview of the process of establishing achievement-level thresholds for the MCAS-Alt is provided in the following paragraphs.

A standard-setting group that included the state's technical advisors and the state's and contractor's special education and assessment specialists met to describe the achievement of students who performed the tasks prescribed by their teachers. By examining each combination of scores that hypothetically could be attained on the MCAS-Alt, the panel discussed and described the different levels of performance for the range of possible score totals for complexity, accuracy, and independence, using the rubric shown in Figure 12.2.

The learning characteristics of each score combination were discussed and described. For example, the performance of a hypothetical student who addressed the standards below grade-level expectations (level of complexity = 3) in a given subject and performed the assigned tasks with more than 75% accuracy (accuracy = 4) and more than 50% independence (independence = 3) could be described as primarily accurate and independent on standards addressed below grade-level expectations. A student who performed the standards below grade-level expectations (level of complexity = 3) but between 25% and 50% accuracy (accuracy = 2) and between 25% and 50% independence (independence = 2) might be described as limited and inconsistent with regard to accuracy and independence; such a student might require frequent prompting and assistance on standards addressed below grade-level expectations.

As a result of examining each score combination and analyzing the characteristics of hypothetical learners who attained those scores, descriptors were used to describe overall student performance within the performance levels of *awareness, emerging,* and *progressing.* Threshold scores were determined for placing students in one performance level or another. A process of reasoned judgment was used to group students into performance-level categories and to describe each student's overall performance. Initial achievement-level classifications were reviewed and validated by panels of special education specialists, other educators, and the state's MCAS-Alt advisory committee. Input from these groups was considered in the development of the final achievement-level thresholds for the MCAS-Alt.

Level of complexity				
1	2	3	4	5
No basis on *Curriculum Frameworks* learning standards	Student addresses social, motor, and communication "access skills" during standards-based activities	Student addresses learning standards below grade-level expectations through "entry points"	Student addresses one or two learning standard(s) at grade-level expectations	Student addresses three or more learning standard(s) at grade-level expectations
Demonstration of skills (accuracy)				
M	1	2	3	4
Strand contains insufficient information to determine a score	Student's performance in this strand is primarily inaccurate and demonstrates minimal understanding (0%–25% accurate)	Student's performance in this strand is inconsistent and demonstrates limited understanding (26%–50% accurate)	Student's performance in this strand is mostly accurate and demonstrates some understanding (51%–75% accurate)	Student's performance in this strand is accurate and of consistently high quality (76%–100% accurate)
Independence				
M	1	2	3	4
Strand contains insufficient information to determine a score	Student requires extensive verbal, visual, and physical assistance (0%–25% independent)	Student requires frequent verbal, visual, and physical assistance (26%–50% independent)	Student requires some verbal, visual, and physical assistance (51%–75% independent)	Student requires minimal verbal, visual, and physical assistance (76%–100% independent)

Figure 12.2. Rubric for scoring Massachusetts Comprehensive Assessment System Alternate Assessment portfolio strands. (From Massachusetts Department of Elementary and Secondary Education. [2008]. *MCAS-Alt: 2008 guidelines for scoring student portfolios* [pp. 10–12]. Malden: Author; reprinted by permission. Included by permission of the Massachusetts Department of Elementary and Secondary Education. Inclusion of this material does not constitute endorsement of this book.)

STRENGTHS AND CHALLENGES OF PORTFOLIOS

As a basis for statewide alternate assessment, portfolios are suitable because they address several important purposes of the assessment:

• Document a relatively large number of tasks

• Show how each student develops and refines his or her knowledge and skills over time; this can be done by including drafts and successive revisions of student work and teachers' data charts showing a record of the student's progress

• Show which standards were actually taught and how well the student learned them (because portfolio products directly reflect instruction)

• Document the level of complexity and difficulty at which the standards are taught

• Show all the steps of the learning process and how each step builds on prior learning

• Provide a window into a classroom, showing precisely how new skills, concepts, and subject matter are taught and how the student can demonstrate and generalize the skill most effectively

There are many technical challenges to implementing portfolio assessments (or other performance-based assessments) on a large scale for relatively high-stakes purposes such as school and district accountability. Concerns about lack of standardization, lack of generalizability, and reliability of scoring are a few issues that must be considered and addressed in the design and implementation of a portfolio assessment system such as the MCAS-Alt. As is commonly the case in large-scale assessments using constructed-response items or performance tasks, reliability of scoring is the least important of these issues and the easiest challenge to overcome. Generalizability of student performance is a key concern, but this concern can be used misleadingly in arguments against portfolio assessment. The extent to which performance on any type of alternate assessment can and should be expected to generalize to the grade-level domain being assessed is an unanswered question regardless of the degree of linkage or alignment with extended content standards that can be demonstrated. Standardization, particularly for comparability of results, is a valid but not paramount concern. Massachusetts has chosen flexibility over standardization in the selection of assessment tasks in an effort to more effectively measure individual student performance and growth.

For the purposes of large-scale assessment and school/district accountability, however, states (Massachusetts included) must provide compelling reasons for their decisions; for example, states must demonstrate why it is beneficial and necessary for educators to make their own judgments in determining specific performance tasks for their own students and how these standards-based, but individualized, tasks can still allow valid comparisons among students and schools. In addition, although the *narrow, but deep* approach typified by portfolio-based systems lends itself quite well to addressing extremely diverse learning needs by allowing a wide range of instructional approaches and contexts, it has been challenging to document the ways in which such a system could assess the full breadth of the curriculum in the way that general assessments do. Therefore, a substantial portion of the technical validity argument for a portfolio-based approach rests with at least the following forms of validity:

- Content validity

- Procedural validity

- Consequential validity

Validity of the content being assessed was relatively easy for Massachusetts to document because it had undertaken such an exhaustive process for defining the essence and entry points of its state curriculum standards. Content experts, assessment (test development and measurement) experts, special educators, and other stakeholders interacted throughout the process to produce authenticated outcomes aligned with grade-level content and customized for students at successive levels of complexity.

The procedural argument allowed the state to document its alternate assessment development process by showing that the right people were at the table when important decisions were being made and that a feedback mechanism had been built into the system to provide continuous improvement. Various constituencies had adequate opportunities to provide meaningful input on the purposes and outcomes of the alternate assessment, and technical advisors played an active role in setting standards, in developing performance-level descriptors, and in other relevant activities.

The consequential validity argument allowed the state to restate the purposes of the alternate assessment and demonstrate that "decisions based on the results of its assessments are consistent with the purposes for which the assessments were designed" (U.S. Department of Education, 2007). Besides determining what students with significant disabilities learned during academic instruction, the assessment results could and should be used to improve instruction and learning for these students, as stated in the original purposes of the MCAS-Alt (Massachusetts Department of Education, 2006a).

Regardless of the type of assessment selected, it was clear from the beginning that the implementation of any alternate assessment system in Massachusetts (or any other state) should occur directly in the classroom and be placed in the hands of teachers working with students with significant cognitive disabilities. It also was clear that ongoing support would be needed to successfully implement the alternate assessment program. As Evelyn Deno wrote in 1973 regarding the implementation of successful instructional programs for students with disabilities,

> In their program designs, they recognized that change and the effort to improve performance quality need continuous support because the pull of tradition is unrelenting and there is a strong tendency to fall back into familiar ways as soon as support for the change directions flags. Those programs were most successful in which technology and mechanisms were developed to sustain chance and commitments were supported strongly at influential administrative levels. (p. 168)

Neither the need for continuous support nor the pull of tradition and appeal of the status quo have diminished in the intervening decades.

Massachusetts has implemented an alternate assessment system designed to impact student learning by integrating and individualizing instruction and assessment at the classroom level. Continuous improvement of the technical characteristics of the individual assessment tasks developed by teachers and the overall validity of inferences drawn about the achievement and growth of individual students is possible through numerous approaches, such as professional development, feedback from portfolio scoring, and the sharing of exemplar tasks, support materials, and so forth. An alternate assessment program designed primarily as an external measure of student attainment of a fixed achievement standard might have demonstrated stronger technical characteristics at the outset. Such a program, however, never would have sufficient precision to measure the wide range of student achievement found among students with significant cognitive disabilities or to provide teachers the level of information needed to make instructional decisions.

ACHIEVING THE ULTIMATE GOAL: INSTRUCTIONAL IMPROVEMENT AND IMPROVED STUDENT LEARNING

Before IDEA 1997, classroom instruction for students with significant disabilities was entirely individualized and only marginally academic at best (Browder et al., 2005). No systematic standards-based instruction was provided to these students because states had yet to implement an effective method of adapting academic instruction for this population. After 1997, an increasing array of educational laws (IDEA 1997, NCLB, the Improving America's Schools Act of 1994 [PL 103-382], and various state education reform laws) were enacted not only to improve learning opportunities for these students but also to include all students meaningfully in standards-based systems of statewide assessment.

Several states identified instructional outcomes known initially as *alternate performance indicators* (APIs), using the terminology of IDEA 1997. This model provided an insightful, though only partial, solution: APIs were set at predetermined cognitive levels and, therefore, were not equally suited to all students with significant disabilities. Other states argued that the functional living skills taught to students with disabilities could be mapped onto the state academic standards and should, therefore, be considered access to the general curriculum; this approach yielded some obvious links to standards but many awkward and far-fetched examples of alignment.

These approaches represented early attempts at improving instruction and learning for students with disabilities; it generally had been acknowledged that academic instruction for these students lacked accountability and consistency and did not provide sufficient opportunities to learn valued academic skills and knowledge. Although neither approach met the states' long-term goals or fulfilled the curriculum access requirements of state and federal laws, both approaches opened doors to other creative solutions that followed. Massachusetts' approach owed much to these early efforts at alignment and adaptation and to the examples provided by states such as Kentucky, New York, Maryland, and West Virginia, which had put similar reform innovations into statewide practice.

Alternate assessments, by themselves, do not necessarily improve teaching and student learning unless intentional measures are taken by states to support the connection between teaching and learning. Teachers must know what standards to teach, how to teach them, and which skills and knowledge are likely to be assessed. Teachers also need explicit guidance from their states on how to move students closer to specific grade-level academic expectations.

In Massachusetts, efforts at improving instruction for students with significant and complex disabilities generally have focused on promoting the self-sufficiency of teachers, using state-approved curriculum guides, and providing reasonable expectations that what is taught is also what will be assessed. Teachers are required to design their own assessment tasks because they have the tools and training to do so. They must align their tasks with the standards, teach at challenging and attainable levels for each student, and document the outcomes of instruction through evidence showing students' performance and progress over time. Assessment tasks for the MCAS-Alt are customized for each student according to each student's level of performance at a given time.

The standardized performance tasks used in some states' alternate assessments may have inconsistent results regarding what students actually learn, or they may be intended for a fixed level of difficulty and, thus, unintentionally exclude some students who have the most significant cognitive disabilities and who will be unable to perform any of the tasks even when prompts are offered. In contrast, the MCAS-Alt directly assesses content and skills at individualized levels that challenge each student.

In Massachusetts, teachers have become adept at providing academic instruction at different levels of complexity, gathering data on student performance, and assembling structured portfolios in the subjects required for assessment. In the process, they have become more effective educators and assessors.

SUMMARY

The alternate assessment format and approaches used by states reflect the purposes of the assessment itself. Assessments that use standardized approaches, such as state-mandated performance tasks and observations, yield results that may make comparisons possible among students and schools but may not be based on skills taught to the student and leave the lowest-performing students unable to perform many of the required tasks. In Massachusetts, by contrast, the required collection of student work samples and performance data over time reflects an emphasis on authentic assessment of skills and knowledge at a level that challenges each student though likely will yield nonstandardized products that make comparisons among students and schools more difficult. An ongoing commitment to professional development, and a policy that encourages choice of assessment tasks by teachers most familiar with students, represents an investment by Massachusetts to promote a primary purpose of the alternate assessment: improved teaching and learning for a student population traditionally excluded from intensive academic instruction.

REFERENCES

Browder, D., Ahlgrim-Delzell, L., Flowers, C., Karvonen, M., Spooner, F., & Algozzine, R. (2005). How states implement alternate assessments for students with disabilities. *Journal of Disability Policy Studies, 15*(4), 209–220.

Commonwealth of Massachusetts. (1993). Massachusetts Education Reform Act of 1993. General Laws of Massachusetts. Chapter 71. Public Schools.

Deno, E.N. (Ed.). (1973). *Instructional alternatives for exceptional children.* Reston, VA: Council for Exceptional Children.

Deno, S.L. (1985). Curriculum-based measurement: The emerging alternative. *Exceptional Children, 52*(3), 219–232.

Hambleton, R.K., Swaminathan, H., Algina, J., & Coulson, D.B. (1978). Criterion-referenced testing and measurement: A review of technical issues and developments. *Review of Educational Research, 48*(1), 1–47.

Improving America's Schools Act of 1994, PL 103-382, 20 U.S.C. §§ 630 *et seq.*

Individuals with Disabilities Education Act Amendments (IDEA) of 1997, PL 105-17, 20 U.S.C. §§ 1400 *et seq.*

Massachusetts Department of Education. (2000–2005). *Curriculum frameworks.* Malden: Author.

Massachusetts Department of Education. (2006a). *MCAS technical report.* Malden: Author.

Massachusetts Department of Education. (2006b). *Resource guide to the Massachusetts curriculum frameworks for students with disabilities.* Malden: Author.

Massachusetts Department of Education. (2007a). *2006 MCAS-Alt: State summary of participation and performance.* Malden: Author.

Massachusetts Department of Elementary and Secondary Education (2007b). *2008 educator's manual for MCAS-Alt.* Malden: Author.

Massachusetts Department of Elementary and Secondary Education (2008). *MCAS-Alt: 2008 guidelines for scoring student portfolios.* Malden: Author.

Nitko, A.J. (1980). Defining "criterion-referenced test." In R.A. Berk (Ed.), *A guide to criterion-referenced test construction.* Baltimore: The Johns Hopkins University Press.

No Child Left Behind Act of 2001, PL 107-110, 115 Stat. 1425, 20 U.S.C. §§ 6301 *et seq.*

Popham, W.J. (1978). *Criterion-referenced measurement.* Upper Saddle River, NJ: Prentice-Hall.

Roeber, E. (2002). *Setting standards on alternate assessments* (Synthesis Rep. No. 42). Minneapolis: University of Minnesota, National Center on Educational Outcomes.

Stiggins, R.J. (1997). *Student-centered classroom assessment* (2nd ed.). Upper Saddle River, NJ: Prentice-Hall, Inc.

U.S. Department of Education, Office of Elementary and Secondary Education. (2007). *Standards and assessments peer review guidance: Information and examples for meeting requirements of the No Child Left Behind Act of 2001.* Washington, D.C.

Wiener, D. (2002). *Massachusetts: One state's approach to setting performance levels on the alternate assessment* (Synthesis Rep. No. 48). Minneapolis: University of Minnesota, National Center on Educational Outcomes.

Wiener, D. (2006). *Alternate assessments measured against grade-level achievement standards: The Massachusetts "competency portfolio"* (Synthesis Rep. No. 59). Minneapolis: University of Minnesota, National Center on Educational Outcomes.

Wiggins, G.P. (1993). *Assessing student performance: Exploring the purpose and limits of testing.* San Francisco: Jossey-Bass.

The Mississippi Alternate Assessment of Extended Curriculum Frameworks

Purpose, Procedures, and Validity Evidence Summary

**STEPHEN N. ELLIOTT, ANDREW T. ROACH,
KRISTOPHER J. KAASE, AND RYAN J. KETTLER**

The Mississippi Alternate Assessment of Extended Curriculum Frameworks (MAAECF) is designed to measure the achievement of students with significant cognitive disabilities as articulated in the Mississippi Extended Curriculum Frameworks (MECFs) for language arts, mathematics, and science. The MECFs represent grade-level alternate content standards that are less complex and more accessible than the state's general education curriculum frameworks. The learning expectations articulated in these curriculum frameworks are intended to support educators in creating standards-based instruction for students with significant cognitive disabilities. The MAAECF is used to assess students in Grades 3–8 and 12 to determine adequate yearly progress (AYP) as required by the No Child Left Behind (NCLB) Act of 2001 (PL 107-110).

PURPOSE AND DESIGN OF THE MISSISSIPPI ALTERNATE ASSESSMENT OF EXTENDED CURRICULUM FRAMEWORKS

Students in Grades 3–8 and 12 who meet the state's definition of significant cognitive disabilities are eligible to participate in an alternate assessment. In general, eligible students are those who have histories of re-

The views expressed in this chapter by Kristopher Kaase, an employee of the Mississippi Department of Education at the writing of this chapter, are solely his own and do not reflect any official policy or position of the Mississippi Department of Education.

quiring extensive individualized instruction and have been classified as having severe to profound intellectual disabilities or pervasive developmental disabilities. During the 2005–2006 and 2006–2007 school years, more than 3,600 students (approximately 600 per grade level) were eligible to participate in the MAAECF. This represents 7.2% of the students with disabilities or 0.8% of all Mississippi public school students in Grades 3–8. The number of 12th-grade students who participated in 2007 was 300.

Introduction and Overview of the Assessment

The MAAECF is a comprehensive rating scale that uses teachers' evidence-based judgments of knowledge and skills typically exhibited by students during daily classroom instructional experiences. Depending on each student's grade-level cluster—elementary, middle school, or high school—teachers rate 58–68 language arts items and 52–60 mathematics items. The results of these ratings are total scores for knowledge and skills in language arts/reading and mathematics. (Starting in the 2007–2008 school year, science scores also will be available.) At each grade level, students' total score achievement in each content area is characterized as being at one of four performance levels: *minimal, basic, proficient,* and *advanced.* Once performance levels are determined to be reliable by two or more raters, they are reported for AYP purposes; achievement at the *minimal* or *basic* levels is reported as *not proficient,* and achievement at the *proficient* or *advanced* levels is reported as *proficient.*

Purposes of the Assessment

The MAAECF is a comprehensive, evidence-based rating scale assessment that is an integral part of the statewide assessment system for all students. The alternate assessment provides a means for students with significant cognitive disabilities to participate in the assessment system and to demonstrate their mastery of knowledge and skills in a manner that is sensitive to the diverse and unique disabilities of these students. Such an assessment is mandated by federal and state laws, and it provides teachers, parents, and other educational stakeholders reliable and valid information in the following areas:

- Individual students' achievement of specific knowledge and skills in language arts (reading and writing) and mathematics, aligned with the state's MECFs and grade-level content standards

- The achievement of students with significant cognitive disabilities, as a group, relative to expectations articulated by alternate grade-cluster proficiency (achievement) standards with grade-specific cut scores

- The progress of students with significant cognitive disabilities, as a group, relative to the expectations for progress set by the state in the form of an AYP index

Content Standards to Guide Instruction and Assessment

To determine which content the alternate assessment in Mississippi should measure, we worked with an alternate assessment workgroup composed of 45 individuals representing regular and special educators, parents, special education advocates, and university faculty from across the state to develop extended content standards: the MECFs. The MECFs clearly articulate important knowledge and skills in the content areas of reading/language arts, mathematics, and science. The MECFs in language arts and mathematics for elementary, middle school, and high school students with significant cognitive disabilities are available to all educators on the Mississippi Department of Education (MDE) web site (http://www.mde.k12.ms.us). The MECFs are organized according to a four-level hierarchical structure, with the most general level being a content area. Each content area comprises multiple content strands that subsume multiple competencies, and, in turn, each competency can be further defined by specific objectives. Figure 13.1 illustrates the relationship among these four levels of content. The collective MECF includes curriculum content to which students with significant cognitive disabilities are expected to be exposed during the course of their education in Grades 3–8 and 12. Experienced consultants from E & R Assessments led the alternate assessment workgroup's efforts to develop the MECFs. The process was influenced by Webb's (1997) sequential development process and universal design principles (Thompson, Johnstone, & Thurlow, 2002). The MECFs are organized by grade cluster: elementary, middle, and high.

The MECFs in language arts comprise a reading strand and a writing strand. The reading strand consists of two competencies and 50 objectives, and the writing strand consists of two competencies and 18 objectives. The mathematics content area consists of five strands with one

---

Content area: Language arts
 Content strand: Reading
  Competency 1. Use word recognition skills and strategies to communicate.
   Objectives. **1A.** Student matches letters and sounds.
     1B. Student matches printed words to objects.
     1C. Student reads and recognizes names of classmates.

Figure 13.1. Example of Mississippi's four-level curriculum framework structure. (From Mississippi Department of Education. [2007, August]. *Technical manual for the Mississippi Alternate Assessment of the Extended Curriculum Frameworks for Students with Significant Cognitive Disabilities* [p. 14]. Jackson: Author; reprinted by permission.)

competency each and a total of 59 objectives. The objectives for both language arts and mathematics were written at a level of specificity and objectivity that allowed them to be translated almost word for word into items on the MAAECF rating scale. An illustration of this translation of MECF objectives to MAAECF rating scale items can be observed in Figure 13.2; Items 5, 8, and 9 function as indicators of Language Arts Objectives 1A, 1C, and 1B from Figure 13.1.

Using the grade-cluster–focused MECF language arts and mathematics objectives to guide the writing of items for the MAAECF resulted in a pool of items. A comparative examination of the various grade-cluster versions indicates a significant amount of overlap among the contiguous versions. This overlap was by design for the first 2 years to document a comprehensive developmental picture of performance for students with significant disabilities. Starting with the 2007–2008 assessment, the amount of overlap was reduced when the items were refined; some common items across levels, however, are essential to enable the assessment to provide progress information as well as AYP achievement status reports. Table 13.1 provides a concise picture of the number of items in each version by content and competency area and the number of items common to various forms.

Conclusions About the Design of a Technically Sound Mississippi Alternate Assessment of Extended Curriculum Frameworks

As described in this chapter, the MAAECF is a standards-focused, comprehensive rating scale used to assess students' achievements. These ratings are based on teachers' observations and evidence samples of students' classroom work. The items for the assessment come directly from the learning objectives in the MECFs. The core elements of the assessment are classroom-based evidence samples for items ideally aligned with students' standards-focused individualized educational programs (IEPs) and scored using objective multidimensional rubrics. Classroom evidence thus serves as an indicator of the knowledge and skills targeted by an item. The evidence for any given item, as described by the activities listed in the MECF documents, is expected to be more complex as students progress through Grades 3–12. Figure 13.3 illustrates the anatomy of an MAAECF rating scale item and situates the evidence for each item as an indicator of the knowledge and skills identified in the grade-cluster content standards.

The MAAECF requires a systematic administration process and teamwork between two raters to ensure high-quality results. The resulting scores for the content areas of language arts and mathematics are interpreted using performance-level descriptors with specific skill examples and cut scores for operationalizing differences in overall levels

Language Arts	IEP Aligned (√)	Work Samples	Tests	Observations	Interviews	Video/Photo	Audio Tape	0 = Nonexistent	1 = Emerging	2 = Progressing	3 = Accomplished
			Evidence Sources						Proficiency Ratings		
Reading Strand: Competency 1. *Use word recognition skills and strategies to communicate.*											
1 Student demonstrates literacy readiness.								0	1	2	3
2 Student attends while teacher reads.								0	1	2	3
3 Student answers yes or no questions in an appropriate modality.								0	1	2	3
4 Student understands letter-sound relationships.								0	1	2	3
5 Student matches letters and sounds.								0	1	2	3
6 Student recognizes functional symbols and signage.								0	1	2	3
7 Student recognizes and reads basic sight words.								0	1	2	3
8 Student reads and recognizes names of classmates, family members, and teachers.								0	1	2	3
9 Student matches print words to objects.								0	1	2	3
10 Student matches words or symbols to common pictures of school and community.								0	1	2	3
11 Student uses pictures for context clues.								0	1	2	3
12 Student decodes phonetically regular words.								0	1	2	3
13 Student makes new words based on word families.								0	1	2	3
14 Student reads printed words.								0	1	2	3
15 Student reads and follows class schedule.								0	1	2	3
16 Student reads simple sentences fluently.								0	1	2	3
17 Student understands and uses abbreviations.								0	1	2	3
18 Student leaves a message on an answering machine.								0	1	2	3

Figure 13.2. Section from the language arts portion of the Mississippi Alternate Assessment of Extended Curriculum Frameworks (MAAECF) rating scale. (From Mississippi Department of Education. [2007, August]. *Technical manual for the Mississippi Alternate Assessment of the Extended Curriculum Frameworks for Students with Significant Cognitive Disabilities* [p. 15]. Jackson: Author; reprinted by permission.) (*Key:* IEP, individualized education program.)

Table 13.1. Mississippi Alternate Assessment of Extended Curriculum Frameworks item count across grade clusters for 2006 and 2007

Content area	Competence	Elem. Grades 3–5	Middle school: Grades 6-8			High school: Grade 12[a]		
		Total # items	Total # items	# Items common w/Elem.	# Items common w/HS	Total # items	# Items common w/Elem.	# Items common w/MS
Lang. Arts	1. Word Recognition	16	18	16	9	13	7	9
	2. Comprehension	29	32	29	19	29	16	19
	3. Writing Process	7	12	7	4	12	3	4
	4. Writing Mechanics	6	6	6	4	9	4	4
Total # LA Items & % Common Items		58	68	58 (85%)	36 (53%)	63	30 (48%)	36 (57%)
Math	1. Numbers and Operations	24	26	24	11	19	9	11
	2. Patterns & Relationships	9	11	9	5	13	5	7
	3. Geometry	7	7	7	4	8	4	4
	4. Measurement	8	10	8	8	13	6	8
	5. Collect & Report Data	4	5	4	4	7	3	4
Total # Math Items & % Common Items		52	59	52 (88%)	32 (54%)	60	27 (45%)	34 (57%)
Total # Items per Rating Scale		110	127	110	68	123	57	70

From Mississippi Department of Education. (2007, August). *Technical manual for the Mississippi Alternate Assessment of the Extended Curriculum Frameworks for Students with Significant Cognitive Disabilities* (p. 14). Jackson: Author; reprinted by permission.

[a]Grade 12 was first used in 2007

Key: Elem., Elementary; HS, High School; MS, Middle School; Lang. Arts, Language Arts; LA, Language Arts.

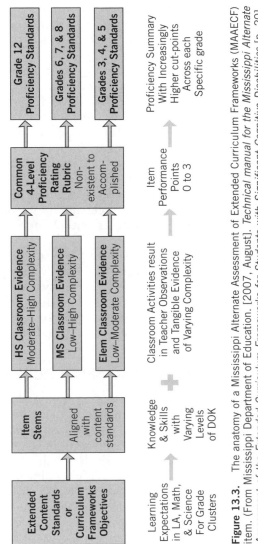

Figure 13.3. The anatomy of a Mississippi Alternate Assessment of Extended Curriculum Frameworks (MAAECF) item. (From Mississippi Department of Education. [2007, August]. *Technical manual for the Mississippi Alternate Assessment of the Extended Curriculum Frameworks for Students with Significant Cognitive Disabilities* [p. 20]. Jackson: Author; reprinted by permission.) (*Key:* HS, high school; LA, language arts; DOK, depth of knowledge.)

of performance. Teachers must attend a daylong professional development workshop and successfully pass an online qualification test before they can be designated as qualified to use the assessment. Teachers' use of the assessment is supported with numerous resource materials such as the *MAAECF Administration Guidebook* and written and digitized (DVD) case studies (materials are available at http://www.mde.k12.ms/maaecf).

The MAAECF is built on time-tested rating scale methodology and features teachers' judgments of students' knowledge and skills that are indicators of valued objectives representative of the state's curriculum frameworks in mathematics, language arts, and science. With training and support, educators can use the MAAECF to document the achievements of students with significant cognitive disabilities. To ensure the integrity of the results of this assessment, the state of Mississippi a) annually conducts a number of regional professional development sessions on the use of the MAAECF and requires teachers who use the instrument to pass a qualification test, b) conducts annual monitoring of the assessments in a representative sample of schools, and c) undertakes studies addressing fundamental validity questions.

Figure 13.4 illustrates the relations among key components of the Mississippi alternate assessment and accountability system and how validity studies provide the foundation on which the system is built. The results of these studies are presented in the last section of this chapter. Before examining them, however, a detailed understanding of the administration and scoring of the MAAECF is provided.

ASSESSMENT INSTRUMENT AND PROCEDURES

The enhanced alternate assessment for Mississippi features an evidence-based rating scale approach that is common to virtually every alternate assessment across the country. Approved alternate assessments from the past several years (e.g., alternate assessments used in Connecticut, Arizona, and Idaho) served as influential models for the MAAECF. The focus and format of the Mississippi approach to a rating scale (see Figure 13.2) highlights that a) items are indicators of MECF objectives, b) evidence to support the ratings of these items must be collected, and c) ratings of the proficiency of each indicator must be made. Key aspects of the MAAECF that further characterize it as a rating scale are the evaluation rubrics that guide item-level ratings and enable translation of total scores in a given content area to a proficiency continuum.

Assessment Process

Before the assessment process begins, a student's IEP team must complete an MAAECF participation checklist to determine whether the stu-

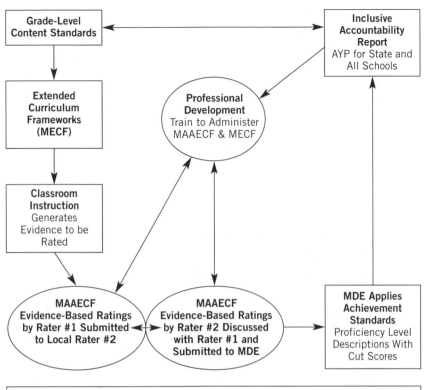

Figure 13.4. The Mississippi alternate assessment and accountability system. (From Mississippi Department of Education. [2007, August]. *Technical manual for the Mississippi Alternate Assessment of the Extended Curriculum Frameworks for Students with Significant Cognitive Disabilities* [p. 8]. Jackson: Author; reprinted by permission.) (*Key:* AYP, annual yearly progress; MECF, Mississippi Extended Curriculum Frameworks; MAAECF, Mississippi Alternate Assessment of Extended Curriculum Frameworks; MDE, Mississippi Department of Education.)

dent is eligible for the MAAECF. As indicated, IEP team members are responsible for deciding whether a student with a disability is eligible to participate in the MAAECF or whether that student should take some or all of the general assessment with accommodations. To be eligible for the MAAECF, the IEP team must answer questions about the student's a) curriculum, b) present level of educational performance, c) need for instructional support, and d) source of difficulty with the general curriculum. Each of the four questions must be considered with respect to each of the content areas being assessed. For a student to be eligible to participate in an alternate assessment in any content area, the IEP team must answer

Yes to each of the four questions. It is possible, but unusual, for a student to take one content area assessment on the general assessment and be assessed in the remaining content areas with the MAAECF.

Once it has been decided that a student will participate in the MAAECF, a five-step process must be followed:

Step 1:   Align MAAECF items with learning objectives to focus evidence collection

Step 2:   Collect performance evidence for a sample of items

Step 3:   Analyze and rate the proficiency of all items

Step 4:   Summarize proficiency scores and performance-level decisions after establishing their reliability

Step 5:   Submit results and evidence sets to the MDE

Key points to keep in mind when conducting an assessment with the MAAECF are discussed in the next several paragraphs.

Aligning MAAECF items with a student's learning goals and objectives requires professional judgment and an understanding of the standards and competencies in the MECFs. One of the key aspects of the MAAECF that makes it a sensitive instrument for assessing individual students' performance is the explicit responsibility it gives teacher evaluators to identify content on the rating scale that is similar to or aligned with each student's learning goals or objectives. An understanding of these curriculum expectations provides a context for the importance of aligning what has been taught with the knowledge and skills assessed on the MAAECF. Students' learning objectives are expected to be influenced by the content in the MECF and, thus, be standards focused and aligned with the MAAECF items.

Alignment does not necessarily mean one-to-one correspondence. It is likely that a student's IEP goals or objectives will have some links to several items in the various content areas (e.g., reading, writing, math). It is important for the rater to look at aligning a student's goals or objectives with the knowledge and skills items that have the strongest connection to a particular content area. It is also important to understand that not all learning goals or objectives appropriate for students with significant cognitive disabilities will align with items on the MAAECF. As more alignment is achieved among standards-based IEP objectives and MAAECF items, however, meaningful instructional access to the general curriculum is more likely to occur.

The alignment of each student's standards-based IEP or other learning goals/objectives with items on the MAAECF rating scale is up to the student's teacher or IEP team members. A specific few questions have been helpful to educators making alignment decisions:

1.　What content area is emphasized in the objective? Is the primary focus reading, writing, or mathematics? Are the knowledge and skills of concern in the student's learning objectives related to any of these areas emphasized in the curriculum frameworks?

2.　Is the knowledge and/or skill that is being taught an entry-level skill in a certain content area?

3.　What are the underlying concepts on which the student is working, and how are those concepts related to a particular knowledge and skill assessed on the MAAECF?

Aligning goals or objectives to items representative of content standards is both an art and a science. Ultimately, it requires teachers to make professional judgments. Over time, it is believed that IEPs and other learning goals or objectives and the content of the MAAECF will have a reciprocal influence on each other and that students will gain more access to the general education curriculum.

Evidence from at least two different categories must be collected and evaluated for each of the items that are aligned with a learning goal or objective. Teachers' ratings and summary performance-level judgments must be based on substantial and tangible evidence or data. In most classrooms, evidence or data about the functioning of students are plentiful. For purposes of the MAAECF, evidence can be categorized into six general areas: work samples, published tests, observations, interviews, videos/photos, and audiotapes. Each aligned goal or objective should have two different kinds of evidence, although it is appropriate to use the same piece of evidence for more than one item. For example, a teacher may have taken a short video of a student writing his or her name and address and then reading it aloud for another person to hear. This video evidence could be used as a basis for rating both an item on the reading strand and an item on the writing strand of the language arts subscale. The teacher also could use some observational record (e.g., narrative recording or a completed recording form) as the second piece of evidence for each of these items.

Ideally, the person gathering the evidence has spent at least 1 month to 6 weeks working with a student before beginning the collection phase of the process. It is important to establish a relationship with the student so that ratings are reliable and representative of the student's learning. In addition, because observations are a valuable source of evidence for many items, teachers need time to observe and record their observations. Many teachers develop excellent progress-monitoring sheets or daily observation records that can provide useful sources of evidence for their summary ratings.

Teachers who correctly complete the MAAECF collect and submit sets of evidence along with evidence worksheets that summarize important attributes of the evidence samples. A set of evidence is defined as two or more pieces of evidence from two different evidence category types (i.e., work samples, tests, observations, interviews, video/photo, audiotape). These sets of evidence are used by the required second rater to establish interrater reliability, for quality control monitoring, and for studies of the validity of the assessment results.

High-quality evidence is relevant (aligned), recent, representative, and can be scored reliably. To support educators in their efforts to collect and document high-quality evidence, each MAAECF evidence worksheet requires the following items:

- The MAAECF rating scale item number for which the evidence is relevant or aligned

- The date each piece of evidence was generated by the student or teacher

- A detailed description of the accuracy of the student's response and the number of settings in which the student provides such a response

- Information about the support or accommodations provided to the student to make his or her responses

In summary, all MAAECF rating scales have to be supported by well-organized and documented evidence samples. At a minimum, teachers are required to collect evidence for one item in each strand of the language arts (four strands) and mathematics scales (five strands). This process results in a minimum of nine sets of evidence with evidence worksheets used to summarize the information for their corresponding items. Starting in 2008, teachers working with 5th-, 8th-, and 12th-grade students also were required to collect evidence for at least one item in each science strand. These evidence requirements are relatively straightforward for students who have one or more standards-based IEP items in each content area strand. When a student does not have an aligned item that routinely provides evidence for the assessment, a teacher must plan ahead and teach material that facilitates the development of the student's knowledge and skills. This instruction can be guided by the many tasks and activities associated with the MECFs and provides tangible evidence about a student's learning.

Teachers are expected to rate all items on the basis of their observations of the student and knowledge of the student's skills. If teachers have not directly observed the student exhibiting the skill, they are expected to attempt to elicit the skill during the assessment period or base their rating on related skills in the same competency domain that they have directly observed. Students are expected to have access to the supports, accommodations, modifications, and assistive technology necessary to demonstrate the extent of their proficiency in the skills and concepts represented by each MAAECF item. Table 13.2 shows the four-level item proficiency rubric used to rate every item on the MAAECF.

The resulting ratings score and proficiency-level determination must be deemed highly reliable or consistent with that of another individual who completes a reliability check before the score can be reported. A second individual must be selected before the assessment and provided a rating form with items checked that have evidence sets to review. This second individual also needs to independently review the collection of evidence assembled by the first rater before completing his or her proficiency ratings. The two individuals then meet to determine the agreement between their ratings and make an overall proficiency-level decision for each content area.

Results of the alternate assessment are summarized using a four-level proficiency framework. The proficiency framework places each stu-

Table 13.2. Four-level item proficiency rubric used to rate every item on the Mississippi Alternate Assessment of Extended Curriculum Frameworks

Item proficiency rating	Descriptive criteria to guide rating decisions
0 = Non-existent (Cannot do currently)	Student is currently unable to perform any part of a skill or demonstrate any knowledge even with full physical prompting in a highly structured setting.
1 = Emerging (Aware & starting to do)	Student attends to task and can respond to some part of the knowledge and skills required by the task given significant physical, verbal, visual, or other form of support. The student may take a long time to respond and is correct or accurate less than 25% of the time in a limited number of settings.
2 = Progressing (Can do partially & inconsistently)	Student is in a stage of building consistency. Performance may be seen as somewhat inconsistent and responses are generally correct between 25%–75% of the time when provided moderate support in several settings. The student shows improvement in acquiring and applying skills with repeated opportunities and feedback.
3 = Accomplished (Can do well & consistently)	Student exhibits the knowledge and skills required by the task and responds correctly more than 75% of the time with minimal support on a regular basis. The student routinely performs the skill in a variety of settings with familiar instructions, materials, or individuals. The student requires little or no supervision in accurately demonstrating the knowledge and skills required by the task.

From Mississippi Department of Education. (2007, August). *Technical manual for the Mississippi Alternate Assessment of the Extended Curriculum Frameworks for Students with Significant Cognitive Disabilities* (p. 20). Jackson: Author; reprinted by permission.

dent on a common criterion-referenced path to the state's content standards and performance levels in the content domains of language arts and mathematics. Results are reported to the Mississippi Office of Student Assessment for purposes of monitoring progress and school-wide accountability. A typical performance-level descriptor is illustrated in Figure 13.5.

Figure 13.6 provides an overview of the connections among the MECF content standards, classroom instructional evidence, the MAAECF rating scales, and performance (achievement) levels—all of which ultimately contribute to AYP decisions.

All summary decisions must be deemed reliable. To estimate the reliability of the performance-level decisions, a second individual who knows the student well is expected to complete a review of the evidence and the first rater's item ratings for items with evidence in each content domain. On the basis of this information, the second individual should make a decision about which performance-level description best characterizes the student's performance. The overall performance-level score decisions of the first rater and the individual who completes the reliability check must be in agreement—they both must result in an overall judgment of either *proficient* or *not yet proficient*—before results can be reported. For purposes of school and statewide educational accountability reports, each student needs a performance level of either *proficient* or *advanced* to achieve the status of *proficient as measured by the MAAECF.* Any student who is functioning at either the minimal level or a basic level is characterized as *not yet proficient as measured by the MAAECF.*

To determine whether acceptable agreement for the fundamental summary decision of *proficient* or *not yet proficient* has been achieved, teachers complete the chart (Figure 13.7) documenting the performance levels determined by the first rater and the individual providing the reliability check. If there is a general agreement, then a decision can be reported. Significant disagreements among raters, however, must be resolved before a performance report is submitted.

If disagreement in professional judgments cannot be resolved through a review and discussion of the evidence and individual item analysis, then the raters must get a third rater (typically, the district special education supervisor) to independently review the evidence and item ratings. The third individual's performance-level decisions should then be compared with the first rater's performance-level decisions to determine whether an acceptable degree of agreement has been reached, in which case a decision can be reported.

Rater 2's Special Role and Responsibilities

Rater 1 is responsible for selecting a second rater (Rater 2) to help ensure that the assessment results are reliable. Rater 2's work begins at Step 4 in the MAAECF process after Rater 1 has finished his or her ratings and has

GRADES 3–5 LANGUAGE ARTS

Language Arts involves development of skills and understanding of concepts in five interrelated strands: (1) reading, (2) writing, (3) speaking, (4) listening, and (5) viewing. The skills and concepts in these five strands vary in complexity and importance for students at each grade level. A critical component at each grade level is text complexity in terms of sophistication of language, context, and syntax. As students progress through the grades, the skills and concepts required to comprehend and compose texts become increasingly complex.

To develop and demonstrate skills in language arts, students require varying levels of support especially as text complexity increases. This support or accommodation is intended to facilitate access and/or responses of knowledge and skills the student has developed.

Minimal	Basic	Proficient	Advanced
Student is able to perform simple skills, but has difficulty communicating, understanding, and demonstrating most discrete pre-literacy skills. Student currently exhibits 1 or 2 of the entry-level skills and knowledge in reading at a barely *emerging* level.	Student attends to language arts instruction and participates in activities. Student responds or performs several skills in at least one language arts strand, typically at the *emerging* level in at least one setting.	Student demonstrates the ability to communicate ideas, and decode and comprehend text. The student's understanding of basic concepts and performance of many skills in two or three language arts strands are typically at the *progressing* level across two or more settings.	Student demonstrates a consistent understanding of the basic concepts and skills contained in the language arts items. He or she performs many of the skills in four or more language arts strands at the *progressing* level and some skills at the *accomplished* level in multiple settings.
Student typically: • Demonstrates very limited understanding of the most basic language arts concepts and skills.	Student typically can: • Attend and respond to texts that are read to him or her by an adult or peer. • Notice pictures in text and use them to make inferences and predictions. • Communicate personal wants, needs, and opinions verbally or through the use of assistive technology.	Student typically can: • Attend to and demonstrate an understanding of texts that are read to them by an adult or peer. • Read basic texts with adult support. • Demonstrate an expanded sight vocabulary and phonological skills. • Use writing, typing, or other mediums to create simple short texts.	Student typically can: • Use a basic sight vocabulary and phonological skills to read unfamiliar words or text. • Make connections between information in a text and previously read materials or life experiences. • Write or type simple stories, journal entries, and letters with minimal support. • Answer appropriately to some comprehension questions.
Gr 3 0---------------8	9----------------------38	39-------------------119	120-----------------174
Gr 4 0---------------9	10--------------------45	46-------------------122	123-----------------174
Gr 5 0-------------11	12--------------------53	54-------------------124	125-----------------174

Figure 13.5. Typical performance-level descriptor showing the four levels of proficiency in language arts for Grades 3–5. (From Mississippi Department of Education. [2007, August]. *Technical manual for the Mississippi Alternate Assessment of the Extended Curriculum Frameworks for Students with Significant Cognitive Disabilities* [p. 4]. Jackson: Author; reprinted by permission.)

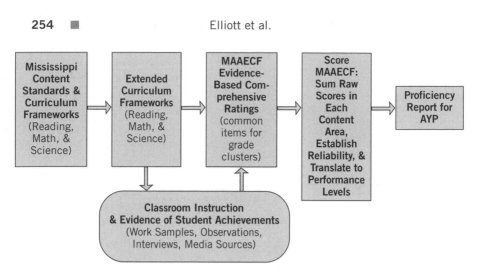

Figure 13.6. Measuring, interpreting, and reporting the academic proficiency of students with significant disabilities using the Mississippi Alternate Assessment of Extended Curriculum Frameworks (MAAECF). (From Mississippi Department of Education. [2007, August]. *Technical manual for the Mississippi Alternate Assessment of the Extended Curriculum Frameworks for Students with Significant Cognitive Disabilities* [p. 28]. Jackson: Author; reprinted by permission.) (*Key:* AYP, adequate yearly progress.)

made a preliminary performance-level decision. Three activities are required of Rater 2; these activities are designed to enhance the reliability of the MAAECF results:

- *Activity 1 for Rater 2:* Review and rate all evidence for items; ensure that the evidence is dated and that information is provided about the correctness of the student's responses, support needed, and number of settings in which the student was able to respond correctly. Rater 2 can request better documentation or more evidence from Rater 1.

- *Activity 2 for Rater 2:* Review all item ratings of Rater 1 to verify that every item has been rated and to learn more about the student's performance in the content area. (Rater 1's additional ratings function as secondary evidence for Rater 2.)

- *Activity 3 for Rater 2:* On the basis of the collected evidence and the ratings of Rater 1, independently select the overall performance level that best characterizes the student's skills. This decision is marked on Rater 1's MAAECF interrater reliability estimates page for each content area assessed. Resolve any disagreements that result in unreliable decisions.

Figure 13.8 provides a visual summary of the five-step assessment process for the MAAECF and the teamwork required to ensure that the resulting scores and performance-level decisions are reliable.

Rater #1's Decision	Reliability Rater's Decision	Inter-rater Outcome		Action to be Taken
Minimal	Minimal or Basic ⟶	Agreement	✓	Report Minimal Performance Level
	Proficient or Advanced ⟶	Disagreement	⟶	Settle Disagreement
Basic	Minimal or Basic ⟶	Agreement	✓	Report Basic Performance Level
	Proficient or Advanced ⟶	Disagreement	⟶	Settle Disagreement
Proficient	Minimal or Basic ⟶	Disagreement	⟶	Settle Disagreement
	Proficient or Advanced ⟶	Agreement	✓	Report Proficient Performance Level
Advanced	Minimal or Basic ⟶	Disagreement	⟶	Settle Disagreement
	Proficient or Advanced ⟶	Agreement	✓	Report Advanced Performance Level

Figure 13.7. Mississippi Alternate Assessment of Extended Curriculum Frameworks outcome decision agreement and reporting chart. (From Mississippi Department of Education. [2007, August]. *Technical manual for the Mississippi Alternate Assessment of the Extended Curriculum Frameworks for Students with Significant Cognitive Disabilities* [p. 18]. Jackson: Author; adapted by permission.)

VALIDATION OF SCORE INTERPRETATIONS AND USES

To achieve the assessment and accountability purposes of the MAAECF and the standards for high-quality tests as articulated in the *Standards for Educational and Psychological Testing* (American Educational Research Association, American Psychological Association, & National Council on Measurement in Education, 1999), the scores from the MAAECF and the decisions based on them must be deemed reliable and valid. In the remainder of this chapter, we provide readers with a summary of the steps taken to develop the MAAECF and the evidence suggesting that the MAAECF yields meaningful and accurate scores concerning students' academic achievement when it is administered with integrity. In the last section of the chapter, we outline current and proposed studies that will facilitate the continued development of evidence to support the claims for the validity of MAAECF scores.

The collection of evidence and the quantification of judgments about students' knowledge and skills on items designed for alignment with the state's content standards (i.e., curriculum frameworks) provide

Rater 1:

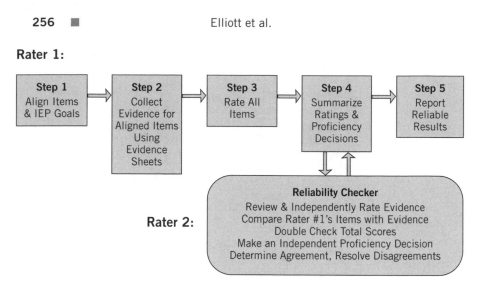

Figure 13.8. Teamwork for reliable results: The roles of Raters 1 and 2. (From Mississippi Department of Education. [2007, August]. *Technical manual for the Mississippi Alternate Assessment of the Extended Curriculum Frameworks for Students with Significant Cognitive Disabilities* [p. 19]. Jackson: Author; reprinted by permission.) (*Key:* IEP, individualized educational program.)

the basis for evaluating the reliability and validity of the resulting scores. Ultimately, a statement about the validity of an assessment involves an evaluative judgment of the degree to which interpretations and uses of the assessment's results—item and total scale scores or proficiency statements—are justified. To make decisions about the degree to which the MAAECF yields valid results, we asked the following five guiding questions and have collected substantial evidence during the past 3 years to answer them.

The Content Question

How well does the sample or collection of assessment tasks represent the domain of tasks to be measured? Most teachers can answer this question by reviewing copies of tests and comparing items with what they teach. The greater the similarity or alignment of the knowledge and skills required by the test items with those taught in the classroom, the more confidence teachers have that the test measures what they value. This question was central to the development of the MAAECF and influenced the alternate assessment workgroup in its efforts to translate the state's curriculum frameworks to items on the MAAECF rating scale.

The Consistency Question

How consistent are the results of an assessment scored by two people? The issue of consistency in scores and scoring is at the heart of the scores' reliability. With a rating scale such as the MAAECF, it is possible to have two or more educators independently rate one student's evidence for a particular item or make summative judgments concerning the student's overall proficiency level. When the raters agree, their ratings are considered reliable. Thus, the consistency question can be answered by examining the interrater reliability of ratings and agreement for levels of proficiency and by examining the internal consistency of the scales the items represent.

The Test–Criterion Relationship Question

How well does a student's performance on the assessment predict future performance or estimate current performance on some valued measure of the knowledge and skills other than the test itself? Most teachers can answer this question by comparing the assessment results with another measure of performance, such as classroom tests or summary observations. The greater the similarity between the test and teachers' other criteria of performance, the more confidence teachers have in the test scores. Progress in answering this question has been made with the completion of a multitrait-multimethod study with known groups of eligible and noneligible students with disabilities.

The Construct Question

How well can teachers interpret performance on the assessment as a meaningful measure of the knowledge and skills the assessment purports to measure? Most teachers cannot answer this question because doing so would require establishing the meaning of the assessment by experimentally determining what factors influence students' performances. Many educators use data on the content and test–criterion relationships as evidence that the test measures a specific construct. Construct validation takes place primarily during the development of a test and is based on an accumulation of evidence from many sources. In the case of a new testing program such as the MAAECF, information about the construct being measured can be gained by reviewing the evidence used to make proficiency judgments and by examining item-to-total score correlations for the various content area rating scales. Results of factor analyses also can provide information on the underlying construct being measured.

The Consequences Question

How well does the use of the assessment results accomplish the intended purposes of the assessment and avoid unintended effects? If an assessment is intended to contribute to improved student learning, the consequences question becomes deceivingly simple: Does it? In trying to answer this question, teachers typically pose many more questions. For example, What impact does the assessment have on teaching? What are the possible negative, unintended consequences of using the assessment's results? Although there is no short or easy answer to these questions, we believe they are worth asking. In fact, these questions often are the first ones many educators ask when confronted with new, large-scale assessment programs. In the annual evaluation of the MAAECF, teachers and parents are asked fundamental questions about the consequences of using the MAAECF on their time, their instruction of students, and their understanding of students' learning.

Issues regarding the validity of the MAAECF results came up before the MAAECF ever was administered, tend to continue after it has been completed, and are always relative to the stated purpose of the alternate assessment program. The typical and seemingly straightforward question—Is the MAAECF valid?—is inappropriately worded and requires some technical knowledge to answer. Better questions are, Is the MAAECF a well-designed assessment that teachers use as intended? and Does the MAAECF yield valid scores when used appropriately? The MAAECF's technical manual is dedicated to documenting efforts to answer these questions with objective data.

As a means of planning and integrating an evidence base to address these practical validity questions, we used the framework illustrated in Table 13.3. As indicated by the numbered items in this figure, at least 11 forms of evidence were targeted as foundations for the validity of the MAAECF scores.

The development and evaluation of the MAAECF has been driven by the design imperatives for technically sound assessments and sensitivity to the challenges confronting students with significant cognitive disabilities and the educators who teach them. According to professional standards and policy documents, assessments used in accountability systems should possess the characteristics of validity, reliability, and usability. Statements about the validity of an assessment involve evaluative judgments of the degree to which interpretations and uses of the assessment's results (scores or proficiency statements) are justified.

Answers to Fundamental Validity Questions

To ensure that the MAAECF encourages meaningful inclusive assessment practices and meets professional guidelines and federal regulations for technical quality, the MDE addressed five validity questions through a coordinated set of validity studies and evidence documenting activities. The questions and key evidence that address them are presented in the next several paragraphs.

How well does the sample or collection of assessment tasks represent the domain of tasks to be measured? Using Webb's (1997) model for

Table 13.3. Validity evidence collection plan

Source of validity evidence	Description of validity evidence to be collected
Evidence based on test content	#1. Alignment analysis with students' IEP goals/objectives and items
	#2. Alignment with content standards, classroom instruction, and content of MAAECF
	A) Importance & instructional relevance ratings by work group members after pilot study cases
	B) Alignment of items with content standards by separate panel of educators
Evidence based on relations to other variables	#3. Correlations among teachers' ratings of students on the MAAECF and the Academic Competence Evaluation Scales (ACES) and the Vineland Adaptive Behavior Scales–II (VABS–II)
	#4. MAAECF ratings correlated with ACES & regular state achievement test results for a sample of 4th & 8th graders; select a random sample of students with disabilities who participated in the regular assessment with and without accommodations and have their teachers complete a MAAECF, an ACES, and VABS–II
Evidence based on internal structure	#5. Conduct a factor analysis of a random subsample of MAAECF cases
Evidence based on consequences of testing	#6. Survey teachers and parents about the acceptability, utility, and meaningfulness of the MAAECF
	#7. Review IEP alignment data from completed MAAECF rating forms & IEP reviews (pre-training & post-training) as an indicator of access to the general curriculum
Evidence based on response process	#8. Results of interviews with teachers who pilot tested the MAAECF and data collected during evidence reviews
Evidence based on reliability of ratings and responses to items	#9. Coefficient alphas on completed MAAECF
	#10. Standard error of measures for each MAAECF scale
	#11. Inter-rater agreement data from completed MAAECF

From Mississippi Department of Education. (2007, August). *Technical manual for the Mississippi Alternate Assessment of the Extended Curriculum Frameworks for Students with Significant Cognitive Disabilities*. Jackson: Author; reprinted by permission.

Key: IEP, individualized educational program; MAAECF, Mississippi Alternate Assessment of Extended Curriculum Frameworks.

alignment, two alignment studies evaluated the connections among the MAAECF rating scale items and Mississippi's language arts and mathematics curriculum frameworks at the 3rd, 5th, 8th, and 12th grades. The collective results of these studies indicated that the MAAECF generally attains Webb's criteria for alignment at all grade levels. In fact, the MAAECF's performance was much stronger than what is typically achieved by large-scale assessments in other states. Independent panels of educators and actual users also reviewed the content of the items and verified that they were nonbiased, objective, and, in many cases, aligned with academic content in students' IEPs.

How consistent are the results of an assessment scored by two or more people? Interrater agreement was calculated by comparing the ratings of the first and second local raters for each case on the standards-focused items on the MAAECF rating scale. Across grade levels, the mean percentage of interrater agreement was between 0.85 and 0.90 in both content areas for the local raters. This same high level of agreement was achieved by a group of well-trained independent raters who did not know the students and only reviewed evidence sets for a subset of items when the evidence was of high quality. Thus, a high level of agreement for item scores and the rule-governed objective procedure for translating these scores to performance levels can result in reliable decisions about each student's achievement on the MAAECF.

How well does a student's performance on the assessment predict future performance or estimate current performance on some valued measure of the knowledge and skills other than the test itself? Concurrent and predictive evidence for the validity of MAAECF scores has been collected as part of the Consortium for Alternate Assessment Validity and Experimental Studies Project. This study examined the relationship between performance on the MAAECF and two nationally normed rating scales (the Academic Competence Evaluation Scales and the Vineland Adaptive Behavior Scales–II). In addition, the MAAECF was administered concurrently with the state's general assessment to a sample of students with disabilities who did not qualify as having significant cognitive disabilities, thus providing some evidence about the discriminant validity of the MAAECF with known groups of eligible and ineligible students. This approach to validation evidence replicates an article (Elliott, Compton, & Roach, 2007) published in *Educational Measurement: Research and Practice.* The preliminary analyses of data from this Mississippi replication indicate that the MAAECF relates to other measures of known constructs in expected ways, although the magnitude of the relations as operationalized by correlations is low to moderate.

How well can teachers interpret performance on the assessment as a meaningful measure of the knowledge and skills the assessment purports to measure? Every teacher who used the MAAECF was required to attend a daylong professional development session and pass an online qualification examination before he or she could be considered a qualified user. Teachers also had access to a number of online resource materials such as the *MAAECF Administration Guidebook* and written and digitized (DVD) case studies with rich evidence examples (see www.mde .k12.ms/maaecf). In addition, many teachers reported that a portion of the language arts and mathematics items were relevant and aligned with some of their students' IEP objectives. Finally, teachers' responses to the survey statement, *The scores and performance-level information result-ing from the MAAECF are meaningful,* was characterized as the most strongly supported among the 12 statements they were asked to evaluate about the MAAECF. Additional evidence regarding this important question was provided in June 2007 by teachers who examined samples of evidence collected by fellow teachers as part of the MAAECF process. Results of this evidence study indicated that evidence quality influences the reliability of ratings and that the instructional activities highlighted in the MECFs and documented with the MAAECF evidence worksheets can result in high-quality information about students' academic achievement that supports the rating process (i.e., increases interrater reliability).

How well does the use of the assessment results accomplish the intended purposes of the assessment and avoid unintended effects? A desired outcome of the MAAECF process is more standards-focused IEPs and increased access to the general curriculum for students with significant cognitive disabilities. The results from the first 2 years of using the MAAECF indicated that teachers were providing more standards-focused academic instruction to most students with significant disabilities. Data from subsequent years will provide additional information on the relationships among the MAAECF rating scale and students' IEP goals and objectives. In addition, nearly 1,000 more students per year have been deemed proficient in language arts and mathematics in AYP reports. There have not been any reports or evidence of negative consequences from the use of the MAAECF.

Integrated Picture of the Evidence for the Validity of the Mississippi Alternate Assessment of Extended Curriculum Frameworks

In this chapter, we have systematically described and examined 3 years of assessment development activities, professional development efforts, formal usage studies, and analysis of extant MAAECF language arts and mathematics results. Many people—more than 3,600 students, nearly 2,500 educators and parents, and more than a dozen professionals from the MDE and E & R Assessments—have been part of these activities. The result has been a substantial amount of quantitative and qualitative information about the psychometric characteristics of the MAAECF. An integrated summary of this psychometric information is provided in Table 13.4, which highlights the validity evidence framework used to guide the development of the MAAECF.

The 21 brief descriptions of evidence for the validity of the MAAECF shown in Table 13.4 are contextualized within the comprehensive expectations for psychometric soundness required by the *Standards and Assessments Peer Review Guidance* (U.S. Department of Education, 2004)

Table 13.4. Validity evidence summary for the Mississippi Alternate Assessment of Extended Curriculum Frameworks (MAAECF)

Type of validity evidence	Sources of validity evidence	Description of validity evidence	USDOE review criteria
Content	Evidence based on test content	• Item development with educator workgroup • Pilot study review of items and IEP alignment analysis • Webb alignment analysis with independent panel of educators in 2006 and again in 2007 • Item difficulty and IEP alignment analysis with all Year 1 and Year 2 data • Item analysis data from factor analysis with all Year 1 data	3.4, 3.5, 3.7, 5.1, 5.2, 5.3, & 5.4
Concurrent; Convergent & Discriminant; Predictive	Evidence based on relations to other variables	• Examination of relationship between MAAECF scores and demographic variables of student race and sex • Concurrent validity study for MAAECF with Academic Competence Evaluation Scales (ACES) and VABS–II for a sample of 85 students who were administered the MAAECF in spring 2007 • Concurrent and discriminant validity study for MAAECF with Mississippi Achievement Test (MAT) for a sample of students with disabilities who do not qualify for the MAAECF but will be administered it by trained raters in spring 2007	4.1, 4.4

Construct	Evidence based on internal structure	• Factor analysis (principal factor method) for all items together with entire grade 3 and grade 8 sample for Y 1 • Follow up factor analyses for all language arts and mathematics scales separately for all grades in Y 1 sample	4.1
Consequential	Evidence based on consequences of testing	• Teacher pilot study survey • Teacher survey post-assessment Y 1 • Parent pilot study survey and post-assessment Y 2 • Achievement level outcomes analysis for all students Y 1	4.3
Content & scoring consistency	Evidence based on response process	• Pilot Study post-assessment survey and focus group discussion • Teacher training sessions with evidence and scoring activities • User qualification examination results for items concerning assessment procedures and scoring • Evidence Quality and Inter-rater reliability study data	4.4
Reliability Estimates	Evidence based on reliability of ratings or responses to items	• Internal consistency data for MAAECF language arts and mathematics scales • Interrater item level and achievement level agreement data • Standard error of measurement estimates for MAAECF language arts and mathematics scales	4.2, 4.4

From Mississippi Department of Education. (2007, August). *Technical manual for the Mississippi Alternate Assessment of the Extended Curriculum Frameworks for Students with Significant Cognitive Disabilities.* Jackson: Author; reprinted by permission.

Key: USDOE, U.S. Department of Education; IEP, individualized educational program; VABS–II, Vineland Adaptive Behavior Scales–II (Sparrow, Cicchetti, & Balla, 2005); Y, year.

and the *Standards for Educational and Psychological Testing* (American Educational Research Association, American Psychological Association, & National Council on Measurement in Education, 1999). The evidence suggests that the MAAECF, when used properly, yields reliable and valid scores that inform educators and parents about students' achievement in language arts and mathematics. There is no evidence to suggest any negative consequences for students, educators, or others using this information to make decisions about students' instruction or academic performance.

Evidence to Support the Purposes of the Mississippi Alternate Assessment of Extended Curriculum Frameworks

As noted at the outset of this chapter, the MAAECF was developed with three purposes in mind:

> *Purpose 1.* Assess and report individual students' achievement of specific knowledge and skills in language arts (reading and writing) and mathematics that are aligned with the MECFs and some key learning objectives.

> *Purpose 2.* Determine and report the achievement of students with significant cognitive disabilities, as a group, relative to expectations articulated by alternate grade-cluster (achievement) standards with unique grade-level cut scores.

> *Purpose 3.* Report the progress of students with significant cognitive disabilities, as a group, relative to the expectations for progress set by the state in the form of an AYP index.

The MAAECF's first 2 years of use statewide provided substantial evidence (as documented in this chapter) to support the assessment's continued use among students with significant cognitive disabilities for these three purposes. Of course, more evidence is needed to support the continued use and development of the MAAECF. Data for an important concurrent validity study were collected and are in the preliminary stages of analysis, and virtually all of the analyses conducted with Year 1 data have been or are being repeated with the Year 2 MAAECF data set for students in Grades 3–8 and 12. Plans to ensure continued development and improvement of the MAAECF for students with significant cognitive disabilities and the standards-based accountability system for educators have been made and will contribute to the already substantial and growing technical soundness of this instrument.

NEXT STEPS IN THE DEVELOPMENT OF THE MISSISSIPPI ALTERNATE ASSESSMENT OF EXTENDED CURRICULUM FRAMEWORKS

Although substantial evidence exists regarding the reliability and validity of MAAECF language arts and mathematics scores, especially with students in Grades 3–8, there is room to improve the assessment procedures, and a need remains for ongoing efforts to examine the effects of changes on the technical soundness of the resulting scores. In this final section of the chapter, we look forward and outline areas in which plans have been established and actions are underway that are designed to refine and improve the technical and instructional validity of the MAAECF for students with significant disabilities. We are focusing our current efforts on five areas:

1. Refinement of items across the grade-cluster versions of the MAAECF

2. Refinement of the evidence collection and submission requirements for the MAAECF

3. Refinement of the procedures for second raters

4. Refinement of professional development materials

5. Refinement of the MECF documents

Two additional initiatives that may receive more attention are a) a comprehensive survey of parents of students with significant disabilities to discern their reactions to the MAAECF and the assessment's instructional effects on their children's education and b) an examination of classroom activities and related MAAECF items that are more sensitive to the abilities of a small subgroup of students with the most severe disabilities.

The remainder of this section summarizes the plans to address each of the five refinement or improvement areas for the MAAECF.

Refinement of Items Across the Grade-Cluster Versions

Many common items exist across the grade-cluster levels of the MAAECF. From the outset of the MAAECF's development, it was expected that these common items would be valuable initially in providing a baseline and developmental picture of academic performance for students. It was expected, however, that after 2 years the number of common items could be reduced to facilitate a more streamlined assessment while still allowing the opportunity to examine progress over time on common items, should the state move to a *status plus progress* model of performance.

The item reduction work was completed on the language arts and mathematics scales. As documented in Table 13.5, the word recognition competency in language arts and the numbers and operations competency in mathematics are the primary areas for item reduction. Both these areas had many items and were reduced by 25%–30% without significantly impacting overall alignment or psychometric indices.

This item refinement work was data driven and sensitive to the standards. We examined item difficulty and depth of knowledge levels, recalculated the alignment of the scales with the content standards when items have been removed, and reran analyses to ensure that the reliability of each scale was maintained. This item refinement work resulted in shorter but still well-aligned scales.

Refinement of the Evidence Collection and Submission Requirements

This refinement work began with an evidence and interrater reliability study in which a random sample of evidence sets for 83 students in the elementary, middle school, and high school levels were examined in detail by a workgroup of teachers experienced in the administration of the MAAECF. This group concluded that the evidence collection worksheets and the evidence collection requirements implemented during Year 2 were good but could be improved. Refinements to the four worksheets have been completed. Previously, one item per competency required the review of an evidence set by a second rater. Data from the Year 2 administration of the MAAECF indicated that, on average, teachers submitted evidence sets for two items per competency. This evidence typically represented one or two skills within a broad competency such as reading comprehension or measurement.

To increase the validity of the teacher ratings of student performance, the MAAECF was revised to require evidence representing the entire breadth of the content area. To facilitate this evidence collection, the MAAECF items were organized within each competency into clusters of related knowledge and skills (see Table 13.6). The items were grouped into clusters not only in recognition of the similar knowledge and skills represented but because students often demonstrate more than one knowledge or skill with a performance. Typically, a student who can demonstrate proficiency in a higher skill also must have proficiency in the lower-level skills. As illustrated in Table 13.7, a student who can demonstrate proficiency in *reads simple sentences fluently* also demonstrates the lower-level skills of *reads printed words* and *recognizes and reads basic sight words.* This organization of knowledge and skills into clusters encourages teachers to develop evidence that demonstrates a

Table 13.5. Draft of Mississippi Alternate Assessment of Extended Curriculum Frameworks item count; proposed reductions in items are implemented

Content area	Competencies	Elem. Grades 3–5 Total # items	Middle school: Grades 6-8 Total # items	# Items Common w/Elem.	# Items common w/HS	High school: Grade 12 Total # Items	# Items Common w/ Elem.	# Items Common w/MS
Lang. Arts	1. Word Recognition	12	14	9	9	13	4	9
	2. Comprehension	18	28	14	19	29	7	19
	3. Writing Process	5	10	4	4	12	2	4
	4. Writing Mechanics	5	5	4	4	9	3	4
Total # LA Items & % Common		40	57	31 (54%)	36 (62%)	63	16 (25%)	36 (57%)
Math	1. Numbers & Operations	19	17	12	9	17	4	9
	2. Patterns & Relationships	6	11	6	6	12	2	6
	3. Geometry	6	7	6	3	7	2	3
	4. Measurement	6	10	6	7	12	4	7
	5. Collect & Report Data	4	5	4	4	7	3	4
Total # Math Items & % Common		41	50	34 (68%)	29 (58%)	55	15 (27%)	29 (53%)
Science	1. Inquiry	7	8	5	2	9	1	2
	2. Earth and Space Systems	12	17	0	13	22	0	13
	3. Life Science	14	14	7	7	25	2	7
	4. Physical Sciences	8	10	6	6	12	3	6
Total # Science Items & % Common		41	49	18 (37%)	28 (57%)	68	6 (9%)	28 (41%)
Total Rating Scale		122	156	83 (53%)	93 (60%)	186	37 (20%)	93 (50%)

From Mississippi Department of Education. (2007, August). *Technical manual for the Mississippi Alternate Assessment of the Extended Curriculum Frameworks for Students with Significant Cognitive Disabilities* (Chapter 8). Jackson: Author; reprinted by permission.

Key: Elem., Elementary; HS, High School; MS, Middle School; Lang. Arts, Language Arts; LA, Langauge Arts.

Table 13.6. Sample Mississippi Alternate Assessment of Extended Curriculum Frameworks language arts item clusters for elementary, middle school, and high school levels

Elementary: Grades 3–5	Middle School: Grades 6–8	High School
	Language Arts [Number of items follows the cluster name.]	

Competency 1: Word Recognition (Elementary)

Cluster
A. Initial Interactions with Symbols 2
B. Phonics 2
C. Recognizing Words 3
D. Using Symbols & Visual 5

12

Competency 2: Comprehension (Elementary)

Cluster
A. Responding to Text & Other Messages 5
B. Vocabulary & Conceptual Understanding 3
C. Listening & Conversation 4
D. Conveying Information 4

16

Competency 1: Word Recognition (Middle School)

Cluster
A. Symbols, Pictures, & Environmental Print 4
B. Phonics 3
C. Reading Words & Sentences 5

12

Competency 2: Comprehension (Middle School)

Cluster
A. Responding to Text & Other Messages 6
B. Vocabulary & Conceptual Understanding 3
C. Listening & Conversation 3
D. Answering Comprehension Questions 3
E. Using Resources to Get Information 4

19

Competency 1: Word Recognition (High School)

Cluster
A. Recognizing Words 4
B. Word Use Strategies 4
C. Reading Words & Sentences 4

12

Competency 2: Comprehension (High School)

Cluster
A. Responding to Text & Other Messages 6
B. Vocabulary & Conceptual Understanding 6
C. Listening & Conversation 4
D. Answering Comprehension Questions 7
E. Uses Media & Other Information 3

25

Competency 3: Writing Process

Cluster

A. Words & Symbols 4
B. Writing for an Audience 3

7

Competency 4: Writing Mechanics

Cluster

A. Spelling & Grammar 3

3

Item Total = 38 / Evidence Sets = 11

Competency 3: Writing Process

Cluster

A. Creating a Message 4
B. Researching Information 4
C. Revising and Using Tools 2

10

Competency 4: Writing Mechanics

Cluster

A. Writing Mechanics 5

5

Item Total= 46 / Evidence Sets = 12

Competency 3: Writing Process

Cluster

A. Creating a Message 5
B. Researching Information 4
C. Revising and Using Tools 3
D. Personal Information 2

14

Competency 4: Writing Mechanics

Cluster

A. Spelling & Punctuation 5

5

Item Total = 56 / Evidence Sets = 13

From Mississippi Department of Education. (2007, August). *Technical manual for the Mississippi Alternate Assessment of the Extended Curriculum Frameworks for Students with Significant Cognitive Disabilities* (Chapter 8). Jackson: Author; reprinted by permission.

Table 13.7. Sample content area item clusters for language arts and mathematics

Example elementary grades language arts cluster using symbols & visuals	Example middle grades cluster collecting and reporting data
Student recognizes and reads basic sight words.	Student creates a simple text or meaningful picture to report findings.
Student reads and recognizes names of classmates, family members, and teachers.	Student creates a graph, table, or chart from data.
Student matches print words to objects.	Student explains terms *always, sometimes,* and *never.*
Student reads printed words.	Student interprets a graph, table, or chart.
Student reads simple sentences fluently.	Student uses basic probability concepts to make predictions about an event.

From Mississippi Department of Education. (2007, August). *Technical manual for the Mississippi Alternate Assessment of the Extended Curriculum Frameworks for Students with Significant Cognitive Disabilities* (Chapter 8). Jackson: Author; reprinted by permission.

student's highest level of performance and that integrates the knowledge and skills represented by the cluster. This organization also supports performances that are more authentic and representative of the student's level of sophistication instead of requiring separate evidence to demonstrate each discrete skill/item.

Refinement of the Second Rater Procedures and Refinement of Continued Professional Development Materials

These two areas for improvement have been conceptualized as interrelated and were the central focus of a funded proposal the state made to the IDEA General Supervision Enhancement Grant competition (Priority B in Catalog of Federal Domestic Assistance [CFDA] 84.373X). The abstract for this project read

> To enhance the overall technical quality of the Mississippi Alternate Assessment of Extended Curriculum Frameworks (MAAECF), the Mississippi Department of Education (MDE) will develop a collaborative team consisting of experts in the field of alternative assessments for students with significant cognitive disabilities and experts in the field of assessment development, scoring, and reporting. The Mississippi Department of Education aspires to develop a comprehensive system for ensuring the technical soundness of results from its alternate assessment for students with significant cognitive disabilities. A key element in the proposed system is a center for evaluating the quality of evidence submitted by teachers to (a) document students' knowledge and skills for content included in the Mississippi Extended Curriculum Frameworks (MECF) *and* (b) establish the reliability of teachers' proficiency ratings of students on the MAAECF. This Center for Alternate Assessment Review of Evidence and Scoring (CAARES) will be located at Mis-

sissippi State University (MSU) and will work directly with the MDE Office of Student Assessment. In addition, this new Center will coordinate with a Research and Validity Studies Team and a Professional Development Support Team from the state's current vendor for the development of the MAAECF. Collectively, the CAARES staff and the teams of psychometric experts from E & R Assessments will work with MDE staff to enhance the overall technical quality of the MAAECF for students with significant cognitive disabilities. This collaborative effort is expected to result in (a) more rigorous and independent reviews of teacher collected evidence and students' proficiency scores, (b) more focused and pragmatic professional development designed to enhance both instruction and assessment, and (c) more comprehensive investigations of reliability estimates and related validity evidence for students' scores. These are important results that will contribute to the continued improvement of the Mississippi Alternate Assessment of Extended Curriculum Frameworks for students with significant cognitive disabilities and for the educators who work with them daily to provide access to the general curriculum and the skills needed for success in life after school.

This project builds on the existing alternate assessment system and significantly enhances it through the addition of the CAARES at MSU's Research and Curriculum Unit. The efforts of the CAARES staff, in collaboration with the MDE Student Assessment Office and teams of experts focused on professional development and validity studies, enables more integrated and comprehensive reviews of the classroom evidence used to anchor teachers' proficiency scores, ensures an independent two-rater scoring process, provides all teachers with feedback and professional support to enhance instruction-generated evidence, and integrates all of this information into the ongoing efforts to maintain and document the technical soundness of the MAAECF. The shaded elements in Figure 13.9 indicate how the CAARES enhanced alternate assessment components advance instruction, assessment strategies, and the technical quality of the resulting alternate achievement scores.

Scoring

In the updated system, teachers continue to score all the items for each content area as they did previously on the MAAECF. The average across all items for a cluster represents the cluster score. The cluster average is calculated by machine (i.e., there is no place to report the average cluster score on the reporting form).

In the previous versions of the MAAECF, teachers' ratings were validated by local independent raters. The refinement in the second rater procedures requires all evidence for all students to be sent to the CAARES state scoring center for an independent rating by raters trained by the state to evaluate evidence quality and to rate student performance

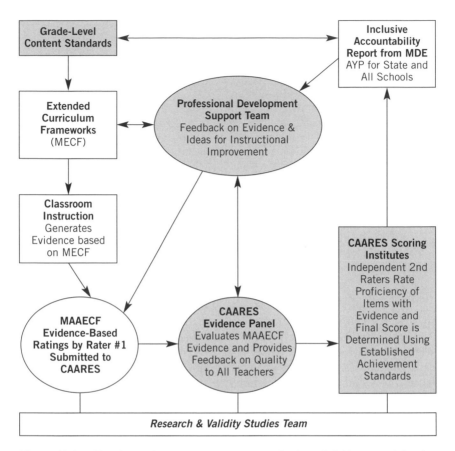

Figure 13.9. The Center for Alternate Assessment Review of Evidence and Scoring (CAARES) enhanced Mississippi alternate assessment and accountability system. (From Mississippi Department of Education. [2007, August]. *Technical manual for the Mississippi Alternate Assessment of the Extended Curriculum Frameworks for Students with Significant Cognitive Disabilities* [p. 8]. Jackson: Author; reprinted by permission.) (*Key:* MDE, Mississippi Department of Education; AYP, adequate yearly progress; MECF, Mississippi Extended Curriculum Frameworks; MAAECF, Mississippi Alternate Assessment of Extended Curriculum Frameworks.)

according to the submitted evidence. Many of these state-level raters will be teachers of students with significant cognitive disabilities who completed the assessment process at the local level. These state-level raters will be trained to evaluate evidence for a) alignment with the MECFs, b) recency (i.e., evidence reflects student performance during the assessment period), c) representativeness (multiple pieces of evidence with a detailed description of the accuracy of the student's response and the number of settings in which the student provides such a response), and d) reliability (information about the support or accommodations provided to the student to make his or her responses). State-level raters will be trained to evaluate evidence quality and accurately score evidence and then to accurately evaluate and rate a qualifying set before serving as raters. State-level raters will be assigned carefully so that they will not be reviewing assessments for students from their own school districts or regions.

The state-level rater first will determine whether the evidence is aligned. If the evidence is not aligned, it will be considered nonscorable. If the evidence is scorable, then the state-level rater will assign a proficiency rating to each cluster. State-level cluster scores will be compared with the cluster average provided by each student's teacher. If the scores are in agreement or within an acceptable range of difference (e.g., adjacent), then the teacher's original ratings will stand. If there is not agreement, then a second state-level rater will evaluate the assessment. If the state-level raters agree, then the state-level rater scores will be assigned to the student.

Because of the number of students for whom evidence will be submitted (more than 3,000) and the state's resources, a matrix sampling approach to the state-level review of evidence and comparison of scores will be employed. This sampling design will ensure that a) all teachers and b) all content areas (but not necessarily all clusters within a content area) are sampled.

Professional Development

Professional development will be grounded in the work of the state scoring center. By evaluating evidence for both quality and scoring accuracy, patterns of teacher strengths or weaknesses in these areas within and across content areas can be identified. Weaknesses will be targeted for professional development activities, which may include face-to-face training sessions and online training or resources. The rich evidence base will provide examples of superior evidence that can be shared as models for teachers.

Refinement of the Mississippi Extended Curriculum Frameworks Documents

The collection of the MAAECF evidence at the state level will provide a rich database of information about the performance of students with significant cognitive disabilities in language arts, mathematics, and science. As teachers better adapt to the instructional needs of these students, student performance will increase. Student performance also will provide feedback on the academic content standards and indicate areas for refinement. We expect that such refinement will be necessary within a couple of years of implementing the refinements identified above.

SUMMARY

The technical soundness and instructional utility of the MAAECF is an important part of the Mississippi assessment and accountability system. The current assessment is working well, and, with the refinements outlined in this chapter, it will improve and will provide reliable and valid annual summaries of the academic achievements of students with significant cognitive disabilities.

REFERENCES

American Educational Research Association, American Psychological Association, & National Council on Measurement in Education. (1999). *Standards for educational and psychological testing.* Washington, DC: Author.

DiPerna, J.C., & Elliott, S.N. (2000). *Academic Competence Evaluation Scales (ACES).* San Antonio, TX: Pearson Assessment.

Elliott, S.N., Compton, E., & Roach, A.T. (2007). Building validity evidence for scores on a state-wide alternate assessment: A contrasting groups, multi-method approach. *Educational Measurement: Issues & Practice, 26*(2), 30–43.

Mississippi Department of Education. (2007, August). *Technical manual for the Mississippi Alternate Assessment of the Extended Curriculum Frameworks for Students with Significant Cognitive Disabilities.* Jackson: Author.

No Child Left Behind Act of 2001, PL 107-110, 115 Stat. 1425, 20 U.S.C. §§ 6301 *et seq.*

Sparrow, S.S., Cicchetti, D.V., & Balla, D.B. (2005). *Vineland Adaptive Behavior Scales, Second Edition (Vineland-II).* Circle Pines, MN: AGS Publishing.

Thompson, S.J., Johnstone, C.J., & Thurlow, M.L. (2002). *Universal design applied to large scale assessments* (Synthesis Report 44). Minneapolis: University of Minnesota, National Center on Educational Outcomes. Retrieved March 12, 2009, from http://education.umn.edu/NCEO/OnlinePubs/Synthesis44.html

U.S. Department of Education. (2004, April). *Standards and assessments peer review guidance: Information and examples for meeting requirements of the No Child Left Behind Act of 2001.* Washington, DC: Author.

Webb, N.L. (1997). *Criteria for alignment of expectations and assessments in mathematics and science education* (NISE Research Monograph No. 6). Madison: University of Wisconsin-Madison, National Institute for Science Education.

CHAPTER 14

Test Design and Validation of Inferences for the Oregon Alternate Assessment

DIANNA CARRIZALES AND GERALD TINDAL

Although alternate assessments have relatively brief references in federal regulations, they have become an important component of state large-scale assessment systems.

INTRODUCTION AND BACKGROUND: LEGISLATIVE AND EMPIRICAL BASIS OF ALTERNATE ASSESSMENTS

With fewer than 10 years of implementation, alternate assessments have become a field unto themselves. To the credit of those enacting the legislation and regulation and those conducting the research, the measurement field has expanded to include alternate assessments. It seems likely that students are benefiting, though the results are not all accounted for yet, and outcomes from the implementation of alternate assessments need to be monitored carefully. Nevertheless, students taking alternate assessments are participating in the academic reforms that are present in general education, and the research agenda on measures sensitive to this group of students—students with the most significant cognitive disabilities—is increasing. This research is rapidly establishing the validity of the inferences that can be made from assessments that are linked to grade-level standards. Although the legislation and regulation preceded the research, which often was concurrent with adoption and changes in practice, federal peer review of state assessment systems provided the significant impetus for change.

Legislation and Regulations on Alternate Assessments

Five significant legislative and regulatory efforts have resulted in a curious conundrum of educational measurement. The Individuals with Disabilities Education Act Amendments (IDEA) of 1997 (PL 105-17), the No Child Left Behind Act (NCLB) of 2001 (PL 107-110), the 1% and 2% announcements (discussed later in this chapter), and peer reviews of statewide assessment programs systematically have made the assessment of students with disabilities *a part of,* instead of *apart from,* educational practices in measuring the learning outcomes of public schools. These reforms have the potential not only to change educational practices but also to modify fundamentally how educators view measurement.

1. IDEA 1997 ushered in a significant reform in educational assessment: Students with disabilities would need to be included in large-scale testing programs and be provided access to the general education curriculum (Olsen, 1998). This initial legislation allowed certain students accommodations or modifications in the tests they took. At that time, the idea of test accommodations had been studied but was in its nascent stages (see Tindal & Fuchs, 1999). Since then, considerable research has been conducted on making changes to testing so that the essential test constructs do not change and the scores can be aggregated with those of nonaccommodated tests (Thompson, Johnstone, & Thurlow, 2002).

2. On January 8, 2002, President George W. Bush signed NCLB into law. NCLB significantly changed the manner in which participation in large-scale testing would be considered. Simple participation was no longer emphasized; rather, critical thresholds had to be reached such as 95% participation of student populations disaggregated by poverty levels, race, ethnicities, disabilities, and limited levels of English proficiency. This disaggregation meant that improvement no longer could be achieved at the expense of averages that would mask the performance of students in these groups.

3. On December 9, 2003, regulatory guidance was issued from the U.S. Department of Education. For students with the most significant disabilities, up to 1% of students could be counted in measures of a state's adequate yearly progress (AYP) if they were deemed proficient on an alternate assessment based on alternate achievement standards (AA-AAS; see Federal Register, 2003). At the time, alternate assessments had many methodologies, and it was assumed that the grade-level content standards would be the essential base for achievement of standards but that alignment would entail reduced breadth, depth, or complexity:

An alternate assessment must be aligned with the state's content standards, must yield results separately in both reading/language arts and mathematics, and must be designed and implemented in a manner that supports use of the results as an indicator of AYP. (Federal Register, 2003, p. 68699)

4. On May 10, 2005, Education Secretary Margaret Spellings announced that states would be allowed to develop alternate assessments judged against modified achievement standards (AA-MAS) for students with persistent academic disabilities served under the IDEA. States also would be allowed to count proficient scores from such assessments in making AYP decisions, but the number of such scores would be capped at 2% of the total tested population. This population of students would be judged against grade-level content standards, and off-grade testing would not be allowed. Nevertheless, this form of participation would involve some reduction in complexity (for the research base used in defining this population, see U.S. Department of Education, 2005).

5. In the 2005–2006 academic year, states were required to submit their entire large-scale testing programs for peer review, in which a number of criteria would be invoked to document various components of technical adequacy. Based essentially on the *Standards for Educational and Psychological Testing* (American Educational Research Association, American Psychological Association, & National Council on Measurement in Education, 1999), the criteria considered various aspects of reliability and validity evidence (U.S. Department of Education, 2004).

Research on Alternate Assessments Concurrent with State Adoptions

While the legal and regulatory language was being adopted and practice was being changed, some limited research was also being conducted. This literature on assessment of students with significant disabilities, however, was limited primarily to portfolio assessments and seldom addressed measurement or scaling issues. For example, Kleinert, Kearns, and Kennedy (1997) described a number of standards for evaluating alternate assessments with scoring dimensions aligned to performance, support, settings, interactions, contexts, and domains (each referenced to a professional literature base). They reported on the reliability of the alternate portfolio approach across 3 years, with agreement indices of 57%, 49%, and 49% achieved on a four-point scale. They also reported a correlation of .45 between a measure of program quality and performance on the alternate portfolio (a finding also reported by Turner, Baldwin, Kleinert, & Kearns, 2000). Kampfer, Horvath, Kleinert, and Kearns

(2001) reported on 206 teachers' perceptions of time and effort associated with a number of variables relevant to the operation of the alternate assessment: eligibility, materials sent out, schedules, entries, progress, social relationships, access to multiple settings, and development of natural supports. They reported teachers spending 25–35 hours outside of instructional time to complete the portfolios. Modest relationships were found among outcome performance and a number of these operational variables. These early studies were bold new efforts to bring a population of students to large-scale assessments and to document outcomes. These studies on reliability and inclusiveness provided critical findings that supported further research into issues of measurement and scaling.

Oregon's Response

During these early days of research prior to and immediately following the release of new regulations on alternate assessments, Oregon's response to legislative and regulatory requirements for the meaningful measurement of all students was to develop two AA-AAS. One was designed specifically for students whose needs were defined primarily by their performance toward functional or life skills goals, and the other assessment was designed for students whose individualized educational programs (IEPs) included academic content that addressed emerging basic academic skills linked to standards in early grades not assessed by the general assessment—that is, kindergarten, first, or second grade. Between 2000 and 2005, development on these assessments continued to be refined and enhanced using empirical research that drew from instructional techniques, assessment approaches, and best practices for serving students with disabilities (Browder et al., 2003).

By 2005, Oregon had established two distinct approaches toward alternate assessment: the Extended Career and Life Roles Assessment System and the Extended Subject Area Assessments. Each testing approach assessed students in material linked to the four subject areas—reading, writing, mathematics, and science—across all the grades tested by the general assessment. Approximately 900 students were taking the Extended Career and Life Roles Assessment System, and 3,000 students each were taking Oregon's Extended Reading and Extended Mathematics assessments; fewer students were taking the Extended Writing assessment because of its more limited grade-level application. The Extended Science assessment was piloted in 2003 and implemented in 2004 with about 1,000 students. Since their inception in 2000 until 2005, these assessments evolved not only in response to federal requirements for more inclusive models of instruction and assessment but also in response to developments in research specifically for students with disabilities. One of the most significant evolutions was the shift from life-skills assessments to applications addressing students' academic skills.

Researchers at the University of Oregon had conducted several studies on the alternate assessments, particularly the extended measures in the basic skills. Reliability and criterion validity studies were conducted in reading and math (Tindal, Glasgow, Gall, VanLoo, & Chow, 2002; Tindal et al., 2003). Almond, Tindal, Arnold, Stolp, and McCabe (2003) used a multitrait, multimethod matrix (Campbell & Fiske, 1959) and Yin's (1989) case study design to study assessments across several states. Crawford, Tindal, and Carpenter (2006) studied Oregon's alternate writing assessment to determine whether its internal structure accurately reflected the six areas identified as tasks that students had to complete during the assessment. Finally, Yovanoff and Tindal (2007) scaled reading performance tasks to a 25-item statewide reading test to extend the lower measurement range.

Peer Review and the Need for Change

In 2005, a national peer review of statewide assessment systems (including alternate assessments) clarified the NCLB performance expectations for students with significant disabilities. The gradually pervading philosophy of assessment and instruction for this population asserted that all students should have expectations that could be linked demonstrably (via empirically designed alignment studies) to grade-level content. The nation's alternate assessments, therefore, were cemented as tools for determining student performance toward grade-level content.

The clarification of federal expectations for alternate assessments and the resultant need for detailed technical documentation fueled assessment conversations across the nation about students with significant disabilities. Some of these conversations were philosophical and soul searching: *What should we expect of these students? What are we taking from these students if we ask teachers to reduce their focus on the life skills and routines that the students will need for relative independence? What critical academic standards should all students know and master?* Other conversations addressed empirical issues: *Can mastery of the mathematical principle of dilation be demonstrated accurately when using graphical and verbal supports is not offered to students in the general population? Can an assessment item that is supported with a series of scaffolds for this population be considered comparable with a similar item with no such supports?* Assessment geared only toward measuring student progress in skills such as dressing and greeting was to be replaced with assessments that incorporated obvious links to grade-level content. Gone, too, were assessments that allowed students to take out-of-level tests that targeted standards at lower grade levels.

In Oregon, the issues generated by the peer review led to a statewide redefinition of the population taking alternate assessments; the state took a two-pronged approach that linked items to grade-level content standards and that was appropriate for students with significant cognitive disabilities who needed a) significantly reduced breadth, depth, and complexity of academic content and b) additional supports and scaffolds to access the assessments.

The redevelopment of Oregon's alternate assessment system was founded on the belief that students with the most significant cognitive disabilities were not defined by any categorical disability classification. Instead, this population would be identified by characteristics defined broadly at a state level but identified more accurately and specifically by experts closest to each student. Students who took alternate assessments in Oregon could fall into any of the federal disability categories; they would not be prevented from or required to participate in alternate assessments on the basis of disability categories. The needs of each student would be the primary basis for decision making about his or her participation in an alternate assessment.

A second principle was that broad and varied supports would be available to students participating in Oregon's alternate assessments. Three main types of support and access were considered before the actual development of the measures:

1. An assessment was required that reflected universal design principles in its construction. In developing Oregon's alternate assessments, we emphasized universal design principles by reducing complexity, developing scaffolds of prompting, and using clear, specific graphics.

2. Assessments could be administered with any of the state-allowable accommodations. Such accommodations included the presentation of materials (more space, repeat of an item prompt or removal of an item prompt) and the types of responses recorded and scored.

3. Students' prerequisite skills would need to be assessed at the time of testing to maximize the involvement of students. Because students with the most significant cognitive disabilities often have interfering behaviors that can negatively impact inferences made during standardized assessments, a separate assessment was incorporated to determine the level of support that a student might need to minimize his or her potential confounding behaviors.

UNIVERSAL DESIGN OF ALTERNATE ASSESSMENTS, ACCOMMODATIONS, AND PREREQUISITE SKILLS

The specifications for Oregon's alternate assessments were based on guidelines of universal design to ensure that all students, regardless of disability, could access the assessments to the greatest extent possible.

The specifications were enhanced further by incorporating state-approved accommodations into the test design. Finally, the test design ensured that the information provided by the proximal assessment of prerequisite skills would be used meaningfully.

Universal Design for Assessment and Universal Design for Learning

Universal Design for Assessment (UDA) is a test development system with the potential to address issues in developing alternate assessments. Nationally, UDA is recognized as a powerful tool for supporting the needs of the diverse student population. UDA is a measurement system that provides customized tests based on individual needs. As such, UDA captures the knowledge and abilities of the widest range of students with the least amount of external accommodations or modifications to the test structure or format (Thompson et al., 2002). UDA systematically embeds format changes within the assessment tool and anchors these changes to student performance by providing a multimethod design to accurately assess basic skills. Thus, UDA provides direct access to content information and student performance data without retrofitting existing materials or relying on imprecise decision-making methods.

The broader concept (beyond UDA) is Universal Design for Learning (UDL), a framework developed by the Center for Applied Special Technology (CAST) to guide construction of curricula and assessments that are flexible and supportive of all students (Dolan & Hall, 2001; Meyer & Rose, 1998; Pisha & Coyne, 2001; Rose, 2001; Rose & Dolan, 2000; Rose & Meyer, 2000, 2002; Rose, Sethuraman, & Meo, 2000). The universal design movement in architecture inspired the concept of UDL. This movement called for the design of structures that anticipated the needs of individuals with disabilities and accommodated these needs from the outset. Universally designed structures also offered unforeseen benefits for all users. Curb cuts, for example, served their intended use for people in wheelchairs, but they also were beneficial to people pushing strollers, carts, and even average walkers. Designing from the start for individuals with disabilities led to improved usability for everyone.

For the past 15 years, CAST has developed UDL theory through an ongoing program of research and development (e.g., the National Center on Accessing the General Curriculum, the Strategic Reader Project, the Engaging the Text Project, the Thinking Reader Project). UDL recognizes the extensiveness of individual differences and uses curriculum flexibility to optimize learning in the face of these differences. *Universal* does not mean *one size fits all;* instead, it means that learning is conceived and designed to accommodate the widest possible range of learner needs and preferences. The UDL framework guides the development of adaptable curricula by means of supporting 1) recognition learning by providing multiple, flexible methods of presentation, 2) strategic learning by providing multiple, flexible methods of expression, and 3) affective learning by providing multiple, flexible options for engagement.

UDL also is based on brain research regarding learning and individual differences. These three principles parallel three fundamentally important learning components and three distinct learning networks in the brain: recognition, strategy, and affect (Rose & Meyer, 2002). The common recommendation of these three principles is to select goals, methods, assessments, and materials to minimize barriers and maximize flexibility. In this manner, the UDL framework structures the development of curricula that fully support every student's access, participation, and progress in all three essential facets of learning.

Accommodations to Ensure Construct Assessments

Although UDA and UDL were considered before assessment construction, they cannot absolutely ensure valid inferences from testing grade-level achievement. Unanticipated issues may still arise in the manner in which tests are administered or taken. A growing body of literature on such test changes (or accommodations) is becoming established in the field of large-scale assessments. Generally, it is thought that such changes can lead to valid inferences if they a) do not change the constructs being assessed, b) provide unique advantages to students who need them, and c) do not provide any advantages to students who do not need them.

To date, test accommodations are made by retrofitting existing assessments. Teachers, publishers, and test developers typically impose accommodations onto previously created materials designed for the general education population. Although this process may remove some barriers to accessing the information, student performance may suffer as a result of inappropriate changes (Fuchs et al., 2000). For accommodations to be beneficial, format changes must be specific to individual needs (Helwig & Tindal, 2003). For example, a student with a visual impairment may benefit from information presented in large text or braille; however, the same student may find auditory presentation of information a barrier. An individualized approach to selecting accommodations may significantly increase student access to information, resulting in improved student performance.

Students with diverse needs are provided external testing accommodations designed to remove physical, cognitive, or sensory barriers that may inhibit understanding or expression of domain-specific knowledge. These personal attributes may prohibit successful interactions with information or instructional tasks. For example, students with limited reading proficiencies encounter significant difficulties when taking multiple-choice mathematics tests (Helwig, Rozek-Tedesco, Heath, Tindal, & Almond, 1999).

Accommodations mediate the effects of inhibitory characteristics without altering the constructs under investigation. By changing the medium through which information is presented, allowing alternate response formats, altering the external environment, or adjusting the timing of the testing situation, accommodations allow students direct access to the targeted domain (Elliott, Kratochwill, & McKevitt, 2001). With well-suited accommodations, the accuracy of the assessment results increases, leading to more appropriate inferences about student skills and knowledge. Although consistent with the theories supporting UDA, the mechanisms of delivery and placement decisions differ across these support-based systems. As most states require students to be familiar with their accommodations before they take assessments, it becomes imperative to consider classroom use; in this focus, a natural bridge extends from testing to teaching and from UDA to UDL.

Oregon maintains a list of accommodations that have been approved by a state-facilitated panel of experts for use by all students during statewide assessments. These accommodations promote and allow greater access for all students participating in the assessments without impacting the constructs being assessed. Any student taking the state's general or alternate assessment is permitted to use an accommodation without invalidating his or her final score.

Prerequisite Skills

Students with the most significant disabilities often have interfering behaviors that may inhibit the use of singular response systems. Some students have sensory impairments that prevent them from seeing or hearing directions; others have orthopedic impairments that prevent movement or inhibit their responses. To follow the principles of universal design and all requisite flexibilities, a series of four levels of independence was considered.

The first level (assumed as the default level) is *independent* (coded 4), signifying that the student can successfully complete the item with no assistance. The second level, *verbal–visual–gestural* (coded 3), indicates that the student requires some assistance to orient or focus but that, once engaged, the student can complete the item successfully. The third level is *partial physical prompting* (coded 2), indicating that the student needs a physical prop or prompt to successfully complete the item. The final and fourth level is *full physical* assistance (coded 1) and is given when the teacher provides hand-over-hand assistance to ensure the student's success on the item.

The prerequisite skills component of Oregon's Extended Assessments estimates the level of support each student needs in taking the assessment. Teachers use these items to determine what level of support they have permission to use in determining what the students know and can do. Performance on the prerequisite skills component does not impact students' achievement levels on the content knowledge and skills portion of the alternate assessment. Rather, in the content knowledge and skills section of the test, content prompts (the assessment items linked directly to grade-level standards) are presented using the levels of support determined from the prerequisite assessments, with students given equal opportunity to answer correctly or incorrectly (i.e., levels of independence did not influence accuracy).

With universal design, allowance of accommodations, and very specifically tailored assessments to ascertain prerequisite skills, the design and development of Oregon's alternate assessment system was structured around the content of grade-level standards. This design, however, could not have been completed without the prior articulation of these guidelines.

DESIGN AND DEVELOPMENT OF THE OREGON EXTENDED ASSESSMENT

Oregon's alternate assessments were designed by reducing the depth, breadth, and complexity of the grade-level content standards to create items that linked to the content standards yet more accessible to students with the most significant cognitive disabilities.

Reduction in Complexity

In the development of Oregon's alternate assessment system, steps were taken to increase the cognitive accessibility of each item by analyzing and removing potential barriers for students with significant cognitive disabilities. Additional administration allowances were developed during the course of review and pilot administration. Using the same general profile of students who take alternate assessments as recommended by IEP teams, the test developers created items to address the concerns listed in Table 14.1.

Reduction in Depth

Reduction in depth in Oregon's Extended Assessment was achieved by carefully considering the skills required at each item level. Depth of knowledge was measured using a four-point scale (see Table 14.2) representing a hybrid of Webb's four levels (Tindal, 2006; Webb, 2006) but extended downward to include the range of cognitive demands required of students participating in alternate assessments. Each point on the scale has several associated verbs to help raters distinguish among levels of complexity.

Table 14.1. Development and administration steps taken to reduce the complexity of test items in Oregon's alternate assessment system

Development steps toward reducing complexity
- Select the most appropriate word with the smallest number of syllables
- Reduce number words used in item, directions, and passages
- Use independent clause structure instead of dependent clause structure in passages
- Develop prompts with minimal wording
- Ensure more opportunities for modeling
- Provide more examples when possible
- Create clear (not tricky) distractors
- Provide explicit textual information with reduced requirements for extended inference
- Provide rules rather than exceptions
- Use careful sequencing so that potentially similar/confusing information is not presented adjacent to similar information
- Provide multiple-choice options for items when possible or appropriate for item construction

Administration steps toward reducing complexity
- Employ appropriate pacing
- Supply performance-neutral praise statements for teacher to use regularly throughout assessment (e.g., *You are working so hard!*)
- Provide additional wait time after the presentation of an item
- Provide alternative means of demonstrating accuracy (e.g., *Raise your hand/nod/ blink if you see a match*)

From Oregon Department of Education. (2008b). *Technical manuals volumes 1–8*. Retrieved April 9, 2009, from http://www.ode.state.or.us/search/page/?id=1305; reprinted by permission.

Reduction in Breadth

Oregon's content standards are organized according to a hierarchical structure. Score reporting categories are the broadest category, followed by standards (sometimes referred to as domains), which in turn are followed by individual objectives. Reduction in breadth of standards coverage was a component of item development for this population.

For 2006–2007, reduction in breadth was achieved systematically by selecting standards for development based on the vertical alignment of content standards. Verticality or reach was defined in two ways: a) The same standard appeared across the grades in the span (e.g., the same standard was found in Grades 3, 4, and 5 for the elementary test) or b) the standards, as they appeared across grades, indicated a distinct progression of that standard in keeping with developmental expectations. This assurance of verticality allowed for the development of a single cross-grade item that referred to a single standard or progression of standards. As noted, in some cases, the standards were very clearly additive in complexity across the grades, noting depth in more detail or in more broad domains (e.g., in

Table 14.2. Depth of knowledge codes, labels, and definitions based on sample behaviors

Code	Label	Sample behaviors	Tindal adaptation	Oregon application
1	Recognition and reproduction	Attend: *Touch, look, vocalize, respond, attend, recognize.* The student responds to limited stimuli (e.g., always the same cue, always the same stimulus such as his or her name).	"A 'behavior event' with 1:1 correspondence completed in a single context" (p. 42). The materials (context) in which student performance is in response to a stipulated form that is heavily practiced, reflecting rote behavior.	*Attention:* Touch, look, vocalize, respond, attend, recognize
2	Skill or concept	Recall: *List, describe, identify, state, define, label.* The student responds to a (limited) general case range of cues (e.g., attends to several different forms of words or reads different words, some of which represent rule variations of each other—lop, pop, stop, drop, etc.).	"A 'behavioral event' with more than 1:1 correspondence in more than one context with correct or incorrect responses" (p. 42). The materials (context) in which student performance is in response to alternate forms, reflecting fluency or automaticity with a basic skill.	*Memorize/recall:* List, describe, identify, state, define, label

| 3 | Strategic thinking | Comprehend: *Explain, conclude, group, restate, review, translate.* The student responds with different behaviors in a multiple-step sequence with behavior that reflects a range of rules (e.g., reads or listens to sentences and responds with answers—for example, *Who is the main character?*). | "A multiple step 'behavioral event' executed in more than one context with more than 1:1 correspondence and with partial correct scoring of responses" (p. 42). The materials (context) in which student performance is in response to alternate forms and the student must use a (complex) sequence of steps that reflects general(ized) knowledge. | *Comprehension:* Explain, conclude, group, restate, review, translate |
| 4 | Extended thinking | Apply: *Compute, organize, collect, classify, construct, solve, operate, use, generalize.* The student is presented a problem and must arrange the stimulus differently from what was presented to determine how to respond in addition to the correct response (e.g., reads or listens to multiple sentences and then is asked an abstract question in which the student must consider several alternatives and then respond—for example, *What is the main idea of this story?*) | "A multiple step 'behavioral event' executed as an approach (of many) to completing a task that occurs in multiple" contexts (p. 42). The materials (contexts) in which student performance is in response to alternate forms and the student must set up the problem before answering it through a (complex) sequence of steps that reflects general(ized) knowledge. | *Application:* Compute, organize, collect, apply, classify, construct, solve, operate, use, generalize |

Source: Tindal (2006).

mathematics, integers were the target in early grades, then fractions, and, finally, real numbers with decimals; see Table 14.3a). In other cases, the content of the standards did not change at all, and it was assumed that the content of the assessment was based on grade-level difficulty (see Table 14.3b). Finally, a number of standards required some interpolation, as in the example shown in Table 14.3c. When we analyzed these data, we found considerable agreement in the degree to which content judges determined the vertical alignment to be defensible (see Table 14.4).

Standard Setting

Alternate achievement standards were set for Oregon's Extended Assessments using Item Response Theory scaling procedures. A panel of representative educators and assessment specialists reviewed the content of the Extended Assessments in light of the achievement-level expectations

Table 14.3a. Alternate assessment vertical alignment additive complexity

Grade 2	Grade 3	Grade 4
Read, write, order, model, and compare whole numbers less than 100.	Read, write, order, model, and compare whole numbers less than 1,000.	Read, write, order, model, and compare whole numbers versus one million, common fractions, and decimals to hundredths.

Table 14.3b. Alternate assessment vertical alignment same standard

Grade 4	Grade 5	Grade 6
Identify and/or summarize sequence of events, main ideas, and supporting details in literary selections.	Identify and/or summarize sequence of events, main ideas, and supporting details in literary selections.	Identify and/or summarize sequence of events, main ideas, and supporting details in literary selections.

Table 14.3c. Alternate assessment vertical alignment interpolated links

Grade 5	Grade 6	Grade 7
Identify and analyze text that uses prioritization as an organizational pattern (e.g., newspaper articles).	Identify and analyze text that uses compare-and-contrast and cause-and-effect organizational patterns.	Analyze text to determine the type and purpose of the organizational structure being used by the author (e.g., description, sequential/chronological, categorization, prioritization, compare-and-contrast, or cause-and-effect).

From Oregon Department of Education. (2008b). *Technical manuals volumes 1–8.* Retrieved April 9, 2009, from http://www.ode.state.or.us/search/page/?id=1305; reprinted by permission.

Table 14.4a. Grade 3–5 ratings of alignment

Rating	Reading		Writing		Mathematics	
	Count	%	Count	%	Count	%
Loosely aligned	0	0	2	10	10	19
Fairly well aligned	5	9	4	19	11	21
Very well aligned	52	91	15	71	31	60
Total	57	100	21	100	52	100

Table 14.4b. Grades 6–8 ratings of alignment

Rating	Reading		Writing		Mathematics	
	Count	%	Count	%	Count	%
Loosely aligned	5	8	5	10	2	2
Fairly well aligned	11	19	2	4	22	21
Very well aligned	43	73	41	85	82	77
Total	59	100	48	100	106	100

From Oregon Department of Education. (2008b). *Technical manuals volumes 1–8.* Retrieved April 9, 2009, from http://www.ode.state.or.us/search/page/?id=1305; reprinted by permission.

associated with each of the assessed grades. A bookmarking process was used to determine cut points in item-ordered booklets, and cut scores for each of four achievement categories (*Does not meet, nearly meets, meets, exceeds*) were determined. Degrees of impact on students for each grade were evaluated according to the percentages of students who would fall into each of the achievement categories. Once cut scores were determined, panel members were presented with impact data and allowed to adjust cut scores according to passing rates for each grade (the number of students meeting or exceeding the standard). Levels of impact by grade and achievement categories for the Extended Reading and Extended Mathematics assessments are shown in Table 14.5.

Scaffold Administration

Oregon developed an alternate administration option of its Extended Assessments that (for each subject area) provided a series of additional supports (beyond universal design principles and reduction methods) to the administration rules for students whose IEP teams determined that such additional supports were necessary. In a scaffold administration version of the assessment, whenever possible, items were preceded by brief additional language (referred to as the *preamble*) that provided extra information relevant to the content of the items; any additional information (or graphic support) that might help students access the information cognitively also was presented. For example, a geometry item that required students to calculate the missing value of a side in a triangle might have

Table 14.5a.   Extended reading impact by grade 2006–2007

Grade	Does not yet meet (%)	Nearly meets (%)	Meets (%)	Exceeds (%)	Meets or exceeds (%)
3	13	21	41	25	66
4	26	15	35	24	59
5	26	20	37	17	54
6	23	15	38	24	62
7	25	20	41	14	55
8	33	22	32	13	45
10	35	28	23	14	37

Table 14.5b.   Extended mathematics impact by grade 2006–2007

Grade	Does not yet meet (%)	Nearly meets (%)	Meets (%)	Exceeds (%)	Meets or exceeds (%)
3	22	42	23	13	36
4	51	14	15	20	35
5	54	15	19	12	31
6	56	28	13	3	16
7	65	18	14	3	17
8	77	12	9	2	11
10	73	16	10	1	11

From Oregon Department of Education. (2008b). *Technical manuals volumes 1–8.* Retrieved April 9, 2009, from http://www.ode.state.or.us/search/page/?id=1305; reprinted by permission.

asked (with a supporting graphic), *The perimeter of this triangle is 13 inches. What is the length of Side C?* If the content standard was designed to address perimeter, the supporting language before that question might have provided the additional information, *A triangle has three sides,* which would not impact students' knowledge of the content standard under assessment but would allow students to consider this information in making their determinations. In addition to such preambles, the scaffold administration version was enhanced by the inclusion of more supportive graphics when necessary. For example, a bar graph may have reflected only numbers and symbols in the standard administration version, but in the scaffold administration version it might have been accompanied by numerically accurate representations of the objects in each of the bars. Figure 14.1 provides two examples in reading and mathematics that illustrate the use of graphics.

Prerequisite Skills Assessment

In designing the assessment of content knowledge and skill, a separate assessment was conducted to ascertain each student's prerequisite skill levels and independence in completing the tasks. Each student begins the test by being assessed on a task of 10 items (the prerequisite skills

Standard Version *Scaffold Version*

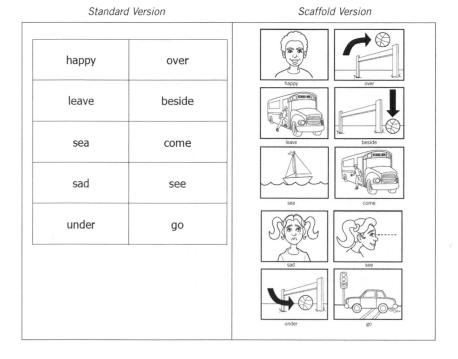

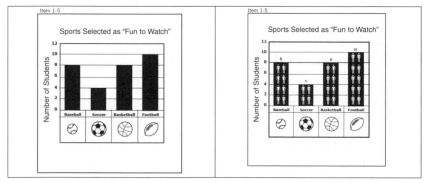

Figure 14.1. Examples illustrating the use of graphics in standard and scaffold versions of reading and mathematics assessments. (From Oregon Department of Education. [2008a]. *Oregon's Extended Assessment Test specifications and blueprints* [p. 18]. Salem: Author; reprinted by permission.)

task) to ascertain the level of support necessary for them to be successful on those items. Items were developed so that teachers could support students in one of four ways (1 = *independent*, 2 = *verbal–visual–gestural*, 3 = *partial physical*, 4 = *full physical*). If a student functioned independently, the teacher could use a code of *A* to indicate that the stu-

Prerequisite skills	Independence for success						
1. Attention: Here are some materials (ascertain attention).	A	I	R	1	2	3	4

Figure 14.2.　Scoring band for measuring prerequisite skill levels and independence. (From Oregon Department of Education. [2008b]. *Technical manuals volumes 1–8*. Retrieved April 9, 2009, from http://www.ode.state.or.us/search/page/?id=1305; reprinted by permission.)

dent *already* had the skill in question. This last option was provided to maintain student engagement and motivation and to make the administration of the test more efficient. As noted in the scoring band shown in Figure 14.2, teachers also may determine that an item in the prerequisite skills task was *inappropriate* (*I*) or that a student *refused* to respond (*R*). In the prerequisite skills task, it was not possible to code tasks as too difficult (only *I* or *R*, along with the levels of independence for success).

During administration of an Extended Assessment, once a student has taken all 10 prerequisite skills items, the teacher uses a frequency count to determine the level of support used most often to bring the student to a successful conclusion on the item. The support most frequently needed during the administration of the prerequisite skills items is used to indicate what type of support a teacher might provide for the student to access the content items of the assessment.

OUTCOMES FROM THE OREGON EXTENDED ASSESSMENT

In the documentation for the peer review submitted in August 2008 (Oregon Department of Education [ODE], 2007), a number of analyses established the reliability of the measures and the validity of the inferences made from the Oregon Extended Assessment. We followed the guidelines described in the white paper by the Technical Work Group on Including Students with Disabilities in Large-Scale Assessment (2006) to make a claim and support it by documenting evidence on content coverage, response processes, internal structure, and relations to other variables as recommended by the American Educational Research Association, American Psychological Association, and National Council on Measurement in Education (1999). The claim was that

> the alternate assessments based on alternate achievement standards are aligned with grade level academic content, generate reliable outcomes at the item, task, and test level, include all students, have a cogent internal structure, and fit within a network of relations within and across various dimensions of content related to and relevant for making proficiency decisions. (ODE, 2007, p. 6)

Content-Related Evidence and Training

Content-related evidence included an extensive alignment study (both with the grade-level standards and with the coverage of breadth, depth, and complexity) as part of the blueprint and test specifications. We also described a series of test development and review procedures in which content experts in each subject area (17 in science and 25 each in reading and mathematics) reviewed all the items for their focus on grade-level standards, their accuracy, and their clarity. At least two individuals reviewed every item and recommended whether to accept, revise, or reject the item. An internal evaluation was provided by the office responsible for defining and maintaining the state's content standards within ODE to ensure that the standards were vertically aligned and focused on the most important standards:

> Following initial review, standards review, and pilot administration . . . four regional trainings were conducted. During the trainings of approximately 170 teachers, detailed feedback was requested on the following features of the assessment: format, scoring, administration, teacher scripting, teacher materials, student materials, content, and relevance to the population. (ODE, 2007, p. 13)

A sensitivity and bias review ensured that the items and test were appropriate for students who were deaf, hard of hearing, blind, or visually impaired. Additions were recommended to include a) more descriptive language to accompany graphics (particularly for the science assessment) and b) cleaner language for adequate Braille transcription, with minor adaptations made to ensure that students who were blind could respond without compromising the constructs under assessment. The Braille version of the test (in each subject area) was designed as a nearly exact replica of the test, with all items made accessible. On a few items, the consultant noted that no adaptation was possible (ODE, 2007, p. 14).

Throughout the process of item and task development, we also piloted various versions with small samples of students. Just before the final version of the test was published, 12 content teachers and special educators provided one final review, focusing on sensitivity, bias, content, and language.

We conducted the training in two phases. Cadre I teachers were trained in regional 2-day workshops with approximately 20–50 teachers in attendance. Staff from ODE and Behavioral Research and Teaching conducted the training. Then, just before the test window opened, video-streamed training was conducted from an ODE studio during the course of 2 days. The previously trained (Cadre I) teachers visited regional sites to help deliver training to local teachers from each region (labeled Cadre II). Each workshop (for Cadre I and II) was evaluated for content knowledge using a 10-item scale at the beginning and at the end. A pre–post test of change was computed and found that significant gains in content knowledge occurred through this training.

Reliability of Items, Tasks, and Test Performance Levels

Reliability included both internal consistency and item correlations. Cronbach alpha for items was positive and sufficiently high (at least .80 was judged as adequate for standardized tests). Virtually all reliability coefficients were above this level and typically ranged in the high .80s and mid .90s.

We analyzed the performance levels for each grade and subject area at the prerequisite skill and content knowledge levels.

1. In reading and mathematics prerequisite skills, students averaged just above 150 raw points (of 200 possible points). In writing prerequisite skills, students averaged about 120 points (of 140 possible points). In science prerequisite skills, students averaged 165 points (of 200 possible points).

2. On the content knowledge tasks in reading, elementary students scored just above 60% of the possible raw points (100), with students in the middle and high school grades slightly lower (averaging 50%). On the content knowledge tasks in writing, performance in the elementary grades was about 30 points (of 70 possible points) and 35 points (of 80 possible points) in the middle and secondary grades. Mathematics content knowledge tasks were somewhat difficult, reflecting about 25%–40% correct (of 100 possible points). Finally, in science, students averaged about 50%–65% correct (of 100 possible points).

Response Processes

We conducted several analyses of the response processes to better understand how (versus how well) students performed on the tests. First, we looked at the patterns of participation. In the test administration, teachers had the option of not administering items that they thought were too difficult or that they deemed inappropriate (e.g., a blending task for a student who was deaf). Teachers also could choose which tasks to administer and were directed to ensure that each student completed at least five tasks (with five items) to be counted for participation; of course, with this rule, a number of tasks and items also were not administered. In the end, the percentages of items judged too difficult ranged from a few percentage points to nearly a quarter of the items (mathematics and writing had more items judged too difficult). The percentage of items deemed inappropriate was quite low (reflecting only a few percentage points) in each subject area. Second, we analyzed participation by levels of support (*independent, visual–verbal–gestural, partial physical,* and *full physical*). The vast majority of students took the test either independently or with just visual–verbal–gestural supports. Only a very small percentage of students required any type of physical support.

Internal Structures

For valid test score interpretations and validity generalization, it is expected that a) the items show some level of internal consistency (Standard 1.11), b) the internal structure of the test remain stable across major reporting groups (p. 15), and c) the internal structure of the test remain stable across alternate (hopefully equivalent) forms of the same test (ODE, 2007, pp. 51–52). We conducted exploratory factor analyses on the various subject area tests and with each grade band. An exploratory factor analysis was implemented with maximum likelihood factor extraction and varimax factor rotation if more than one factor was extracted. Goodness-of-fit indices were used to test how well the estimated factor model accounted for the observed data. In each of the subject areas and grade bands, we typically found four factors to account for most of the variance but one factor to be most substantial; the factor structures were closely (and uniquely) associated with specific tasks. We could account for 43%–70% of the variance with reference to these four factors.

Criterion-Related Evidence

The final form of evidence we collected to support our claim was criterion related. We completed two analyses, comparing performance by a) tasks and b) disability. For the comparison by tasks, we used Campbell and Fiske's (1959) multitrait (multimethod) analysis to document the relation among tasks within a subject area, and we compared these values with those between subject areas. For example, the different reading tasks were compared with each other and with the various mathematics tasks. We conducted this analysis in reading versus mathematics, writing, and science. In all correlations, the values within tasks were much higher than the values between tasks. For the disability analysis, we compared performance (at each grade band and for each subject area) across 11 categories similar to those reported by Tindal et al. (2003). For categories that had sufficient sample sizes, we found the patterns to be consistent (e.g., students with the most significant disabilities, such as traumatic brain injury, performed less well than those with less significant disabilities, such as communication disorders, severe learning disabilities, emotional disturbance, or autism). In contrast, we also found that students with sensory impairments performed quite well relative to the entire grade-level population, suggesting that the test functioned well for the full spectrum of primary disabilities.

Functional Decision Making and Inferences from Type of Administration

Because we had developed two administration options for each test (scaffold and standard), the last form of validity evidence compared the administration options for each subject area and grade band. This form of evidence can be considered a specific form of response process (stan-

Table 14.6a. Results from Task 4 (Reading vocabulary item) ($\eta^2 = .473$)

Test administration type	Mean	Standard deviation	N
Standard	7.3338	2.30322	2963
Scaffold	5.1394	3.60681	2174
Total	6.4051	3.12075	5137

Source	Type III sum of squares	df	Mean square	F	Significance	Partial η^2
Corrected model	23645.644(a)	2	11822.822	2301.417	.000	.473
Intercept	1056.029	1	1056.029	205.565	.000	.038
Prerequisite	17607.315	1	17607.315	3427.420	.000	.400
Test administration type	788.588	1	788.588	153.506	.000	.029
Error	26374.342	5134	5.137			
Total	260767.000	5137				
Corrected total	50019.986	5136				

Table 14.6b. Results from Task 6 (Math graph item) ($\eta^2 = .346$)

Test administration type	Mean	Standard deviation	N
Standard	4.3027	2.94170	2329
Scaffold	2.4950	3.12437	2196
Total	3.4254	3.16319	4525

Source	Type III sum of squares	df	Mean square	F	Significance	Partial η^2
Corrected model	15657.707(a)	2	7828.853	1195.678	.000	.346
Intercept	29.485	1	29.485	4.503	.034	.001
Prerequisite	11964.167	1	11964.167	1827.252	.000	.288
Test administration type	558.077	1	558.077	85.233	.000	.018
Error	29608.370	4522	6.548			
Total	98360.000	4525				
Corrected total	45266.077	4524				

From Oregon Department of Education. (2008b). *Technical manuals volumes 1–8.* Retrieved April 9, 2009, from http://www.ode.state.or.us/search/page/?id=1305; reprinted by permission.

Key: N, total number in sample; *df,* degree of freedom; *F,* Fisher's *F* ratio; η^2, eta squared.

dard versus scaffold, controlling for level of prerequisite skill). Consistently, we found that although students performed significantly higher on the standard administration (compared with the scaffold administration), levels of prerequisite skill accounted for most of the variance. For example, in the reading vocabulary and mathematics tasks depicted previously in this chapter, most of the variance was in prerequisite skills and not in type of administration (standard versus scaffold; see Table 14.6).

SUMMARY

We analyzed the alternate assessment system in Oregon by making a claim and then providing evidence to support the claim. Through the alignment of the test with grade-level standards, the use of test specifications to operationalize the task and item development, and the systematic training of teachers, we felt confident that students with the most significant disabilities took tests that adequately addressed relevant content. The analysis of reliability provided evidence that items were consistently functioning within tasks; performance levels also were consistent within and across grade bands in each subject area. Our analysis of response processes reflected the very principles of universal design that we had considered even before test design (particularly the use of multiple forms of participation with a scaffold version). Internal structures of the tests were documented through factor analyses that consistently reflected dimensionality in accordance with the tasks. Finally, criterion-related evidence was noted through a multitrait analysis along with an analysis by disability. Although further improvements were necessary, primarily in the expansion of the grade-level expectations to include high school, we believe the tests provided an initial beginning to validation of the inferences made on grade-level content standards.

REFERENCES

Almond, P., Tindal, J., Arnold, N., Stolp, P., & McCabe, P. (2003, June). *Alternate assessment: Research findings and implications for state practice.* Paper presented at the 2003 Large Scale Assessment Conference, San Antonio, TX.

American Educational Research Association, American Psychological Association, & National Council on Measurement in Education. (1999). *Standards for educational and psychological testing.* Washington, DC: Author.

Browder, D.M., Spooner, F., Algozzine, R., Ahlgrim-Delzell, L., Flowers, C., & Karvonen, M. (2003). What we know and need to know about alternate assessment. *Exceptional Children, 70*(1), 45–61.

Campbell, D.T., & Fiske, D.W. (1959). Convergent and discriminant validation by the multi-trait, multi-method matrix. In W.A. Mehrens & R.L. Ebel (Eds.), *Principles of educational and psychological measurement: A book of selected readings* (pp. 273–302). Chicago: Rand McNally & Company.

Crawford, L., Tindal, G., & Carpenter, D.M., II. (2006). Exploring the validity of the Oregon extended writing assessment. *The Journal of Special Education, 40*(1), 16–27.

Dolan, R.P., & Hall, T.E. (2001). Universal design for learning: Implications for large-scale assessment. *IDA Perspectives, 27*(4), 22–25.

Elliott, S.N., Kratochwill, T.R., & McKevitt, B.C. (2001). Experimental analysis of the effect of testing accommodation on the scores of students with and without disabilities. *Journal of School Psychology, 39*(1), 3–24.

Federal Register. (December 9, 2003). *Title I—Improving the academic achievement of the disadvantaged: Final rule* [pp. 68697–68708]. Volume 68, Number 236.

Fuchs, L.S., Fuchs, D., Eaton, S., Hamlett, C.L., Binkley, E., & Crouch, R. (2000). Using objective sources to supplement teacher judgments of reading test accommodations. *Exceptional Children, 67*, 67–82.

Helwig, R., Rozek-Tedesco, M., Heath, B., Tindal, G., & Almond, P. (1999). Reading as an access to mathematics problem solving on multiple-choice tests for sixth grade students. *The Journal of Educational Research, 93*(2), 113–125.

Helwig, R., & Tindal, G. (2003). An experimental analysis of accommodation decisions on large-scale mathematics tests. *Exceptional Children, 69*(2), 211–225.

Individuals with Disabilities Education Act Amendments (IDEA) of 1997, PL 105-17, 20 U.S.C. §§ 1400 *et seq.*

Kampfer, S., Horvath, L., Kleinert, H., & Kearns, J. (2001). Teachers' perceptions of one state's alternate assessment: Implications for practice and preparation. *Exceptional Children, 67*(3), 361–374.

Kleinert, H.L., Kearns, J.F., & Kennedy, S. (1997). Accountability for all students: Kentucky's alternate portfolio assessment for students with moderate and severe cognitive disabilities. *The Journal of the Association for Persons with Severe Handicaps, 22*(2), 88–101.

Meyer, A., & Rose, D.H. (1998). *Learning to read in the computer age.* Brookline, MA: Brookline Books.

No Child Left Behind Act of 2001, PL 107-110, 115 Stat. 1425, 20 U.S.C. §§ 6301 *et seq.*

Olsen, K. (1998). *Alternate assessment issues and practices.* Lexington, KY: Mid-South Regional Resource Center.

Oregon Department of Education. (2007). *2006–2007 technical report—Oregon's alternate assessment system: Reliability and validity.* Salem: Author.

Oregon Department of Education. (2008a). *Oregon's Extended Assessment Test Specifications and Blueprints.* Salem: Author.

Oregon Department of Education. (2008b). *Technical manuals volumes 1–8.* Retrieved April 9, 2009, from http://www.ode.state.or.us/search/page/?id=1305

Pisha, B., & Coyne, P. (2001). Smart from the start: The promise of universal design for learning. *Remedial and Special Education, 22*(4), 197–203.

Rose, D. (2001). Universal design for learning: Deriving guiding principles from networks that learn. *Journal of Special Education Technology, 16*(1), 66–70.

Rose, D., & Dolan, B. (2000). Assessment. *Journal of Special Education Technology, 15*(4). Retrieved March 12, 2009, from http://jset.unlv.edu/15.4/asseds/rose.html

Rose, D., & Meyer, A. (2000). Universal design for learning. *Journal of Special Education Technology, 15*(1), 67–70.

Rose, D.H., & Meyer, A. (2002). *Teaching every student in the digital age: Universal design for learning.* Alexandria, VA: Association for Supervisors of Curriculum Development.

Rose, D., Sethuraman, S., & Meo, G. (2000). Universal design for learning. *Journal of Special Education Technology, 15*(2), 56–60.

Technical Work Group on Including Students with Disabilities in Large-Scale Assessment. (2006). *Including students with disabilities in large-scale assessment: Executive summary.* Eugene: Behavioral Research and Teaching, University of Oregon.

Thompson, S.J., Johnstone, C.J., & Thurlow, M.L. (2002). *Universal design applied to large scale assessments* (Synthesis Rep. No. 44). Minneapolis: University of Minnesota, National Center on Educational Outcomes.

Tindal, G. (2006). *Alignment of alternate assessments using the Webb System: Alignment report 2.* In *Aligning assessment to guide the learning of all students: Six reports on the development, refinement, and dissemination of the Webb Alignment Tool.* Washington, DC: The Council of Chief State School Officers.

Tindal, G., & Fuchs, L. (1999). *A summary of research on test changes: An empirical basis for defining accommodations.* Lexington, KY: Mid-South Regional Resource Center.

Tindal, G., Glasgow, A., Gall, J., VanLoo, D., & Chow, E. (2002). *Oregon extended assessment: Technical adequacy analysis summary.* Salem: Oregon Department of Education.

Tindal, G., McDonald, M., Tedesco, M., Glasgow, A., Almond, P., Crawford, L., et al. (2003). Alternate assessments in reading and math: Development and validation for students with significant disabilities. *Exceptional Children, 69*(4), 481–494.

Turner, M., Baldwin, L., Kleinert, H., & Kearns, J. (2000). The relation of a statewide alternate assessment for students with severe disabilities to other measures of instructional effectiveness. *The Journal of Special Education, 34* (2), 69–76.

U.S. Department of Education. (2004). *Standards and assessment peer review guidance: Information and examples for meeting the requirements of the No Child Left Behind Act of 2001.* Washington, DC: Author.

U.S. Department of Education. (2005). *Raising achievement: Alternate assessments for students with disabilities.* Retrieved from http://www.ed.gov/print/policy/elsec/guid/raising/alt-assess-long.html

Webb, N. (2006). *The web alignment tool: Development, refinement, and dissemination.* In *Aligning assessment to guide the learning of all students.* Washington, DC: Council of Chief State School Officers.

Yin, R. (1989). *Case study research: Design and methods.* Thousand Oaks, CA: Sage Publications.

Yovanoff, P., & Tindal, G. (2007). Scaling early reading alternate assessments with statewide measures. *Exceptional Children, 73*(2), 184–201.

CHAPTER 15

The South Carolina Alternate Assessment

LORIN MUELLER, STEVE FERRARA,
SUZANNE SWAFFIELD, AND DOUGLAS G. ALEXANDER

In 2004, the South Carolina Department of Education (SCDE) contracted with the American Institutes for Research (AIR) to develop a new system for assessing students with disabilities. SCDE desired the new assessment to suit four purposes. First and foremost, SCDE wanted the assessment to capture and evaluate the performance of students who previously had been left out of the statewide assessment program. Second, SCDE wanted the assessment to help improve the instruction of these students. Third and fourth, SCDE wanted the assessment to satisfy state and federal accountability requirements, respectively. AIR and SCDE began development of the new South Carolina Alternate Assessment (SC-Alt) in September 2004.

CONTENT OF THE SOUTH CAROLINA ALTERNATE ASSESSMENT

The new assessment is linked to South Carolina's academic standards, which provide the basis for alignment across the state for district and school curricula, classroom instruction, and learning outcomes. To supplement the academic standards, SCDE created a set of Assessment and Measurement Guidelines (ASMGs) to extend the academic standards for the SC-Alt and to inform classroom instruction.

The SC-Alt comprises four content areas: English/language arts (ELA), mathematics, science, and social studies. The ELA assessment comprises three subtopics: reading, writing, and communication. In addition, high school students are assessed on physical science within the science assessment, consistent with the general state assessment. The ASMGs describe the relation of the academic standards to the SC-Alt in each of these areas. The ASMGs were developed through an extensive process involving committees of special educators and content experts. These committees identified the key academic standards that were most important for students.

ASSESSMENT DESIGN

SCDE underwent a careful process to design the new SC-Alt, taking into account the state's previous experience with alternate assessments. The previous alternate assessment system had used portfolio-based assessments for students in Grades 3–8 and performance tasks for students in Grade 10. SCDE wanted to avoid portfolio-based assessments for the new SC-Alt because of the expensive and time-consuming scoring processes required by portfolio formats. There also were concerns regarding the comparability of portfolios and teachers' abilities to ensure that appropriate student performance examples were included in portfolios. SCDE conducted several teacher focus groups and classroom observations and solicited advice from their technical advisory committee to further inform the design of the SC-Alt.

The final design consists of a series of performance tasks, with four to six items within each task. Each task uses a common introduction and set of materials to save test administrators some time. The assessment is individually administered and follows a specific script. The items are linked to grade-level academic standards in three grade bands: 3–5, 6–8, and 10. Table 15.1 shows the age ranges for students taking each form. Each item has a scaffold scoring procedure, with the number of score points ranging from one to four. For example, on a four-point item, if a student is able to respond correctly to the question with no additional clarification from the administrator, the student receives four points. If the student responds incorrectly, the administrator makes the item easier by taking away an attractive response option or providing a scripted clue. If the student is then able to respond correctly, he or she receives three points. This process continues until the student is able to respond correctly or the administrator exhausts all script options.

Table 15.1. Age ranges for each grade-band form

Form	Age in years, as of September 1
Grades 3–5	8–10
Grades 6–8	11–13
Grade 10	15

Source: South Carolina Department of Education (2008).

ITEM DEVELOPMENT

AIR worked with SCDE to create item-writing teams for the SC-Alt. Item-writing teams consisted of content experts and special educators who all had been trained using the U.S. Office of Special Education Programs' *Designing from the Ground Floor: Alternate Assessment on Alternate Achievement Standards.* They also were provided with the test specifications and an item writer's manual that described guidelines for creating reliable and valid achievement test items. Each item was pilot tested using AIR's cognitive laboratory facilities. Items that seemed to function as expected were then administered to students in South Carolina using small-scale field tryouts before field testing. On the basis of these administrations, we revised the items, task structure, and administration script before the full field test. Before constructing field test forms, SCDE and AIR conducted reviews of content, sensitivity, and bias with teacher committees to ensure that the items were linked to academic standards and valid for measuring student achievement across gender and ethnic subgroups.

The ELA, math, and science assessments were field tested in the spring of 2006. After field testing, the items were reviewed to ensure that their psychometric properties were consistent with expectations and did not exhibit differential item functioning. A separate alignment study was conducted by SCDE to ensure that the final assessment adequately covered the academic standards.

ADMINISTRATION

To facilitate the administration process, the assessment is highly scripted. There is a separate administration manual to familiarize teachers with the entire assessment, the administration process, common issues with the assessment, and how to get help with the administration. The administration script is highly prescriptive. It gives specific directions on how to set up manipulatives and response cards, directions for scoring student responses, adaptive instructions, and how to deal with items that pose access limitations to students. Each task follows a common format. First, the materials and setup are detailed. Second, adaptive instructions are provided and are followed by directions for dealing with access limitations. Instructions are pictographic whenever possible to minimize the reading load on test administrators. Figure 15.1 provides an example of pictographic instructions. Scripts were specified to ensure standardized administration. A redacted example script is shown in Figure 15.2.

Several common adaptations and accommodations are offered for students. Specific examples are that 1) administrators can say response options aloud, 2) administrators can point to all of the response options

Figure 15.1. Pictographic instructions indicating the keyed response with an arrow. (The Picture Communication Symbols © 1981–2008 by Mayer-Johnson LLC. All Rights Reserved Worldwide. Used with Permission. Boardmaker® is a trademark of Mayer-Johnson LLC.)

or concrete objects, 3) students may touch or hold the objects, 4) administrators may place the objects in specific locations or orientations for students who have limited visual fields or reach, and 5) administrators may change the backgrounds. In addition to these accommodations, administrators may opt to use Mayer-Johnson Picture Communication Symbols, which are used throughout the tasks and items. If a student uses a different symbol for the same word, the test administrator may substitute the more familiar word for the one provided. The test administrator may also replace response cards with concrete objects. The objects must be similar in size, shape, and color and not change what is being measured.

Script:

Say: **We're going to talk about** _____.

Do: Give the student the _____.

OR

Say: ***Show (tell) me which one means*** _____. ***This one*** [indicate

the _____ card], ***this one*** [indicate the _____

card], ***or this one*** [indicate the _____ card]?

Figure 15.2. This figure shows an example item script for the teacher to follow when administering an item, including alternate wording.

These materials also must be age- and grade appropriate. Braille and tactile maps are provided for some tasks.

Because the assessment is individually administered, possibly across multiple testing sessions, and because of the wide range of accommodations, allowed SCDE allows a 7-week administration window.

STUDENT PLACEMENT QUESTIONNAIRE

Because the assessment is individually administered, saving time is important. For this reason, the assessment has three entry points; these entry points are designed so that students only are administered items that are best suited to their individual achievement levels. Achievement levels are determined using a Student Placement Questionnaire (SPQ), which allows teachers to quickly describe the levels of support students require to perform specific activities linked to the academic standards. Teachers make judgments regarding how much support their students need and then assign each student a starting point within the assessment. Teachers' judgments are captured by adding the sum of the teacher responses (on a four-point scale, with zero points indicating something a student cannot do and three points indicating something the student almost always can do independently of teacher support). The sum of these responses is then matched against the score ranges corresponding to starting points for the assessment.

Each starting point requires students to complete at least five tasks: tasks 1–5, 3–9, or 6–12. If a student is able to successfully complete the final task corresponding to his or her starting point, the administrator is instructed to administer the next task and continue until the student is unable to respond successfully. Successful task performance is defined as getting at least one point on three items within a task.

To ensure accurate assignment of students to starting points within the assessment, we used a Rasch-based Item Response Theory (IRT) model to scale the SPQ items to the SC-Alt scale for each content area. We then determined the optimal dividing points on the theta scale that differentiated items included within each starting point range on the test. Then, using a score conversion table, we determined the raw scores on the SPQ that corresponded to the dividing points on the theta metric. This process resulted in a simple rule for teachers to follow when selecting starting points for the assessment and assigning students to take the items best suited to their achievement levels. Investigations of this process suggested a very high degree of classification accuracy for this method (typically above 85% for each grade and subject), and correlations between SPQ scores and student achievement ranged from .70 to .75. The SPQ also included instructions for moving a student forward or back in the assessment if the content did not seem appropriate to the administrator.

SCORING

One of the key features of the SC-Alt is that student responses are scored by the test administrators—typically students' teachers, who are familiar with their students' response styles and any accommodations their students require. Scoring is scaffolded from the maximum score point to the point at which a student would receive a score of zero for no response. Figure 15.3 shows an example of a scaffolded scoring process.

Within the lowest starting range for each content area, engagement items are used to determine whether a student is ready to engage in the academic task. These items measure extended focus and involvement in the assessment. The administrator assigns a score according to the following rubric:

- Four points for sustained involvement

- Three points for generally maintained involvement

- Two points for intermittent/irregular involvement

- One point for fleeting awareness with little or no involvement

- No response (zero points) if the student does not demonstrate awareness

ADMINISTRATION REQUIREMENTS

Every teacher who administers the SC-Alt assessment is required to attend an SCDE or district test administration training session before administering the test. This training orients teachers to the assessment, administration manual, and scoring procedures.

In addition to trained test administrators, each administration must be observed by a monitor. The role of the monitor is to observe the test

---

TRY 1
If the student answers correctly, record 2 and move to the next item.
If the student answers incorrectly, remove the incorrect response choice and move to
    TRY 2.
If the student does not respond, remove [specified response option] and move to **TRY 2**.

TRY 2
If the student answers correctly, record 1 and move to the next item.
If the student answers incorrectly, record 0 and move to the next item.
If the student does not respond, record NR and move to the next item.

Figure 15.3.   An example of scaffolded response scoring with three response options.

session, verify the use of proper procedures, authenticate student responses, and sign the security agreement and affidavit. The test administrator security affidavit must be signed by the administrator and monitor and validated by the principal. This document is completed during the assessment administration and is used to record the dates and lengths of each administration session.

To validate test administration procedures, a stratified random sample of teachers was taken across districts to participate in a 10% sample of videotaped administrations. The results of this study were extremely positive for the assessments of Grades 3–5 and 6–8. For Grades 3–5, video raters agreed with the teachers' scoring decisions approximately 90% of the time, and they assigned at least an adjacent score approximately 99% of the time. For Grades 6–8, video raters agreed between 76% and 95% of the time and assigned at least adjacent ratings between 95% and 99% of the time. For Grade 10, the level of exact agreement dipped slightly to 65%, and adjacent agreement was approximately 80%.

PSYCHOMETRICS

The SC-Alt assessment was designed to provide a single, vertically linked scale from Grades 3 to 10 with a minimal amount of administration time required. To accomplish this, we included a series of within-grade linking tasks and across-grade linking tasks. This design is specified in Table 15.2. A significant number of linking items span across difficulty ranges within a grade band and subject area and also across grade bands. Within–grade-band linking items were those within tasks that overlapped between starting points within the assessment (i.e., tasks 3–5 to link the low-difficulty range to the moderate-difficulty range, and tasks 6–9 to link the moderate- and high-difficulty ranges).

Cross–grade-band linking items represented appropriate content for both grade bands. These were placed throughout the assessment, although in general they occurred earlier (in terms of item order) in the higher-grade assessments. Cross–grade-band linking tasks were used in adjacent grade bands only; no tasks linked Grades 3–5 to Grade 10 directly.

Each content area was scaled using a simultaneously calibrated Rasch IRT model across grade bands. Using precalibration from the 2006 field test, forms were designed to be slightly more difficult (in terms of mean item location) for higher grade bands. The average item location within tasks was used to order tasks within the assessment. Using the simultaneous calibration, estimated student achievement rose across grade bands, suggesting that the scale operated as expected. Marginal reliabilities (interpreted similarly to alpha coefficients for two-stage tests) were also high: above .75 across grade bands and starting points.

Table 15.2. Summary of linking design

Subject	Test description			Starting positions									
	Grade band	Items	Tasks	Low		Within-grade-band linking (low to moderate)		Moderate		Within-grade-band linking (moderate to high)		High	
				Items	Tasks	Items	Tasks	Items	Tasks	Items	Tasks	Items	Tasks
English/ language arts	3–5	68	12	32	5	19	3	38	7	19	4	36	7
	Cross-grade-band linking (29)												
	6–8	65	12	31	5	17	3	39	7	22	4	34	7
	Cross-grade-band linking (24)												
	10	64	12	28	5	16	3	37	7	21	4	36	7
Math	3–5	53	12	23	5	14	3	30	7	16	4	30	7
	Cross-grade-band linking (37)												
	6–8	55	12	23	5	14	3	31	7	17	4	32	7
	Cross-grade-band linking (29)												
	10	60	12	24	5	15	3	34	7	19	4	36	7

Science	3–5	58	12	26	5	16	3	35	7	19	4	32	7
	Cross-grade-band linking	(25)											
	6–8	60	12	28	5	17	3	36	7	19	4	32	7
	Cross-grade-band linking	(20)											
	10	56	12	26	5	15	3	33	7	18	4	30	7
Social studies	3–5	82	19	29	7	12	3	33	8	8	2	40	9
	Cross-grade-band linking	(37)											
	6–8	80	19	29	7	12	3	33	8	9	2	39	9
	10	X	X	X	X	X	X	X	X	X	X	X	X

From American Institutes for Research. (2008, Spring). *South Carolina Alternate Assessment technical report.* Washington, DC: American Institutes for Research; adapted by permission.

SCORE REPORTING

Scores for the SC-Alt are reported in two ways: as scale scores and as achievement levels. Scale scores ranged from 260 to 740 for each content area. The simultaneous calibration of items across grade bands resulted in a single, vertical scale, which allows student achievement to be tracked over time.

Using the scale scores, students can be assigned to achievement levels for each content area. Each achievement level is specified in the South Carolina Descriptions of Achievement Levels (DALs). The DALs specify the knowledge and skills of test takers within each performance or achievement level on the SC-Alt. They are designed with the expectation that students will grow and achieve more from year to year and that they will be able to demonstrate these skills as they receive more instruction. As such, the DALs explicitly assume that a student must know and be able to do more at higher grade bands than at lower grade bands to achieve the same achievement level. However, the DALs are constructed to capture a wide enough range of achievement that they cover the range of achievement across grades within a grade band (i.e., from Grades 3 to 5 within the Grade 3–5 band).

The DALs were designed to fit the following template when compared with the ASMGs:

- Level 4: Students must demonstrate and apply academic skills and competencies.

- Level 3: Students must demonstrate increasing academic skills and competencies.

- Level 2: Students must demonstrate foundational academic skills and competencies.

- Level 1: Students may demonstrate emerging academic skills and competencies.

Levels 3 and 4 are considered *proficient* for adequate yearly progress calculations. Table 15.3 presents an example of one DAL.

DALs were linked to scale scores by way of the ID-matching standard-setting process (see Cizek & Bunch, 2006; Ferrara, Perie, & Johnson, 2002). This process is similar to the bookmark method in that it uses an ordered item booklet (in this case, each score point was ordered) and asks panelists to identify the item (or score point) that best differentiates the items aligned with one DAL compared with an adjacent DAL. The ID-matching process differs from the bookmark method in two important ways. First, panelists are allowed to note some overlap in items that are aligned with each DAL in the ordered item booklet; this is called the *area of uncertainty* and is where panelists should look for items on which to place cut scores. Second, panelists make no probability judgments; these are set as policy beforehand.

Table 15.3. Grade 3–5 descriptions of achievement levels for English/language arts

Students performing at Level 4 demonstrate and apply academic skills and competencies. They should be able to
- Identify story elements such as the main idea and cause and effect
- Make predictions and draw conclusions about text
- Read and understand the main idea of a simple paragraph
- Create and edit personal written products
- Follow multistep oral or signed directions
- Take turns appropriately during conversation or discussion

Students performing at Level 3 demonstrate increasing academic skills and competencies. They should be able to
- Identify story elements in text (e.g., characters, settings, events, cause and effect, problem solution)
- Read words and simple sentences
- Generate an idea and use words, pictures, or oral language to write
- Follow one-step oral or signed directions
- Communicate agreement or disagreement appropriately

Students performing at Level 2 demonstrate foundational academic skills and competencies. They should be able to
- Participate in reading activities by telling or showing what the text is about, using objects, pictures, or words
- Identify individual words and story elements (e.g., main idea, events, setting, characters)
- Use oral and written language to describe; choose topics and generate ideas for written communication
- Focus attention on a speaker and listen without interrupting; participate in conversations by responding appropriately

Students performing at Level 1 demonstrate emerging academic skills and competencies. They should be able to
- Attend to a variety of text read aloud as evidenced by facial expressions, gestures, or sounds
- Attend to a writing activity using objects, pictures, or letters
- Respond to conversations using facial expressions, gestures, or sounds; attend to a speaker

From American Institutes for Research. (2007, Summer). *South Carolina Alternate Assessment Spring, 2007 standard setting, setting standards in grade bands 3–5, 6–8, and 10, for ELA, mathematics, and social studies technical report.* Washington, DC: American Institutes for Research; adapted by permission.

Standards were set using teacher panels that consisted of special education teachers and content experts. Each content panel comprised two subpanels that set standards at the anchor grades (2–5 and 10), and the standards for Grades 6–8 were set by the whole group using the anchor grades as a guide. Once all provisional standards had been set within each content group, a meta-panel was convened to ensure that the standards were consistent across grade bands and content areas. Tables 15.4–15.7 show the final recommended scale scores and percentages of students in each category.

Table 15.4. Estimated percentage of students at each performance level—English/language arts

Performance level	Scale score cut score	Estimated percentage in level	Estimated cumulative percentage (at and above) for each performance standard
Grades 3–5			
Level 1	—	12.6	100.0
Level 2	403	25.4	87.4
Level 3	466	21.9	62.0
Level 4	491	40.1	40.1
Grades 6–8			
Level 1	—	12.9	100.0
Level 2	417	23.3	87.2
Level 3	477	14.9	63.9
Level 4	501	49.0	49.0
Grade 10			
Level 1	—	13.4	100.0
Level 2	429	23.6	86.6
Level 3	487	12.5	63.1
Level 4	514	50.6	50.6

From American Institutes for Research. (2007, Summer). *South Carolina Alternate Assessment Spring, 2007 standard setting, setting standards in grade bands 3–5, 6–8, and 10, for ELA, mathematics, and social studies technical report.* Washington, DC: American Institutes for Research; adapted by permission.

Table 15.5. Estimated percentage of students at each performance level—Math

Performance level	Scale score cut score	Estimated percentage in level	Estimated cumulative percentage (at and above) for each performance standard
Grades 3–5			
Level 1	—	14.3	100.0
Level 2	413	30.8	85.7
Level 3	476	29.3	54.9
Level 4	526	25.7	25.7
Grades 6–8			
Level 1	—	15.9	100.0
Level 2	425	28.5	84.1
Level 3	489	25.9	55.6
Level 4	534	29.8	29.8
Grade 10			
Level 1	—	16.1	100.0
Level 2	434	30.1	84.0
Level 3	498	28.9	53.9
Level 4	541	24.9	24.9

From American Institutes for Research. (2007, Summer). *South Carolina Alternate Assessment Spring, 2007 standard setting, setting standards in grade bands 3–5, 6–8, and 10, for ELA, mathematics, and social studies technical report.* Washington, DC: American Institutes for Research; adapted by permission.

Table 15.6. Estimated percentage of students at each performance level—Science

Performance level	Scale score cut score	Estimated percentage in level	Estimated cumulative percentage (at and above) for each performance standard
Grades 3–5			
Level 1	—	19.8	100.0
Level 2	430	18.2	80.2
Level 3	469	17.5	62.0
Level 4	496	44.5	44.5
Grades 6–8			
Level 1	—	22.1	100.0
Level 2	447	18.5	77.9
Level 3	489	15.3	59.3
Level 4	514	44.0	44.0
Grade 10			
Level 1	—	25.3	100.0
Level 2	463	25.0	74.7
Level 3	506	16.1	49.7
Level 4	535	33.6	33.6

From American Institutes for Research. (2007, Summer). *South Carolina Alternate Assessment Spring, 2007 standard setting, setting standards in grade bands 3–5, 6–8, and 10, for ELA, mathematics, and social studies technical report.* Washington, DC: American Institutes for Research; adapted by permission.

Table 15.7. Estimated percentage of students at each performance level—Social studies

Performance level	Scale score cut score	Estimated percentage in level	Estimated cumulative percentage (at and above) for each performance standard
Grades 3–5			
Level 1	—	19.3	100.0
Level 2	423	32.7	80.7
Level 3	492	30.1	48.1
Level 4	549	18.0	18.0
Grades 6–8			
Level 1	—	19.7	100.0
Level 2	439	27.3	80.3
Level 3	503	34.1	53.0
Level 4	560	19.0	19.0

From American Institutes for Research. (2007, Summer). *South Carolina Alternate Assessment Spring, 2007 standard setting, setting standards in grade bands 3–5, 6–8, and 10, for ELA, mathematics, and social studies technical report.* Washington, DC: American Institutes for Research; adapted by permission.

SUMMARY

The SC-Alt was designed to address SCDE's need to track student progress over time for accountability purposes and to help improve student instruction. The performance task–based design of the assessment facilitates the comparability of scores and the standardization of administration. Items were developed with content experts and special education teachers. The administration is designed to facilitate standardization and score comparability while minimizing the burden of administration on teachers. This was accomplished by a unique linking design and by allowing teachers to administer only the items that are best suited to students' individual achievement levels, which are determined by using the SPQ. Administration is simplified by using pictographic instructions and a highly specific script with scaffolded items. Cross–grade-band and within–grade-band scores are compared using a simultaneously calibrated vertical scale. Scores are reported using a scale score and a DAL. The DALs were linked to scale scores through the ID-matching standard-setting process. The result was a coherent system of standards for alternate assessments of eligible students in South Carolina from Grades 3 to 10.

REFERENCES

American Institutes for Research. (2007, Summer). *South Carolina Alternate Assessment Spring, 2007 standard setting, setting standards in grade bands 3-5, 6-8, and 10, for ELA, mathematics, and social studies technical report.* Washington, DC: American Institutes for Research; adapted by permission.

American Institutes for Research. (2008, Spring). *South Carolina Alternate Assessment technical report.* Washington, DC: American Institutes for Research.

Cizek, G.J., & Bunch, M.B. (2006). *Standard setting: A guide to establishing and evaluating performance standards on tests.* Thousand Oaks, CA: Sage Publications.

Ferrara, S., Perie, M., & Johnson, E. (2002, September). *Matching the judgmental task with standard setting panelist expertise: The item-descriptor (ID) matching procedure.* Colloquium presented for the Board on Testing and Assessment of the National Research Council, Washington, DC.

South Carolina Department of Education. (2008). *SC-Alt Assessment Standards and Measurement Guidelines (ASMGs).* Retrieved March 31, 2009, from http://ed.sc.gov/agency/Accountability/Assessment/old/assessment/programs/SWD/SC-AltAssessmentStandardsandMeasurementGuidelines.html

South Carolina Department of Education. (2008, Spring). *South Carolina Alternate Assessment Test administration manual.* Columbia: Author.

U.S. Office of Special Education Programs. *Designing from the ground floor: Alternate assessment on alternate achievement standards.* Web site: http://www.osepideasthatwork.org/toolkit/ground_floor.asp

For more information on Picture Communication Symbols:

Mayer-Johnson LLC	Telephone: 1-800-588-4548
2100 Wharton Street	Fax: 858-550-0449
Suite 400	E-mail: mayerj@mayer-johnson.com
Pittsburgh, PA 15203	Web site: www.mayer-johnson.com

The Future of Alternate Assessment

CHAPTER 16

Considering the Consequences of Alternative Assessments

PETER BEHUNIAK

Establishing the validity of any test is the primary challenge in the design and development of educational assessments. The appropriateness of employing procedures intended to validate measures of educational achievement for a general student population has been the subject of much research and debate within the measurement community. However, the difficulties encountered in collecting and interpreting validity evidence are even greater when the instrument of interest is an alternate assessment. This chapter examines some of the ways in which current validity theory and practice apply to alternative assessments. An argument is presented that encourages the greater use of one aspect of validity, consequential or impact evidence, when attempting to validate an alternative assessment.

GENERAL OBSERVATIONS ON TEST VALIDITY

The nature of validity theory and practice is always evolving. This is evident in changes described in the current edition of the *Standards for Educational and Psychological Testing* (American Educational Research Association [AERA], American Psychological Association [APA], & National Council on Measurement in Education [NCME], 1999) when compared with the four earlier editions of 1955 (AERA & National Council on Measurements Used in Education), 1966 (APA), 1974 (APA), and 1985 (AERA, APA, & NCME). The seminal work of Messick (1989) advocated, among other changes, a unified conceptualization of validity. More than a decade later, Kane (2006) suggested further adjustments to the conceptual validity framework in describing the advantages of an argument-based approach.

The current environment in the field of measurement virtually ensures that more changes, perhaps even more extensive, are to be anticipated. One issue of *Educational Researcher* (AERA, 2007) was devoted almost entirely to discussing the perceived adequacy of concepts of validity and to describing changes that might occur in the future. Also, plans are underway to begin the multiyear process of developing the sixth edition of the *Standards for Educational and Psychological Testing*. As these efforts indicate, the measurement field will dedicate much attention to standard concepts and practices in the test validity arena.

One aspect of validity theory and practice that has received and continues to receive much attention concerns the various types of validity evidence and the ways in which these types should be conceptually related. Messick's (1989) unitary conceptualization transformed the way the measurement community thought about test validity. An article by Lissitz and Samuelsen (2007) questioned the utility of this approach and proposed elevating the status of content evidence and lowering reliance on construct evidence. Others responding in the same journal (Embretson, 2007; Gorin, 2007; Moss, 2007) argued for the continued importance of construct validity and, to varying degrees, supported the continued conceptual role of a test's construct in a unitary validity framework.

This dialogue about validity is healthy and should lead to a better understanding of validity research and improved practices of gathering validity evidence. However, it also means that, in the next few years, there may be less agreement in the field about the best ways to proceed with validation practices for educational assessments. This is a predictable side effect when theory and practice enter a transitional phase. Although these developments have implications for all assessments, there are several reasons to be particularly concerned with how the developments affect alternate assessments. The next section examines a number of these considerations.

VALIDITY CONSIDERATIONS
FOR ALTERNATE ASSESSMENTS

The increasing prevalence of alternative assessments in public education has increased the challenges faced by theorists and practitioners working to ensure the validity of these measures. One factor that contributes to the challenge of validating alternate assessments is that these measures must be considered as parts of larger assessment systems. In order to better understand these challenges, it is instructive to begin by considering the validation practices used for the general assessments with which the alternate assessments are paired.

It is common for large-scale educational assessments to include evidence of reliability—typically, internal consistency and rater consistency (when appropriate). Evidence of content validity is also frequently provided because these assessments are usually based on published content standards. This content evidence can take many forms, including procedural descriptions (e.g., committee and expert reviews), links among test specifications and content standards, and alignment studies. Evidence of the successful use of a specific psychometric model (e.g., three-parameter Item Response Theory) is also a typical element in the technical documentation.

It is less common to see criterion or construct evidence provided to support validity arguments. The reasons for this vary from program to program. Evidence of criterion validity, such as concurrent or predictive studies, may be viewed as less important for a standards-based assessment using the reasoning that as long as sufficient evidence is available to document that the measure is closely linked to the underlying content standards, relationships with other achievement tests are not necessary. This view was, in part, the perspective of Lissitz and Samuelsen (2007) when they stated, "Our thesis is that the internal characteristics [of the test] should be determined to be the content validity of the test and that these do not depend upon external factors" (p. 437).

The rationale for having little or no construct evidence is likely quite different. One understandable limitation would be available resources because all of these deadline-driven programs must establish priorities, which necessarily omits some desirable but nonessential psychometric steps. Another reason is potentially more problematic: For many assessments, empirical evidence regarding the construct being assessed would not be likely to support the intended use of the instrument. For example, consider a reading test that is intended for fifth-grade students and is based on the state's content standards. The state's standards indicate several reading elements to be part of the fifth-grade standards, such as *recognizing the author's stance* and *making a personal connection*. It is unlikely that empirical studies such as factor analysis would confirm the intended structure of the assessment. This would place the state agency in the untenable position of being required (possibly by both state and federal mandates) to base the assessment on state content standards despite evidence that the agency's best efforts fall short of accomplishing this task. A common technique for dealing with this issue is to rely on the acceptable fit of the test items to the psychometric model on which the assessment is created to support the claim of a single construct being measured (in this case, reading) based on the unidimensionality assumption of the model.

So, what should be done about the validation of alternate assessments? The first impulse might be to model the practices used with the paired general assessment—that is, to lean heavily on reliability and content validity evidence to develop a validity argument. Unfortunately, these components do not lend themselves to use with alternate assessments in the same way that they do with general assessments.

Reliability evidence for alternate assessments poses a challenge for at least two very different reasons. In some programs, the nature of the instrument and the nature of the student population being assessed make it difficult to achieve traditionally acceptable levels of consistency. Obtaining adequate levels of reliability when using an assessment model such as a portfolio can be difficult under the most desirable circumstances. When a portfolio model used as an alternate assessment is applied to a very diverse student population and monitored by each student's own teacher, the realization of acceptable levels of reliability evidence becomes that much more difficult to attain. In addition, there are frequently small numbers of students within each grade or subgroup, presenting another obstacle to collecting suitable validity evidence.

A different type of obstacle exists when an alternate assessment consists of an observational instrument or checklist. In most cases, the design of these assessments requires administration by each student's own teacher. Although it is technically possible to calculate internal consistency estimates, the resulting estimates are frequently at or approaching 1.0. These results are generally uninterpretable with regard to the reliability of the instrument because the estimates almost certainly reflect the administrative procedures and the familiarity of each teacher with his or her own students.

This leaves the possibility of relying on content validity to support alternate assessments. This is probably the most common practice. It is troubling, however, that the mandates and requirements that led to the widespread creation and use of alternate assessments actually limit the utility of content validity evidence to support the technical adequacy of these measures. The No Child Left Behind Act of 2001 (PL 107-110) requires states to base their alternate assessments on the same content standards as their general assessments at each grade (U.S. Department of Education, 2003). This might seem innocuous, but in practice it presents a significant additional obstacle.

To understand the problem, consider the following thought experiment. A fully qualified team of measurement experts and content specialists receives a set of content standards for a specific grade and content area, such as sixth-grade reading. They are charged with designing an assessment that is as valid as possible; they may use whatever item formats or assessment techniques they deem necessary. They are given wide discretion with regard to practical limitations such as available resources and a suitable test length. When the team members finish designing the assessment, they are given a new charge: Design a second assessment that is based on the same content standards but that will serve as an alternative to the first. However, additional constraints are placed on the team as they begin their work. The second assessment cannot be a parallel measure. Some item formats are not allowed. Due to certain characteristics of the student population targeted by the assessment, some test administration procedures need to be modified or prohibited. It should be clear that because of the more restrictive conditions imposed, the content validity of the second assessment would almost certainly be lower than that of the first assessment.

This does not mean that the second assessment must be devoid of content validity. Evidence of content validity should still be gathered and evaluated. However, this scenario, which closely resembles the current environment for the development of many alternate assessments, does present a challenge to those responsible for designing valid measures. What better source of validity evidence exists to help support the available content validity evidence? The next section explores the possibility that evidence of consequential validity offers a suitable opportunity.

EVIDENCE OF CONSEQUENTIAL VALIDITY

There has long been widespread support for collecting evidence of how an assessment affects examinees or their environment. Messick (1989) observed that "the general evidence supportive of score meaning [must] be enhanced by specific evidence for the relevance of the scores to the applied purpose and for the utility of the scores in the applied setting" (p. 63). Specifically focusing on the consequences of an assessment, Messick (1989) also argued that "the appropriateness of the intended testing purpose and the possible occurrence of unintended outcomes and side effects are the major issues" (pp. 83–84). Kane (2006) added, "Consequences, or outcomes, are the bottom line in evaluating decision procedures, which are always designed to achieve some desired outcomes or to avoid some undesirable outcomes" (p. 54).

It is interesting that the debate over certain aspects of validity, such as the utility of the unitary conceptual approach, does not diminish the perceived importance of examining sources of consequential validity. Lissitz and Samuelsen (2007) elaborated on their perspective:

> The class of impact evaluation studies, which involve the consequences of using a test or assessment device . . . is also an important kind of research. . . . Another example is the case where testing is introduced to change what teachers do in the classroom. If that is the impact that was intended, then verifying that it actually occurs would be an important step. (p. 445)

This is precisely the intention of the mandate to incorporate alternate assessments into each state's assessment program. Alternate assessments are believed to offer students who previously were excluded from mainstream educational programs a number of potential advantages, such as increasing the accountability of schools for student achievement and improving classroom instruction (Almond, Lehr, Thurlow, & Quenemoen, 2002).

It is proposed here that the validation of alternate assessments would be more effectively addressed through an increased focus on their intended purposes and the unintended outcomes associated with their use. The basis for this strategy has both negative and positive aspects. On the negative side, the absence of other types of validity evidence or the additional difficulties associated with collecting this evidence (as discussed earlier) suggests that a focus on consequences may be warranted. On the positive side, the purposes of implementing alternate assessments support research regarding the degree to which these measures affect the students who take them. Collecting evidence regarding the consequences of alternate assessments can greatly advance our understanding of the impact of these instruments.

So what would be the best way to establish a program of research into the consequences of implementing alternate assessments? There is no shortage of discussion in the literature regarding the requirements, obstacles, and methods associated with examining the consequences of educational assessments (Chudowsky & Behuniak, 1998; Haertel, 1999; Kane, 2006; Linn, 1997; Mehrens, 2002). When the issues regarding the consequences of assessments are considered in relation to the unique aspects of the different types of alternate assessments, it is clear that many different paths could be taken to obtain evidence of consequential validity. The remaining part of this chapter discusses some of the possible avenues that could prove useful in developing research into the consequences of alternate assessments.

Educational Consequences

Most educational assessments are intended to improve achievement directly or indirectly. For example, students can receive added instruction in weak areas, new instructional methods can be introduced, curricula can be adjusted, or students can be assigned more relevant work. In the case of alternate assessments, a frequent goal is the inclusion of students with disabilities in mainstream classes and exposure to the regular curriculum. All of these possibilities provide opportunities to examine the implementation of alternate assessments. These and other programmatic and instructional changes provide a realistic starting point in the study of consequences.

Of course, the ultimate measure of changes in student achievement would surpass these process and environmental factors and, instead, focus directly on indicators of achievement. Direct indicators might include such techniques as the use of performance activities or observations of student behavior habits in and outside of the classroom. Because research involving direct indicators is time consuming and costly to implement, it may not be feasible initially (or at all) for some programs. However, it appears likely that carefully designed research studies based on the judicious use of samples of students might overcome many of these practical constraints.

Defining the Target Content

Content validity is not typically considered to be directly associated with consequential validity, and it is not my intention to (overly) blur the lines between these two types of evidence. However, for reasons discussed earlier, there is a special relationship between the target content and the nature of alternate assessments that provides a window of opportunity for researchers investigating the consequences of employing alternate assessments. Consider the early steps in the process of test development (and recall the thought experiment described earlier). After test developers are provided the content standards on which the test will be based, they must determine the nature of the alternate assessment (e.g., portfolio, performance activity, or checklist).

The next step involves reformulating the content to render it suitable for the structure of the alternate assessment format. This must be accomplished while still maintaining a reasonable degree of fidelity to the original content standards. An example of this occurs when a set of content standards, which might include 50 or 100 elements, is the basis for a portfolio-style alternate assessment. In order to make the portfolio manageable, there must be some reconceptualization of the content based on a set of decisions and priorities that may or may not be explicitly stated. The reformulated content standards will usually consist of a smaller number of elements that might be defined more broadly. This reformulation of the target content provides an opportunity to examine a new set of consequences of the alternate assessment.

Presumably, the content is modified on the basis of decisions that are closely tied to the characteristics of the students participating in the assessments and their educational programs. Some of the considerations that typically are weighed are students' physical and cognitive disabilities, each student's individualized education plan, and other related environmental factors. These considerations often produce test specifications that differ to varying degrees from the specifications used to guide test development for the general assessment. Some of the differences may well be related to test format differences, such as when the general assessment consists of many selected response items and the alternate assessment is a portfolio. The differences of interest, however, are those related to modifications made purposefully to render the alternate assessments appropriate for the target student population.

Modifications in the descriptions of an alternate assessment's content standards can be examined for clues regarding the curricular priorities for participating students. For example, if several curriculum standards (e.g., strands, objectives, learning expectations) in the original content standards are combined into one, broader standard, then comparing these two ways of representing similar content may prove instructive. If certain curriculum standards receive greater emphasis or are eliminated in the reformulation process, these changes could be similarly informative. Other investigations of the consequences of modified descriptions of content in such areas as teacher perception, curricular emphasis, and instructional methods could provide additional valuable information regarding the effects of alternate assessments.

The Relationship of Stated Purposes and Score Inferences

It is safe to assume that everyone would like each student to do well on the assessments that he or she takes. When a student does not do well, it is presumed to be an indication that something needs to change: Educators and parents begin considering the appropriateness and effectiveness of the student's class placement, instructional approaches, courses of study, need for remediation, and a variety of other factors. Even when a student performs well on an assessment, a similar sequence of interpretation and review might be initiated. Questions may be raised regarding whether the academic material presents enough of a challenge to the student or whether the student's course of study should be broadened or enriched. This is part of the useful cycle that occurs when testing is used to guide instruction and inform educational decision making.

The process of drawing inferences based on test scores and examining how well these inferences further the stated purposes of the program provide another opportunity for studying the consequences of assessments. The purposes of alternate assessments generally fall into two main categories. One set of purposes mirrors those that exist for regular assessments, such as improving student achievement or promoting school reform. A second set of purposes is unique to the population of students and teachers involved in alternate assessments, such as improving the academic rigor of programs for students with cognitive disabilities or increasing the amount of time students with disabilities spend in mainstream classrooms. Examining the degree to which these purposes are facilitated by alternate assessments certainly would qualify as evidence of consequential validity.

There also may be productive areas of research that are more subtle and somewhat indirectly linked to the stated purposes of using alternate assessments. One such area is the way in which teachers perceive and work with students with disabilities. Because students with disabilities are often the recipients of one-to-one instruction, it would be particularly compelling to consider the possible effects on the teacher–student relationship brought about by the use of alternate assessments. Kane (2006) described how teachers refine their views of students by using feedback from assessments and other sources:

If a teacher's expectations fail for many students in many situations, the teacher may need to rethink some of his or her basic assumptions. On the other hand, if the teacher's conceptual frameworks are working reasonably well for most students but are failing for a particular student, the teacher is more likely to rethink the assumptions being made about that student. (p. 48)

A study of changes in perceptions, assumptions, and practices among teachers of students participating in alternate assessments could provide important information about the consequences of using these measures.

Social Consequences

Educational consequences are easier to study, but social consequences may be more important, at least in some situations. It is certainly relevant to consider whether a reading program in Kindergarten through Grade 3 prepares students adequately for the class work and assignments they will receive in the middle grades and in high school. However, few would argue with the view that a critical reason for teaching reading to all students is to prepare them for what comes after high school, be it the demands of higher education, the requirements established by employers in the workplace, or the need for at least minimal skills to be functionally literate. It seems particularly relevant to consider the social consequences of using alternate assessments because many of the students who take these assessments are enrolled in programs that are designed to prepare them for the situations they will encounter outside of the classroom.

The study of some social consequences simply may not be possible due to the time and other resources that would be required. However, examining the degree to which students increase the transfer of some of their academic skills to extracurricular settings does seem manageable. Parents could be included in studies involving focus groups or similar research techniques to gather evidence regarding students' behavior habits outside of school. Even the nature of the home–school relationship could be considered a type of social consequence suitable for investigation.

SUMMARY

This chapter has discussed many aspects of the concept of validity as it pertains to the development and use of alternate assessments. The chapter identified some of the difficulties encountered when attempting to validate alternate assessments, particularly when these difficulties are differentially applied to alternate assessments and the regular assessments with which they are paired. A greater focus on collecting evidence regarding the consequences of alternate assessments would be a valuable advancement toward validating these instruments. This argument is not intended to suggest that less effort or interest should be directed to other types of validity evidence. Instead, it is proposed that research regarding the intended and unintended consequences of introducing alternate assessments into classrooms is currently underutilized and could provide a needed improvement in our understanding of how valid these measures really are.

REFERENCES

Almond, P.J., Lehr, C., Thurlow, M.L., & Quenemoen, R. (2002). Participation in large-scale state assessment and accountability systems. In G. Tindal & T.M. Haladyna (Eds.), *Large-Scale Assessment Programs for All Students.* (pp. 341–370). Mahwah, NJ: Lawrence Erlbaum Associates.

American Educational Research Association. (2007, November). *Educational Researcher, 36*(8).

American Educational Research Association, American Psychological Association, & National Council on Measurement in Education. (1985). *Standards for educational and psychological testing.* Washington, DC: Authors.

American Educational Research Association, American Psychological Association, & National Council on Measurement in Education. (1999). *Standards for educational and psychological testing.* Washington, DC: Authors.

American Educational Research Association & National Council on Measurements Used in Education. (1955, January). *Technical recommendations for achievement tests.* Washington, DC: National Education Association.

American Psychological Association. (1966). *Standards for educational and psychological tests and manuals.* Washington, DC: Author.

American Psychological Association. (1974). *Standards for educational and psychological tests.* Washington, DC: Author.

Chudowsky, N., & Behuniak, P. (1998). Using focus groups to examine the consequential aspect of validity. *Educational Measurement: Issues and Practices, 17*(4), 28–38.

Embretson, S.E. (2007). Construct validity: A universal validity system or just another test evaluation procedure? *Educational Researcher, 36*(8), 449–455.

Gorin, J.S. (2007). Reconsidering issues in validity theory. *Educational Researcher, 36*(8), 456–462.

Haertel, E.H. (1999). Validity arguments for high stakes testing: In search of the evidence. *Educational Measurement: Issues and Practices, 18*(4), 5–9.

Kane, M.T. (2006). Validation. In R.L. Brennan (Ed.), *Educational measurement* (4th ed., pp. 17–64). Westport, CT: Praeger.

Linn, R.L. (1997). Evaluating the validity of assessments: The consequences of use. *Educational Measurement: Issues and Practices, 16*(2), 14–16.

Lissitz, R.W., & Samuelsen, K. (2007). A suggested change in terminology and emphasis regarding validity and education. *Educational Researcher, 36*(8), 437–448.

Mehrens, W.A. (2002). Consequences of assessment: What is the evidence? In G. Tindal & T.M. Haladyna (Eds.), *Large-scale assessment programs for all students* (pp. 149–177). Mahwah, NJ: Lawrence Erlbaum Associates.

Messick, S. (1989). Validity. In R.L. Linn (Ed.), *Educational measurement* (3rd ed., pp. 13–103.). New York: American Council on Education and Macmillan.

Moss, P.A. (2007). Reconstructing validity. *Educational Researcher, 36*(8), 470–476.

No Child Left Behind Act of 2001, PL 107-110, 115 Stat. 1425, 20 U.S.C. §§ 6301 *et seq.*

U.S. Department of Education. (2003). *Title I—Improving the academic achievement of the disadvantaged, final rule* (34 C.F.R. Part 200). Washington, DC: Author.

CHAPTER 17

Which Came First—The Curriculum or the Assessment?

DIANE M. BROWDER,
SHAWNEE WAKEMAN, AND CLAUDIA FLOWERS

Most states have experienced several iterations of their alternate assessments based on alternate achievement standards. One reason for the changes made to these assessments has been to strengthen the alignment between the assessments and the states' academic content standards. The Individuals with Disabilities Education Act Amendments (IDEA) of 1997 (PL 105-17) required that all students have access to the general curriculum and that students who were unable to participate in large-scale assessments receive alternate assessments. As described in Chapter 5, thinking about curriculum for students with significant cognitive disabilities has evolved since the 1980s. Given this evolution and the changing nature of alternate assessments, it can be difficult to identify whether the development of alternate assessments for students with significant cognitive disabilities stemmed from new thinking about curriculum or whether it created this thinking. Which came first—the curriculum or the assessment?

In the context of special education prior to 1997, many students were tracked into one of three curricula: a) the general curriculum with expectations for grade-level achievement, b) a remedial academic curriculum (e.g., an eighth grader working on second-grade math), or c) a functional life skills curriculum. Prior to 1997, only the first group, who were expected to show grade-level achievement, participated in the states' large-scale assessment programs. Remedial academics were characterized as off grade level and focused primarily on reading and math. Students in upper grades often received instructional applications to life skills (e.g., consumer mathematics). Functional life skills curricular planning used a catalog approach. Similar to making selections from a clothing catalog, individualized educational program (IEP) teams selected skills that were needed and preferred. Also, in this life skills approach, an IEP could be a student's entire curriculum. Although planning efforts considered students' chronological ages, there was no grade-level differentiation. Any academics taught were limited to those immediately usable in daily life (functional academics). Sometimes, IEP teams used decision models to determine who would or would not receive academic instruction. For example, substantial life skills deficits and slow progress in academics might be reasons to omit academics from IEPs. Ironically, there was no research to show that mastering functional life skills (e.g., hand washing, dressing, cooking) was a prerequisite to academic learning.

Between IDEA 1997 and the No Child Left Behind Act (NCLB) of 2001 (PL 107-110), which required the reporting of adequate yearly progress in academic content areas, there was a brief era of confusion about what alternate assessments were meant to measure. As noted by Thompson, Thurlow, Johnstone, and Altman (2005), some states' alternate assessments were based on their academic content standards, some on extensions of these standards, some only on functional life skills, and some on functional life skills meant to backmap to state standards. Browder, Flowers, et al. (2004) did a content analysis of 31 states' performance indicators for their alternate assessments and found a variety of curricular philosophies reflected. In contrast, those identified by content experts as having the strongest links to the content areas had a clear academic focus. That is, backmapping did not always work well in creating alignment with state standards.

Once NCLB required the reporting of adequate yearly progress in academic content areas, states needed alternate assessments with measurable outcomes in language arts, mathematics, and science that linked to grade-level content standards. For students to have a fair assessment, they obviously also needed academic content instruction. Many educators had to shift their thinking not only about alternate assessments but also about curricular planning and instruction for students with significant disabilities. For example, educators needed to think about sequences of skills for grade-level or grade-band differentiation versus the former catalog approach. The IEP could not be the entire curriculum, but it needed to be standards based. IEP teams needed to determine how to balance students' ongoing needs to learn functional life skills with new academic content priorities. Academic content needed to be extended from grade-level content rather than borrowed from early grades or preschool.

For educators whose context was planning between the general curriculum or an alternate curriculum (functional or remedial academic), the requirement of alternate assessments that linked to academic content probably did precipitate the changes in curriculum. Nevertheless, this was not the only curricular context in 1997. Educators working in inclusive contexts had been moving toward greater curricular integration for some time. For example, Ryndak and Alper (1996) described how to blend content from the general curriculum and functional life skills in planning IEPs. Similarly, Downing and Demchak (1996) described how to address individual needs with general education curriculum. Even early resources on alternate assessment described how to integrate these procedures with the general curriculum (Burdge et al., 2001). For students receiving instruction in inclusive contexts, teaching skills that linked to general curriculum content was often already in the planning. The challenge of federal policy was that all students receiving instruction in all contexts would have access to the general curriculum and be assessed with alternate assessments if they were unable to participate in the general assessment with or without accommodations.

Although some students may have had access to general curriculum content already in their educational plans, NCLB also required students to show achievement of state standards. Access was not enough; students needed to demonstrate learning of the content. In the early era of alternate assessments, some states focused on access more than learning. In other words, a student's score may have been combined with considerations of program quality. For example, a rubric used to score a portfolio assessment might include ratings for opportunities to learn with typical peers or use skills of self-determination. Sometimes, the term *access skills* was used to refer to general motor or communication skills that students could use in general education settings that were not necessarily academic. Even for students who were fully included in general education contexts, the increased focus on demonstrating learning of content that linked to grade-level standards required some new thinking about curriculum planning.

Our work at the University of North Carolina at Charlotte on the alignment of alternate assessments began in the late 1990s during the early era of alternate assessments. We began by examining how the requirement of alternate assessment was affecting the dual priorities of academic and functional content, using less complex models of alignment in which content experts completed global ratings of state materials (Browder, Flowers, et al., 2004; Browder, Spooner, et al., 2004). In this early work, we tried to help the field reflect on how the new policies were intersecting with a changing landscape of curricular priorities. Next, we tried applying an existing alignment methodology to see how states with the strongest links to their state standards would fare (Flowers, Browder, & Ahlgrim-Delzell, 2006). Although the participating states found the information useful for future planning, we did not think existing methodologies were asking about the elephant in the room. That is, were the alternate assessments linking to academic content standards? Were the alternate assessment items even academic (what we dubbed *really reading* and *really math*)? Next, we worked with our content experts at the university to define what alternate achievement standards could mean (Browder, Wakeman, et al., 2007). The criteria we developed in that conceptual piece became the underpinning for the new alignment model called Links for Academic Learning that we developed and field tested with states (Flowers, Wakeman, Browder, & Karvonen, in press). A close reading of these studies reveals that our thinking has evolved in the last decade from simply asking, *Is it academic?* to *Does it match the content of the state standard?* and *Is the student showing learning?* (See Chapter 5 for more details about the criteria for alignment.)

All states have alternate assessments based on alternate achievement standards. Many of these states have participated in alignment studies to determine whether their alternate assessments link with their states' academic content standards. What is less clear is whether curricular alignment is present. Given the curricular context in the last decade, especially for students in self-contained special education classrooms, it is uncertain whether students are receiving instruction in the academic content to be assessed. Karvonen, Wakeman, Browder, Rogers, and Flowers (2008) surveyed 123 teachers in five states using the Curriculum Indicator Survey about their professional development and instructional strategies in teaching academic content to students with significant cognitive disabilities. Teachers reported receiving less professional development in instructional strategies and content standards in science and math than they did in English/language arts instructional strategies and content standards. Teachers identified the priorities for instruction within English/language arts to be beginning reading, discussion, and questioning/listening/contributing. Priorities identified in math appeared to be in number sense, measurement tools, operations, and patterns, relations, and functions. No common priorities emerged in science; no topic in any strand was taught intensively to more than one third of the target students identified by the teachers. This preliminary work suggests that teachers need much more professional development on how to teach to grade-level content standards.

SUMMARY

To answer the question of which came first—the curriculum or the assessment—the groundbreaking work on how to teach general education content can be found in resources on inclusion of students with severe disabilities that predate federal policy (e.g., Downing & Demchak, 1996). Alternate assessments came next but with variations in content focus that reflected the changing curricular landscape of the era (Browder, Spooner, et al., 2004) As part of NCLB, states have had to show how their alternate assessments link to academic content standards. Thus, the expectation that every student, even those with significant cognitive disabilities, would show yearly progress in language arts, mathematics, and science was ushered in by this policy. To catch up with this expectation, many states began to create curricular resources demonstrating how to adapt content for students with complex disabilities (e.g., Massachusetts Department of Elementary and Secondary Education or South Dakota Department of Education). What is not yet known is the extent to which all students have access to general curriculum content, appropriate assistive technology, and other means to demonstrate learning.

REFERENCES

Browder, D., Flowers, C., Ahlgrim-Delzell, L., Karvonen, M., Spooner, F., & Algozzine, R. (2004). The alignment of alternate assessment content to academic and functional curricula. *Journal of Special Education, 37*(4), 211–223.

Browder, D.M., Spooner, F., Ahlgrim-Delzell, L., Flowers, C., Karvonen, M., & Algozzine, R. (2004). A content analysis of the curricular philosophies reflected in states' alternate assessment performance indicators. *Research and Practice in Severe Disabilities, 28*(4), 165–181.

Browder, D., Wakeman, S.Y., Flowers, C., Rickelman, R.J., Pugalee, D., & Karvonen, D. (2007). Creating access to the general curriculum with links to grade level content for students with significant cognitive disabilities: an explication of the concept. *Journal of Special Education, 41*(1), 2–16.

Burdge, M., Groneck, V.B., Kleinert, H.L., Longwill, A.W., Clayton, J., Denham, A., et al. (2001). Integrating alternate assessment in the general curriculum. In H.L. Kleinert & J.F. Kearns, *Alternate assessment: Measuring outcomes and supports for students with disabilities* (pp. 49–75). Baltimore: Paul H. Brookes Publishing Co.

Downing, J.E., & Demchak, M. (1996). First steps: Determining individual abilities and how best to support students. In J.E. Downing, *Including students with severe and multiple disabilities in typical classrooms: Practical strategies for teachers* (pp. 35–61). Baltimore: Paul H. Brookes Publishing Co.

Flowers, C., Browder, D.M., & Ahlgrim-Delzell, L. (2006). An analysis of three states' alignment between language arts and math standards and alternate assessment. *Exceptional Children, 72*(2), 201–215.

Flowers, C., Wakeman, S., Browder, D., & Karvonen, M. (in press). An alignment protocol for alternate assessments based on alternate achievement standards. *Educational Measurements: Issues and Practice.*

Individuals with Disabilities Education Act Amendments (IDEA) of 1997, PL 105-17, 20 U.S.C. §§ 1400 *et seq.*

Karvonen, M., Wakeman, S., Browder, D.M., Rogers, M.S.A., & Flowers, C. (2008). *Academic curriculum for students with significant cognitive disabilities: A decade after IDEA 1997.* Manuscript submitted for publication.

No Child Left Behind Act (NCLB) of 2001, PL 107-110, 115 Stat. 1425, 20 U.S.C. §§ 6301 *et seq.*

Ryndak, D.L., & Alper, S. (1996). *Curriculum and assessment for students with significant disabilities in inclusive settings.* Boston: Allyn and Bacon.

Thompson, S.J., Thurlow, M.L., Johnstone, C.J., & Altman, J.R. (2005). *2005 state special education outcomes: Steps forward in a decade of change.* Retrieved December 7, 2005, from http://education.umn.edu/NCEO/OnlinePubs/2005 StateReport.htm

CHAPTER 18

Key Issues in the Use of Alternate Assessments

Closing Comments to Open More Discussion and Exploration of Solutions

STEPHEN N. ELLIOTT

I have been involved with alternate assessment research and development for a decade, working with a number of state assessment teams, conducting independent research, and publishing a number of validity studies and conceptual papers. During this time, federal policies and regulations have evolved, as have the expectations for students with significant disabilities and the educators who teach these students and assess their achievements. Several technical and practical issues, however, persist and require more attention if we are to improve our assessments of students with the most significant disabilities and provide educators with meaningful information to guide instruction. In this chapter, I identify four of the most pressing issues or concerns that we confront with alternate assessments and provide bullet points summarizing the empirical justifications as to how these issues may be addressed by well-trained educators. Andrew Roach and I have addressed a couple of these issues (Elliott & Roach, 2007), but there is much more to be examined and discussed by those involved in the design and use of alternate assessments that are both technically sound and instructionally useful.

ISSUE 1: TEACHERS AS RELIABLE JUDGES OF STUDENT PERFORMANCE

- Research indicates that teachers are highly reliable judges if they are provided structures for reporting what they have observed.

- Teachers make hundreds of judgments about students' academic and social behavior habits. There have been more than 20 data-based articles published in major refereed journals documenting teachers' ability to reliably estimate students' academic knowledge and skills (e.g., Demaray & Elliott, 1998; Hoge & Coladarci, 1989; Hurwitz, Elliott, & Braden, 2007). The research, in fact, indicates that the majority of teachers, when inaccurate, underestimate students' skills!

- Many published rating scales that utilize teachers as the primary source of data about students' social and academic behavior habits are used daily in schools across the country. Many of these provide evidence for decisions about special education status—a decision with significant consequences for students, their families, and teachers.

- Teachers' judgments are highly valued and trusted for a) aligning the content of assessments with content expected to be learned and b) deciding how much students need to know and be able to do to achieve a "proficient" level of achievement.

- Teacher judgments are part of every approach to alternate assessment; some of these judgments are about needed support, some are about prompting, some are about students' responses, and some are about the quality and type of evidence.

- High-quality assessment training of teachers can facilitate reliable ratings of students' academic skills. Teachers in Mississippi are trained and must past a qualifying test to be able to administer and score the Mississippi Alternate Assessment of Extended Curriculum Frameworks (MAAECF).

- Teachers (or anyone, for that matter) are more reliable judges when the evidence they are asked to review is organized according to standardized and salient dimensions of relevance, recency, and representativeness and also when the scoring criteria are clear and objective. Thus, structure in the form of evidence presentation and scoring criteria enhance reliable judgments.

ISSUE 2: RELIABILITY OF TEACHERS' RATINGS AND THE CONCEPT OF INDEPENDENCE

- The reliability of decisions about students' academic proficiency is very important and should be managed in a way that minimizes error in the final judgment: *proficient* or *not proficient.*

- Teachers' ratings and subsequent decisions about students' achievement levels must be reliable. To determine whether these ratings and decisions are reliable, the consistency of the ratings can be examined a) for many items by one rater and b) by two raters on a common set of items. To achieve high levels of agreement or reliability, both raters must have a common understanding of each student they rate. This common understanding usually is achieved with classroom work samples and direct observations. High-quality evidence, training, and monitoring of raters influence the degree to which two raters agree.

- Confidence in the reliability of ratings by two or more raters is increased when it is known that the raters functioned independently. Independence can be achieved in a number of ways: a) professional training, b) separation of the individuals when they are doing their ratings, and/or c) disallowing direct communications among raters.

ISSUE 3: STANDARDS-BASED INDIVIDUALIZED EDUCATIONAL PROGRAMS AND THE DEVELOPMENT AND COLLECTION OF EVIDENCE

- The alignment of curriculum, instruction, and assessment are desired goals of standards-based reform. Individualized educational programs (IEPs) are key instructional documents for students with disabilities and provide insights into what academic skills are valued and most salient for individual students.

- The skills called for by academic content standards that also appear on students' IEPs should be expected to generate classroom work samples and opportunities for teachers to observe what their students understand and can do. Thus, IEP objectives that align with both content standards and items on an assessment should be excellent and practical sources of classroom-based work evidence for making decisions about students' academic knowledge and skills. IEPs do not limit the objectives aligned with the content standards; rather, they indicate which objectives are a priority for each student. No student's learning is limited to the objectives in his or her IEP.

- IEP objectives provide evidence about the degree to which students are gaining access to content expected of learners in the general education curriculum.

ISSUE 4: AMOUNT AND
QUALITY OF CLASSROOM EVIDENCE
NEEDED FOR VALID RATINGS OF PROFICIENCY

- The alternate assessments for students with significant cognitive disabilities in several states (e.g., Arizona, Connecticut, Hawaii, Idaho, Indiana, Mississippi) are based on teachers' ratings of students' work and classroom performance records for each school year. The evidence teachers collect and rate must illustrate knowledge and skills that are relevant to the item that the evidence is intended to support. In other words, the evidence must be aligned with the content standard that is being assessed. This evidence also must be recent and representative, and the resulting ratings must be reliable to be reported for accountability purposes.

- "The evidence teachers collect influences the inter-rater reliability" of the assessments. "In general, the more comprehensive the evidence collected, the higher the likelihood that two or more raters will agree on the proficiency ratings they provide . . . [each] student." As stated in the MAAECF Rating Scale (Version 2.0):

  > Evidence must be collected and documented with Evidence Worksheets for each competency in a content scale. Evidence from at least 2 different categories must be collected and evaluated for each of the items that are aligned with an IEP goal or objective. If there is no IEP aligned item in a given competency, then evidence must be collected for another non-IEP aligned item. Meaningful evidence of a student's knowledge and skills already exists in most classrooms (e.g., work samples, teacher-made or published tests, observations, interviews, videotapes/photos, or audiotapes). This evidence must be from the current school year and kept one year for monitoring purposes. (see Mississippi Department of Education, 2007)

- High-quality evidence is relevant, recent, representative, and can be scored reliably. To support educators in their efforts to collect and document high-quality evidence, evidence worksheets are recommended. The evidence worksheets used in Mississippi are good examples. They include the following information:

  1. The MAAECF rating scale item number for which the evidence is relevant or aligned

  2. The date each piece of evidence was generated by the student or teacher

3. Multiple pieces of evidence with a detailed description of the accuracy of the student's response and the number of settings in which the student provides such a response

4. Information about the support or accommodations provided to the student to make his or her responses

• Given the characteristics of high-quality evidence, the four-level evidence rubric shown in Table 18.1 was created to functionally communicate that the evidence quality varies. It is very important to create evidence samples that meet or exceed the expected standards. I encourage each teacher who is conducting an alternate assessment to use this rubric as a self-guide to enhance the quality of the evidence collected and the documentation provided to others about the evidence.

• Many states use an evidence sampling approach. All rating scales must be supported by well-organized and documented evidence samples. It is difficult to specify how much evidence and how many items should be sampled; yet, with well-designed reliability and validity studies, one can establish the degree to which a subset of items and evidence predicts the overall ratings on a given scale. Thus, questions regarding the ideal amount of evidence and number of items can be answered empirically, and they should.

Table 18.1. Four-level evidence rubric for the Mississippi Alternate Assessment of Extended Curriculum Frameworks

Significantly below standard (1)	Approaches standard (2)	Meets standard (3)	Exceeds standard (4)
The knowledge and skills represented by the evidence are clearly irrelevant to the item they are intended to support. The amount and type of evidence is limited or lacks clarity and cannot be reviewed reliably. Finally, the recency of the information is questionable.	The knowledge and skills represented by the evidence are of questionable relevance to the item they are intended to support. The amount and type of evidence may be minimally appropriate or lack clarity, so the evidence is difficult to review. Some but not all of the material is recent.	The knowledge and skills represented by the evidence are relevant to the item they are intended to support. The amount and type of evidence is acceptable, and the evidence is easy to review. All of the material is dated or seems recent.	The knowledge and skills represented by the evidence are relevant to the item they are intended to support. The amount and type of evidence is substantial, and the evidence is highly organized, easy to review, and has dates.

SUMMARY

- Train and support teachers to conduct sound assessments.

- Provide teachers with a clear set of learning expectations for their students and ways to generate tangible evidence that reveals what students have learned.

- Trust teachers who have been trained and who present high-quality samples of evidence.

- Establish a verification (monitoring and validation) process.

SUPPORTING REFERENCES

Demaray, M.K., & Elliott, S.N. (1998). Teachers' judgments of students' academic functioning: A comparison of actual and predicted performances. *School Psychology Quarterly, 13*(1), 8–24.

Doll, E., & Elliott, S.N. (1994). Consistency of observations of preschoolers' social behavior. *Journal of Early Intervention, 18*(2), 227–238.

Elliott, S.N. (1998). Performance assessment of students' achievement: Research and practice. *Learning Disabilities: Research and Practice, 13*(4), 233–241.

Elliott, S.N., Compton, E., & Roach, A.T. (2007). Building validity evidence for scores on a state-wide alternate assessment: A contrasting groups, multi-method approach. *Educational Measurement: Issues & Practice, 26*(2), 30–43.

Elliott, S.N., & Roach, A.T. (2007). Alternate assessments of students with significant disabilities: Alternative approaches, common technical challenges. *Applied Measurement in Education, 20*(3), 301–333.

Gerber, M., & Semmel, M.I. (1984). Teacher as imperfect test: Reconceptualizing the referral process. *Educational Psychologist, 19*(3), 137–148.

Hoge, R.D., & Coladarci, T. (1989). Teacher-based judgments of academic achievement: A review of the literature. *Review of Educational Research, 59*(3), 297–313.

Hurwitz, J.T., Elliott, S.N., & Braden, J.P. (2007). The influence of test familiarity and student disability status upon teachers' judgments of students' test performance. *School Psychology Quarterly, 14*(2), 115–144.

Mississippi Department of Education. (2007, August). *Technical manual for the Mississippi Alternate Assessment of the Extended Curriculum Frameworks for Students with Significant Cognitive Disabilities.* Jackson: Author.

Roach, A.T., & Elliott, S.N. (2006). The influence of access to the general education curriculum on the alternate assessment performance of students with significant cognitive disabilities. *Education Evaluation and Policy Analysis, 28*(2), 181–194.

Roach, A.T., Elliott, S.N., & Berndt, S.A. (in press). Teacher satisfaction and the consequential validity of an alternate assessment for students with significant disabilities. *Journal of Disability Studies.*

Roach, A.T., Elliott, S.N., & Webb, N. (2005). Alignment of an alternate assessment with state academic standards: Evidence for the content validity of the Wisconsin Alternate Assessment. *Journal of Special Education, 38*(4), 218–231.

CHAPTER 19

Psychometric Rigor for Alternate Assessments

For the Sake of Interpretation, Not Rigor

STEVE FERRARA

We all agree, I believe, that alternate assessments should meet psychometric rigor requirements, at least to the degree that grade-level content area assessments do. In short, alternate assessments must conform to the *Standards for Educational and Psychological Testing.* I admit a personal psychometric inconsistency (some colleagues may call it a shortcoming): I am proud to work on alternate assessments even though their technical quality typically falls short of the *Standards for Educational and Psychological Testing.* Alternate assessments enable inferences from test performances (i.e., they provide evidence) about what students know and can do in academic content areas. I want psychometric rigor for all assessments because I want to be able to infer from test performance what students know and can do beyond the specific testing conditions. For alternate assessments, I seek attainable psychometric rigor to support reasonable interpretations.

Because they are part of a coherent system, all standards-based achievement assessments enable interpretations about what students know and can do. Such systems include the following components:

- Content standards—descriptions of content area knowledge, skills, and conceptual understanding that students should learn

- Performance-level descriptors (PLDs)—descriptions of what students should know, be able to do, and understand in a content area

- Assessment items and tasks—academic tasks that, we hope, elicit from examinees the content area knowledge, skills, and understandings described in the content standards and PLDs and delineated in test and item specifications

- A scoring and reporting system to link student test performance to the PLDs

The first two elements help to define the achievement construct that is the target of inference. The latter two elements enable inferences from test performances about a student's status on the construct—or, more directly, what students know and can do in relation to the content standards and PLDs. The degree to which these elements align determines the validity of interpretations made from test scores about what students know and can do. For example, if the items on a fifth-grade mathematics assessment are highly aligned (using peer review terminology) with the content standards and PLDs they target, then we can feel confident in inferences about what students know and can do. In this context, saying that inferences are *valid* means that they are dependable, trustworthy, accurate, and so forth. Students who reach the *Proficient* level on a fifth-grade mathematics test might be expected to perform proficiently as they do arithmetic calculations and reason mathematically in fifth- and then sixth-grade mathematics, in retail situations, at home, and elsewhere.

These four elements provide a backdrop for my comments about alternate assessments; although alternate assessments do not conform to the *Standards for Educational and Psychological Testing* to the same degree that grade-level content area assessments do, they still provide useful information about what students know and can do.

APPLICABILITY OF PERFORMANCE-LEVEL DESCRIPTORS TO ALL STUDENTS WITH SIGNIFICANT COGNITIVE DISABILITIES

The interpretive situation for students with significant cognitive disabilities is complicated. The population of students who are eligible for alternate assessments is more diverse cognitively than that of students who participate in grade-level assessments. The lowest-achieving students who perform on grade-level assessments well enough to get onto score reporting scales function quite similarly to the highest-achieving students. Both groups have highly developed communication skills, and both acquire grade-level content area knowledge, skills, and understanding. In contrast, we are not quite sure yet to what degree students with the most significant cognitive disabilities can engage in their immediate environments independently or how much communication skill they can develop. The highest-functioning of their peers (in cognitive, communication, and social senses) do acquire some academic skill, communicate verbally, and develop some independence. Although it is reasonable to interpret performance on grade-level tests for all eligible examinees using a single set of PLDs, it probably is not reasonable to do so for students with the most significant cognitive disabilities.

Two different sets of PLDs—one for most students who participate in alternate assessments and another for those with the most significant cognitive disabilities—may be necessary. PLDs for students with the most significant cognitive disabilities could represent a subset of knowledge, skills, and understanding or additional reductions of depth and breadth beyond the reductions in complexity for alternate achievement standards. Or, reasonable growth standards might be appropriate (see Chapter 6). Here, rigor for the sake of interpretation implies that PLDs must be appropriate for the wide range of students who are eligible for alternate assessments, and that may mean that multiple sets of PLDs are necessary even for a single alternate assessment.

INFERRING COGNITION AND ACADEMIC KNOWLEDGE AND SKILL FROM LIMITED BEHAVIORAL EVIDENCE

Students who have communication skills and academic skills can convey what they know and can do in their responses on alternate assessments. Though they may not always communicate clearly and consistently, they can produce enough clear evidence to enable judgments about the quality of their work and inferences about what they know and can do in a given content area. On the other hand, interpreting communication, physical behaviors, and indicators of attention of students with the most significant cognitive disabilities can be tenuous. Teachers who work with these students often can discern their likes and dislikes and their physical needs, and they even may be able to engage their students in limited two-way communication. However, interpreting the eye gaze of a student with physical disabilities as a selection among multiple response choices may require more inference than reliable observation. And determining a student's choice among options, knowing that that student perseverates on the first or last thing said or presented, also requires judgment. Here, rigor for the sake of interpretation implies that we may have to accept that interpreting test-responding behavior as evidence of what students know and can do may be tenuous for students with the most significant cognitive disabilities.

LIMITED GENERALIZABILITY FROM
TEST PERFORMANCE TO OTHER SITUATIONS

The regulations of the No Child Left Behind Act (NCLB) of 2001 (PL 107-110) acknowledge the appropriateness of adjusting expectations for students who are eligible for alternate assessments. These adjusted expectations are called *extended standards,* meaning that grade-level standards are extended downward. *Downward* is not intended to mean *easier.* Rather, the complexity of grade-level content standards is reduced by narrowing the depth and breadth of the standards so that they are accessible to students with disabilities, who in turn can learn them. As a consequence, inferences about what students know and can do based on their performance on alternate assessments are limited to extended content standards that are less complex than grade-level standards. That is stating the obvious, of course. In this case, the NCLB regulations themselves require rigor for the sake of interpretation.

INCONSISTENCY OF PERFORMANCES
OVER OCCASIONS AND SITUATIONS

Making cautious generalizations to other occasions and situations is related to the amounts and types of supports that students eligible for alternate assessments require in learning and assessment situations, across different tasks, and on different days and times of the day. These students exhibit fatigue, wandering attention, anxiety, and resistance just as their peers who are working on grade level do (often even more so). Their cognitive and physical performance also may be less internally consistent than that of students with no cognitive disabilities. As a consequence, students need various forms of support to complete tasks. Support may range from hand-over-hand assistance and scaffolding of tasks in learning situations to verbal encouragement, repeated prompting to complete a task, and some physical prompting to encourage a student to focus on a task. Here, rigor for the sake of interpretation implies that generalizing conclusions about what students know and can do from a specific testing occasion to other situations outside of the testing environment must account for possible inconsistencies in performance.

TEST ADMINISTRATOR CONSISTENCY AND ACCURACY

Alternate assessments often require classroom teachers to adapt tasks (e.g., scaffolding items to reduce complexity for students who cannot respond successfully) and to score student responses. These decisions usually are made on the fly, while the teacher administers the assessment and manages the student's attention, physical behaviors, and well-being.

Though test administration training may be rigorous, managing all of that is a considerable challenge. In some cases, an independent observer may record and evaluate the assessment administration process for evaluation purposes. But this practice only can detect procedural and scoring errors; it cannot correct the errors before they influence student test scores. Here, rigor for the sake of interpretation implies that administration and scoring accuracy may be influenced negatively by situational variables, perhaps for some students more than others, and that effective training and rehearsal are minimum requirements.

IMPLICATIONS FOR DESIGNING ALTERNATE ASSESSMENTS AND EVALUATING THEIR PSYCHOMETRIC RIGOR

The most common designs for alternate assessments fall short of conforming to the *Standards for Educational and Psychological Testing*. For example, alternate portfolio assessments typically sample narrowly from the extended grade-level standards that might be assessed. Rating scales with supporting evidence cover eligible extended standards adequately, but the requirements for supporting evidence typically sample narrowly from the extended grade-level content standards. Furthermore, scores that are based only on observer ratings can be questionable, which is why rating scales now typically require supporting evidence. And, tailored assessments based on scaled performance tasks have their own limitations. (For disclosure purposes, I should mention that I worked on assessments of this type for South Carolina and New Mexico.) For example, because only those tasks that are appropriate for a student's academic proficiency level are selected from the full collection of tasks, students may not be assessed on all extended content standards. Further, all three of these approaches are sound technically only to the degree that teachers score student responses consistently and accurately and adapt administration of assessment tasks without undermining valid inferences about what students know and can do on their own.

SUMMARY

There is little to be gained and much to be lost from applying the *Standards for Educational and Psychological Testing* harshly, without regard for the uniqueness of students with significant cognitive disabilities and the inferences we wish to draw about what they know and can do. I accept that I must use caution beyond the levels I use in interpreting scores from grade-level academic achievement tests when I infer what students know and can do from an alternate assessment. In fact, I am glad to adapt the *Standards for Educational and Psychological Testing* to the alternate assessment environment—but not abandon them—because even tenuous interpretations are better than no large-scale assessment information at all.

REFERENCES

American Educational Research Association, American Psychological Association, & National Council on Measurement in Education. (1999). *Standards for educational and psychological testing.* Washington, DC: American Psychological Association.

No Child Left Behind Act of 2001, PL 107-110, 115 Stat. 1425, 20 U.S.C. §§ 6301 *et seq.*

CHAPTER 20

Does the Emperor Have New Clothes?

CLAUDIA FLOWERS

I was first introduced to alternate assessments based on alternate achieve-ment standards (AA-AAS) 6 years ago while examining the alignment of 31 states' AA-AAS with academic content standards (Browder et al., 2004; Browder et al., 2003; Flowers, Browder, & Ahlgrim-Delzell, 2006). My colleagues' and my private name for this research was *The Emperor's New Clothes,* which reflected our uncertainty about what content was being measured by these new types of assessments. Our major research questions were, *Is this really reading?* and *Is this really math?* Though our findings indicated that many of the AA-AAS were not measuring reading and math, we found, to our surprise, that several states' AA-AAS were assessing reading and math. These findings opened our eyes to what was possible and to how states could design academic assessments for students with significant cognitive disabilities despite the limited re-search on teaching academic subjects to this student population.

Since those initial studies, the questions that educators are asking about AA-AAS have changed. Instead of questioning whether students with significant disabilities should be included in large-scale accounta-bility programs, now we are asking how best to assess these students on academic content. AA-AAS (or the 1% assessment) allow students with significant disabilities to be included in states' accountability systems and provide access to the general curriculum for students who histori-cally have been excluded. The presentations at the Eighth Annual Mary-land Conference at the University of Maryland College Park on October 11 and 12, 2007, focused on how assessments can be designed, adminis-tered, and interpreted.

I had two takeaway messages from the conference. First, much more work is needed to describe the content domain of AA-AAS. Simply re-ducing the depth and complexity of the grade-level content standards will not provide enough information and guidance for improving teaching and learning. Second, there is no correct measurement model to apply to all AA-AAS. The following sections provide more details about these takeaway messages.

TAKEAWAY MESSAGE 1: DEFINING THE CONTENT DOMAIN

The foundation and starting point for all assessments is a rich description of the content domain. Ideally, the content domain should be based on theoretically sound principles of student learning, but there is limited research about how students with significant cognitive disabilities learn academic knowledge and skills (Browder, Spooner, Ahlgrim-Delzell, Wakeman, & Harris, 2006; Browder, Wakeman, Spooner, Ahlgrim-Delzell, & Algozzine, 2006; Courtade, Spooner, & Browder, 2007). Despite the limited research, all states are required to develop and administer AA-AAS.

States have used a variety of approaches to reduce the depth and complexity of grade-level content standards. Some states see special educators as the best personnel for determining the academic needs of their students. These states train special educators to start with grade-level content standards and then design assessment items, activities, or work products that align with the standards. In other states, committees of content experts and special educators extend the grade-level content standards to illustrate how students with significant cognitive disabilities can have access to grade-level content. These committees either extend all the grade-level content standards or select specific strands that are judged to be the most meaningful for students with significant cognitive disabilities. These are good first steps to defining the content domain for students with significant cognitive disabilities.

Another dimension that is not typically considered in the content domain is level of independence. For students with significant disabilities, good teaching requires additional supports that are faded over time to promote student independence and mastery of academic tasks. Ideally, students work independently during assessments. However, many students need physical supports and modifications when they participate in assessments. Some states describe how supports are incorporated into their grade-level content standards and even take level of independence into account when scoring AA-AAS.

The heterogeneity of students' needs and skills must be considered when defining the content domain. Simply knowing students' disability categories provides little information about their academic abilities. Symbolic levels of communication—the extent to which students use symbols to communicate—provide a promising taxonomy for thinking about academic instruction. Most academic learning requires symbolic communication, but many students with significant disabilities need to build their use of symbols as they work on academic learning. Extending the content domain to include descriptions of how some students communicate at nonsymbolic levels (i.e., hard-to-interpret vocalizations with no clear cause and effect) allows all students with significant disabilities to participate in AA-AAS.

TAKEAWAY MESSAGE 2: NO SINGLE CORRECT MEASUREMENT MODEL

There is no silver bullet for evaluating the validity of the interpretation and use of AA-AAS. Each state has to decide which model to apply according to its purposes, definitions, and assumptions about its AA-AAS. Two states that presented at the conference, South Carolina and Georgia, illustrated the different approaches that states might take to evaluate their AA-AAS. South Carolina has a performance-based assessment with state-designed items/tasks and standardized instructions for teachers. South Carolina intentionally designed assessment tasks with withdrawal of scaffolding as the students correctly responded to the tasks. Because of this standardization of content standards, assessment , and administration, South Carolina can use many of the tools (e.g., Item Response Theory, vertical scales) that typically are found in general education assessments.

Georgia uses a portfolio assessment that allows teachers to design the activities and work products included in students' portfolios. Multiple entries for each content strand are required to provide replication in the portfolio for evaluating reliability. Realizing the importance of teachers for its AA-AAS, Georgia started training teachers on extending grade-level content standards and designing assessment activities 3 years before the AA-AAS was implemented. Evidence for evaluating the technical quality of Georgia's AA-AAS was different from what is traditionally found in large-scale assessment systems. For instance, Georgia used a standard-setting approach that blended body-of-work and profile approaches for setting cut scores across 192 different potential student profiles. In many ways, Georgia took greater risks with its AA-AAS format, charting new territory in looking at evidence to support the inferences, but the designers of this assessment feel strongly that this approach is best for the state's students.

SUMMARY

Given the complexities of students' disabilities, heterogeneous performance levels, lack of academic curricula, and limited research about how students with significant cognitive disabilities learn and develop in academic areas, it is not surprising that AA-AAS continue to challenge measurement experts. But these challenges should not discourage anyone. As AA-AAS mature, they can be expected to stand up to criticism, and states will have accumulated evidence to support inferences regarding the interpretation and use of these unique assessments.

REFERENCES

Browder, D., Flowers, C., Ahlgrim-Delzell, L., Karvonen, M., Spooner, F., & Algozzine, R. (2004). The alignment of alternate assessment content to academic and functional curricula. *Journal of Special Education, 37*(4), 211–223.

Browder, D.M., Spooner, F., Ahlgrim-Delzell, L., Flowers, C., Karvonen, M., & Algozzine, R. (2003). A content analysis of the curricular philosophies reflected in states' alternate assessment performance indicators. *Research and Practice for Persons with Severe Disabilities, 28*(4), 165–181.

Browder, D.M., Spooner, F., Ahlgrim-Delzell, L., Wakeman, S.Y., & Harris, A. (2006). A meta-analysis on teaching mathematics to students with significant cognitive disabilities. *Exceptional Children, 74*(4), 407–432.

Browder, D.M., Wakeman, S.Y., Spooner, F., Ahlgrim-Delzell, L., & Algozzine, B. (2006). Research on reading instruction for individuals with significant cognitive disabilities. *Exceptional Children, 72*(4), 392–408.

Courtade, G., Spooner, F., & Browder, D.M. (2007). Review of studies with students with significant cognitive disabilities which link to science standards. *Research and Practice in Severe Disabilities, 32*(1), 43–49.

Flowers, C., Browder, D., & Ahlgrim-Delzell, L. (2006). An analysis of three states' alignment between language arts and mathematics standards and alternate assessments. *Exceptional Children, 72*, 201–215.

CHAPTER 21

Assessment Population

Implications for the Validity Evaluation

JACQUELINE F. KEARNS AND ELIZABETH TOWLES-REEVES

Using the National Alternate Assessment Center (NAAC)'s enhanced model (Marion & Pellegrino, 2006) from Pellegrino, Chudowsky, and Glaser (2001) as a theoretical model for assessment design suggests that three vertices—cognition, observation, and interpretation—align in high-quality assessment design. For alternate assessments based on alternate achievement standards (AA-AAS), population characteristics and theoretical understanding of how the population acquires competence in the cognition vertex are especially important for evaluating the validity of these instruments in large-scale assessment and accountability systems. As such, two important questions emerge. First, is the assessment appropriate for measuring the extent to which the intended population is acquiring the specified competence in the academic domains? Second, are the appropriate students participating in the assessment? The first question concerns the purpose and use of the assessment instrument, whereas the second question speaks to the role these assessments play in accountability decision making. The results of these questions may have both intended and unintended consequences.

For example, if an AA-AAS measures the academic content appropriately, students with significant cognitive disabilities, if given the appropriate communication supports, will respond to items on the assessment. Because AA-AAS may be more restrictive in terms of access to the range, depth, and breadth of content standards, it is important that the assessments be administered only to the appropriate student population. This is particularly important if the assessment system as a whole is to provide accurate information about teaching and learning academic content.

In an effort to provide information about the assessed population in terms of these two questions, the NAAC's Learner Characteristics Inventory (Towles-Reeves, Kearns, Kleinert, & Kleinert, 2009) was designed to enhance the demographic information collected about the assessment population based on observed and validated characteristics of these learners. As presented in Chapter 1, the analysis of these student characteristics provided essential descriptive data about students in this population in terms of how they communicate receptively and expressively and also about benchmark reading and math items validated by the severe disabilities research literature (Browder, Wakeman, Spooner, Ahlgrim-Delzell, & Algozzine, 2006).

These data verified that the population described in the literature is highly diverse in terms of communication, disability category representation, and reading and math skill levels, although the majority of students use oral speech to communicate, have sight word vocabularies, and use calculators to solve math problems. However, a small percentage of the population communicates expressively and receptively at very early levels of communicative competence at all levels in Grades 3–11. We also learned that the percentages of students advancing in their levels of symbolic language use were not changing, and many of these students were not using augmentative and alternative communication systems. Without basic communication systems and advancing levels of communicative competence, true access to the general curriculum is virtually impossible to achieve.

Given the effect of accountability systems, the importance of *highest achievement standard* is also an assessment population concern. With a very short history of teaching academic content to this population, the assumptions about what students know and can do in academic content will most certainly be challenged, as will questions of how these students achieve competence in academic domains. The percentages of students who fall within the achievement categories of *basic, proficient,* and *advanced* must be delicately balanced in order to fairly represent the achievement of the population. A large percentage of students scoring basic or below may have the unintended consequence of complacency; their teachers might think, "They will never get there, so why bother considering their learning results?" Schools that have high percentages of students scoring proficient or higher risk the same unintended consequence of complacency, which begs the question of whether we are underestimating the achievement potential of the population. Careful analysis of the population and consideration within the design and implementation of an assessment system can help achieve this very important balance.

Although the data from the Learner Characteristics Inventory presented in Chapter 1 reveal some unique findings from a descriptive analysis, we are hopeful that coupling those results with state assessment results will reveal more about the extent to which students with various characteristics respond to test items as well as whether the performance distribution makes sense given the characteristics of the population. This will allow educators not only to design better AA-AAS instruments but also, from an accountability point of view, to better ensure that the achievement standards set for the population do in fact represent the highest achievement standards possible (U.S. Department of Education, 2005).

SUMMARY

Finally, remember that the hypothetical students described in Chapter 1 who exemplify these unique characteristics—Megan, Jason, Leslie, and Skyler—also very much resemble typical kids in terms of their interests and their social and cultural needs. Because academic performance is highly valued in U.S. society, it is imperative that we make that value accessible to all. As one parent quipped, "A bad day of testing once a year pales in comparison to multiple years of low expectations for achievement." What professionals learn from these students has the potential to enhance learning for all.

REFERENCES

Browder, D., Wakeman, S., Spooner, F., Ahlgrim-Delzell, L., & Algozzine, B. (2006). Research on reading instruction for individuals with significant cognitive disabilities. *Exceptional Children, 72*(4), 392–408.

Marion, S., & Pellegrino, J. (2006). A validity framework for evaluating the technical quality of alternate assessments. *Educational Measurement: Issues and Practices, 25*(4), 47–57.

Pellegrino, J., Chudowsky, N., & Glaser, R. (Eds.). (2001). *Knowing what students know: The science and design of educational assessment.* Washington, DC: National Academies Press.

Towles-Reeves, E., Kearns, J., Kleinert, H., & Kleinert, J. (2009). An analysis of the learning characteristics of students taking alternate assessments based on alternate achievement standards. *Journal of Special Education, 42*(4), 241–254.

U.S. Department of Education. (2005). *Alternate achievement standards for students with the most significant cognitive disabilities: Non-regulatory guidance.* Washington, DC: Author.

CHAPTER 22

Some Key Considerations for Test Evaluators and Developers

SCOTT F. MARION

The previous chapters included many interesting discussions and analyses designed to improve the field's understanding of alternate assessment. In this chapter, I offer the following points for test users and evaluators to consider when evaluating the technical quality of states' alternate (and general) assessment systems:

- Technical quality evaluations must center on validity.

- Consequences are essential.

- Reliability, alignment, and other typical approaches are important, but they are not as important as validity.

- An argument provides a useful and important framework.

- It is important to prioritize and get going.

VALIDITY IS CENTRAL

When evaluating the technical quality of alternate assessments (or any assessment, for that matter) it is important to focus on the validity of test-based inferences. Technical evaluations and technical manuals have certainly improved since 2001—due, in part, to the No Child Left Behind (NCLB) Act peer review requirements—but they are still often collections of unrelated statistics and documentations of various procedures. This information is important, but its impact and quality would be significantly enhanced if the studies were designed and organized to contribute to evaluations of validity arguments. The purpose of technical documentation is to provide data for critically evaluating inferences from AA-AAS scores and the logic of interpretative arguments.

CONSEQUENCES ARE ESSENTIAL

There might be a lingering theoretical debate about whether consequences are integral to construct validity, but I, among many others, argue that consequences are as much a part of validity as is content or any other source of evidence. However, whether or not one agrees with this view of validity, alternate assessments are used for important decisions, and the consequences of these decisions must be considered in validity evaluations. Furthermore, alternate assessments on alternate achievement standards (AA-AAS) were initiated for social justice reasons to ensure that students with significant cognitive disabilities were properly included in educational programs. If this is a value of AA-AAS systems—and I believe it is for most of them—then evaluations of technical quality must include critical examination of the intended positive and unintended negative effects of the uses of the systems' test scores.

We focused almost exclusively on consequential evidence when first evaluating the technical quality of alternate assessments, but we realized that if alternate assessments were to be seen as something more than nice activities for students with significant cognitive disabilities, then we needed to pay attention to more traditional aspects of technical documentation so that alternate assessments might be considered legitimate. Nevertheless, consequences of these assessments must be part of any validity evaluation of states' alternate assessment systems.

OTHER TECHNICAL CRITERIA

What about reliability, alignment, comparability, and other traditional criteria? There is no question that reliability is important for us to have confidence that our inferences from an assessment system might be generalized to more than one occasion or to a different sample of assessment events. However, this criterion might be overrated, especially in the narrow way that reliability has been applied in AA-AAS evaluations. Most often, reliability for alternate assessment systems is conceived simply as interrater agreement among scorers or misapplied coefficient alpha (or analogous approaches). Just because correlations can be computed does not mean that their values should be reified. There is no question that we need more appropriate ways to evaluate reliability and incorporate this evidence into a comprehensive validity argument, but until then we should limit our enthusiasm for reliability coefficients.

Alignment has received considerable attention as several organizations—notably the University of North Carolina Charlotte—have adapted alignment methods for use with alternate assessments. These studies were very useful in guiding states toward focusing their assessments on academic content, but in and of themselves most alignment studies provide only partial content-related validity evidence. However, if pursued at a deep level, high-quality alignment studies can provide useful evidence about the nature of the construct.

IMPORTANCE OF A VALIDITY ARGUMENT

One of the most important reasons for articulating a validity argument is that it helps test users and evaluators better structure the studies and evaluate the results. Similar to the way in which a well-developed schema helps learners incorporate new concepts to create deeper understanding of a domain, a validity argument helps guide the validity evaluation and subsequent synthesis to produce a comprehensive evaluation. Like a theory of action, the interpretative argument makes the values explicit through specific propositions such as the following:

1.   Observed scores will increase for students in response to high-quality instruction.

2.   The quality of school-level instruction will increase as a result of appropriate use of test scores to target professional development.

3.   As a result of decisions based on AA-AAS scores, the educational opportunities of students will improve.

These all lead to important validity inquiries. It is critical, however, that state leaders and evaluators move beyond vague statements and assumptions to specific propositions and explications of the mechanisms. Simply saying that an AA-AAS is being designed to fulfill NCLB and Individuals with Disabilities Education Act (IDEA) requirements is inadequate. For example, the second suggestion in the preceding list is a good start, but it would be inadequate if it stopped there. The evaluator and/or test user must specify the logical connections among the various components of the system and articulate the mechanism(s) by which this proposition could be supported. In this case, the theory of action might specify, for instance, that the test scores will be used in school leadership meetings to guide teachers' sharing of best practices and establishing mentoring relationships to address needs identified by AA-AAS scores.

SUMMARY

Several validity theorists and others, as discussed in Chapter 7, offered suggestions for prioritizing and focusing validity evaluations. There is no right way to do this, but unfortunately there are many wrong ways. States and other test users need to develop validity study plans that are based on the interpretative argument (or another legitimate organizing framework) to organize the studies and the synthesis of evidence. Many of these studies—particularly consequential studies—need early planning and data collection. So, in other words, prioritize and get started!

REFERENCES

Individuals with Disabilities Education Improvement Act of 2004, PL 108-446, 20 U.S.C. §§ 1400 *et seq.*

No Child Left Behind Act of 2001, PL 107-110, 115 Stat. 1425, 20 U.S.C. §§ 6301 *et seq.*

CHAPTER 23

Toward a Straighter Road

RACHEL F. QUENEMOEN

The development of alternate assessment since the late 1980s has been challenging, but many of the twists and turns have been legitimate and necessary steps. The shifts in understanding what students with significant cognitive disabilities really know and can do, based on the surprising evidence of their learning, has made how to measure their learning a moving target. We should celebrate those shifts. How many times have we had the privilege to witness transformations in understanding and expectations that were led by the students themselves? Teachers often tell me, "I had no idea that my students could learn this content, that they would be engaged and entranced by the same things their typical peers were learning. Who knew?" These teachers and students provide the beginnings of a map that will help straighten the road to effective alternate assessments, but a great deal of leadership and collaboration has to occur in order to translate their discoveries into effective assessment practice.

State departments of education have the major leadership role more so than federal policy makers, measurement experts, university researchers, or test companies. State departments of education have the necessary blend of policy, practice, expertise, and opportunity to change how and on what content students with disabilities are assessed at the state level. They also have the obligation and the ability to intervene at the district and school levels to change how and what content these students are taught. Cross-discipline collaborative planning, thinking, designing, training, and implementation are the keys to developing assessments that hold schools accountable for the "right" things. Only then can accountability actually result in improved outcomes for students.

In my observations as a technical assistance provider to states, very few states have all the partners at the table, and even fewer have all the partners committed to moving these students and their teachers firmly into high expectations in a standards-based system. Most have some partners who understand and are committed to real change; others have multiple partners but are still finding either disinterest or, occasionally, resistance.

If you are a state leader in special education, curriculum, assessment, or a related field, take some time to reflect on what you know and can do to build on the evidence that students with significant cognitive disabilities and their teachers are benefiting from standards-based reform and accountability. Although the focus of this book is on alternate assessments based on alternate achievement standards, as states grapple with these assessments it is inevitable that reform of instruction and assessment practices for all students with disabilities will emerge as needing focused attention. Thus, these comments are applicable to practices related to all students with disabilities and, specifically, about how students with disabilities access and learn the content covered by assessments—the general curriculum.

Special education leaders in some states have stepped up to lead their field into standards-based reform. Many special education teachers and administrators (as well as many general education teachers and administrators) cling to an understanding of what the general curriculum is that predates the Individuals with Disabilities Education Act Amendments (IDEA) of 1997 (PL 105-17). As a consequence, many students are not taught an enrolled-grade, standards-based curriculum. As I work with teachers in many states, I ask them, "What percentage of students with disabilities—not just those with significant cognitive disabilities— are getting the services, supports, and specialized instruction they need to succeed in their enrolled-grade curriculum?" I rarely hear responses that are higher than 30%. It is more than a decade since IDEA was refocused in 1997 to ensure that students with disabilities would get the services, supports, and specialized instruction they needed not just to access but also to make progress in the curriculum built on the same goals and standards as those intended for all other students. The No Child Left Behind Act of 2001 (PL 107-110) and the Individuals with Disabilities Education Improvement Act of 2004 (PL 108-446) reinforced those requirements in the context of standards-based system accountability. Why have we not seen more focus on the changes needed to make that happen? How do we make the shift from a special education curriculum to a standards-based curriculum and instructional focus? How do we link arms with our valued curriculum and instruction partners and bring all of our students and all of our teachers into the standards-based system of professional development and support? Some states have done so, and it is time for all states to rethink their practices of separate instruction, curriculum, and professional development support for special education. Special education has been "special" (and, I would suggest, separate and unequal) for too long; it is time to put a rigorous focus on "education."

State leaders in curriculum offices can offer their substantial knowledge and skills about the knowledge and skills all children should know and be able to do. As I work in state offices, I generally find the curriculum staff to be absolutely enthusiastic about helping create paths to their content for all students, once they understand that these paths are intended to help all students. The best curriculum staffers love their content and love helping teachers understand how to make the content come alive for all students. Without their help, assessment and special education offices struggle—and make significant errors—as they try to figure out what is essential for all learners.

As a state assessment leader, it is time to acknowledge that educational soundness is an essential test of the appropriateness of testing options, instead of past reliance on primarily technical expertise for design choices. As evidenced by every chapter in this book, the educational soundness of alternate assessments for students with significant cognitive disabilities is a moving target. Design decisions must consider not only technical expertise but also expertise and emerging understanding in the fields of severe disabilities, curriculum, and instruction. Given that most states' technical advisory committees (TACs) are primarily from academic measurement backgrounds, it will be important for assessment staffers to challenge their own TACs to think outside the box about the technical adequacy and validity arguments related to these assessments. Bringing a multidisciplinary team together on a TAC will strengthen their recommendations, and it also will make your meetings a lot more interesting in the process!

SUMMARY

The long and winding road of alternate assessments has led to a point at which students with significant cognitive disabilities are joining their peers in the standards-based reform movement. In the process, it has led us to ask why all students with disabilities do not have access to the challenging general curriculum. In some states, districts, and schools, these questions have led to the correction of these historical inequities. Has any other K–12 testing initiative during the last several decades resulted in a similar powerful effect to raise expectations for a group of students? We have much to celebrate in our work thus far!

REFERENCES

Individuals with Disabilities Education Act Amendments (IDEA) of 1997, PL 105-17, 20 U.S.C. §§ 1400 *et seq.*

Individuals with Disabilities Education Improvement Act of 2004, PL 108-446, 20 U.S.C. §§ 1400 *et seq.*

No Child Left Behind Act of 2001, PL 107-110, 115 Stat. 1425, 20 U.S.C. §§ 6301 *et seq.*

CHAPTER 24

How Should States Move Forward?

SUSAN L. RIGNEY

Our understanding of how students with significant cognitive disabilities learn—and, consequently, our understanding of the appropriate curriculum and assessments for them—is changing rapidly. As states devise effective alternate assessments based on alternate achievement standards (AA-AAS) and other data-gathering instruments, many long-standing assumptions are being contradicted. How should states move forward?

- Borrow from the best. This book describes many innovative practices that can serve as models for states that are rebuilding or revising AA-AAS. For example, an excellent technical manual is available from the Georgia Department of Education, Maryland implemented a rigorous procedure for evaluating mastery objectives linked with grade-level standards in order to ensure alignment, and Connecticut produced scorer training videos. New products and procedures are being completed through state grant projects and funded technical assistance centers such as the National Alternate Assessment Center.

- Provide extended support for individualized education program (IEP) team decisions. This is undoubtedly one of the greatest unmet needs associated with AA-AAS. IEP teams require effective ongoing training in order to make consistent and appropriate eligibility decisions based on a thorough understanding of the assessments available and the students eligible for each. In addi-

---

This chapter is intended to promote the exchange of ideas among researchers and policy makers. The views expressed in it are part of ongoing research and analysis and do not necessarily reflect the position of the U.S. Department of Education.

tion to understanding assessment administration procedures, IEP teams also can benefit from professional development focused on academic content and pedagogy, standards-based IEPs, and understanding the change process.

- More well-designed validation studies are urgently needed. The initial documentation of technical quality for AA-AAS generally focused on scoring consistency and linkage of the assessments with grade-level academic content. Practitioners, policy makers, and parents need to understand in greater detail whether and how AA-AAS have influenced teaching and learning for students with significant cognitive disabilities. We also need to know how the implementation of federal policy has affected the beliefs of stakeholders—including the students themselves—regarding the abilities of this student population. States are urged to share the information they have collected and the decisions that have resulted so that others can build on their efforts.

SUMMARY

As a result of their work on the AA-AAS, states have made substantial progress in addressing the technical challenges of designing and implementing measures of the academic progress of students with significant cognitive disabilities. Teachers have gained a new, and often surprising, understanding of these students' abilities. Our next efforts should focus on refining the accuracy and meaningfulness of the data collection tools we have developed, and using the information they provide to support teaching and learning that enriches students' lives.

CHAPTER 25

Principles Unique to Alternate Assessments

WILLIAM D. SCHAFER

In the school context, assessments are used for at least two important purposes. First, tests gauge the degree to which students, individually or in groups, have attained the academic competencies they are supposed to have learned. This sort of information is useful for reporting progress to parents and for directing curricular and instructional reform. Second, tests are used to make judgments about the success or value of educational programs. Particularly in the context of statewide tests, whether or not they are for the purposes of regulatory agencies—for instance, the U.S. Department of Education's administration of the No Child Left Behind Act (NCLB) of 2001 (PL 107-110)—this function of assessments forms the basis of accountability programs that help public agencies determine the value of educational institutions. Thus, all assessments used for accountability must be judged at least in part by their ability to support evaluations about whether schooling has been successful.

In this chapter, I develop three principles about alternate assessments in the accountability context. These points are controversial, and whether they are satisfied can serve to differentiate alternate assessments from each other:

- Alternate assessments should be based on individual learning goals.

- The outcomes that alternate assessments measure should be available at the beginning of instruction.

- We should not expect to see a relationship between aptitude and achievement over the measured outcomes.

INDIVIDUAL LEARNING
GOALS FOR ALTERNATE ASSESSMENTS

In an earlier publication (Schafer, 2004), I proposed a fundamental accountability principle: to assess every student on what he or she is supposed to be learning. There are two important elements in this principle.

First, every student is to be assessed. This is a reasonable expectation for schools because they receive funding to educate all students—not just some of them. In this regard, the Individuals with Disabilities Education Improvement Act of 2004 (PL 108-446) and NCLB legislation, which mandate the testing of all students regardless of disability, represent desirable directions for assessment and accountability programs.

Second, the assessments should cover what a student is supposed to be learning. For the regular assessment, that is relatively easy to accomplish. Student outcomes are well developed through content standards that apply to all who take the tests, and the assessments are evaluated in part by the degree to which they are aligned with those content standards. Further, achievement expectations are described—especially at the *proficient* level that is used to administer NCLB programmatic decisions—and related to standards (operationalized as cut scores) on the assessments.

For alternate assessments, however, this criterion is not as straightforward. Every student who takes an alternate assessment has an individualized educational program (IEP), which often specifies what learning goals are appropriate for him or her. Even when the IEP does not specify learning goals, expectations other than those developed for regular students would be more appropriate. Thus, what any given student is supposed to learn often varies from student to student. For an alternate assessment, this likely means that flexible (i.e., individualized) goals are best. This brings me to my first principle for alternate assessments: Whereas regular assessments have common learning expectations for all students who take them, *alternate assessments should be based on individual learning goals.* Students and their teachers should be accountable for learning expectations that are tailored to each student's unique capabilities and needs and not to the capabilities and needs of other students who may be very much unlike him or her.

This is not to say that different learning domains are needed for alternate assessments. Student expectations may be developed for the domains of reading, math, science, and any other academic area, as well as for nonacademic areas. Which of these are measured is a matter of public policy. However, within each discipline (reading/language arts, math, and science in order to comply with NCLB as administered by the U.S. Department of Education), a connection must be drawn to grade-level content standards for the regular assessment, but that does not imply that the same content expectations are required.

AVAILABILITY OF ASSESSED OUTCOMES AT THE BEGINNING OF INSTRUCTION

A valuable by-product of an assessment program is clarification of the learning goals for which teachers are providing instruction. In general education programs, content and achievement standards serve to define end points that students are expected to achieve on the assessments. The clearer the end points, the better teachers can visualize what their students should know and be able to do. For general education assessments, transparency is needed regarding which domains a test will cover. There are various ways to ensure transparency; some states even release each year's tests to help clarify what they assess and how they assess it.

Because alternate assessments should allow flexibility in learning expectations, there is less clarity in what they cover, especially for each individual student. However, to capitalize on the ability of assessments to define educational goals, I introduce my second principle for alternate assessments: like regular assessments, *the outcomes that alternate assessments measure should be available at the beginning of instruction;* they should not be determined at the time of assessment. For the most positive results possible, the goals of instruction should be visible and attainable. A teacher can hit a learning target only when it is clear and consistent.

ALTERNATE ASSESSMENT ACHIEVEMENT SHOULD NOT DEPEND ON APTITUDE

My final principle has to do with evaluating alternate assessments, and it is a distinction between the general education and alternate contexts. In general education assessment programs, we naturally expect students who have higher aptitudes to score higher because all students are learning the same expectations. Therefore, a positive correlation would be expected between aptitude and achievement. But, for alternate assessments, because each student is working toward individualized learning goals, *we should not expect to see a relationship between aptitude and achievement over the measured outcomes;* rather, the goals themselves should take aptitude (or degree of cognitive disability) into account. Indeed, a positive correlation could indicate that the assessment of achievement is confounded with degree of disability—a violation of the individualization principle.

SUMMARY

I have argued here that alternate assessments are most useful, both for the formative purposes of assessment-driven instruction and the summative purposes of educational program evaluation, when the assessments cover individualized educational goals that are available at the beginning of instruction. Thus there will be only trivial association between aptitude (or degree of cognitive disability) and assessment results. Indeed, the latter could be a criterion for valid inferences about program success from alternate assessments.

The principle that alternate assessments should measure flexible learning goals and, thereby, respond to individual student challenges has other implications, particularly for evaluating alternate assessments. These are explored further in Schafer (2005), which provides further reading on this topic of documenting the psychometric properties of alternate assessments.

REFERENCES

Individuals with Disabilities Education Improvement Act (IDEA) of 2004, PL 108-446, 20 U.S.C. §§ 1400 *et seq.*

No Child Left Behind Act of 2001, PL 107-110, 115 Stat. 1425, 20 U.S.C. §§ 6301 *et seq.*

Schafer, W.D. (2004). Review the book *Large-scale assessment programs for all students: Validity, technical adequacy, and implementation. Contemporary Psychology, 49*, 622–625.

Schafer, W.D. (2005, August). Technical documentation for alternate assessments. *Practical Assessment Research & Evaluation, 10*(10). Retrieved January 26, 2009, from http://pareonline.net/getvn.asp?v=10&n=10

CHAPTER 26

Reflections on the Alternate Assessment in Oregon

GERALD TINDAL

The naming conventions in large-scale testing programs depict constructs that are largely confined to the language of state grade-level standards designed to reflect levels of achievement. Yet, the contextual nature of the assessments to allow access for students with significant cognitive disabilities or sensory impairments also needs to be considered: Assessments reflect complex bundles of access skills, prerequisite skills, and target (content) skills.

SUPPORTS NEEDED FOR PARTICIPATION IN THE TEST

One of the most significant challenges to the latest changes made in the Oregon Alternate Assessment was ensuring its applicability to a diverse population. A guiding principle for all tasks and test administration guidance was to provide any level of support necessary to access the target skill. We viewed access as irrelevant to the construct and, therefore, provided two explicit strategies to teachers. First, they used a preassessment to ascertain students' independence levels (prerequisite skills). Second, they could assess students using either of two formats to ensure access to a communication system: a standard or scaffold administration.

The Oregon Department of Education developed a set of items that were placed as the first 10 and that were related to the skills needed to show proficiency in each subject area. These items were administered to determine an appropriate level of support needed to administer the test and were developmental in leading to the content items. They were administered by bringing students to success in answering each item: four points (answered independently by the student), three points (student needed a verbal, visual, or gesture support), two points (student needed partial physical support), or one point (student needed full physical support). Furthermore, a scaffold version of the test provided additional supports that might be needed to overcome any access problems in taking the test due to communication systems. In a scaffold administration, the language preceding the item provided students with additional context to understand what was being asked. Scaffold administration items also included graphics to provide additional support for the item without interfering with the construct being tested.

TYPES OF EVIDENCE TO SUPPORT INFERENCES OF PROFICIENCY

Validity needs to be considered as a form of argumentation as described in the White Paper commissioned by the Office of Special Education Programs in 2005 (see http://www.osepideasthatwork.org/toolkit/models.asp). In this paper, equal emphasis is given to procedural evidence and empirical–statistical evidence. This paper also emphasizes the need for strong hypotheses and disconfirmability and falsifiability, particularly because most large-scale assessment conclusions are very one-dimensional. Large-scale assessments typically focus only on outcomes with conjectures of cause supported by documentation of population sampling, measurement (scaling), and analysis. Rarely does the research design drive the question; independent variables are postulated and concurrent dependent measures are largely ignored while controlling variables are only casually addressed. As specified in the *Standards for Educational and Psychological Testing* (American Educational Research Association, American Psychological Association, & National Council on Measurement in Education, 1999), multiple lines of evidence are needed as part of the validation process.

Content-Related Evidence

This type of evidence is entirely driven by state grade-level standards. In the latest (second) version of the Oregon Alternate Assessment, the Oregon Department of Education conducted an alignment/linkage study that addressed the depth of knowledge of the items and standards and the alignment/linkage between them.

Internal Structures

The Oregon Department of Education approached internal structures at two levels: 1) items within tasks and 2) tasks within tests. The focus on items was needed for continuous improvement, taking into account several dimensions of each item to ascertain how well the items worked; the focus on tasks reflected the integrity of the constructs in relation to the standards.

Criterion-Related Evidence

A rather significant problem in establishing evidence that supports the relation of alternate assessments with other measures is the singularity of the domain for sampling items. Typically, this population of students is very diverse, with spillover in learning across subject areas. Therefore, evidence was analyzed on the proficiency levels of various disability categories and on the relation of proficiencies across subject areas.

Response Demands

In Oregon, this dimension of the validation process was one of the most important to ensure that the content being tested was accessed fairly using formats for interaction that were universal in design. Given the state's need to develop a single assessment that had previously consisted of four separate assessments (career and life skills, juried assessments, challenge down, and an extended assessment of basic skills), levels of independence and provision of scaffold administration were considered essential to better understand this dimension of validity.

COHERENCE OF THE TESTING PROGRAM

We may be witnessing the "Balkanization" of special education, in which the entire field of disabilities has been falsely divided into populations with different labels (e.g., *students with severe retardation* became *students with significant cognitive disabilities* and now are known as the *1% population*). Yet, the new frontier is likely on the intersections of these labels (students who are between the lowest 1% and 2% groups or between the 2% and accommodated administration of the general education test). Although the most current special education movement, response-to-intervention, appears "quarantined" in terms of giving students labels, the concept has transportability into working with all populations. Including students with disabilities in large-scale testing programs is a relatively recent phenomenon that has resulted in new perspectives about the validation process. Using Messick's (1989) perspective on validity as a unitary construct and Kane's (2001) logic of an argument-based claim with supporting evidence, the technical manual (Oregon Department of Education, 2007–2008) submitted for peer review provided the following perspective to organize all documentation.

Proficiency is established and confirmed through an explicit process that uses content and special education teachers who understand the demands of the test and the achievement-level descriptors. This proficiency uses the same language as that appearing with the general education, but the inference is significantly conditioned by using tasks that are reduced in breadth, depth, and complexity. This proficiency, however, reflects application of the same grade-level standards that are used throughout the entire statewide assessment system. Further supporting this inference is an application of the same technical analyses that are applied to the general education test. Finally, the reporting system is entirely transportable across both the alternate and general education assessment systems.

SUMMARY

Alternate assessments represent a recent form of large-scale testing that allows states to include ALL students, even those with the most significant cognitive disabilities. This population is comprised of students with a range of access problems (sensory, motor, and behavioral) that need to be considered in administering and scoring any kind of test.

In the Oregon Alternate Assessment, access was provided by first assessing students' level of independence and prerequisite skills. This step allowed the test administrator to appropriately assist the student to take the test without interfering with the construct being tested. Teachers could then use either a standard or scaffold administration to ensure appropriate communication of item content. Both dimensions of access were investigated along with documentation of several types of validity evidence: content of standards, internal structures, criterion relations, and response demands. Although validation was reported in a technical manual for this specific population, the Department of Education considered the entire population of all students in the educational accountability system (Grades 3–8 and high school) for understanding the coherence of the testing program.

REFERENCES

American Educational Research Association, American Psychological Association, & National Council on Measurement in Education. (1999). *Standards for educational and psychological testing.* Washington, DC: Authors.

Kane, M. (2001). *The role of policy assumptions in validating high-stakes testing programs.* Paper presented at the annual meeting of the American Educational Research Association, Seattle.

Messick, S. (1989). Validity. In R.L. Linn (Ed.), *Educational measurement* (3rd ed., pp. 13–103). New York: American Council on Education.

Oregon Department of Education. (2007–2008). *Technical report—Oregon's Alternate Assessment system reliability and validity.* Salem, OR: Author.

CHAPTER 27

Essential Truths About Alternate Assessments

DANIEL J. WIENER

As director of a state alternate assessment program since 1998, I was asked to provide a brief and thoughtful message summarizing the key points for researchers, state assessment coordinators, and others interested in the lessons learned, in Massachusetts and across the country, regarding the assessment of students with significant disabilities. In Chapter 12, Charlie DePascale and I discussed the purposes of alternate assessments and the promises and opportunities presented by alternate assessments to improve instruction and learning for this difficult-to-assess population. However, those opportunities to improve teaching and learning must be built into assessment systems intentionally, and they must be nurtured and supported throughout the process, or else alternate assessments will become simply tools to measure the status quo.

In our state, fundamental questions addressed by stakeholders during development of the Massachusetts Comprehensive Assessment System Alternate Assessment (MCAS-Alt) resulted in important decisions that shaped the system. Was the purpose of the alternate assessment to measure students' performance, or should it also assess progress over time, perhaps across one or more academic years? Should the alternate assessment be integrated with instruction to encourage a greater understanding of standards-based instruction by educators of students taking alternate assessments? Implicit in the federal requirement for alternate assessment was the assumption that standards-based instruction for these students had not occurred uniformly (if at all) and that states would be required to develop systems to ensure that students with significant disabilities participated fully in the academic activities and resources of schools. This assumption led us to develop an alternate assessment that did more than simply weighing and measuring students; our assessment also improved daily instruction and student learning.

The views expressed in this chapter by Daniel J. Wiener, an employee of the Massachusetts Department of Elementary and Secondary Education at the writing of this chapter, are solely his own and do not necessarily reflect any official policy or position of the Massachusetts Department of Elementary and Secondary Education.

The "1 percent rule" that went into effect in 2003 changed the method used to calculate adequate yearly progress in schools and districts in which students took alternate assessments, and it went far in raising the profile of these students. But states also had to acknowledge that most special educators were not extensively trained to teach modified academic content to students with a range of disabilities. States were forced to be clear about their expectations that academic skills and content would be taught to this population, that these students would participate in academic assessments, and that their results would be included in the accountability system.

Instructional improvement, then, is part of this equation, and alternate assessments represent an important lever to make it happen. However, it also is necessary to acknowledge some essential truths about alternate assessments and the population who use them:

- In most cases, alternate assessments do not measure the same breadth and depth of standards measured by standardized tests. Portfolios in particular represent only core samples of the learning that has occurred in a classroom, although, if done well, they do show progress over time and the instructional approaches used to assess performance. This apparent shortcoming may not be relevant, however, since students with significant disabilities are generally not taught standards at the same breadth, depth, and complexity as other students.

- Although more standardized in their approach, performance assessments purportedly assess a broader range of standards, but, in contrast to portfolios, they tend not to include all students because many students require full prompting and assistance to complete the tasks. Therefore, the results will provide only limited information on the skills students are able to perform.

- Alternate assessments are simply measurement tools for a difficult-to-assess population. Alternate assessments do not necessarily or inherently improve student learning unless mechanisms for doing so are intentionally built into their systems.

Given this final point, how can states best focus their efforts to improve instruction to promote both the self-sufficiency of teachers and the expectation that the content they teach reflects the content that will be assessed?

It is important for educators to understand what their state wants them to teach, and they should have access to ongoing professional development opportunities in adapting curriculum and instruction for students with significant disabilities. Educators also should know whether their state's alternate assessment actually will measure what has been taught (as now occurs in states in which teachers design tasks specifically for the assessment of their students) or whether their state will prescribe a discrete sample of skills for assessment.

For states to nurture instructional improvements, teachers need to become familiar with the standards, learn how to identify the standards' entry points for each student, and know how to effectively move students from their baseline levels of achievement toward grade-level expectations, even though this goal may seem out of reach. This goal has implications for states regarding the kinds of educational resources they develop for schools, especially in terms of describing the standards that must be taught, how to adapt them, and how they will be assessed. States must think carefully about how they might use their alternate assessments for purposes beyond simply weighing and measuring students, and expanding these assessments to enhance learning.

The state of Massachusetts has maintained the following structures and processes that have encouraged not only educational improvements but also a sense of ownership and buy-in on the part of educators:

- Teachers receive a concrete guide to the learning standards, including instructional ideas and a methodology for their individual adaptation. The state's expectation must be clear that standards will be implemented regularly in classrooms. However, without a roadmap, content will be hit-or-miss.

- Educators are taught data collection skills to increase the pace of instruction, identify goals that are realistic, and determine when mastery has been achieved.

- Intensive, ongoing professional development opportunities promote the state's expectations for instruction, curriculum, and assessment. The relatively high turnover among special educators (25%–30% annually in Massachusetts) ensures a perpetual need for state-sponsored training activities.

- The state promotes an understanding of how to design appropriate standards-based activities that yield high-quality assessment products, particularly when the assessment tasks will be designed by teachers. In contrast, when alternate assessment tasks are designed by the state, a bank of potential tasks and/or items should be made available to teachers beforehand for practice and review and to ensure that valued skills will be taught.

- The following opportunities are also made available to Massachusetts teachers with prior alternate assessment experience:

    Become expert trainers to assist colleagues in learning the alternate assessment process, particularly when constructing portfolios is a requirement

> Collaborate with colleagues in designing and sharing effective standards-based curriculum, instruction, and alternate assessment activities
>
> Assist in developing resource materials that identify effective instructional strategies and approaches
>
> Review and score alternate assessments under the state's close supervision

- The state promotes the involvement of teachers in recommending continuous improvements to the system.

These efforts require a commitment of time, energy, creativity, and resources by the state, but, in concert with federal mandates for the inclusion of all students in assessments and accountability, they already have had a major impact on improving teaching and learning.

SUMMARY

Effective, research-based methods are now used in some states to ensure that alternate assessment serves as a vehicle for instructional improvement. Opportunities to improve teaching and learning must be built intentionally into assessment systems and be constantly nurtured by the state; otherwise alternate assessments become tools only to measure the status quo. Implicit in the federal requirement to conduct alternate assessments was the assumption that standards-based instruction for students with significant cognitive disabilities had not occurred previously and that full participation in the academic curriculum by these students was now required. However, the rush to meet recent federal review criteria has led many states to retool their assessments in ways that may not lead to improved learning opportunities. States should not lose sight of the original goal to develop alternate assessments that do more than simply weighing and measuring students; assessments should also improve instructional opportunities and student learning. Without strong training for teachers, and a commitment by the state to ensure a direct link between instruction and assessment, the ultimate goal of improving learning will not be realized.

Index

Page numbers followed by *f* indicate figures; those followed by *t* indicate tables.